P9-EDU-436

THE LEAGUE FOR SOCIAL RECONSTRUCTION: INTELLECTUAL ORIGINS OF THE DEMOCRATIC LEFT IN CANADA 1930–1942

MICHIEL HORN

The League for Social Reconstruction: Intellectual Origins of the Democratic Left in Canada 1930–1942

UNIVERSITY OF TORONTO PRESS
Toronto Buffalo London

Toronto Buffalo London
Printed in Canada
ISBN 0-8020-5487-0

Canadian Cataloguing in Publication Data

Horn, Michiel, 1939-
The League for Social Reconstruction

Includes index.
ISBN 0-8020-5487-0
1. The League for Social Reconstruction – History.
2. Socialism in Canada – History. 3. Radicalism – Canada – History. 4. Right and left (Political science). I. Title.
HX101.L43H67 335′.00971 C80-094689-8

TO W.H. CAZANT AND D. CAZANT–VAN OORT

Preface

The League for Social Reconstruction has an important place in the history of Canadian radicalism. It was the first organization of social-democratic intellectuals in Canada. It had a strong influence on the Co-operative Commonwealth Federation, the farmer-labour-socialist party that took shape in the Depression. It helped to popularize ideas of social and economic change ultimately adopted by the two major political parties. Its most obvious contributions to Canadian intellectual and political life were its two books, *Social Planning for Canada* (1935, reissued in 1975) and *Democracy Needs Socialism* (1938). But the LSR deserves to be remembered too for its preservation of *The Canadian Forum*; when the monthly was about to succumb to extreme poverty in 1936, the league purchased it and kept it alive.

After a decade of activity, the LSR disappeared early in 1942. However, it had counted in its membership some of Canada's best and most generous minds. Its memory is treasured by its alumni, who include distinguished scholars, jurists, journalists, diplomats, politicians, and other public servants. Among them are four current companions of the Order of Canada. This book is the first published account of the organization they founded, its history, ideas, contemporary influence, and continuing importance.

At a time when state intervention in the economy and the prerogatives of the central government are under attack and when corporate concentration in Canada is more pronounced than ever before, a history of the LSR serves a useful purpose. It should remind readers, if they need reminding, of some of the reasons for the expanded role of government in the economy and society; it should suggest that in Canada the power of the corporations is more to be feared than that of democratic government and that the fragmentation of the latter enhances the former.

The men and women of the LSR believed in a positive state and a planned economy, although they linked both closely to the increased equality and co-operation of a socialist commonwealth. They argued that in Canada only the central government was able to check the growth of corporate concentration and protect minority rights adequately. Some of their ideas have a special relevance in the 1980s.

This book is based mainly on archival and printed primary sources. In the use of the latter I have drawn no over-rigid distinction between LSR publications and the writings of the league's leading members. 'The work of the Fabian Society consists of the work of individual Fabians,' Sidney Webb once said. Much the same was true of the LSR. It did not, could not, impose the kind of discipline that would, despite internal disagreements, have allowed it to speak with a single voice.

A further argument for taking a broad view of its work is that there was a tendency at the time for observers to identify the statements of prominent members with the LSR itself. 'We have to realize now,' Frank Scott told Frank Underhill in December 1935, not long after the publication of *Social Planning for Canada*, 'that when any of us puts pen to paper we are scarcely individuals any longer, but voices of a movement. We and the LSR are all judged by whatever any of the seven authors does or writes.' This may have been an exaggeration intended to control the occasionally acerbic Underhill. There was enough truth in it, however, to warrant the inclusion here of some of the non-scholarly writings of Scott, Underhill, and others as part of what the LSR wanted to say to Canadians.

I have not relied on written and printed materials alone. My work has benefited from interviews, conversations, and correspondence with several dozen people who were active in the LSR or knew those who were. I owe substantial debts to former members of the league who opened their personal files, reached into their memories to try to clarify matters left obscure by the written record, commented on what I was thinking and writing, and encouraged me to push the book through several redrafts to completion. Three stand out for their unfailing interest and help: Leonard Marsh, Frank Scott, and Graham Spry. I am grateful to them and to all the others.

The project began as a doctoral dissertation, completed in 1969 under the supervision of Ramsay Cook. I am obliged to him for his advice at that stage and also to my examiners. In 1972 I resumed my research, Frank Underhill's papers having in the meantime become available as a result, sadly, of his death. During the next few years I incurred debts of gratitude to staff members of libraries and archives across the country. To those who assisted me at the University of British Columbia, Carleton University, the University of Guelph, Queen's University, the University of Toronto, York University, the Public Archives of Ontario, the National Library, and, above all, the Public Archives of Canada, my warm thanks.

Elizabeth McRae pulled together my research notes and cross-indexed them, thus setting the stage for writing. Patricia Law and Joanne Robinson ably and expeditiously typed different drafts of the manuscript. Jack Granatstein, Roger Hutchinson and Jos. Lennards read parts or all of the manuscript at different stages and commented helpfully. Suggestions, most though not all of them useful, also came from readers for the University of Toronto Press and the Social Science Federation of Canada. Roger Hall and Sandra Martin offered sound advice on matters of style. At the press, Rik Davidson was a source of encouragement who seemed to retain confidence in the ultimate outcome even when once or twice I lost it. Susan Kent was a most skilful copy editor. All these people contributed to the worth of this book; any errors or weaknesses that remain are my responsibility.

Several people helped to make the work of research and writing more agreeable than it might otherwise have been. Rob and Alayne Hamilton provided me with a place to stay in Ottawa and were fine company. Steven Horn was also a generous host. During my sabbatical year Jack and Annètje Horn were a source of great comfort and warmth. As a bachelor I have no wife to thank for her endless patience and support, but I do want to express my appreciation to some delightful friends and companions.

I dedicated my first book to my parents. This volume I dedicate to two people who were at one time like parents to me; I am grieved that one of them did not live to see it.

The project was assisted financially by the Research Grants Committee, Glendon College of York University, and by the Canada Council, which awarded me a leave fellowship in 1974–75. The book is published with the help of a grant from the Social Science Federation of Canada, using funds provided by the Social Sciences and Humanities Research Council of Canada, and of a grant from the Andrew W. Mellon Foundation to the University of Toronto Press.

M.H.

Contents

THE LEAGUE FOR SOCIAL RECONSTRUCTION: INTELLECTUAL ORIGINS OF THE DEMOCRATIC LEFT IN CANADA 1930–1942

Frank H. Underhill

King Gordon

Elmore Philpott

Irene M. Biss

Kenneth Taylor

Escott Reid

Hume Martyn

F.R. Scott

Edgar McInnis

H.M. Cassidy

Ruth Reid

[illegible] Gregory

Beatrice Cassidy

W.C. MacGregor

J.F. Parkinson

Lorne McInnis

A.F. Wynne Plumptre

E.A. Havelock

G.G. Coote

Henry A. Holman

J.S. Woodsworth

E.J. Garland

Eugene Forsey

Graham Spry

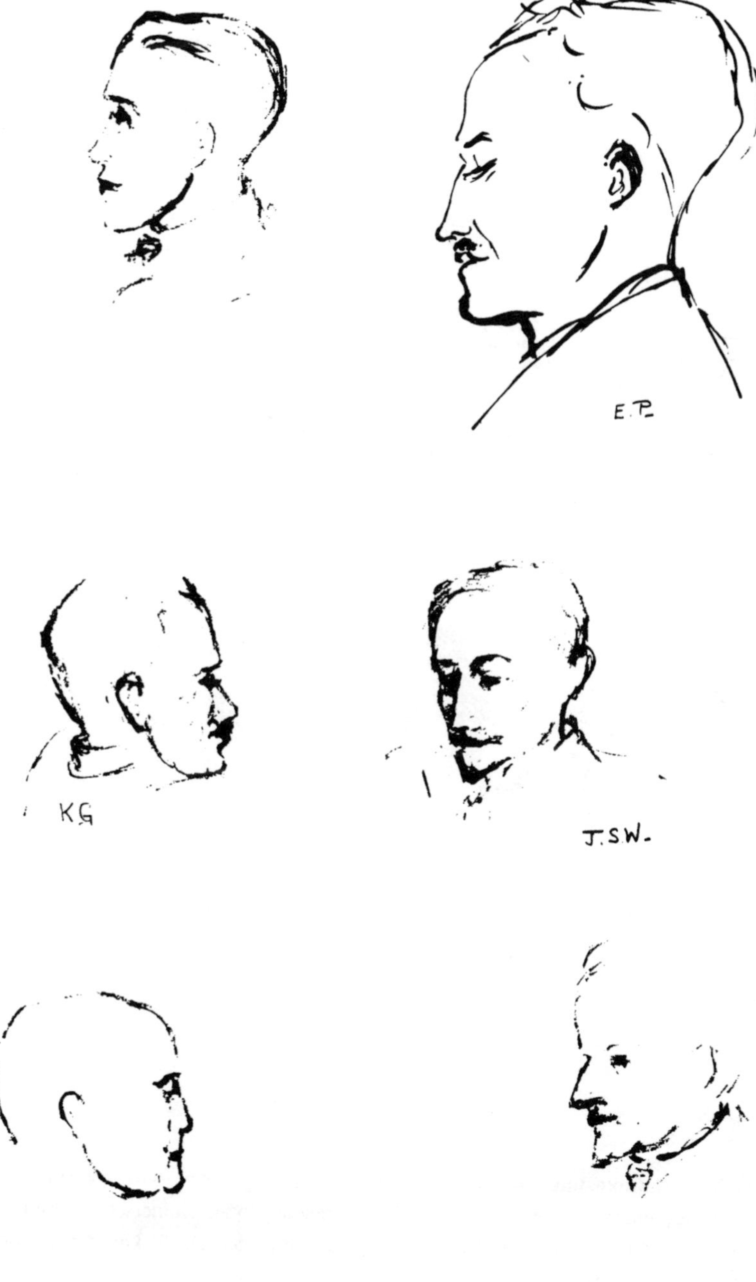

E.P.
KG
J.S.W.
F.H.U.
J.S.W.

The sketches and signatures reproduced on the preceding pages formed part of 'a memento of an historic gathering' given after the Burlington meeting to Mrs Somerset in April 1933 and now in the Public Archives of Canada. They are reproduced here by kind permission of Professor Blair Neatby.

1

Canadian intellectuals and the Depression

Winter, the bleakest so far of the Depression, had ended. On the eve of the last week-end in April 1933, the small town of Burlington in southern Ontario was tinged with that delicate pale green that proclaims, exhilaratingly, the arrival of spring. In mid-week it had been windy and cool, but by Friday the temperature was climbing. At the local country club the professional and groundsmen got ready for the season's first wave of golfers. In nearby Hamilton shabby men on park benches closed their eyes, turned their faces to the sun, and dreamed of jobs.

Unemployment was close to the minds of many Canadians as that week-end approached. Almost one in three wage earners was out of work; many of them had not had a job for a year or more. In Toronto, fifty kilometres east of Burlington, little less than a quarter of the population had received some assistance from the House of Industry during the previous year. By March 1933 more than 30 per cent of Montrealers were drawing direct relief. In other, smaller towns across the country, especially those dependent on a single dominant industry, the proportion of relief recipients was as high as one-half.[1]

Unprecedented and appalling, these figures were matched by the destitution of drought-stricken Saskatchewan and neighbouring areas of Manitoba and Alberta. There hundreds of thousands of farming folk were forced on to the relief rolls. Since the crash of the stock and commodity markets in October 1929 the country had become steadily poorer and many of its people increasingly discouraged. Would there ever be an end to this Depression?

The Depression and the way out of it were the subjects that occupied two dozen men and women who on Thursday, 27 April, gathered in Burlington for four days of meetings. They were members of the League for Social Reconstruction (LSR), an organization that had taken shape in Montreal and Toronto in the fall and winter of 1931–32. They were now meeting at a farm that belonged to Mrs W.B. Somerset, a well-to-do member of the LSR's Toronto branch. A book with the tentative title 'Reconstruction – A Plan for Canada' was the main item on the agenda. With several politicians associated with the Co-operative Commonwealth Federation (CCF) in attendance, however, the discussion not infrequently turned to the affairs and prospects of this new political movement.

Chairman of the sessions was Frank Underhill, a waspishly witty professor of history at the University of Toronto. At age forty-three a decade older than most of the other participants, Underhill was the national president of the LSR. Guest of honour at Burlington and often the centre of attention was the grave and ascetic-looking member of Parliament from Winnipeg North Centre, James Shaver Woodsworth. Not long from his fifty-ninth birthday, he had been a parliamentary spokesman for labour since 1921. He was the leader of the young CCF; he was also the honorary president of the LSR.

The two men were surrounded by young people in their late twenties and early thirties, fairly recent graduates of Canadian and English universities. More than half held university teaching posts; six had been Rhodes Scholars. From McGill University came that ebullient patrician, poet, and professor of law, Frank Scott, and the voluble Eugene Forsey, lecturer in economics. With them from Montreal had come King Gordon, a controversial United Church minister who taught Christian Ethics at United Theological College. He was under notice of dismissal, his position having been eliminated ostensibly on budgetary grounds. Some thought his outspokenness on uncomfortable subjects was the real reason.

Among the faculty members from the University of Toronto were three economists, Irene Biss, Harry Cassidy, and Joseph Parkinson. Eric Havelock, an intense classicist given to pacing around like a caged bear, taught in Victoria College. From McMaster University, recently moved from Toronto to Hamilton, had come another economist, the precise Kenneth Taylor. Others in attendance included Graham Spry, a journalist bubbling over with ideas, Escott Reid, the brilliant young political scientist who had recently become national secretary of the Canadian Institute of International Affairs, and Edgar McInnis, a historian from the University of Toronto.

Passionately those present argued about the contents of the proposed book. The country was in a mess; the LSR must make prescriptions for change. Perhaps the CCF would be able to carry them into effect. But what sort of change was necessary? Should and could Canada move towards socialism? What precisely did that mean? How much could be accomplished through the existing political system? Every night debate raged until the small hours. Even during the walks that people took to clear their heads the discussions continued.

As the week-end drew to a close, the participants signed a sheet of paper on which someone had drawn some pencil sketches of Woodsworth, Underhill, and others. It was presented to Mrs Somerset 'as a momento [sic] of an historic gathering.' Apparently at least one person felt sure that Canada would undergo reconstruction and that the LSR would help to guide the process. The architects of the new order went home on Sunday, their heads 'still buzzing with four solid days of argument.'[2] They were convinced that the book would soon be ready. It was not the only one of their expectations that was doomed to disappointment.

II

The Depression was the most disruptive in a series of economic slumps that for more than a century had periodically tested the pocketbooks and spirits of farmers, industrial workers, businessmen, and others. In Canada, deflated prices for the products of agriculture and the extractive industries, a tightening of credit, and increased unemployment were the chief manifestations of these slumps. On occasion they produced serious crises in public finance.

The impact of depressions had increased as Canada underwent industrialization and urbanization. The urban unemployed were incapable of looking after themselves and their families once their savings, meagre if they existed at all, ran out. They then become charity cases, usually charges on local government. Embarrassingly, those charges tended to be most numerous when, as a result of reduced tax revenue during a slump, local governments were least likely to be able to support them. This was clear before the 1930s. During the post-war depression of 1920–23 the Dominion government provided relief funds to the provinces, which in turn alleviated the financial difficulties experienced by a number of municipalities.

In the 1920s the image of an essentially rural and agricultural country lingered, but the reality had changed. The census of 1931 showed that, of Canada's population of 10,377,000, rather more than half lived in communities of one thousand or larger. In Ontario and Quebec, the industrial heartland, almost six in ten did. Of those gainfully employed fourteen years of age and over, 29 per cent now worked in agriculture compared with approximately 33 per cent ten years earlier. Trade and finance, service and clerical occupations were taking a growing share of the labour force. So was manufacturing. Among exports, agricultural products were becoming less important, though they were still crucial to the welfare of several regions and industries. Fed by the rapid development of hydro-electric power after the turn of the century, pulp and paper and metal mining had become major export industries, while exports of manufactured goods were also growing.

There was, however, a general failure to accept the full consequences of the changing economic reality. On the whole Canada was politically unimaginative, culturally and intellectually a backwater. Political caution reflected the social conservatism of a majority of both legislators and voters. The working-class inhabitants of Hugh Garner's *Cabbagetown*, although poor, 'believed in God, the Royal Family, the Conservative Party and private enterprise, [and] were suspicious and a little condescending towards all heathen religions, higher education, "foreigners" and social reformers.' Even intellectuals* had, with few exceptions, scarcely faced the problems of dependency and want that arose out of urbanization and the new industrial order.

Not that anyone necessarily paid much attention to what intellectuals had to say about economic matters. In a young country, in which activities intended to enhance personal or national wealth assumed great urgency, intellectuals were at the periphery of most concerns. Some were valued for what they could do to accelerate economic growth or to assist in the making and safeguarding of money, others for what they were believed to be able to do in preparing the soul for another world. In other capacities they might be useful, decorative, or entertaining, but not of much importance, their opinions not particularly worth getting.

The modest esteem in which intellectuals were generally held was reflected in, and at the same time was due to, the relatively low incomes most of them enjoyed. Those who earned a living by cultural or intellectual work usually did so in the employ of institutions that did not have much money. Few Canadian intellectuals were of independent means: Goldwin Smith's case *was* unusual.

Lack of wealth was something of a stigma in a country to which most people had come in the hope of providing for themselves and their own to an extent not possible in the Old World. 'If you're so smart, why ain't you rich?' was a question heard not only in the United States. To be sure, respect was accorded to preachers, teachers, scholars, and other clerks, if only because of the length and expense of their education and training. However, long before the 1920s, that go-getting decade when the status of businessmen reached its zenith, intellectuals were clearly not the equal of men of affairs. Certainly very few businessmen regarded them as such.

The social problems of economic and industrial change were, under the British North America Act, the responsibility mainly of provincial and municipal governments. In some cases, as in that of old-age pensions after 1926, financial support was provided by the Dominion government. In no jurisdiction were social and labour legislation well developed at the outset of the Depression. Halting steps

* 'I have considered as intellectuals all those who create, distribute and apply *culture*, that is, the symbolic world of man, including art, science and religion. Within this group there are two main levels: the hard core or creators of culture – scholars, artists, philosophers, authors, some editors, and some journalists; and the distributors – performers in the various arts, most teachers, most reporters. A peripheral group is composed of those who apply culture as part of their jobs – professionals like physicians and lawyers.

'When Europeans speak of the *intelligentsia*, they mean all three categories.' Seymour Martin Lipset, *Political Man* (Garden City, NY 1963) 333.

only had been taken towards a 'welfare state,' one that, in Gunnar Myrdal's words, has 'fairly explicit commitments to the broad goals of economic development, full employment, equality of opportunity for the young, social security, and protected minimum standards as regards not only income, but nutrition, housing, health, and education for all people of all regions and social groups.'[3] Indeed, there were those who believed that even those halting steps were in the wrong direction. Canadians were obliged to look after themselves as best they could and to look to the state reluctantly and only as a last resort. Most of them believed that this was as it should be.

The LSR was to refer to a 'pioneer mentality,' unreflectingly individualistic and optimistic. 'A university president might question progress,' W.L. Morton writes of the 1920s, 'but the popular mind in Canada accepted without thought the doctrine of continual, automatic progress, moral as well as material. One had only to persevere in the plain, hard way, and all would be well.'[4] Want was easily seen as evidence of idleness, improvidence, or vice. Even misfortune could be interpreted as being somehow the victim's fault. In case of unavoidable need one turned to relatives or friends. It was a disgrace to ask for public relief, a confession of incompetence or sinfulness, of friendlessness and failure.

Rooted in rural life, these attitudes persisted in the towns and cities. Parents, schools, and popular literature all shored up the old verities. If human beings laboured and saved, God and nature would provide.

Yet the gospel of hard work, frugality, and sturdy self-reliance – in co-operation with those close to one, to be sure – was by the 1920s largely irrelevant to the condition of many Canadians. They depended on badly paying and often seasonal jobs. (Some depended on tariff protection, subsidies, and other socially sanctioned forms of public assistance, but Canadian manufacturers need not concern us here.) They were at the mercy of economic forces they could not control and of decisions they could not influence. Illness, industrial accident, or death could upset the best-laid plans; the prospect of old age emphasized the need for savings to people who were often quite unable to save. Most important, in cities much more than in the country it was very hard to provide for self and family if anything went wrong.

On the farm misfortune had to be grim or protracted before it became catastrophe. Subsistence could usually be maintained for a considerable time even while the enterprise was losing money. The landless urban labourer had no such protection. If he became disabled or unemployed, he very soon stared pauperism in the face. Often his wife was already working in order to secure an adequate family income. The margin for error or plain bad luck was slim, especially for the unskilled or semi-skilled worker.

The Great Depression brought misfortune on a colossal scale. It devastated Canada, and it has not yet been forgotten. More than forty years afterwards the occasional headline – 'The worst unemployment since the Depression' – continues to draw it to public attention.

The economic downswing began in the summer and autumn of 1929 – the Wall Street Crash was symbol as well as contributory cause – and ended in the winter and spring of 1933. The recovery that followed was uneven: prairie agriculture hardly shared in it. Moreover, it was interrupted by a renewed downturn in 1937–38. When war came in September 1939, many Canadians looked back on ten lean and hungry years.

War brought the fulfilment of hopes too long delayed. Providentially, the drought in Saskatchewan ended. Commodity prices rose. The armed forces and war industry began to absorb man- and womanpower: by 1941 unemployment was no longer a serious problem. A harsh prediction made by the LSR in 1935 had come true: 'It will be the mocking irony of our economic system if it presents as the ultimate, moral, "Christian" solution for unemployment – another war.'[5]

This is not the place for a detailed account of the economic impact of the Depression on Canada.[6] However, one of its aspects is worth describing because it was of considerable importance in the founding of the LSR. A larger proportion of Canadians was unemployed, and for longer periods of time, than in any economic slump before or since. The Dominion Bureau of Statistics estimated that on 1 June 1933, approximately 19 per cent of the total civilian labour force (agricultural as well as non-agricultural, self-employed as well as employed, salary as well as wage earners) were out of work. From then on the proportion decreased, but four years later one in eleven was still unemployed. In what remained of the pre-war period joblessness rose again.

Unemployment among wage and salary earners was lowest in managerial, professional, and commercial-financial occupations and in government and education. It was higher in transportation, manufacturing, and merchandising, and it was highest in the building trades and export industries, metallic mining excepted. Above all, the unskilled and the young suffered.

Of course, many of those who kept their jobs had to accept cuts in their wages and salaries – cuts at least partially mitigated by a decrease in the cost of living – or submit to a deterioration of working conditions. Extreme was the experience of teachers in rural Saskatchewan, where salaries plummeted and often were paid not in cash but in promissory notes of highly dubious worth. Max Braithwaite's *Why Shoot the Teacher* is a harrowing though humorous account of what this meant to one twenty-year-old fresh out of normal school. (One suspects that little of the humour was immediately obvious at the time.) But Braithwaite's experience differed only in degree from what happened to many working people elsewhere, in other regions and different jobs.

Yet few Canadians would have said that it was better not to work at all than to work for low wages at disagreeable tasks. Not only did unemployment often bring pauperization in its wake; it also tended to undermine the self-respect and self-confidence of the unemployed. Young people, from public-school drop-outs to university graduates, competed eagerly for scarce jobs; older men were usually prepared to do anything legal, and sometimes illegal, in order to get back to work.

Canada lacked any well-designed means of coping with mass unemployment, little having been learned in this respect from previous depressions.[7] Unemployment insurance did not yet exist. It would in any case have been of no use to those who were looking for their first job or those who had been unemployed for years. There was poor relief, but it was a local responsibility, often indifferently administered and inadequately funded. It was not intended to cope with the hundreds of thousands who became public charges in the 1930s.

It did not take many of the unemployed long to exhaust their resources. They had lived at the ragged edge of poverty even when they were working. As the 'Roaring Twenties' drew to an end, one-half of Canadians were at the poverty level or below it: approximately $1,000 per year for an urban family, lower on the farm. They were not helped by a system of taxation that relied heavily – for 90 per cent in 1930 – on indirect and property taxes that were more burdensome to the poor than to the better off. Many Canadians had no savings to speak of. After they had pawned or sold any valuables they might have, exhausted their credit with grocers and fuel merchants, could borrow or beg no more from relatives and friends, had their utilities cut off, and underwent or faced eviction from their homes, they would be forced to apply for relief.

Relief was usually far from easy to get. It involved a demonstration that the applicant was destitute and quite incapable of providing for his family. In many communities single people could not get it: one had to have dependents. Getting relief was a very mixed blessing, however. Life 'on the pogey' was meagre and humiliating, disliked and even hated by those who experienced it, feared by many others. Especially white-collar people and the better-paid artisans often tried to move heaven and earth in an attempt to stay off the relief rolls. Yet it increasingly became the family man's only licit alternative to starving and freezing in the dark with his wife and children. A woman's employment, if she could find it, rarely paid well enough by itself to sustain a family. Within two years of the onset of the Depression private charitable agencies were quite unable to meet all the demands for help.

Talleyrand observed that a married man with family will do anything for money. Certainly the destitute family man can ill afford pride. Most working people already knew this. In the 1930s thousands of white-collar Canadians, even some business and professional men, learned the same bitter lesson. They accepted relief with reluctance, but they accepted it.

Single people learned the lesson also, but in a somewhat different way. Ineligible in most cases for conventional relief, they could remain dependent on their parents or they could hit the road. Transiency, especially among single young men, increased dramatically after 1929. Although life on the road permitted a lingering sense of self-reliance, it offered no lasting solution to the problems of pauperism. Recognizing this, several of the provinces as well as the Dominion government opened relief camps for single unemployed men. Many young men swallowed their pride and entered them.

Because destitution was a virtual prerequisite for obtaining relief, it is startling to find that in April 1933, even as the LSR was meeting in Burlington, more than one and a half million Canadians depended on direct relief for physical survival. That was 15 per cent of the population! Two years later the figure was still one million. At the end of the decade Leonard Marsh of McGill University warned that a tenth of Canadians was drifting into chronic indigence.[8] By some who had become virtually unemployable even though 'able-bodied,' life on the dole was increasingly regarded as no worse and probably better than the menial, fitful, and ill-paid jobs that had been theirs. In any case, lengthy spells of unemployment and relief did nothing to qualify them for other kinds of work. Furthermore, impaired educational and economic opportunity had considerable effect on their children. Masked for a time by the wartime economic boom, the 'welfare trap' of more recent times was already taking shape.

III

The LSR was called forth by economic distress and dislocation on an unprecedented scale. Some of those who joined the league had been attracted by some form of socialism, Christian, Fabian, even Marxist, well before the Depression. But they did not link up or try to recruit others until 1930–32, as Canada and the world lurched ever further into crisis. Appalled by the suffering, particularly that of the urban unemployed, small groups of young and well-educated men and women got together, initially in Montreal and Toronto, to survey the mounting wreckage and explore the prospects for change. That a sizable proportion of them, as much as a third, was in education, social work, or the ministry was no accident. In the lives of their students, their clients, their parishioners, they were witnessing the demoralization of Canada, the undermining of her people.

Increasingly convinced that much of the competition in the economic realm was ultimately destructive, even of competition itself, they hoped that Canadians would learn to value co-operation more highly. They saw as part of their educational role the encouragement of co-operation. The LSR sought to replace 'monopoly' capitalism with a new economic order that the league came to call socialist and that it also described as the co-operative commonwealth. Although the league did not help to found the CCF, its association with the new political movement soon became very close.

In the service of its social and economic goals, the LSR sought to replace the loose federation that Canada had become with one in which economic matters, at least, would be firmly controlled from the centre. Peace being held to be essential to the establishment of the co-operative commonwealth, the LSR opposed the imperial tie because of its potential to involve Canada in a war. Many of its members also came to oppose the international obligations that accompanied membership in the League of Nations.

The LSR was a new phenomenon in Canadian intellectual life. Before the 1930s there had been no radical intelligentsia to speak of. Intellectuals were little drawn to the small radical and socialist movements and parties that existed from the late nineteenth century on. Generally they either shared the prevailing faith in progress and property or they did not draw attention to their doubts. The intellectual as social critic was not unknown, but he was usually a traditionalist excoriating society for its crass materialism and its failure to take seriously 'higher concerns.' Few intellectuals questioned the institution of private property, the dominance of capital over labour, or the benefits of a market economy.

By the 1920s socialism had made some inroads into Protestant clerical circles, notably among the clergy of the Methodist Church and its successor (in 1925), the United Church of Canada. Several ex-clergymen were active in radical politics: J.S. Woodsworth and William D. Irvine as Labour MPs, A.E. Smith in the Communist Party of Canada. Other intellectuals showed little interest, however. For example, 'an attempt made by Professor R.M. MacIver of the University of Toronto to launch a movement of social reconstruction in 1917 misfired.'[9] The Progressive movement among Ontario and western farmers got as little support from intellectuals as labour movements did. What support there was consisted of isolated individuals.

One reason why social radicalism found few adherents among the intelligentsia was that it challenged firmly established ideas and practices concerning property and contracts. Another was that it fell foul of strong feelings of attachment to the British Empire. Just as in the nineteenth century radicalism was linked, in people's minds if not in fact, to republicanism, democracy, and pro-Americanism, so by the end of the Great War it was coming to be associated with Bolshevism and the Soviet Union. And the Soviets had come by the mid-1920s to seem just as serious a menace to the integrity of the Empire as ever the Americans had been.

Frank Underhill once described the issue of imperial loyalty as a red herring that distracted the attention of Canadians from the economic, social, and political problems facing the country. Red herrings are evidently a potent species of fish! The issue did affect English Canadian intellectuals, however: the accusation of disloyalty to the British connection was damaging. In French Canada, where this sort of disloyalty was not so serious a fault, an ultra-conservative Roman Catholic hierarchy effectively checked radical tendencies among intellectuals.

The schools did little or nothing to foster the development of a critical cast of mind. T.W.L. MacDermot, then a historian at McGill and later headmaster of Upper Canada College in Toronto, commented in 1931 on the strong tendency of the educational system to discourage independence of thought. Neither school-teachers nor university professors had as yet organized themselves to protect academic freedom. For employees of all kinds there was no tradition of free political involvement or even the free expression of opinion. 'Men keep their doubts to themselves lest they get the sack – though doubts are not necessary to get that now – or be ostracized, or quietly immolated in the machine that employs them.'[10] That is, if they *had* doubts. We have no reason to suppose that many Canadians or, for that matter, many Canadian intellectuals were covert critics of the established order. Probably the great majority of them shared the prevailing ideas and beliefs without thinking much about them. It was the safe, sensible, natural course.

And yet: the issue of imperial loyalty was losing its power to distract. The Great War had raised questions about the value of the British connection. As the result of a conflict in which Canada would hardly have been involved had it not been for her ties with Britain, we had experienced great loss and divisiveness. The crisis over conscription had gravely endangered the country. Anti-imperialist feeling gained a certain legitimacy in the federal Liberal party, which was led in the interwar years by William Lyon Mackenzie King and depended on the support of French Canadians. With 'national unity' a primary concern to the political heir of Sir Wilfrid Laurier, the British connection was in official circles regarded with some misgiving.

At the same time, the pattern of Canadian economic relations was shifting from one of dependence primarily on British markets and sources of investment to one of dependence on the United States. As a result of the impact of mass-circulation magazines and, later, films and radio, cultural relations with the United States were also becoming stronger. Decades of migration, from Ontario, Quebec, and the Atlantic provinces into the States, and from the republic into Canada's West, had among Canadians weakened the fears of the nineteenth century. Increasing numbers came to think of themselves as North Americans first and to downplay the practical if not the symbolic significance of their status as British subjects.

The deepening Depression undermined, to some extent, faith in capitalism, the market economy, and the lords of private enterprise. The prestige of businessmen, very high in the 1920s, declined in the early 1930s.[11] It became clear to a growing number of Canadians that businessmen had no real answers to the questions raised by the slump. They purveyed bromides, saw silver linings to clouds and lights at the ends of tunnels, but these responses failed to cope with the realities of rising unemployment and agricultural distress.

A good many working people and farmers had lost confidence in the established order long before *this* Depression. So had a very few intellectuals. Now, however, a growing number of them were reaching the conclusion that they could do better than businessmen and business-oriented politicians. Some intellectuals were ready to assume roles of leadership. Where business ethics and expertise were failing, a different ethic and a different kind of expert might succeed. By 1932, in the midst of spreading economic disorder, a group of intellectuals was at last proclaiming the end of an era of progress under capitalism.

A similar though more emphatic shift to the left was taking place among intellectuals in Britain and in the United States. The political scientist Neal Wood notes that 'a British radical intelligentsia, comparable to the long-established continental intelligentsias, did not appear until the 1930s.'[12] In the United States those years have been described as 'the Red Decade' because of the spread of leftist ideas in intellectual circles. Liberal intellectuals came into their own during the 1930s, one historian writes: 'During this period, also, the left wing became an increasingly important segment of American liberalism as a whole.'[13]

In the two larger countries the Marxist and communist paths attracted more travellers than they did in Canada. Most Canadian intellectuals who turned left embraced the democratic socialism of the LSR and CCF. The Soviet Union found admirers in all three countries, but in Canada, at least, intellectuals rarely linked that admiration to support of the domestic Communist party.

About the Communist Party of Canada (CPC) there hung an aura of conspiracy, disloyalty, criminality. The arrest under Section 98 of the Criminal Code of Tim Buck and seven other Communists in 1931, and their conviction on the charge of criminal sedition, meant that the CPC was technically illegal until the repeal of Section 98 five years later. In view of this and of the low incidence of radicalism among Canadian intellectuals before the Depression, it is unsurprising that very few of them found their way into the CPC. It was a bit daring to join even the LSR!

IV

A distinctly donnish flavour permeated the league. Although they constituted less than 10 per cent of its membership, academics from the beginning and throughout its ten-year existence were highly conspicuous in the leadership of the LSR. Of the six national presidents only one, Louise Parkin of Montreal (1939–40), did not hold a university teaching post. Of the six men who served as vice-president only two, Graham Spry, and Everett Hall of London, Ontario, were not professors. (See appendix three.) This dominance by the academic element resulted mainly from the central place that education occupied in the LSR's purpose and activities. It owed a good deal, too, to the personal accomplishments and prestige of most of the academics in the LSR.

Other groups heavily represented among the members were schoolteachers, clergymen, social workers, as well as housewives and university students. The league was overwhelmingly college-educated, urban, anglophone, and central Canadian. The branches in Montreal and Toronto were by far the largest and most active: each had two hundred members or more throughout the 1930s and sponsored full programs of speeches, panel discussions, seminars, and so on. The annual national convention was never held in any other cities. At various times, however, and especially in the early years, before 1935, the LSR had branches in more than twenty other towns and cities in Ontario and the four western provinces. In the Atlantic region no branch ever really got properly off the ground. Members from rural Canada were rare; French Canadian members were rarer still. At no time did the total membership of the LSR reach one thousand.

The league's immediate audience was little more representative of Canadian society than its membership. This was not because the LSR sought to exclude anyone. Its meetings were open to the public; its books, pamphlets, and radio broadcasts were intended to reach as many Canadians as possible. But discussion of the need for social change is an esoteric hobby. The small minority of Canadians pursuing that hobby was not enlarged by the noticeably academic tone of much of LSR writing, a tone that persisted in spite of attempts to popularize the socialist argument.

Whether in book and pamphlet form or in *The Canadian Forum*, the main conduit of LSR views on current events, the league's writings captured neither of their potential audiences in trying to attract both. Those writings were not 'popular' enough to reach a large readership; they were not systematic enough to qualify as important contributions to the literature of socialism. To this generalization *Social Planning for Canada* (1935), the most comprehensive statement of the LSR's program, constitutes at least a partial exception. It sold three thousand copies, a number by no means negligible given that its price was high by contemporary standards. It was judged by reviewers, in Canada and abroad, to be a significant socialist statement, an assessment that the passage of time has modified but little.

Although the LSR's immediate public impact was small, its influence was substantial. The program and policy statements of the CCF during its first decade were designed or heavily influenced by the LSR. So, after 1935, was the CCF's organization. The Regina Manifesto of 1933 was drafted by league members led by Frank Underhill, and was firmly based on the LSR's own manifesto. Because CCF politicians used in their public statements material provided by the LSR, its ideas gained a much wider audience than the league was able to find for itself.

Another aspect of the LSR's influence is harder to assess. The group did not work in isolation. Membership, full or associate, was taken up by some people who were by no definition socialists and who did not support the CCF. Generally they did not stay for long, but they carried ideas with them when they left. Then there were the friends and acquaintances of LSR members who knew what the league stood for and who, while thinking some of its proposals extreme, agreed with others. These they may have adapted to their own ends. Intellectual influences are often impossible to trace with accuracy; who is to say, however, that Liberal politicians like Brooke Claxton and Vincent Massey, Conservative politicians like J.M. Macdonnell and Roland Michener, were not influenced by their acquaintanceships with LSR members and their awareness of ideas put forward by the league? And if they *were* influenced, who can say what consequences that had for the Canadian people?

The spread of the LSR's proposals was aided by the involvement of its members in other organizations, many of them founded in the 1920s and 1930s, that had an interest in studying the world and Canada, in enlightening them or improving them. These included the Canadian Political Science Association, the Canadian Institute of International Affairs, the League of Nations Society, the Canadian Institute on Economics and Politics, the Canadian Radio League, the Canadian Association for Adult Education, the Canadian Youth Congress, the Civil Liberties Union, the Committee To Aid Spanish Democracy, and the Fellowship for a Christian Social Order. Although none of these groups was narrowly partisan, almost all of them had political overtones and interests. They brought about constant contact between members of the LSR and others and encouraged the joint examination and sharing of ideas. Though much nearer its left bank than its right, the LSR was within a broad intellectual stream.

In spite of its rather short life the league was an important contributor to the intellectual and political life of Canada. Attempts made after the Second World War to revive it failed. The same absorption in the affairs of the CCF that, in the late 1930s and early war years, had led people to abandon the LSR prevented its rebirth. In a sense, however, the league lived on in the CCF and later in the New Democratic Party.

The LSR is primarily remembered as a group of intellectuals who enunciated the Canadian socialism of the CCF. Some of its importance, however, rests in its formulation of ideas concerning social welfare and fiscal policy in Canada, ideas that were deemed to be relevant to a capitalist economy in a transitional stage on the road to socialism. They were also held to presage key features of the co-operative commonwealth. But the ideas and policies derived from them were not in themselves socialist and hence were available for borrowing by Liberals and Conservatives. Beginning in the 1930s the major political parties in power in Ottawa and the provincial capitals introduced measures that over time brought about the modern welfare state in most of its essentials. Many of these measures were first proposed by the LSR and CCF.

A causal link between the league's ideas and their eventual, if often partial, implementation is probably impossible to demonstrate. In some cases it may simply not exist. Social democrats are not the only people who can think up serviceable reforms. However, the CCF, which championed many policies proposed by the LSR, is widely conceded the role of idea-giver in Canadian politics from the 1930s into the 1950s. Several measures of reform introduced by the Dominion government during the Second World War were prompted largely by the growing popularity of the CCF and constituted an attempt to steal some of its thunder.[14]

The LSR was a band of intellectual pioneers and sappers, trying with limited success to undermine aging citadels of thought and policy and to construct new ones. Even though a number of its once-radical notions have since become law or practice, however, its hopes for a co-operative commonwealth remain unsatisfied. The lost causes of the past repay study, Paul Goodman has reminded us, not least when those causes remain with us as unfinished business.

'Romantic' and 'innocent' the men and women of the LSR may have been in their diagnosis of the ills of society and the economy, their prescriptions for change, their attempt to reconcile freedom and the constraints of co-operation. Frank Underhill, looking back on the LSR in 1966, confessed as much.[15] An examination of what league members said and wrote, however, reveals at least as much shrewdness and hardheadedness as innocence in their assessment of the economic, social, and political problems of a country and a world in depression. Some of their ideas are still worth taking seriously, particularly in a period of renewed high unemployment as well as exacerbated regional and international disparities and divisions. The LSR was for a time a conscience to a country that so far has found neither social justice nor itself. The league's usefulness is not exhausted.

2

Bright beginnings

The Depression brought into existence the first organization of left-wing intellectuals in Canadian history. As the evidence of economic dislocation mounted, some of the younger intelligentsia became vocally critical of the inability of government and business to cope with it. For reasons partly personal, partly social, a few intellectuals took the unusual steps of protesting against aspects of their society that they considered to be unjust and challenging several of its basic assumptions. By the second year of the Depression of couple of small groups based in Toronto and Montreal were taking shape, consisting mainly of young men and women in the professions who asserted that the country could no longer go in the old way.

One such group came to life in Toronto in 1930. Writing in November to John W. Dafoe, editor of the *Manitoba Free Press* and a prominent Liberal, the historian Frank Underhill noted that a group of 'radically minded [professors]' was meeting at the University of Toronto. Their president was Underhill himself.[1]

It was this group that a few months later circulated what quickly became known as 'the letter of the sixty-eight professors.' This was a protest against the interference by Toronto police with public meetings. Led and inspired by their rabidly anti-communist Chief Constable D.C. Draper, the police had since the beginning of 1929 routinely prevented or broken up meetings deemed to be communistic. For almost two years no more than an occasional voice of protest was raised by the Toronto intelligentsia. This changed towards the end of 1930, however. The Fellowship of Reconciliation, a recently established, ecumenical organization of pacifists with international links, challenged the Police Commission to defend its policy in open debate. The chief constable and one of the commissioners dismissed the proposed public forum as evidently 'a communistic meeting under thin disguise.' The police furthermore induced a worried theatre owner to cancel his agreement with the fellowship, which had to meet at Carlton Street United Church instead.

Loud were the complaints that Sunday evening. Several fellowship members were clergymen; a few others taught at the University of Toronto. It was outrageous to be accused of communism, to lose one's intended meeting place. What business did the police have to interfere with meetings, anyway?

Soon afterwards, on 15 January 1931, a letter critical of the commission appeared in the four Toronto newspapers. It was signed with sixty-eight names, quickly recognized as those of teachers at the University of Toronto, a number of them senior. The letter had been drafted mainly by Underhill; it asserted 'that the right of free speech and assembly is in danger of suppression in this city' and deplored the policy of the Toronto Police Commission over the previous two years as 'short-sighted, inexpedient, and intolerable.' The signatories affirmed their 'belief in the free public expression of opinions, however unpopular or erroneous.'[2]

The result was a furore that did not die down for a full month. Three of the newspapers, the *Globe*, the *Mail and Empire*, and the *Evening Telegram*, were joined by leading citizens in regretting and deploring that 'communist sympathies' seemed to exist among a group of people whose claims to gentility had hitherto been beyond serious question. Editors and readers who wrote letters to them worried about the damage that radical professors might do to the minds of impressionable students. Only Joseph Atkinson's *Toronto Star* took the side of the sixty-eight. Although the professors had taken care not to state their affiliation with the university, the Board of Governors in due time thought it necessary publicly to dissociate the university from their action. It was a tempest in a teapot, perhaps. The sensation of being under attack, however, fostered a feeling of solidarity among some of the signers, while the tenor of the attack led them to become more critical of the established order.

What sixty-eight academics did in Toronto, one did in Montreal. Late in January 1931 two speakers at a meeting of the Canadian Labour Defence League, a Communist-run organization, were arrested and charged with sedition. On 3 February the Montreal *Gazette* published a letter by Frank Scott protesting the police action in this and similar cases and questioning the legality as well as the wisdom of what the police were doing. The Montreal police chief and the press were quick to inform Scott that the right of free speech had limits. The seditious and blasphemous utterances of communists must be curbed. 'I cannot allow this sort of thing to take place in Montreal,' the police chief said. 'There should be no place for communism in this country,' the *Gazette* added. Objections of the kind raised by Scott or by the Toronto professors were 'gratuitous' and even 'dangerous' insofar as they might lead students to be tolerant of the communist evil.[3] To Scott and others the message was clear: the beneficiaries and guardians of privilege would abuse the legal system in order to suppress certain kinds of criticism.

As the Depression worsened, the need for criticism and change became more pressing. One of the signers of the letter of the sixty-eight, Harry M. Cassidy, certainly thought so. An assistant professor of social science who was then studying unemployment in Ontario, he was becoming convinced that social scientists must become more radical and political. In May 1931 he wrote to J.S. Woodsworth to suggest that some economists at the University of Toronto might soon be of use to Woodsworth and the ginger group of Labour and Farmer MPs in the House of Commons.[4]

This was music to the politician's ears. For years he had been hoping that 'something more or less corresponding to the English Fabian Society' might be founded in Canada.[5] Through it university men might be of help to persons like himself. In 1929, when Woodsworth expressed this hope, the time had not yet come. Two years later, however, the man to whom he had expressed it, Frank Underhill, was ready to have a go at creating such an organization.

In 1931 Frank Hawkins Underhill (1889–1971) had already gained a certain notoriety, primarily because of his anti-imperialist iconoclasm and a ready wit that struck his detractors as acerbic. A slight man with a remarkably open face, bespectacled, with eyes that usually smiled, he was as kind to his students as he could be harsh in writing about some businessman or politician who annoyed him. 'He could be exasperating, but it was hard not to love him,' a student recollects. 'He was absolutely the most stimulating of teachers.' More than once in the 1930s and early 1940s the loyalty of his students required demonstration, for Underhill's commentary on current events kept him in trouble throughout those years.

Born into an artisan's family in Stouffville, just northeast of Toronto, 'a North York Presbyterian Grit,' as he later called himself, Underhill had studied classics and history at the University of Toronto and Balliol College, Oxford – he had won a Flavelle Scholarship – before the war. His teaching career began at the University of Saskatchewan, but he soon enlisted, fought in France as a second lieutenant in a British territorial regiment, and was wounded in the German offensive of March 1918. After teaching in Khaki University, part of the Canadian war effort, he returned to Saskatoon in time for the 1919 fall term.

Underhill returned to a country in turmoil. Throughout the world the year 1919 was one of revolution and counter-revolution, and though conditions in Canada were less extreme than in Europe they caused worry to many solid citizens. The Winnipeg General Strike in May and June was the most spectacular manifestation of the post-war malaise. The historian had more sympathy for another upheaval, which had its origins in the course of economic development before the war – the agrarian revolt in western canada. His early politics were Liberal, but at Oxford he had joined the Fabian Society as well as the Russell and Palmerston (Liberal) Club. He now became a supporter of the new Progressive movement. To a degree he learned to see central Canada through prairie eyes; he saw Toronto in a new, unflattering light. He also married a western woman, Mary Ruth Carr.

All the same, he did not feel at home in the West and in 1927 gladly took the opportunity to return to Toronto as professor of history. He liked his job, but the city, its social and intellectual stuffiness, its pretence of being more British than Britain, the money-grubbing of the men who set its tone: all these now irritated him. This irritation soon found relief, and Underhill's interest in politics an expression, after he was in 1929 asked to write a monthly column for *The Canadian Forum*. The main outlet for the writings of progressive intellectuals in the twenties, the *Forum* was in the decade and a half that followed to carry uncounted thousands of words by Underhill. Political commentary was greatly to his liking; he wrote easily and crisply. The tartness of his pieces earned him enemies as well as admirers, however. One Toronto newspaper, the *Mail and Empire*, demanded in 1931 that the historian be disciplined. It was not the last time that this demand was to be heard.

Tall, self-confident, capable of great charm, a *bon vivant* with a sometimes faintly condescending manner, Francis Reginald Scott was ten years Underhill's junior. At age thirty-two he was already one of Canada's better-known poets. Born into a well-established upper-middle-class family in Quebec, he was the son of Archdeacon F.G. Scott, also a poet and during the Great War chaplain to the First Division of the Canadian Expeditionary Force. The younger Scott had studied history at Bishop's College in Lennoxville, Quebec. After teaching school for a year he entered Magdalen College, Oxford, with a Rhodes Scholarship in 1920. He loved history but, after teaching it again at Lower Canada College upon his return, he was persuaded by his older brother, a lawyer, that there was more future in the law. In 1928, after a year of practice Scott took a teaching post in the Faculty of Law at McGill, the university where his paternal grandfather had taught anatomy. In 1928, too, Scott married a promising artist, Marian Dale.

Unlike Underhill, Scott had been little interested in politics before the Depression; he *was* impressed by the Christian socialism of R.H. Tawney's *The Acquisitive Society* (1921). For most of the 1920s he was mainly occupied with his studies and his poetry. One of the new Montreal school of poets, he was co-founder with Leo Kennedy, A.M. Klein, and A.J.M. Smith of the *McGill Fortnightly Review*. He also published poems in other journals, including *The Canadian Forum*. Towards the end of the decade Scott's horizon was expanding, however. Partly this was the result of his belonging to 'the Group,' an informal non-partisan discussion club consisting mostly of young men who had been at Oxford. Among its other members were Terry MacDermot and Eugene Forsey, as well as Brooke Claxton and an investment counsellor named Raleigh Parkin. In 1930 they were at work on a book that would 'deal with political, economic and social problems of the country' by offering remedies to them.[6] Scott was only one of its intended contributors; others included MacDermot and Forsey as well as Graham Spry, national secretary of the Association of Canadian Clubs, and Underhill. This book was never published, for reasons that none of its contributors have been able to recall. However, his participation in the project quickened Scott's interest in Canada. His expanding awareness of his country and his world was further nourished by his membership in the Montreal branch of the newly established Canadian Institute of International Affairs. The Depression radicalized him. By the summer of 1931 Scott was ready for a political movement and a cause.

In August Scott and Underhill met each other in person for the first time. The occasion was the annual Institute of Politics at Williams College in Williamstown, Massachusetts. From the very first the two men hit it off. They enjoyed each other's style; both had sharp minds and knew how to use them. More important, they saw the problems that beset Canada in much the same light and were groping towards similar solutions. They had met at the right time.

One Sunday morning the two of them, accompanied by Percy Corbett, dean of McGill's Faculty of Law, walked up Mt Greylock. At just over a thousand metres Greylock is the tallest peak in the Berkshire range, but it is not particularly dangerous or daunting. Scores of hikers were on their way to the top that day. It was a bracingly active day's excursion, with the promise of a solid dinner back in Williamstown at the end. Alas, with prohibition still in effect, a good drink was harder to obtain.

Those who dwell in the plains often get heady in the mountain air. Visions of a vitalized Canada appeared. Underhill stressed the need for a sort of Fabian society in Canada. He believed that a new political party would soon arise, with support from farmer and labour organizations. There should be a group of intellectuals that could provide the new party with a coherent platform. This in turn might prevent the party from disappearing in the same way the Progressive movement of the 1920s had melted away.

Scott responded with enthusiasm as the historian outlined his ideas. Although Corbett largely shared the concerns of his two companions, he became almost a spectator as Scott and Underhill bounced ideas off each other. With every step upward, social change came to seem more possible. As the men surveyed the hills around them and the world below, they undertook to launch a national organization of intellectuals. They descended to their evening meal with growing hunger and a warm sense of accomplishment.

Underhill and Scott agreed that the first goal of the proposed organization should be the enunciation of new ideas. These would influence public opinion and guide politicians. To these ends they thought the publication of a series of pamphlets to be most suitable. When they returned to Canada, however, they found that not everyone was impressed with this plan. 'Frank Scott has brought back the product of your joint climb up Greylock,' Terry MacDermot shortly afterwards wrote Underhill: 'It seems to be simply a serial production of the book. Claxton is inclined to think that pamphlets will not be so effective ... I incline in my turn to agree. On the other hand, it may be the only way of getting anything out at first. The main thing is to get something written – we, down here at all events, spend at least 90% of our energies in talking about and organizing for what we are going to do.'[7] The self-criticism was unsurprising. Intellectuals are apt to accuse themselves of talking rather than doing, generally with reason.

In the planning for the new organization MacDermot and Claxton soon took a back seat. By the early autumn Scott's main collaborators were Eugene Forsey, King Gordon, a young minister who had recently been appointed to the staff of United Theological College, and a law student named David Lewis. Forsey and Gordon were to be centrally important in the LSR, the CCF, and an organization of Christian socialists called the Fellowship for a Christian Social Order (FCSO); Lewis later in the decade became the key employee of the national CCF.

Eugene Alfred Forsey, excitable, contentious, equipped with a keen intellect, already had the habit of being quick to correct the mistakes of others, often at considerable length. This made him less than universally popular. He was a fine raconteur who could delight listeners with his gifts of mimicry. His face and voice were both marvellously expressive, especially when he disagreed strongly with someone. Rarely was he able to suffer fools in silence; sometimes he regretted this.

Born in Newfoundland in 1904, the son of a Methodist clergyman, Forsey grew up in Ottawa in the home of his maternal grandfather, W.C. Bowles, who was the chief clerk of the House of Commons. To this Forsey owed a lasting taste for the intricacies of government. He took his BA and MA degrees in economics and political science from McGill, going to Balliol College, Oxford, on a Rhodes Scholarship in 1926. Three years later he joined the faculty of McGill as a sessional lecturer in political economy. Although he had a heavy teaching load and was also trying to complete a doctoral thesis, his restless energy, capacity for moral outrage, and sense of Christian duty carried him well beyond his university work. He was an active layman in the United Church of Canada. His political convictions were also strong: at Oxford he became eager to help build a more co-operative, more equitable, more Christian social order. He saw the organization proposed by Scott as one possible means.

John King Gordon shared many of Forsey's passions, but added to them patience and the ability to disagree in argument without giving offence. 'He had a great sense of humour which kept fanaticism in check,' a friend recalls. A tireless worker, he invariably took the part of the underdog. This trait he owed to his parents and particularly to his father, Rev. C.W. Gordon, better known as the popular novelist Ralph Connor. A Presbyterian minister in Winnipeg who served as a chaplain during the war, Dr Gordon was a man of great magnanimity who, more by example than by preaching, instilled in his son and daughters a sense of Christian love and duty and an immense interest in people.

Born in 1900, King Gordon studied at Manitoba College and went to Oxford on a Rhodes Scholarship in his twenty-second year. There he was influenced by the neo-idealism of his tutor, F.L. Ogilvie, and by the Christian socialism of R.H. Tawney. Gordon returned to Canada to study theology at Wesley College and served for some years as a United Church minister in several prairie charges. The fall of 1929, when Wall Street peaked and then crashed, found him a spectator in New York, where he studied at Union Theological Seminary. He was most impressed by two teachers who became his friends, the radical theologians Reinhold Niebuhr and Harry Ward. By the time he was appointed to teach Christian Ethics in Montreal two years later, Gordon was a vigorous critic of capitalist society.

David Lewis already was one when he entered university. Short of stature, with intense, dark eyes in a lively face, he was twenty-two years old in 1931. He was affable and extraordinarily well-spoken, with that touch of self-importance that often attaches to students who have gained the respect and confidence of their teachers. Born in Russian Poland, he had come to Canada as a small child. His father had encouraged him to read socialist books, and even as a teenager the younger Lewis was active in politics. He had ties with organized labour in the Montreal garment district; soon after entering college he became the secretary of the McGill Labour Club. A brilliant student, he came to the attention, first of Forsey and later, after he entered law school in 1931, of Scott. The latter was particularly impressed with the young Jewish immigrant and urged him to apply for a Rhodes Scholarship. By 1932 the successful Lewis was studying law at Oxford. Before he left, however, he added a note of realism to the discussions of the academics who were planning the work of the proposed organization.

In Toronto, Underhill found upon his return that things had already begun to move. Some of the members of the discussion group formed the previous fall were already working on a manifesto for the sort of Fabian Society he had proposed to Scott. Among them were Harry Cassidy, Eric Havelock, Lorne T. Morgan, and J.F. Parkinson, all but Havelock economists at the University of Toronto. Morgan did not stick around for long: the organization that was taking shape was apparently too tame for him. Later in the 1930s he was to become a trenchant critic of social democracy. His place among the planners was taken by yet another young economist, Irene Biss.

Harry Morris Cassidy (1900–1951), immensely able and industrious, was during its first two years one of the key figures in the LSR. A handsome and slim six-footer who loved sports and played tennis avidly, he was generous with his time where students, good causes, and his friends were concerned. He and his wife Beatrice entertained often: the Cassidys and their home on Cottingham Street in the Summerhill area of Toronto were popular with other junior faculty members.

A native of Vancouver, Cassidy had attended the University of British Columbia and the Robert Brookings Graduate School of Economics and Government in Washington, DC. He was uncommon among the LSR's academics in having gone to the United States for his advanced studies and in holding the PH D degree. After teaching economics south of the border for two years, he landed a position at the University of Toronto in 1929. Keenly interested in welfare economics, he was by 1931 also secretary and research director for the Unemployment Research Committee of Ontario. He wrote its report, *Unemployment and Relief in Ontario 1929–1932*; this and his subsequent work for the Lieutenant-Governor's Committee on Housing Conditions in Toronto helped to establish him as perhaps Canada's foremost expert on social-welfare policy.

In 1934 the Cassidys left Toronto to return to the west coast: Cassidy had accepted appointment to the directorship of Social Welfare for the Province of British Columbia. His socialism was never deeply red, and he craved the opportunity to try to put some of his ideas into practice. He left his mark on the LSR, however, and, as a co-drafter of the Regina Manifesto, on the CCF as well. And he was not completely lost to the LSR: he continued to help with the league's book, *Social Planning for Canada*.

Several members of the Toronto inner circle were recent immigrants from England. Eric Alfred Havelock, twenty-eight years of age in 1931, was the oldest among them. Slightly built, with a restrained manner, he possessed a brilliant mind and a sardonic wit. This sometimes made him a less than comfortable companion. Although he usually had his temper well under control, he could get carried away by emotion and by his own very considerable eloquence.

After studying at Leys School and taking a degree in Greats at Cambridge, Havelock had come to Canada in 1926. He taught at Acadia University, Wolfville, NS, for three years and then joined the Department of Classics at Victoria College. As an undergraduate he had eagerly read G.D.H. Cole, Harold Laski, and G.B. Shaw; a few years later, in 1930, he was deeply impressed when he met J.S. Woodsworth. He had come to see himself as a Christian socialist and to feel the lack of something like the Fabian Society. He joined Underhill's little group of radical professors and helped to draft the letter of the sixty-eight. If there was to be an organization of left-wing intellectuals, Havelock wanted to be part of it from the beginning.

So did Joseph Frederick Parkinson. A handsome man with a beautifully chiselled face and a fine voice, he was almost universally liked. One sometime collaborator calls him 'thoughtful, tolerant, wise.' He was endlessly helpful to his students, and their plight upon graduation, their inability to get employment commensurate with their education or, indeed, to get any employment at all, distressed him deeply. Born in 1904, he was easily young enough to empathize closely with them.

A graduate in commerce from the London School of Economics, Parkinson had come to Canada in 1929 in order to take a position in the Department of Political Economy at the University of Toronto. A man with an orderly cast of mind, he was attracted by the notions of central planning that socialists were developing at that time. These he soon fused with the advocacy of counter-cyclical monetary and fiscal policies. He was eventually to become a great admirer of the *General Theory* of John Maynard Keynes.

Irene May Biss was quite as popular as Parkinson. 'An extraordinarily pretty woman, tall, with sparkling eyes, lovely curls, and a smile which constantly played around the corners of her mouth,' one man remembers; 'She had a beautiful, low-pitched voice, and a fine English wit. She was also very intelligent, but didn't show off.' She was, and is, charming.

Biss's background was cosmopolitan. Born in South Africa in 1907, she had lived in India for a number of years before going to England, where she read economics at Girton College, Cambridge. After taking her degree in 1928 she obtained an MA in social research from Bryn Mawr College in Pennsylvania before becoming a lecturer in the Department of Political Economy at Toronto in 1929. The salary was very low, and for the next nine years the young economist made ends meet by serving as a don in residence.

Her father was a member of the British Labour party, and while at Cambridge Biss belonged for a time to the Labour Club. The coming of the Depression reinforced her interest in thorough-going social reform. Like Parkinson and others in the department, she signed the letter of the sixty-eight. The new organization proposed by Underhill and Cassidy seemed to her to be overdue.

Progress was now rapid. In October, Graham Spry – he did not know it yet, but seven years later he would marry Irene Biss – wrote to Underhill: 'I hear that a sort of Fabian Society is being formed, and that you are behind it ... In this connection I have some plans which might interest you ... I am negotiating for the purchase of an erstwhile radical paper.'[8] It was *The Farmer's Sun*, organ of the United Farmers of Ontario, which Spry was intent on buying. The weekly was in financial difficulties and he was confident that he could make a good deal.

A tall, athletic, square-jawed man, steady-eyed, animated, and emphatic in his speech, Graham Spry was always in motion. His fertile brain was ever hatching new schemes for the benefit and improvement of his fellow countrymen. Since there was a healthy dash of ego in Spry's make-up, he usually cast himself prominently in these schemes. He was a born organizer with a circle of friends and acquaintances that, by 1931, stretched clear across Canada.

Born into an old Canadian family in 1900, Spry grew up in Manitoba and went to university there. While taking his BA he worked as a reporter and editorial writer for the *Manitoba Free Press*. As a nineteen-year-old with some military training behind him, he served in the special constabulary during the Winnipeg General Strike, an interlude not predictive of his later sympathies for labour. Three years later he entered University College, Oxford, on a Rhodes Scholarship. He joined the Liberal as well as Labour clubs; this, in addition to a year spent working for the International Labour Organization in Geneva, confirmed his growing tendency to see things from labour's point of view.

Upon his return to Canada in 1926 Spry became national secretary of the Association of Canadian Clubs. For the next five years he travelled a great deal and made contacts everywhere. These proved very useful when, in the fall of 1930, with his good friend Alan Plaunt, he founded the Canadian Radio League. Spry skilfully organized the effort to establish public broadcasting in Canada. At the same time, however, he was becoming increasingly perturbed both by the effects of the Depression on the country he loved and by the prospect of his own future. He was thirty years old – time for a new job, a new challenge?

To a newspaper friend, George Ferguson, Spry wrote in 1931 that he was inclined to take a gamble, to quit his safe job and become 'a rather socialistic, yet not purely agrarian agitator: public ownership, low tariff, etc ...,' to use his journalistic skills on behalf of 'the poor bozos' of Canada. The time seemed right for a change. He wanted to get into politics, Spry told Brooke Claxton: 'There will either be a third party or the Liberal party will move to the left. In either case the farmer's movement in Ontario, as well as in the West, will be of vital consequence ... If I own the Farmer's Sun ... I am free to work with but not under the Farmer movements and to ride with if not partly to drive farm opinion towards one or other result, a Liberal party that is liberal, or a third party.'[9] Armed with $10,000 put up by the independently wealthy Alan Plaunt, Spry purchased the *Sun* in January 1932 and resigned his position with the Association of Canadian Clubs. Thus began for Spry five exhilarating but ultimately deeply frustrating years.

While Spry was negotiating for the takeover of the weekly, the two small groups that Scott and Underhill had got together in Montreal and Toronto were trying to draft a program or manifesto. At least five drafts went back and forth between September and January. The main difficulty lay in deciding just how radical the document ought to sound. Too strident a tone would scare off potential members, it was feared, but the dangers of sounding polite were also great. Who would want to join a bunch of tame tigers?[10]

By and large, restraint conquered passion, not least because the Montreal group was in charge of the final draft. Scott, Forsey, and company had hopes of attracting membership from French as well as English Canada. It therefore seemed advisable not to sound too radical. On the week-end of 23 January 1932 five Montrealers – Forsey, Gordon, Lewis, Scott, and a lawyer named J.K. Mergler – travelled to Toronto in order to iron out some organizational questions and agree upon a name.

They were not the only delegation from Montreal to visit Toronto that winter week-end. The McGill basketball team defeated the Varsity squad in a 'slow and cautious' game on Friday night; the Montreal Canadiens got a more hostile reception on Saturday, as the Maple Leafs blanked them 3–0. On the same evening Mayor W.J. Stewart of Toronto said in a radio message that 'rigid economy' must be exercised if 'sound city credit' was to be maintained. This was the sort of penny-wise–pound-foolish policy that the LSR would come to criticize. For the moment, however, its founders stuck to the business at hand. The meeting came to be regarded as the first national convention of the LSR.

The Montrealers argued for an organization along ostensibly Fabian lines, with three classes of membership: full, associate, and subscribing. In a cosmopolitan mood, they favoured the name 'League for Economic Democracy' as 'an adaptation from the League for Industrial Democracy' in the United States. Neither of these suggestions was adopted. Two kinds of membership only, full and associate, were decided upon at the Toronto meeting. The name was left open. The Torontonians preferred 'League for Social Reconstruction' over the 'American-sounding' name proposed by their Montreal associates. Both were clumsy, Scott thought. 'Couldn't some of you devote an evening to heavy drinking in the hope of achieving an inspiration' and a better name, he asked Underhill in February.[11] Evidently either the spirits or the inspiration failed.

Wymilwood Hall, Victoria College, once the mansion of the millionaire financier E.R. Wood, was the site of the league's first public meeting. The evening of 23 February was more than seasonally cold, with a few snowflakes straggling from the clouds. By contrast, the seventy-five men and women who turned up were warm with enthusiasm. Most promptly took out membership at two dollars per year and approved the manifesto and constitution that had been adopted by the founding groups.

The meeting received no attention from the *Globe* the following morning. The paper's readers were, however, told of an address to the members of the Advertising Round Table on 'the possibilities of television in the advertising field.' Its author, B.A. 'Bert' Trestrail, will reappear in this history as the author of a spirited, if belated and inaccurate, attack on the LSR. To the advertising men on 23 February he had predicted 'that the day might not be far off when people in their own homes would be able to see products in motion, and asked his audience to consider what that would mean from an advertising standpoint.' It was mind-boggling: let it not be said that banality lacks imagination. At Wymilwood, meanwhile, the intellectuals shunned the sort of catchy name an advertising man might have thought up and christened themselves the League for Social Reconstruction.

In Montreal approximately seventy-five people attended the first meeting, held on 11 March 1932. Reluctantly the name chosen by the Torontonians was adopted; what else could be done? The manifesto and constitution were more cheerfully approved. A provisional national executive had been appointed in January, consisting of Gordon, Havelock, Parkinson, Scott, Underhill, who became the first president, and Isabel Thomas, first secretary-treasurer. Remembered as a striking and dynamic woman, Isabel M. Thomas (1899–1953) was the head of the English department at York Memorial Collegiate in Toronto. Educated at the University of British Columbia and the University of Toronto, where she earned the MA degree, she was the daughter of Rev. Ernest Thomas, the secretary of the Board of Evangelism and Social Service of the United Church; to him in part she owed her strong sense of social responsibility and sympathy for the underdog. These she shared also with the man chosen as honorary president of the LSR, J.S. Woodsworth. No one in Montreal was likely to quarrel with these choices, and no one did.

Although it was born of compromise and sought to avoid language that might unduly limit its appeal, the manifesto that emerged from these early meetings remains an effective summary of most of the LSR's concerns throughout its life. The preamble describes the league as 'an association of men and women who are working for the establishment in Canada of a social order in which the basic principle regulating production, distribution and service will be the common good rather than private profit.' The capitalist system is 'unjust and inhuman, economically wasteful, and a standing threat to peace and democratic government.' Wealth has been concentrated 'in the hands of a small irresponsible minority of bankers and industrialists,' to whose interests those 'of farmers and of wage and salaried workers – the great majority of the population – are habitually sacrificed ...' Poverty and insecurity have not been banished in spite of an abundance of resources; catastrophic depression still follows feverish boom. This will continue so long as 'private profit is the main stimulus to economic effort.' Canada needs 'a new social order which will substitute a planned and socialized economy for the existing chaotic individualism ...,' one that will end 'the present glaring inequalities' and thus 'eliminate the domination of one class by another.'

The manifesto lists nine 'essential first steps towards the realization of this new order' (1) Public ownership and operation of utilities and other industries approaching monopoly condition; (2) Nationalization of banks and other financial institutions; (3) Further development of co-operative enterprises, especially in agriculture; (4) Legislation providing social services to the worker as well as giving him 'an effective voice in the management of his industry'; (5) Publicly organized health, hospital, and medical services; (6) Steeply graded income and inheritance taxes; (7) A national planning commission; (8) 'The vesting in Canada of the power to amend and interpret the Canadian constitution so as to give the federal government power to control the national economic development'; and (9) A foreign policy aimed at securing international co-operation and promoting disarmament and peace. Within a few months one more plank was added: it provides for the establishment of boards that will regulate imports and exports.

The document concludes with an undertaking to establish study groups and to inform the public by means of pamphlets, articles, lectures, and the like. The LSR 'will support any political party in so far as its programme furthers the above principles; and will foster co-operation among all groups and individuals who desire in Canada the kind of social order at which the League aims.' The road to the future was to be travelled in the coach of mutual assistance. (See appendix one.)

In retrospect two omissions are striking. One is the absence of a plank on civil liberties. This did not reflect a lack of interest: the letter of the sixty-eight and Scott's protests in 1931 against the prosecution of Communists demonstrate a clear concern. 'I suspect that we were just more concerned with the immediate economic issues,' Professor Scott comments, 'and that the increasing decline in civil liberties only induced us to make statements about it when we came to drafting the Regina Manifesto.'[12]

Minority rights constitute the second omission. 'Legitimate provincial claims to autonomy' – they were not spelled out – were not to be infringed. About the protection of the French language or the cultural rights of French Canadians, however, the manifesto is silent. Possibly the feeling was, in this case as in that of civil liberties, that a document that addressed economic and political matters should not be unduly cluttered up with other concerns. Certainly Scott, for one – he was not alone – was conscious of the French Canadian presence. 'The CCF is likely to encourage the learning of French,' he told the Regina Convention in 1933: 'There is no reason why we might not come out with a bi-lingual currency.'[13] He also promised, however, that provincial rights in education would in no way be affected by the CCF. Later, in the draft of a revised LSR manifesto in 1938, protection of both civil liberties and minority rights was clearly spelled out.

Another omission is not surprising. The manifesto carefully avoids the term *socialism*. Given the wish of the LSR's founders not to scare off the cautious so long as it was possible to attract the more radical, the document was bound to pull punches. Brooke Claxton commented to a friend: 'I have read the platform of Frank's movement with immense surprise. It hardly differs by so much as a comma from those of all political parties in Canada.'[14] There was truth in the exaggeration.

The constitution of the LSR was short and snappy. It defined the league, stated its purpose, and set forth the functions of the national executive, the national convention, and the local branches. The executive, elected annually by the convention, would exercise 'a general control ... over the activities of the League,' and have 'an absolute discretion in regard to publications put out under the name of the League or any of its branches.' The national convention was to be the supreme governing body. It consisted of the members of the executive as well as delegates, one from each branch and additional delegates at the rate of one for each twenty-five branch members. Only the convention would have the power to amend the manifesto or the constitution.

Local branches could be organized wherever ten or more people were gathered together in the name of social reconstruction. Branches were mostly free to operate as they saw fit, so long as they abided by the general directives of the convention and executive and paid their annual capitation fees of fifty cents to the national office. Associate membership was open to those who wanted only to express a general sympathy with the aims of the league. Provision was also made for people who lived in places where branches could not be organized: they could become members-at-large. Finally, students could form their own college groups or join a local branch; a capitation fee of only twenty-five cents was due. (See appendix two.)

Membership grew rapidly at first. By the beginning of April the branch in Toronto had one hundred members; Montreal reached that number in June. In the early summer branches were organized in Victoria and Vancouver. The latter branch shortly published a pamphlet that suggested an additional plank to the manifesto. It looked to measures that would have to be adopted to ensure the supply of essential goods and services to the population in case of emergency. (What emergency was anticipated the Vancouverites did not make clear.) Elsewhere in the West, branches also grew up rapidly in 1932.

Assistance in spreading knowledge that the league existed was provided by some of the Labour and Farmer MPs who made up the ginger group in the House of Commons. Probably more useful was an incident that supports Claud Cockburn's observation: 'Roars of applause are nice too, but there is historical evidence for the belief that you get, in the end, better service out of a sound piece of denunciation and insult by some properly accredited reviler.'[15] The LSR's unexpected benefactor was the prime minister, R.B. Bennett; the occasion was the budget debate in April 1932. Having somehow got hold of a copy of the league's manifesto, the prime minister read it to the other members of the House of Commons and triumphantly identified its author as none other than Vincent Massey, president of the National Liberal Federation. This was 'the new parlour socialism' of the Liberal party, Bennett crowed, designed 'to take advantage of ... the unrest and the distrust incident to the present economic condition and to capitalize it for party advantage ...' J.S. Woodsworth soon set the record straight. Massey was innocent; the manifesto was the work of some university people in Toronto and Montreal. Woodsworth used the occasion to inform the House of the nature and purpose of the LSR and identified himself as its honorary national president. 'Premier Bennett ... rather flattered the movement by associating the name of Vincent Massey with it,' the *Ottawa Citizen* commented. 'The actual organizers seem to be younger people without social prominence or high place in Canadian public life.' Other newspapers also picked up the story. The 'younger people' could only agree with Woodsworth that 'the LSR has certainly had some good advertising.'[16] And at the right time, too.

By the beginning of 1933 there were seventeen branches, Victoria and Vancouver on the coast; Calgary, Edmonton, Breton, and Taber in Alberta; Regina, Prince Albert, and Biggar in Saskatchewan; Winnipeg and Dauphin in Manitoba; Toronto, Ottawa, Kingston, and Belleville in Ontario; Montreal and Verdun in Quebec. Most of these were small, many of them barely having the ten required members. Toronto and Montreal, on the other hand, had at least one hundred and fifty members each.

We know most about the members, full and associate, of the branch in Toronto. Among the names on the membership lists in 1933 and 1934 we find those of Geoffrey Andrew, a teaching master at Upper Canada College, J.B. Bickersteth, the warden of Hart House, University of Toronto, Dr Salem Bland, the controversial United Church minister whose column appeared in the *Toronto Star* under the by-line 'The Observer,' Rev. William B. Creighton, editor of *The New Outlook*, the weekly paper of the United Church of Canada, William Dennison, the remedial-speech teacher who was soon to become prominent in municipal politics, Rev. C.H. Huestis, general secretary of the Lord's Day Alliance, D.M. LeBourdais, author and journalist, Joseph McCulley, headmaster of Pickering College, D. Roland Michener, a lawyer who eventually became governor general, Alan Plaunt, philanthropist with wide interests, Mrs C.B. Sissons, active in a number of left-wing causes in the 1930s, Rev. Ernest Thomas, the secretary of the Board of Evangelism and Social Service of the United Church, S.B. Watson, Canadian manager of the publishing house of Thomas Nelson & Sons, and J.F. White, for some years editor of *The Canadian Forum*. Not all of these people stayed with the LSR for long: Roland Michener, for one, had already left in mid-1934. By that time the branch had 219 full and associate members – no division between them is available – forty-five of them members-at-large.[17]

A breakdown was made of the Toronto membership at the end of 1933. It reveals that among the 202 members, there were 33 schoolteachers, 30 housewives, 19 university professors, 12 social workers, 11 clergymen, 10 physicians and nurses, 5 accountants, 2 lawyers, 2 engineers, 2 architects, and a single librarian, as well as 11 university students and 64 persons described only as 'miscellaneous.'[18] A few of the members were self-employed but most were evidently from the middle and upper levels of white-collar workers, the 'new' petite bourgeoisie. The old petite bourgeoisie of small businessmen, shopkeepers, artisans, and the like, contributed almost no members to the LSR.

Few of the LSR's members were unemployed. Even fewer were wealthy. Most had jobs that provided them and their families with more or less adequate incomes. That the economy was incapable of providing many Canadians with such incomes seemed disgraceful. Those who joined the LSR had at the very least begun to wonder whether the capitalist system was to blame for the want and the despair.

Frank Underhill, a full professor earning $4,700 a year – this fell to just over $4,000 in 1933 when all civil-service and university salaries were reduced – recalled years later: '... For the first and only time in my life I belonged to a small social group who enjoyed a superior status, economic and social.' In the 1930s university professors in Toronto '... had a secure income, not a very big one, but secure ...'[19] The LSR's members typically became critical of the status quo not so much because they were suffering materially themselves as because of the suffering they witnessed, whose spread they feared. The teachers and professors among them knew well what faced young people leaving school. Unemployment seemed such an incredible waste of people and their skills.

Human motives are rarely unmixed. The desire for wealth may be acquired; the desire for recognition and approval assuredly is not. It is innate. A society oriented towards commercial pursuits and money-making does not accord the highest prestige or recognition to teachers, clergymen, and social workers (to say nothing of housewives). Is it surprising that LSR members should have had misgivings about their society, that they should have hoped to inaugurate one in which the helping professions, the nurturers, stood higher in the sight of men? The social scientists among them dreamed of the day when their expertise should have its full reward.

Then, too, thinking people cannot enjoy the awareness that their livelihood is dependent on the favour of others, that the honest expression of oneself may endanger that livelihood. Most human beings crave security; for intellectuals material security takes its place alongside intellectual freedom and integrity. In his fifty-year-old classic, *The Psychology of Socialism*, Hendrik de Man writes: 'The intellectual inclines towards socialism in proportion as he feels that the capitalist organization of society puts hindrances in the way of the fulfilment of his desire to work after his own fashion.' De Man cites dislike of attempts in industrial enterprises to bureaucratize and specialize the functions of the 'brainworker,' the dismay that a professional man or artist may feel in view of the indignity involved in having to sell his skill or talent, 'usually to persons incapable of understanding its true worth,' and the sense that administrative personnel may have that their desire to serve the public is being subordinated to the wishes 'of others whose sole interest is acquisitive.'[20]

De Man is not concerned with 'declassed intellectuals,' the self-appointed 'unrecognized geniuses' who constitute 'the ragtag and bobtail of Bohemia.' His interest is in 'engineers, men of science, school teachers, able civil servants,' and so on, 'persons who, far from being social failures, hold premier positions in industry, the State, and the educational world.' It was precisely these people whom the LSR in 1932 set out to reach. From among them the league's membership was largely drawn.

De Man asserts that 'the idea of socialism sprang, not so much from the physical distress of manual workers, as from the moral distress of mental workers.' Why, then, have so few intellectuals become socialists? 'Very few ... are able, on their own initiative, to amplify their special motive of work for its own sake into a constructive social motive. This psychological evolution needs an above-average development of the social sentiment, that is to say an above-average capacity for understanding that the individual lot is an integral part of the lot of the community.'[21] If this interpretation is correct, and if, as I hope to show, the LSR became an organization of socialists, the 'above-average development of the social sentiment' of many LSR members undoubtedly owed much to their religious convictions or background. Too many of them were children of the manse or belonged to the Fellowship for a Christian Social Order for the historian to ignore.

De Man's statement rejects the Marxist view of intellectuals as mere camp followers in the socialist movement unless they wholly adopt and internalize the attitudes and mentality of the proletariat. As a result of his experiences in the Belgian socialist movement, de Man had become critical of the prevailing suspicion of intellectuals with bourgeois or petit-bourgeois antecedents. Self-preoccupied as it may in part have been, however, his explanation of the intellectual's place in the socialist movement is useful. It helps to clarify the attitude of the LSR to a society that attaches a price tag to a man's labour and to the works of his mind.

This attitude was rarely more emphatically expressed than in *Social Planning for Canada*, the LSR's main publication:

There is a third group in the community [in addition to farmers and wage-earners] who might naturally be expected to be attracted to a socialist programme ... This is composed of the extensive middle class of professional men and women, – teachers, scientists, engineers, physicians, dentists, clergymen, nurses, social workers, etc., – and of the managers and skilled technicians in the ranks of industry. Most of these have to a considerable extent in their individual lives eliminated the profit motive from their activities. Most of them are painfully conscious of the vulgarization and degradation which are inherent in a society dominated by money-making; and they would welcome the emancipation of creative energies which would come to them if they were active members in a planned and socialized community. For they feel themselves thwarted and perverted now by the necessity of serving mammon as well as following their own professional ideals.[22]

The allegations of professional uneasiness were quite unsubstantiated. They were, in fact, the products mostly of wishful thinking. Much of the Canadian middle class served – and serves – Mammon in considerable comfort and complacency. However, the passage is revealing about the sort of people who joined the LSR. Pecuniary motives bothered them. They were not indifferent to the need for an income, but they were apt to feel themselves above mere money-grubbing.

A cynic – 'a man who knows the price of everything, and the value of nothing,' as Oscar Wilde put it – might observe that the people who joined the league were simply making a virtue of necessity. Perhaps. But the convictions of many LSR members were deeply rooted in that form of Protestantism that takes seriously the Biblical warnings concerning the love of money and the problems likely to be experienced by rich men seeking to enter the Kingdom of God. The profit motive, the LSR believed sincerely, turns men away from the common good. Adam Smith's 'invisible hand' does not exist, or cannot work the good expected of it. The need for a new co-operative ethic seemed plain.

It seemed plain at least to the few hundred men and women who joined the LSR during 1932. Other Canadians would need enlightening; from the beginning the founders of the LSR undertook to provide the necessary instruction. A research committee was established in the autumn, its chairman the tireless Harry Cassidy.

Thoughts of pamphlets were temporarily put aside. 'The committee proposes to prepare a book, comparable in scope to the British Liberal "Yellow Book," containing a detailed statement of the LSR programme,' Cassidy reported to the national convention in January 1933. 'It is hoped that this book, which will be essentially an amplification of the manifesto, will be accepted by the CCF as a semi-official statement of policy, and that it will be ready for circulation during the coming summer.'[23] This was a pious hope, doomed to disappointment. For the time being the only publication was a leaflet with the title *What To Read*, a list of current left-wing literature.

Seventeen months had passed since Scott and Underhill climbed Greylock, twelve since the organizational meeting in Toronto. In that time, the national executive confessed, '... the League has not done very much to contribute new political and social ideas to Canadian life. Nor has it done much in the way of popularizing old ideas.'[24] Self-criticism, often insincere, was in this case genuine enough. The LSR's bright beginning seemed already tarnished. It was thought the book would change this; it would not, in fact, appear for another two and a half years. None the less, the LSR began significantly to influence public discussion in 1933. The means was the new political movement mentioned by Cassidy, the Co-operative Commonwealth Federation.

3

'If ever there was a time ...'

The League for Social Reconstruction was founded as a non-partisan body. A suggestion that it might itself 'create a new party,' which appeared in an early draft of the manifesto, was weighed and found wanting. Association with any existing political party was also rejected. 'The League would seriously handicap its political usefulness if it were to affiliate itself directly with any political party at the present time,' Scott informed an inquirer. This could only scare off potential members. Frank Underhill told the readers of *The Canadian Forum* that the LSR was intended to appeal to 'those unattached critical spirits who find no haven in either of the two national political parties, and whose circumstances do not make it possible for them to join Labour or Farmer political movements.' He thought that in due time a party might appear that the LSR would want to support; but, for the present, political independence best served the league's educational purposes.[1]

To the LSR the specific agency of social and economic change mattered less at this time than change itself and its direction. But Underhill's drift was clearly apprehended by Norman McLeod Rogers, a political scientist at Queen's University. He therefore declined Underhill's invitation to join the league. 'I know you do not hold the view that there is any real basis for hope in Canadian liberalism,' Rogers wrote, 'but perhaps our difference of opinion arises from the fact that your radicalism started from a Liberal background, whereas all my earlier associations were Conservative.' Rogers hoped to work for change within the Liberal party – three years later, in 1935, he became Mackenzie King's minister of Labour – while Underhill was already looking beyond it. In 1930 Underhill had dismissed the traditional political party as 'nothing but a bundle of sectional factions held together by a common name and a common desire for ... office.'[2] In Britain the struggle was now between two parties that differed on principle as well as in the interests they served. Here was an example Canada might with profit emulate and adapt.

Underhill was not alone in the LSR in expecting the advent of a new party that would attract support from labour and farmers both. Graham Spry purchased *The Farmer's Sun* in this expectation. Yet no one from the LSR attended the meeting in William Irvine's office in the Centre Block of the Parliament buildings on 26 May 1932, where the 'co-operating independent' MPs decided to form a 'Commonwealth party.'[3] A few league members from the Calgary, Edmonton, and Vancouver branches did attend as observers the conference in Calgary on 1 August, where the new movement got its name, a provisional program, and a national council. At that meeting J.S. Woodsworth, leader of the group, was asked by the LSR observer from Calgary what role the LSR might play in the CCF. He replied that 'it was a matter of established League policy that it should not, as an organization, participate in politics.'[4]

Was this true? To be sure, the national executive of the LSR had so far kept its distance. However, many league members were watching the progress of the new party with enthusiasm. After all, Woodsworth was their own honorary president. Moreover, the eight-point program adopted at the Calgary meeting had much in common with the LSR's own manifesto. Before the summer was out not a few league members wanted to throw the LSR's lot in with the CCF.

Among them was Underhill. He saw an unequalled opportunity to help lay the basis of a class-oriented party with a clearly defined body of principles that would be a real alternative to the Liberal-Tory Tweedledum and Tweedledee. Thus established, the new party would not be able to compromise itself out of existence as easily as the Progressive movement had.

Less sure of the desirability of an alliance was Frank Scott. 'Re Co-operative Commonwealth Fed,' he replied to Underhill in early September, 'This seems like the long looked-for article, and therefore I agree the LSR should help it as much as possible. I am doubtful whether any sort of official connection should be established however. At present I rather favour keeping the LSR at its educational job alone.' When Underhill reported that several members in Toronto were thinking of affiliating the branch there to the CCF, Scott advised against it: 'The LSR should keep itself to itself until it knows itself better.' King Gordon and Joseph Parkinson, both members of the national executive, agreed with him.[5]

The greatest fear of these men was that affiliation with the CCF would interfere with the LSR's attempt to reach the intelligentsia. Woodsworth shared this fear. 'If one Local went in,' he argued with Underhill, 'others would have to bear the brunt of any criticism. This would almost inevitably mean that the Ottawa Local, which is composed in part of Civil Service people, would have to drop out, and also that probably a number of members in Winnipeg, Calgary and Vancouver would have to resign as they went in on the understanding that this was to be primarily an educational organization. Would the formal affiliation compensate for the loss of such groups?' Woodsworth thought not: far better if the LSR gave quiet assistance to the CCF. He therefore asked Underhill and Scott whether they would help with the drafting of a permanent manifesto for the movement.[6] They accepted with alacrity.

Woodsworth also hit upon a method whereby the middle-class members of the league could find a place in the CCF, which was a federation of smaller parties and groups, without subverting the purpose of the LSR. He proposed that a third type of organization be formed that, along with the organized farmers and the labour parties, would become an affiliated member of the CCF. This suggestion led to the formation of the CCF clubs, with D.M. LeBourdais as the organizing genius. By the end of 1932 they were cropping up all over Ontario. In this process Underhill and Eric Havelock were prominent, the former assuming for some months, until forced to resign by the university authorities, the chairmanship of the CCF Club Committee. The clubs expanded rapidly, becoming within little more than a year the most numerous component of the Ontario CCF while spreading to other provinces as well.[7]

Any compelling reason for the LSR to affiliate with the CCF disappeared with the formation of the clubs. Nevertheless, at the national convention held in Toronto on 28–29 January 1933, 'the most lengthy and perhaps the most important discussion ... turned on the question of affiliation with the CCF.' Two delegates from Toronto moved a resolution that called for affiliation at the national level 'as a non-political organization pledged to carry on Socialist education and propaganda.' The resulting debate was not only about affiliation but also about the term *socialist*.

Affiliation, its proponents argued, would give the LSR's discussions and propaganda 'a reality which they would not otherwise possess.' Research and political action ought to feed on each other: the decision of the Fabian Society to join the Labour party was cited in support. Affiliation, furthermore, would enable the LSR to become a conscience to the CCF: 'In a year or two's time, when the CCF has gathered momentum, and may be in danger of transforming itself into a mere populist movement in which guiding socialist principles are not stressed, it may be highly expedient for the LSR to occupy some official position which would at least give it the opportunity to link up its own socialist ideology with the political movement.' Fears that the use of the word *socialist* would frighten off potential members were deprecated. Instead of being afraid of it the league should 'adopt it and give it a definite meaning which would identify the word with the League's own programme.'

The opponents of affiliation were unconvinced. First, they said, political action was likely to be pursued at the expense of research and education; second, individual league members could always join the CCF through the clubs; third, once inside the CCF the LSR might have to compromise its own program in the name of party discipline; fourth, affiliation might offend some branches and would scare off 'certain individuals, notably civil servants and those in official positions, who would be of inestimable value to the League.' Finally, 'the word *Socialist* should be deleted since it has such a variety of meanings as to have no meaning, and to Roman Catholics it has false connotations.'

Opposition to the motion came from two groups. A majority of the delegates from Montreal, hopeful still of drawing in French Canadian members and worried that the resolution, if passed, would blast that hope, were one. The other consisted of those who did not think of themselves as socialists or who did not think it sensible to fly the socialist flag. Edgar McInnis, a young historian who was vice-president of the Toronto branch, had two and a half weeks earlier reminded his fellow branch members that the manifesto 'represented fairly accurately a composite view of the group as a whole.'[8] The moderates now had reason to fear that the left-wingers were running away with the LSR.

Two resolutions eventually passed. The first was unanimous: it welcomed the CCF and expressed a willingness to co-operate with it insofar as this would be consistent with the league's educational purpose. The second passed by the narrow margin of eleven to nine: 'Resolved that the National Executive of the LSR apply to the National Executive of the CCF to be allowed to affiliate with the CCF as an educational organization, pledged to the League's policy of social reconstruction, this resolution to be ratified by twelve of the existing branches within five weeks after receiving the resolution.'[9] Avoided for the time being had been the controversial word *socialist*. Whether this would make a difference to anyone remained to be seen.

The second motion eventually went down to defeat because it was not ratified by the requisite twelve branches. In light of this the Toronto branch executive in April turned down an invitation from the Toronto Labour Conference through it to affiliate with the CCF. Affiliation or no, however, the LSR's sympathies were now abundantly clear. In March the principal of Queen's University, W.H. Fyfe, regretted that he would be unable to attend a meeting of the Kingston branch of the LSR, which his acquaintance Underhill was scheduled to address. 'The LSR,' Fyfe wrote, 'is associated in the popular mind with the CCF.'[10] Respectable men and women, beware.

The association did not trouble most members of the LSR. Indeed, in British Columbia they decided to join the CCF as a group. In the early spring they formed the Reconstruction Party (BC), with its own eleven-point manifesto – not surprisingly it closely resembled the LSR document – and chose as their leader an Anglican clergyman from Victoria, one of the founders of the LSR branch there, Rev. Robert Connell. The group then applied for entry into the provincial CCF.

Members of the Socialist Party of Canada (SPC), the most consciously Marxist of the various groups that were ranging themselves under the CCF banner, had strong misgivings about their would-be allies. 'The socialistic principles of the Reconstruction Party are in a very rudimentary state,' Wallis Lefeaux, a Vancouver lawyer, wrote to Angus MacInnis. The SPC member for Vancouver South counselled patience; the newcomers would learn soon enough 'that amelioration through modification will not ameliorate,' and would become more radical.[11]

This remained to be seen. The junction in the British Columbia CCF of the Fabian and Christian socialism of the LSR and the Marxism of the SPC provided a source of constant conflict. Ideological differences were intensified by personal dislikes. When, after the election of November 1933, Connell was selected as House leader over the SPC's favourite, Ernest Winch, the conditions for a rift were already present. For three more years, however, the alliance would limp along.

II

Work on the LSR book got underway early in 1933. Harry Cassidy was its editor-in-chief, Graham Spry his associate. Irene Biss, Eugene Forsey, and Joe Parkinson took charge of chapters dealing with the economy; Underhill assumed responsibility for politics, Scott for the constitution, and a comparative newcomer, Escott Reid, for the chapter on external affairs.

Boyish, ruddy-faced, Escott Meredith Reid, though not a military type, had a curiously military appearance. It was his unusually erect posture, perhaps, or the direct gaze from his blue eyes. His manner was also direct. While he confronted people bluntly, even dogmatically, however, he always managed to separate people from their opinions; he carried no grudges because of disagreements in argument. In his youth already an intimidating figure to those who did not know him, he was greatly liked and appreciated by those who did. His sense of humour and his intellect were both superb.

Born in Campbellford, Ontario, in 1905, the son of an Anglican clergyman, Reid went to school in Toronto. After taking a degree in political science and law at Trinity College, University of Toronto, he gained a Rhodes Scholarship in 1927. For the next three years he was at Christ Church, Oxford. When he returned to Canada, university teaching jobs had suddenly become very rare; Reid was fortunate in obtaining a Rockefeller Fellowship for two years. Then, in 1932, Vincent Massey made available funds to the Canadian Institute of International Affairs so that it could appoint a national secretary, and the gifted Reid obtained the post. Hitherto his work had been on the Canadian party system and electoral behaviour; he now turned his attention to the international arena.

Reid's radicalism had preceded the Depression. He was impressed by the Christian socialist literature that his father received; at Oxford he had become treasurer of the Labour Club. Sometime in 1932 he heard of the LSR and joined it. The forthright and enthusiastic political scientist was a welcome addition to the group.

It was not intended that Reid and the others would work on the LSR book without assistance. In February 1933 Cassidy approached a number of people for contributions in their fields of competence. The phrasing of the request was tailored to the addressee. Thus he told Angus MacInnis that 'the members of the inner editorial circle want the book to be a genuinely socialist document, and we think that we shall be able to make it conform to this objective.' The appeal to men such as Roland Michener or H.F. Angus – an economist at the University of British Columbia and later in the decade one of the Royal Commissioners on Dominion-Provincial Relations – was much more guarded. (Neither of them was able to help.) 'On the whole we have had a most encouraging response ...,' Cassidy reported to Woodsworth in mid-April: 'Of course we are having our troubles reconciling various points of view, but I think that we shall be able to work out a sufficient degree of agreement on major points without sacrificing the essentially socialist emphasis ...'[12]

On the last week-end of April two dozen people interested in the project met in Burlington, a town of just over two thousand souls ten kilometres east of Hamilton. The recently inaugurated President Franklin Delano Roosevelt was making headlines, and the stock markets were showing signs of recovery. The Depression was very much present, however. Those who that week-end attended the annual meeting of the House of Industry, Elm Street, Toronto, learned that exactly 33,629 city families had obtained 'outdoor relief,' relief supplied outside the House of Industry, at some time during the year ended 31 March 1933. They constituted an estimated 24.8 per cent of Toronto families. Total expenditures were $3,413,742, an average of $101.51 per family. (In 1929–30, a total of $249,258 had been paid to 4,622 families.)

At yet another week-end meeting, this one in Chatham, Ontario, the Conservative MP for Toronto Northwest, John R. MacNicol, was the invited speaker. His subject was the new political party. As reported in the *Globe*, he said that the CCF, 'this socialistic and communistic organization,' was opposed to 'every British tradition and ideal.' It would be 'turned down by the sane, thinking people of Canada.'

By MacNicol's standards those who were meeting in Burlington were neither sane nor thinking. They were none the less an impressively talented group. Predominant was the academic element. From the University of Toronto had come Irene Biss, Harry Cassidy, Eric Havelock, Edgar McInnis, Joseph Parkinson, and Frank Underhill, as well as D.C. MacGregor and A.F. Wynne Plumptre, both of the Department of Political Economy. Eugene Forsey, King Gordon, and Frank

Scott had made the journey from Montreal; Kenneth Taylor had driven in from Hamilton.

Three MPs had come, Woodsworth, E.J. Garland (Bow River), and G.G. Coote (Macleod). Elmore Philpott, the journalist who was shortly to be chosen leader of the Ontario CCF – he resigned within the year – was there; so were Escott Reid and Graham Spry. Others who signed the letter of thanks to Mrs Somerset were Beatrice Cassidy, Lorene McInnis, Ruth Reid, R.C. Guyot, Henry Holman, and Howe Martyn, a recent graduate of Victoria College. Mrs Cassidy recalls that the three wives had come along primarily to help feed the group and clean up after them, and joined the discussion in between times: 'Someone had to help Mrs Somerset, after all.'

The hours were very full and productive. By the time they left the participants had very largely agreed on the contents and main outlines of the book, and most felt confident that the volume, provisionally entitled 'Reconstruction – A Plan for Canada,' would appear before the end of 1933. 'Garland and I felt greatly elated over the conference,' Woodsworth reported to Underhill soon afterwards: 'It will mean everything to our movement to have this book as a guide to our activities.'[13]

Over the summer the contributions came in steadily, and an editorial meeting in August optimistically concluded that only one more meeting would be necessary, a month hence, before the book could go to the publishers. The Canadian manager of Thomas Nelson & Sons, S.B. Watson, was a member of the LSR; his firm would handle the book. But much of the work involved in pulling the book together rested on people who had heavy teaching duties. Four courses and twelve class hours per week were common at that time, and junior faculty members often had greater loads. Class time, preparation, grading, interviewing students, meetings, other projects: these left insufficient time or energy once the university term began. It quickly became clear that publication would have to wait at least until the following year.

During the summer of 1933 members of the LSR were busy in a variety of ways. At least one of these made the league well known, even notorious: the assistance given to the CCF at its convention in Regina in the preparation of the program and manifesto of the movement.

An official invitation from the CCF national council to prepare a draft of the program had come in January 1933. Not until late June was much done about it, however. Underhill, having moved his family and himself to a rented cottage on Rosseau Lake, 150 kilometres north of Toronto, for the duration of the summer, finally got to work. Using the LSR manifesto as a basis, he sketched out a couple of drafts until he had something that he was prepared to show to others. After the Dominion Day week-end he returned to Toronto; there, on a warm and humid evening he and his collaborators, Cassidy, Reid, and possibly Parkinson, drank lukewarm beer – the Underhill refrigerator had been shut off – and went over the draft. A further meeting proved necessary in order to approve some changes Cassidy had made to Underhill's clause on state medicine, now called socialized health services. Underhill then retyped the document and sent copies to Gordon, Scott, and Woodsworth before returning to the Muskoka Lakes.

Gordon, Forsey, and Parkinson had all been invited to participate in a conference on politics held by the Winnipeg YMCA at the Lake of the Woods in the second week of July. They discussed the draft but made only a few cosmetic changes in it. J.S. Woodsworth, for his part, was satisfied with the document as it reached him: '[I] can only hope that the convention will adopt this carefully thought-out statement rather than attempting to throw in a lot of half-baked suggestions.'[14]

With the convention itself scheduled to open on Wednesday, 19 July 1933, the national council gathered in Regina three days earlier. A detailed consideration of Underhill's draft began on Monday morning. Forsey, Gordon, Parkinson, and Scott had been invited to join the council. The three Montrealers would be attending the convention as delegates of the Montreal CCF council in any case, and it made good sense to bring them in early. Parkinson was in Regina in no official capacity, but while at the Lake of the Woods he had received a special invitation from Woodsworth. The CCF leader may have thought that an additional economist could only do good.

The four academics were a great hit. Eloquent and enthusiastic, with a pronounced streak of moral earnestness, they made a great impression on those members of the council who had so far known them or the LSR by name only. In the course of the two days' discussion of the draft manifesto, Scott and company got at least as much as they had expected. Adopted without change were the preamble and the clauses on planning, external trade, and socialized health services. At the opposite end, the clauses on taxation and the emergency program were rejected in their entirety. However, the academics had an important hand in redrafting them. The section on agriculture underwent major change; minor revisions only were made in the remaining seven clauses of Underhill's draft.

On 19 July, the day the convention started, stock and grain prices, which had climbed steadily for weeks, crashed suddenly and steeply. From New York, Montreal, Winnipeg, and Chicago the story was the same: disaster for the bulls, sweet revenge for the bears. The next day, a wire story from New York noted, 'stocks and commodities tumbled ... in the wildest selling rush that has been witnessed in the markets during the past three years.' It was an appropriate background to the CCF convention, convinced as some of the delegates were that capitalism was on its last legs, and others that the trade in commodity futures was one of its more immoral features.

On the nineteenth, too, the national council approved the amended draft manifesto and voted grateful thanks to the LSR. This gratitude was not unanimously shared on the floor of the convention. 'Too socialist' was the reaction of some farmer leaders such as W.C. Good of Ontario, also unhappy because the CCF rejected the idea of group government; 'too revisionist,' thought the Marxists in the party. A group of left-wingers vigorously fought the undertaking to pay compensation to the expropriated owners of socialized industries. The United Farmer delegates insisted on it with equal vigour. In the end, sustained by the votes of representatives from the CCF clubs against attacks from the BC left and the farmer right, the manifesto was adopted very largely in the form approved by the national council. The phrasing was sharpened here and there in response to suggestions made by the British Columbia delegates; added was a section on social justice, which dealt with legal and penal reform.

Few sensations are more satisfying, even if only in the short run, than that of having got pretty well what you wanted. It was with this warm feeling that the professors left Regina. Graham Spry, who had attended the conference as a reporter and delegate from the Ottawa CCF Club, wrote to Harry Cassidy: 'The opinions of Scott, Parkinson, Forsey and Gordon were almost always deferred to.' In his turn Cassidy reported to Kenneth Taylor at McMaster University: 'Frank Scott called me this morning on his way back from the CCF convention ... He said that the LSR had scored a brilliant success at the convention, since the members of our group who were on hand had succeeded in having their views accepted pretty generally with respect to the programme.' This was no self-serving exaggeration. George Williams, a national council member from Saskatchewan, observed on the last day of the Regina convention: 'I have felt that the core of this manifesto is largely the work of a group of eastern university professors ...' Writing to Frank Underhill, J.S. Woodsworth described the convention as 'a wonderful success,' and added: 'We cannot be too grateful to you and Cassidy for the manifesto.' There were congratulations all around.[15]

The Regina Manifesto was, in fact, largely an adaptation and elaboration of the manifesto adopted eighteen months earlier by the LSR. To be sure, there was a shared sensibility between the eight-point program adopted at Calgary and Underhill's draft. A textual comparison reveals, however, that the historian scarcely had reference to the Calgary program. Instead he expanded the LSR document, using its clauses verbatim to form the headings of the various clauses in his draft for the CCF. Of the ten points that the LSR manifesto contained in 1933 only one, on co-operative institutions, did not appear in the document Underhill drafted in the Muskokas. (It had reappeared by the time the national council considered the draft.)

A preamble and fourteen clauses make up the Regina Manifesto in its final form. The preamble was very largely unchanged from the one drafted by Underhill, who evidently used the preamble of the LSR manifesto as his inspiration. Five of the fourteen clauses, on planning, socialization of finance, social ownership, the BNA Act, and external relations, were virtually unchanged from the Rosseau Lake draft to the version approved by the convention.

Significant differences between the LSR and Regina manifestos also exist. The former says little about agriculture and then only under the heading of co-operative institutions. As a result, Underhill's draft plank on agriculture was perfunctory. In truth, neither the LSR's thinkers nor the farmers were very clear in 1932–33 what they wanted to do about agriculture. The Calgary program called for 'security of tenure for the farmer on his use-land,' defining this as 'land used for productive purposes.' For a time 'use-lease' or 'use-hold' land ownership was favoured by the Farmer-Labour party in Saskatchewan, formed under the leadership of M.J. Coldwell in 1932. The government would hold ultimate title to the land, moderate the effects of fluctuating prices and drought, and free the farmer from the threat of mortgage foreclosure. The Saskatchewan farmers had some trouble in clarifying the concept, however. 'The mysterious Saskatchewan CCF plan for land,' Eugene Forsey many years later called it: '"Use-tenure," I think it was called. Gordon and I tried, repeatedly, to find out what it meant, and failed. All we got was a truculent "No one is coming here from the East to water down our socialism"'[16]

If the LSR did not fully understand what the Farmer-Labour party wanted, it seems that farmer delegates from other provinces did. They did not care for use-lease; it would undermine the traditional form of land ownership. A compromise was reached in the wording of the plank on agriculture, which demands 'security of tenure for the farmer upon his farm on conditions to be laid down by individual provinces.' This ran counter to the tendency to centralization in economic matters evident in both the LSR and Regina manifestos, but in 1933 that could not be helped. That it offended against Marxist orthodoxy and ignored the policy of the British Labour party on the land question bothered no one in the LSR and only a few souls in the CCF. The assumption ruled that the family farm was not an enterprise suitable for socialization. Soon even the CCF in Saskatchewan agreed. By 1934 that party was already modifying its land policy; two years later the idea of use-lease was dropped from its platform.

Three clauses not found in the LSR manifesto conclude the Regina document. Two of these were in Underhill's draft. A plank on freedom calls for the protection of civil liberties, the repeal of Section 98 of the Criminal Code dealing with sedition, and an end to deportations. Used against Tim Buck, the Communist leader, in 1931 and against other communists and radical labour organizers, Section 98 was particularly offensive to the LSR and CCF, even though they had no reason to love the CPC.

A plank on social justice was added during the convention. It was the brainchild of Lewis St George Stubbs, the former judge from Winnipeg who in the course of his controversial career on the bench had often shown his sympathy for the underdog.[17] The plank proposes an expert commission on the criminal law, 'in order to humanize the law and to bring it into harmony with the needs of the people.'

Finally, the emergency program outlines the immediate steps deemed necessary to cope with the most pressing problems attendant on the Depression, notably unemployment relief. Such a clause was appropriate for a political party; an educational organization had no need for one. It was rewritten in Regina; only the occasional phrase in the final version reflects Underhill's draft. Nowhere in that draft or in the LSR manifesto is there anything quite so seemingly uncompromising as the final sentence of the emergency program and thus the Regina Manifesto: 'No CCF Government shall rest content until it has eradicated capitalism and put into operation the full programme of socialized planning which will lead to the establishment in Canada of the Co-operative Commonwealth.' Although later described by M.J. Coldwell as 'a millstone around the party's neck,' the statement was not basically out of harmony with the rest of the manifesto. Nevertheless, it did make the document sound rather more radical than it was.[18]

While the Regina Manifesto reflected the LSR's thought, the ideas expressed were in the air. Underhill and his associates formulated them for the CCF and made them to some extent systematic. Things were stated in such a way that other, less intellectually oriented people would be able to say: 'Yes, that's the way it is,' or 'That's the way it ought to be.' The ideas were not being formulated solely by the LSR, however. CCF politicians were contributing to this enterprise as well – William Irvine, for example, and Angus MacInnis, and, above all, J.S. Woodsworth. His was a significant influence on the LSR itself. It was he, moreover, who enabled the league's intellectuals to work out the doctrine of that 'Canadian socialism' that he hailed in his opening speech to the Regina convention. They were following their leader.

Influence was their reward, a certain notoriety their punishment. At Regina a newspaperman smelled a story. George V. Ferguson of the *Winnipeg Free Press*, astute, well informed, an old friend of Graham Spry, was struck by the respect shown to the four professors. The term *brain trust* had recently come into currency to describe the academics and other intellectuals who had flooded into public service in Washington since President Roosevelt's election: was there not a brain trust at the convention? Ferguson thought so. A *Free Press* story on 19 July 1933 referred to a brain trust that had prepared the manifesto.

Not long after the Regina convention came to an end, Ferguson in his column drew further attention to the 'CCF Brain Trust.' The LSR's work, he wrote, constituted 'the more or less formal consolidation of Canadian academic socialist thought.' Canadians working 'towards the planned and socialized economy will have behind them trained thinkers who have a power to express coherent, logical views well based on a prolonged study of socialist philosophy and practice.' The brain truster-in-chief was Frank Underhill; he was supported by a group of younger men (the brain trust averaged 31.75 years of age), six of them Rhodes Scholars, 'whose bond is an ardent faith in the scientific socialism of the present day.'[19]

The LSR members identified by name, Cassidy, Forsey, Gordon, Parkinson, Scott, and Spry in addition to Underhill, were secretly flattered and openly annoyed. The column magnified their work at the expense of that done by others; it also drew undue attention to the LSR and tied it too closely to the CCF. Spry thought his friend had 'badly misnamed' the LSR; Underhill, arguing a year later that one of the CCF's main problems was that it had no proper brain trust, charged that Ferguson had coined the phrase in order 'to amuse himself by taking his friends for a little ride.' The journalist denied it: 'The "CCF brain trust" was first heard by me on the lips of Comrade Spry and Comrade Reid.'[20]

Whoever coined the phrase, it soon was accurate enough. Many LSR members became active in the CCF; the league as a whole stood ready to be of service. Delegates to the national convention in February 1934 were told about 'the remarkable growth of interest in, and some support for, the political movement which was in part inspired by the LSR, and the two manifestos of which both were suggested by, and in part written by, the LSR. The formation of the third section of the CCF, ... the clubs, was initiated by the LSR in Toronto ... CCF leaders have used the research facilities of the LSR on frequent occasions, not only in the national field, but in provincial and municipal fields also.'[21] There is exaggeration here. The LSR did not inspire the formation of the CCF, nor did it have anything to do with the Calgary manifesto. But we do not have to accept this evaluation entirely to recognize the key advisory role that, by the summer of 1933, it had come to play.

Advice extended beyond matters of doctrine and policy to those of organization. The CCF adopted federalism as an unavoidable organizational mode. Affiliation was at the provincial level; the provincial sections enjoyed a good deal of autonomy in their operations and even in their programs. Critical of the looseness of Canadian federalism, Frank Underhill, for one, was soon just as critical of inadequate central direction in the CCF. At the Burlington meeting in April the historian lectured J.S. Woodsworth on the party's need for a strong national office and secretariat, and followed this up with a letter. Woodsworth disagreed: local organization should come first. This struck some league members as quixotic. Escott Reid commented that the CCF 'needed a leader of iron who could weld into one fighting unit a loosely knit and undisciplined federation. It possessed in J.S. Woodsworth an idealistic leader of great genius who believed that party discipline was immoral.' While overstated, the description was not without truth.[22]

While the LSR in 1933 largely got its way so far as the CCF's program was concerned, it proved much harder for the league to make its views on organization prevail. More telling even than Woodsworth's opposition was the lack of money. Adopting policy statements in itself is cheap, but no one can run an effective secretariat without lots of cash. Not until the later 1930s did the means present themselves whereby this obstacle could be overcome.

III

The Depression year 1933: drought on the western plains and high unemployment. Thousands of men riding the rods, looking for work from one end of Canada to the other, while thousands of others were restive in the relief camps that had been set up by provincial governments and by Ottawa. Taxes were rising; profit margins had shrunk. And yet one suspects that for many Canadians it was a year much like other years, in which they got by as best they could and enjoyed themselves in whatever ways their tastes and means permitted.

In at least one way it was an unusual year. Economic and political ideas were discussed with a passionate intensity that in Canada was unprecedented and has not been matched since. In that discussion the LSR and its leading members took a prominent part.

The Depression was primarily responsible for the crescendo of talk that culminated during the summer – the Depression, and the inadequate measures taken by governments to try to cope with it. Faced with rising expenditures, especially for relief, governments at all levels sought to cope by cutting all expenditures that could be cut. The vain hope was that in this way the *summum bonum* of orthodox public finance, the balanced budget, would be achieved. The private sector would then lead the economy towards recovery. Budgets proved impossible to balance, however. By 1933, moreover, it was dawning on a growing number of Canadians that the single-minded attempt to do so had reinforced the distress of deflation and was making the Depression worse, not better.

Orthodoxy was being undermined elsewhere in that troubled year, most spectacularly in the United States. Franklin D. Roosevelt had scarcely been inaugurated when he began to shake up his country. The effect of his New Deal initiatives was as yet hard to assess, but at least his administration was doing something. Almost as much as Americans, Canadians were fascinated. Why should similar things not be happening here?

Perplexing questions were being posed by the Depression and the apparent failure of government and business to secure a recovery. By 1933 people were looking for new answers. The Royal Commission on Banking and Currency, the Macmillan Commission, was one important manifestation of this. The crushing deflation since 1929 had raised serious doubts about the credit-granting policies pursued by the country's chartered banks, the effect of those policies on the money supply, and the limited scope for action by the government in the absence of a central bank. Graham Spry appeared before the commission to present a brief on behalf of the LSR; it advocated a publicly owned central bank, a national investment board, and a policy of controlled reflation. The man largely responsible for writing the LSR's submission, J.F. Parkinson, appeared before the royal commission in his own right and was kept on the witness stand for more than an hour.[23]

Several members of the LSR took a conspicuous part in the political seminars or summer schools peculiar to the summer of 1933. Things had got so bad that even R.B. Bennett was prepared at least to listen to the advice of intellectuals. (Two years earlier he had written to Harry H. Stevens, his minister of Trade and Commerce: 'Do you think I want a lot of long-haired professors telling me what to do? If I can't run this country, I will get out.') Of the twenty speakers who addressed the Conservative summer school at Newmarket, Ontario, no fewer than nine were academics. Harry Cassidy was one of them; his speech, 'An Unemployment Policy: Some Proposals,' the historian Richard Wilbur has suggested, may have influenced Prime Minister Bennett and thus the shaping of his program of reforms in 1934–35.[24]

Cassidy and Frank Scott acted as group leaders at the Liberal summer school in Port Hope, Ontario, and Kenneth Taylor read a paper there. As well, an LSR drop-out, Terry MacDermot, presented a paper that aroused considerable interest, 'The Significance for Canada of the American "New Deal."'

At the YMCA's conference on economics and politics held at Lake Couchiching in August, three of the four discussion-group leaders, Eugene Forsey, Joe Parkinson, and Frank Underhill, were leading figures in the LSR. Several league members served on the Canadian secretariat at the British Commonwealth Relations Conference, which met at the University of Toronto in September. During the year, too, Irene Biss and Cassidy were working as researchers for a commission chaired by Sir Robert Falconer, president of the University of Toronto. Appointed by the Board of Evangelism and Social Service of the United Church of Canada, the commission was seeking to determine how the modern order might be made more Christian. Its report, *Christianizing the Social Order*, appeared in 1934.

The indefatigable Cassidy and Scott were doing some further research at this time that made a contribution to the most controversial official inquiry of the decade. Having been retained by the Canadian Association of Garment Manufacturers and the Amalgamated Clothing Workers' Union, they investigated wages and working conditions in the men's clothing industry in Ontario and Quebec. Assisted by several energetic recent graduates of the University of Toronto, including Harry Wolfson and Stuart Legge, they completed their report late in

1933. Unintentionally, they thereby provided Harry H. Stevens with the ammunition he used to launch his attack on monopolistic practices in Canadian industry.

The Cassidy-Scott report, of which Stevens got an advance copy, described a disorganized and demoralized industry in which both employers and workers suffered grievously. Cassidy presented it to the newly established Parliamentary Committee on Price Spreads and Mass Buying in February 1934. One unamused observer was Premier George Henry of Ontario. 'A man of this type who is definitely associated with the CCF,' he complained to R.B. Bennett, 'may use the information he gets for his own purposes and not for the benefit of people generally, particularly ourselves.'[25] Canada was becoming an uncomfortable place for Tory politicians; one after another, incumbent Conservative administrations were turfed out from 1933 to 1935. The Depression was primarily responsible, but the LSR was doing its bit.

In 1933, too, several LSR members made contact with British socialists. Irene Biss and Eric Havelock were both in England during the summer and welcomed the opportunity to speak to a group of Labour MPs. The meeting was arranged by Sir Stafford Cripps. When Biss and he explained what was happening in Canada, Havelock recalls, 'we encountered some strong criticism from Marxist members present who were members of the Socialist League. ... [William] Mellor was particularly hostile to our stated aim to bring in the farmers, but Cripps was far more pragmatic.'[26]

Graham Spry was also in England during the summer, making contacts with people in the Socialist League and the Labour party and gathering whatever information he thought might be of use to the LSR and CCF. He briefly addressed the annual meeting of the Socialist League at Derby, which he attended as a representative of the LSR. In London he visited the offices of the league, the New Fabian Research Bureau, and the Co-operative Union, as well as Transport House. He met and dined with Stafford Cripps, G.D.H. Cole, George Lansbury, E.R. Radice, Christopher Addison, and others. The British socialists definitely wished 'to keep in touch with developments in Canada through personal contacts, articles in the papers of both movements and representation at meetings by fraternal delegates,' Spry reported to the LSR executive upon his return.[27]

As the summer turned into autumn, LSR members had the pleasant sense that they had become visible, that they were making a significant contribution to public debate. The league should do more, however, an impatient Underhill told the members in October. The CCF having been launched, the opportunities for 'political education' were now almost limitless. What organization was more likely than the LSR to provide educational material sympathetic to the CCF? 'But to carry on such work a permanent full-time secretary with a regular office is essential. The national executive is therefore launching a money raising campaign to make possible the setting up of such an office.'[28] For the LSR as well as the CCF, Underhill and others believed, effective organization was essential.

For several months people had been kicking around the idea of opening a national office. At the Burlington meeting Underhill had linked this notion to his suggestion that the CCF needed a central office, a publicity officer, and a research organization. Graham Spry, with his experience and record of success with the Association of Canadian Clubs and the Canadian Radio League, seemed ideal as a secretary or publicity man. J.S. Woodsworth allowed that Spry 'might do an excellent piece of work' provided the money could be found. Spry himself was enthusiastic about the prospect of becoming national secretary for the LSR and CCF, with the associated possibility of starting an LSR periodical. Before the end of May he put an ambitious scheme before Underhill. It envisaged an office in Ottawa to be shared by the LSR, an LSR paper, *The Farmer's Sun*, and, should it be interested, the CCF.[29]

Two months later Spry reported that one of his acquaintances in Ottawa, the lawyer Russel S. Smart, K.C., believed strongly in the LSR's objectives and was willing to make available, free of charge, an office at 116 Wellington Street. The location was ideal, right across from the Parliament buildings. Spry offered to become 'some sort of an official of the LSR' if he could earn a modest living by it. Although they estimated the annual cost of a national office to be five thousand dollars, Harry Cassidy, Joe Parkinson, and Frank Underhill, at a rump meeting of the national executive in August, decided to go ahead. 'I think that everybody had agreed upon the wisdom of setting up the national office if we could get Graham to take charge of it,' Cassidy wrote to Frank Scott.[30] An able administrator and *animateur* (his editorials in *The Farmer's Sun* had helped to bring the United Farmers of Ontario, however briefly, into the CCF), Spry was the person for the job.

He began his work as national secretary in September, working half-time at one hundred dollars per month, enough for a single man to live on if his tastes were Spartan and his wants few. For the time being Spry continued to use his room in the UFO Building in Toronto. As soon as the LSR's finances permitted he and the office would move to Ottawa, and his salary would double as he went to full time. Even now he visited Ottawa as often as he could, using the space provided by Russel Smart as office and living quarters both. Thus he quickly became the chief contact between the LSR and the CCF members of Parliament.[31]

Whether he would become full-time national secretary depended on the success of the LSR's financial campaign. Its target was $6,300. Of this sum $2,500 was to be raised by Toronto, $1,500 by Montreal, $500 each by Calgary and Winnipeg, $300 each by Vancouver and Victoria, $200 each by Edmonton, Ottawa, and Regina, and $100 by the branch in Belleville, Ontario. 'If ever there was a time when the Canadian public were willing to listen to radical political and economic ideas it is now,' Frank Underhill exhorted the branch executives: 'If the LSR fails now to ... carry on socialist education it will probably never again find such an opportunity open to it.'[32]

Alas, perhaps the opportunity was there, but the money was not. It was soon clear that the reach of the national executive far exceeded its grasp. The branch in Toronto came close to collecting half its quota; the other branches fell a very long way short. By February 1934 net income from the campaign stood at a mere $1,400.

Spry had been over-confident. Now he was discovering, not for the last time, that it was far harder to rally financial support for a left-wing cause than for a non-partisan organization such as the Radio League. Left-wingers are not less generous than other folk, but they tend to have less money. The widow's mites may be more meritorious, but it takes a lot of them to match the gift of one rich man.

For more than two years none the less, into 1936, Graham Spry remained the part-time national secretary of the LSR. He was assisted for some months in 1934 by Stuart Legge, an economics graduate of the University of Toronto in 1930 who had become unemployed. Legge was paid ten dollars per week; Spry's salary stayed at a nominal one hundred dollars monthly, much of which was never paid.

Financing the office and its secretary once the campaign money ran out became a matter of catch-as-catch-can. Sometimes there was cash in the till; usually there was not enough. Legge left with a sigh of relief when he landed a job in the public service of Ontario; Spry kept plugging away. But it was a rough road. 'When I stepped off the sheltered verandah of the Canadian Club,' he confided to Brooke Claxton, 'I stepped into a blizzard. And I am glad I did. But the price, personally, financially, has been heavy.' Just how heavy he told Claxton in February 1935: 'My income ... for the last twelve months has been under $500. As I look back I wonder how I have managed to keep alive.'[33] It is no slur on Spry to note that the great majority of Canadian families on relief received less than he did. Of course, they were not expected to travel and make a respectable impression. Nor did they have to concern themselves with retaining membership in the Rideau Club of Ottawa.

IV

As the year 1933 drew to an end, LSR members looked back with a mixture of pride and dissatisfaction. The CCF seemed to be doing reasonably well. In British Columbia it had after an election in November become the official Opposition, and an LSR member, Robert Connell, had been named House leader of the party. At Regina and elsewhere, the LSR had made its mark in its own right. And the work of the summer was continuing. LSR members were speaking to any organization, political, religious, service-oriented, or whatever, that would invite them. The good word was spreading.

One means of spreading it was radio. Graham Spry's Radio League connections proved useful here. Commencing in late October, nine addresses of fifteen minutes each were broadcast on Sunday afternoons at 2:30 on CRCT, the affiliated station of the Canadian Radio Broadcasting Commission in Toronto. Entitled 'The Depression and the Way Out,' the series began and ended with talks by Frank Underhill. It included subjects such as economic planning, central banking, monetary policy, and the like, by C.A. Ashley, Irene Biss, Alexander Brady, Lorne T. Morgan, J.F. Parkinson, and Wynne Plumptre, all from the Department of Political Economy at the University of Toronto. Political propaganda was not permitted; several of the contributors, furthermore, did not or had ceased to belong to the LSR. All the same, the broadcasts in their totality pointed to economic planning by government as the way out of Canada's troubles. When Underhill wrapped up the series in December he felt he had reason to be pleased.

In December the branch in Montreal sponsored the first LSR week-end conference and seminar. Described by a member of the Montreal branch executive, S.E. Briard, as 'eminently successful,' it featured a well-received speech by King Gordon's friend, the theologian Reinhold Niebuhr, on 'The Challenge of Reconstruction.'[34] (In later years the Montreal and Toronto branches collaborated with the national executive in holding a week-end conference between Christmas and New Year's. The site was Pickering College, just east of Toronto; its headmaster, Joseph McCulley, was an LSR member and an excellent host. These conferences proved a happy fusion of the intellectual and the social.)

A grim year for Canada, then, 1933; a good year for the LSR. And yet: the campaign for funds was stalling; some branches were already moribund; the book was nowhere near completion. There was a nagging sense of inadequacy, of not doing enough, of not being able to drum up the support necessary to reconstruct Canada. When over-achievers become reformers they are bound to feel inadequate. There was a sense, however, that the universe was not unfolding as it should. Could this be changed by a program of publication, by speaking more often, by simply working harder? There was no alternative but to try, and see.

4

Winning a few, losing the big ones

'Yesterday's vote shows how ineffective the LSR has hitherto been.' It was 15 October 1935, the morning after the Dominion general election; a dejected Frank Scott was writing to his friend Underhill.[1] The historian, more given than Scott to bouts of gloominess, hardly needed to be told. The CCF had contested 119 out of 245 seats; it had elected only seven members. It had been shut out in Alberta, where hitherto it had had most of its MPs, and in the Canadian heartland, Ontario and Quebec. King Gordon and Graham Spry had gone down to personal defeat in the general débâcle.

It was a big let-down, all the more crushing because it followed hard upon the LSR's greatest moment of achievement. In September its long-awaited, oft-postponed book had finally appeared: *Social Planning for Canada* had come off the press in a run of fifteen hundred copies. A party in Toronto brought together the jubilant contributors and LSR officers. As they drank toasts and congratulated each other they wondered what effect, if any, the book would have on Canada after the election. On the night of 14 October, as the size of the Liberal majority grew, the answer took shape: in the near term, nothing. As for the long term, who could tell?

For the LSR the book's publication and the election came at the end of a two-year period marked by small victories and bigger disappointments, a time of hard work that was rarely rewarded with the results that were intended. It was a time, too, when the LSR increasingly identified itself as a socialist organization co-operating closely with the CCF. By the end of 1935 those who did not like the change had left the LSR. Some decline in membership was one result; a sharpening of the league's focus was another. Better than in 1932 or 1933 the members knew what meaning they attached to social reconstruction.

Emphasis during the period was very much on education by the spoken and the written word. The first LSR radio lectures had barely been completed when a second series began. Thirteen addresses had been prepared under the auspices of the national office; they began on CRCT in Toronto on 14 January 1934. Among the speakers were Harry Cassidy, Eugene Forsey, Joe Parkinson, Frank Scott, Graham Spry, Ken Taylor, and Frank Underhill, as well as two newcomers, Edward Hume Blake, a Toronto lawyer and businessman, and Humphrey Carver, an architect who was King Gordon's brother-in-law. Among the subjects discussed were central banking, housing, farm debts, and the railway problem. A number of favourable responses reached the LSR, as well as several new recruits.

A third series of radio lectures, the second to be sponsored by the national office, was killed soon after it began on 9 December 1934. The subject was 'Canada and International Affairs,' and the intended speakers were Underhill, Escott Reid, Lorne Morgan, Edgar McInnis, G.M.A. Grube of the Classics Department, Trinity College, and, from Queen's University, the philosopher Gregory Vlastos. The opening talks must have been very controversial. 'Only two or three were given,' Scott jotted on the pamphlet announcing the series; 'then the Radio Commission announced that it could not permit any more free use of the radio for this purpose!' Almost certainly the tone of the lectures was neutralist and critical of British foreign policy; this would have occasioned considerable protest.

From November 1934 into the following March Underhill gave a series of sixteen public lectures in Toronto on 'Canada and the World Crisis.' A modest fee was exacted, although the unemployed were allowed in free of charge. An animated speaker, interested in his subject and given to using striking figures of speech, Underhill attracted from sixty to a hundred listeners to each lecture. A similar series of lectures by Eric Havelock, however, entitled 'Democracy at the Crossroads,' had to be abandoned when the Toronto East End CCF Club that sponsored it ran into financial difficulties.

Lively and well-attended programs were mounted during the period by the two large LSR branches in Toronto and Montreal. As indicated in the branch's record of activities from 1933 to 1936, the monthly meetings in Toronto drew from seventy-five to two hundred people. About a third of them would attend the dinner that usually preceded the meeting; this helped to make the gathering a social as well as an intellectual occasion. Furthermore, because the meal was taken in the convention room of a hotel, the practice had the calculated advantage of securing a free hall for the meeting.

Lecturers, panel discussions, and free-wheeling question periods constituted the bill of fare. In 1934–35, for example, Frank Underhill spoke about current Canadian politics; one Thornton Purkis lectured on 'Russia 1905–1934,' and G.M.A. Grube discussed pacifism. Graham Spry assessed the prospects of the CCF in Ontario; Henri Lasserre, of the Department of French, Victoria College, explained the work of the Robert Owen Foundation – it promoted co-operative enterprises – and E.J. Urwick, head of the Social Science Department of the

University of Toronto, discussed the housing shortage in the city. Finally, a general consideration of 'What should be the functions of the LSR?' was led by Grube, Spry, Underhill, and an advertising executive, W. Carlton McNaught.

Extremely clever in a quiet and sardonic way, George Maximilian Antony Grube was both a scholar and a political activist. Born in Antwerp, Belgium, in 1899, he had received his education in Britain. After serving during the war he read Greats at Emmanuel College, Cambridge. For some years he taught in Wales, but he emigrated to Canada in 1928 in order to become professor of Classics at Trinity College, University of Toronto. In 1931 the promising young man became head of the department; his first book, *Plato's Thought*, was published four years later.

From the Great War Grube had carried a fervent pacifism that he came to link to socialism. A co-signer of the letter of the sixty-eight in 1931, he had joined the LSR soon after its founding. In 1934–35 he was branch president; in due time he became an officer in the Ontario CCF as well.

William Carlton 'Bill' McNaught (1888–1963), tall, well dressed, a distinguished-looking man with a high forehead and a ready smile, was an unlikely recruit to the cause of social reconstruction. He had been born into an Ontario Tory family; his father, W.K. McNaught, was a sometime president of the Canadian Manufacturers' Association who was first elected to the Ontario legislature in 1906. His uncle, C.B. McNaught, was a financier who ranked among the 'Fifty Big Shots' excoriated by the Saskatchewan CCF. The younger McNaught graduated from the University of Toronto with a degree in political science in 1911, the same year as his good friend Frank Underhill. McNaught worked as a journalist in Toronto and Calgary, served overseas during the war, and entered the advertising industry upon demobilization. By the early 1930s he was an account executive with McKim Advertising.

Appalled by the Depression, McNaught came to the LSR at the urging of Underhill. Although his work kept him from taking a prominent position in the league, he became an active and influential member. Good-natured, fond of intelligent conversation, and with a larger income than most league members, he made his home at 103 Blythwood Road in North Toronto and his summer cottage near Beaverton on Lake Simcoe, the centre of many festive occasions for members of the LSR.

Parties, picnics, and teas were popular. There was an occasional complaint, however, that people were too busy to attend study groups. The league was not primarily an earnest little band of ideologues; it was more a group of friends, people with broad interests who were drawn to each other for personal as much as ideological reasons, and who enjoyed a drink and a good talk more than most Canadians. Some who joined were zealots, militant antivivisectionists and teetotalitarians, true believers who would have tested the patience of Job. But most were convivial and able to relax. Fun and good fellowship is what many former members recall – Underhill's mordant wit, Forsey's droll impersonations, Spry's joviality. The parties in Montreal seem to have been particularly good. Not a few of them were at Frank and Marian Scott's, on Oxenden Avenue just northwest of the McGill campus and later on Summit Circle in Westmount. 'Frank Scott especially was always exploding with wit and infectious gaiety,' King Gordon remembers.

Montreal branch meetings had an average turn-out of rather less than a hundred, but they tended to be more frequent than those in Toronto. Among the more active members were Dr J. Stanley Allen, a professor at Sir George Williams College, C.E. French, who worked for the Sun Life Assurance Company ('I think it must have taken a good deal of courage for him to take an active part in the LSR given the general attitude towards left-wing movements at the time,' an acquaintance writes[2]), Helen Howes, a legal secretary who later served for two years (1938–40) as national secretary of the LSR, George Mooney, and Frank Aykroyd.

George Stuart Mooney (1901–65) is best known for the fine work he did from the later 1930s on as executive director of the Canadian Federation of Mayors and Municipalities. Already in his early thirties tending to stoutness, the Toronto native was hearty and well liked. He had great gifts as a public speaker, 'more than all the others in the LSR combined,' one friend, R.E.G. Davis, remembers. Another friend, Humphrey Carver, writes: 'One of George Mooney's most likable characteristics was his quite unabashed enjoyment of his own skills as a "spell-binder" in oratory.'[3]

Largely self-educated, Mooney had in his teens begun working as a clerk at Henry Birks & Sons, the jewellers. The YMCA was a major influence in his life, however, and from volunteer work in the young men's section he moved to full-time employment with the Montreal Y in the 1920s. He stayed with the association until he resigned in order to be able to take the CCF nomination in Verdun in the general election of 1935.

Especially remembered for his enthusiastic distribution and sale of pamphlets was a research chemist with the Dominion Tar and Chemical Company, Frank Aykroyd. A good-looking and charming Anglo-Irishman, sandy-haired and open-faced, Franklyn Milnes Aykroyd (1901–75) had emigrated to Canada in 1924. Born in Dublin, he had been educated there and in Cambridge, where he took a degree in chemistry at Gonville and Caius College. A man with wide interests, he had read socialist literature in the 1920s and joined the LSR soon after its founding. He obtained left-wing pamphlets from Great Britain and the United States; he also handled the distribution of CCF and LSR pamphlets. In 1935 he tried to launch a biweekly LSR newsletter in Montreal but failed. Later in the decade he undertook the distribution of *The Canadian Forum* in Montreal. His interest in co-operative enterprises led him briefly to run a consumers' co-operative as well.

At one point Aykroyd obtained a consignment of French socialist pamphlets; these were examined with a view to their suitability for distribution among French Canadians. This project apparently came to nothing, as did the LSR's efforts to attract French Canadian members. The manifesto was early translated into French, the name transformed into *La Ligue de Réconstruction sociale*. This was later changed to *La Ligue pour la Réorganisation de la Société*. Even clumsier than the mouthful of syllables that made up the name in English, the French version utterly failed to draw French Canadians into the league. The occasional bilingual French Canadian did turn up at branch meetings; the inescapable fact was, however, that neither the LSR's socialism nor its desire for a centralized Confederation appealed to the French Canadian intelligentsia in the 1930s or, indeed, to French-speaking Quebeckers as a whole.

One result was that the CCF in Quebec was largely the creation of the Montreal branch of the LSR. Among those who were involved in this were Aykroyd, Mooney, and Lloyd Almond. Aykroyd and Almond were chairman and treasurer of the tiny Quebec CCF in 1935; Mooney was a CCF candidate in the 1935 election. A French Canadian like Jean Péron was, unhappily, a rare bird indeed.

Outside Montreal and Toronto the branches of the LSR were small, and some of them had started to disappear even in 1933. Keeping track of them was not easy; often they died without anyone informing the national office. Unanswered mail and the non-payment of capitation fees then eventually brought the sad message home.

In mid-summer of 1932 there was an active branch in Edmonton; eighteen months later no more than the nucleus of a group survived. After being launched with fanfare in September 1932 – J.S. Woodsworth spoke at the meeting – the branch in Winnipeg was nine months later described by Woodsworth's daughter, Grace MacInnis, as being 'in a rather moribund condition, owing partly to the depression, partly to the lack of members and more especially to the lack of any general enthusiasm.'[4]

A branch in Victoria, which had several discussion groups in early 1934 and was ambitiously aiming at a membership of two hundred, had petered out two years later. 'Members drifted into other organizations,' was the explanation. That was already an old story. 'Where branches have faded away,' Frank Underhill told the readers of *Saturday Night* in 1934, 'it has usually been because ... their most vigorous members have become absorbed in CCF activities.'[5] He failed to mention another reason: some members were frightened away by the LSR's ever more intimate relations with the CCF.

The Ottawa branch in 1933–34 ran a Bureau of Social Research, which circulated articles to twenty-two periodicals deemed to be sympathetic to the CCF. It was not reported to the third annual convention what proportion of those articles had actually been published. The convention was held in Toronto in February 1934; its tone was generally optimistic. Reports were read from active branches in Victoria, Vancouver, Calgary, Windsor, London, Hamilton, Kingston, and, of course, Toronto and Montreal. Branches or their nuclei were claimed by the national secretary to exist in Edmonton, Breton, and Taber in Alberta; Prince Albert, North Battleford, and Regina in Saskatchewan; Dauphin and Winnipeg in Manitoba; St Catharines, Niagara Falls, Barrie, Belleville, and Ottawa in Ontario; and Sackville, NB. This added up to twenty-three groups, a number that, though unquestionably inflated, marked the LSR's widest expansion. Having added 'a considerable number' of members-at-large to the regular Toronto membership, the national secretary later in 1934 estimated the total membership across the country to be close to six hundred.[6] Of these, at least half lived in Toronto or Montreal. How many were full and how many associate members is not known.

Delegates to the convention heard an address by E.R. Radice of the New Fabian Research Bureau in London; he spoke on the prospect of the socialist movement in Great Britain. The national president, Frank Underhill, also spoke, and used the occasion to parade the skull before the feast. As yet the LSR was not doing nearly enough to spread left-wing ideas, he asserted, while the CCF was faltering. (Just at this time the Ontario CCF was going through a debilitating conflict about the propriety of participation in Canadian Labour Defence League rallies on behalf of Tim Buck and other imprisoned Communists. The upshot was that the UFO left the CCF *en masse*, while several Labour members had to be expelled.) With six CCF MPs in the audience – J.S. Woodsworth, Angus MacInnis, G.G. Coote, E.J. Garland, William Irvine (Wetaskiwin), and Henry Spencer (Battle River) had made the journey from Ottawa – Underhill derided the organizational and educational efforts of the CCF; these were 'primitive.' 'Most of us here feel that the CCF has now gone about as far as it can go upon the wave of emotional resentment against current conditions ...,' he subsequently pressed Woodsworth: 'If it is to become a permanent movement, it must achieve a more effective organization and must develop new techniques of public education and propaganda. The fact that Canada is little more than a loose collection of particularist sectional areas does not absolve us from the attempt to overcome the difficulties of sectionalism.'[7] Leadership must come from the centre: the CCF must have an effective national secretariat that would co-ordinate the activities of the parliamentary group and those of the provincial organizations.

In his reply Woodsworth politely reiterated his conviction that local and provincial bodies must be solidly established before a secretariat in Ottawa made much sense.[8] For the time being the CCF national office stayed in the West. Until

1934 it was located in the headquarters of the UFA in Edmonton, with Norman F. Priestley as national secretary; it was then moved to Regina, where M.J. Coldwell assumed the secretarial duties in addition to his work as leader of the Saskatchewan CCF.

Underhill continued to oppose these makeshifts. At the CCF's convention in Winnipeg in July 1934 he found vindication for his views: organizationally, the movement was a mess. Underhill and Frank Scott were both worried beforehand about what the convention, preparations for which seemed to be haphazard, might do about an election platform; and Scott felt 'very strongly that some one at least of our group should be there. it will look bad if we all evaporate in the second year.' Unable to go himself, Scott sent a list of suggestions to Woodsworth instead. Underhill did go and was predictably distressed. 'When Graham Spry and I arrived on Saturday morning, the 14th, the National Council had no idea of what they were going to lay before the Convention,' he grumbled to Scott. Although the two LSR leaders were opposed to drafting an election program immediately, William Irvine had talked the council into doing it. 'So we got to work and drafted it. It is short but not snappy, having been amended by the Council and then again by the Convention, which spend [sic] 1½ days debating it. The National Council have no sense of unity at all and they spent as much time moving individual amendments to their own document as did the rest of the convention put together. Altogether, not a very good show.' If only the national council had been properly prepared, he lamented, the immediate program, dealing with finance, agriculture, labour and social services, and foreign policy, could have been much more effectively phrased.[9]

There were other aspects of the convention that made Underhill unhappy: 'The drivel talked on finance was terrible ... but they did turn down Social Credit as part of the party policy.' But the failure to prepare for and organize the meeting properly remained the chief object of his annoyance. To J.S. Woodsworth he suggested, with an air of 'I told you so,' that strong central leadership was the obvious corrective. 'I hope you do not think that I am being too critical or am losing enthusiasm,' he concluded his post-convention missive, 'But I do feel very strongly that the movement must advance beyond the stage of being a collection of individual missionaries and must get more organisation and more conscious direction at the centre. The only way I know how to make myself useful is to be constantly critical.'[10]

Critical he was, in public and in private. The disarray of the CCF, most plainly evident in the Ontario provincial election in the spring, Underhill judged in an article for the American radical weekly *The Nation* to be one of three great obstacles to the party's electoral success. (Canada's sectionalism and absence of a radical tradition were the others.)[11] It would be another two years, however, before the CCF began to respond to this sort of criticism.

II

Two English socialists visited the LSR during 1934, fall-out of the contacts Irene Biss, Eric Havelock, and Graham Spry had made in their visits to the Old Country in the previous year. After hearing that E.R. Radice would be in North America early in 1934, Spry made certain that he would pass through Toronto, where he addressed the LSR national convention.

A bigger catch came the league's way two months later. Sir Stafford Cripps had been Spry's host in 1933; he had also entertained Biss and Havelock. When Spry became aware that Cripps was planning to visit the United States the following year he urged him to make a detour to Canada under the LSR's sponsorship.

From the LSR's point of view the British socialist's sojourn in Canada was a spectacular success. From 4 to 10 April Cripps spoke at fourteen public and private meetings in Montreal, Ottawa, and Toronto. He addressed a thousand people at a meeting in Montreal; an estimated fifteen hundred heard him in Toronto's Massey Hall. In Ottawa he met R.B. Bennett and H.H. Stevens – oddly enough he seems to have missed Mackenzie King – and the CCF members of Parliament. 'Sir Stafford's visit,' Graham Spry crowed, 'is undoubtedly one of the most important contributions the LSR has made to public discussion of socialist principles.'[12]

Cripps was in Canada again briefly in April 1935, when he shared the platform at the opening of the Ontario CCF convention with William Irvine, MP, and the American socialist leader, Norman Thomas. After his first visit he had noted that Canadian socialists were 'only too ready to listen to propagandists from the Old Country, and the CCF and LSR are anxious to welcome as many as can make the visit.'[13] A few others did, including Fenner Brockway and the Earl of Tavistock. No formal ties developed from these contacts although British socialists occasionally contributed to *The Canadian Forum* after it passed into the hands of the LSR in 1936. On the whole the Canadian movement aroused little interest in British left-wing circles. The publication of *Social Planning for Canada* was an exception: Cripps gave it a long and favourable review in the *New Statesman*.

The men and women of the LSR, for their part, were keenly interested in the British scene. The *New Statesman* was read widely; books by British socialists were almost invariably reviewed in *The Canadian Forum*. Some LSR members joined the Left Book Club, although its enthusiasm for the Popular Front found few supporters here. The Webbs, Harold Laski, G.D.H. Cole, R.H. Tawney, John Strachey, and the others: here were names to conjure with.

Always ready to listen to visitors from abroad, the LSR gained half a travelling lecturer of its own when King Gordon lost his teaching post in 1934. (Budgetary grounds were given for his dismissal but, as will become clear in a later chapter, there was justification for the belief that Gordon's radical views were not irrelevant to the decision.) His misfortune became an opportunity for Canadian social democrats to spread the gospel. During the next three years, sustained more or less adequately with funds donated by friends and sympathizers, he travelled the country for the LSR and the Fellowship for a Christian Social Order. In 1935 he became national secretary of the FCSO. 'I was speaking and preaching from Antigonish to Victoria, and some crumbling clippings suggest that the papers were reporting me wherever I went,' he reminisces. 'And this was true of most of us in the LSR and FCSO. In churches, universities, community organizations, trade unions we found response: in fact, in a real sense we were articulating what they felt about the system which was causing so much suffering and unhappiness.'[14]

An organization that has since its demise in the mid-1940s received scant attention from historians and political scientists, the Fellowship for a Christian Social Order was founded in April 1934. It represented the fusion of two small groups, the Movement for a Christian Social Order in Toronto and the Fellowship of Socialist Christians in Montreal, which had a small associated group in Kingston. The motivating spirits were Professor John Line of Emmanuel College in Toronto and King Gordon in Montreal.

Twenty-three charter members, among them Gordon, Line, Eugene Forsey, Eric Havelock, and Gregory Vlastos, adopted this statement of purpose: 'Believing as we do that there are no distinctions of power and privilege in the Kingdom of God, we pledge ourselves in the service of God and to the task of building a new society in which all exploitation of man by man and all barriers to the abundant life which are created by the private ownership of property shall be done away.'[15] Most of the FCSO's members – by mid-1937 there were 265 in Canada and Newfoundland – were drawn from among the clergy and laity of the United Church of Canada. An Anglican such as Andrew Brewin was uncommon.

To call the United Church of the Depression years a hotbed of radicalism would be silly. Nevertheless, its more conservative communicants had cause for distress. In 1933 both the Montreal-Ottawa and Toronto conferences passed resolutions that called for the introduction of a Christian social order; the Toronto conference also, by a narrow vote, condemned capitalism as unchristian. The following year, on the other hand, the General Council of the church failed to adopt the report of the Falconer Commission, *Christianizing the Social Order*. This was the report that Irene Biss and Harry Cassidy had helped to prepare: its recommendations were evidently too radical for a church that, in the main, shared the prevailing social conservatism. All the same, several church leaders belonged to or sympathized with the FCSO, among them the secretary until 1936 of the Board of Evangelism and Social Service, Ernest Thomas, his successor, J.R. Mutchmor, the editor of *The New Outlook*, William B. Creighton, and the moderator of the church from 1934 to 1936, Richard Roberts. Creighton and Thomas also belonged to the LSR. Small wonder that some laymen believed the higher reaches of the church, and its weekly paper, to be 'dangerously pink.'[16]

Until the early years of the war the relations between the LSR and the FCSO were close: occasionally, local branches met jointly. The most important statement of the fellowship's ideas was *Towards the Christian Revolution*, published in Chicago in 1936 and in London by Victor Gollancz – it was an alternate selection of the Left Book Club – in July 1937. The volume was written and edited by men who belonged to both organizations. R.B.Y. Scott, professor of Old Testament at United Theological College in Montreal, and Gregory Vlastos of Queen's University were the editors and also wrote chapters; other chapters were contributed by John Line, Eugene Forsey, King Gordon, Eric Havelock, H. Martyn Estall ('Propheticus'), and two United Church ministers, R. Edis Fairbairn and J.W.A. Nicholson. Estall was, like Vlastos, a philosophy professor at Queen's University. Not surprisingly, most of the economic analysis in the book was straight out of *Social Planning for Canada*.

III

Early in 1934 the LSR broke into print at last. When it became clear in the fall of 1933 that the publication of the book would be delayed at least until the summer, the research committee revived the idea of publishing pamphlets. Thomas Nelson & Sons published four of them in March. The first, Eugene Forsey's *Dividends and the Depression*, showed that dividends, especially in the tariff-protected and naturally sheltered industries, had dropped less rapidly than wages. *Combines and the Consumer*, written anonymously by A.S. Whiteley, an economist with the Dominion Bureau of Statistics, argued that the distribution practices in several Canadian industries were inefficient and unnecessarily costly to the consumer. *The Church and the Economic Order* was a compilation by Ernest Thomas of statements critical of capitalism made by various Christian leaders and churches. Finally, Frank Scott's *Social Reconstruction and the B.N.A. Act* pointed out the constitutional problems that awaited a socialist government in Ottawa, and assessed the capacity of the British North America Act to accommodate change.

More than one LSR member may have agreed silently with a generally sympathetic reviewer who took 'the intellectual giants on the mental mountain' to task for having 'laboured so long to bring forth these handsful [sic] of sense.' What had happened to the book? 'It is badly needed,' George Grube said at the 1934 convention: 'A much longer delay would have very serious consequences, especially psychologically, upon the whole of our membership.' '[We have our] hands absolutely full,' Harry Cassidy replied.[17]

In truth, the research committee had badly underestimated the difficulties involved in pulling together into 'a unity, rather than merely a symposium' the work of more than twenty different contributors. These difficulties were compounded when the two editors resigned. In the late spring Harry Cassidy left for Victoria to become director of Social Welfare for the Province of British Columbia. As for Graham Spry, his ample energies were during 1934 fully absorbed by other projects.

One of these was the reorganization, in collaboration with J.S. Woodsworth and Angus MacInnis, of the Ontario CCF. The UFO had left the movement; Elmore Philpott had resigned as its leader. In April Spry was elected vice-president of the provincial CCF Council. Soon afterwards the provincial election campaign required his assistance. Very late off the mark in contrast with the Liberals under their flamboyant leader, Mitchell Hepburn, the CCF still suffered from the effects of the winter's troubles. It managed to nominate only thirty-seven candidates, leaving fifty-three seats uncontested. This undermined the party's claim to be the only genuine alternative to the pseudo-choice between Hepburn and Premier George Henry. Badly underfinanced and understaffed, the CCF on 19 June polled a mere 7.1 per cent of the popular vote and gained the election of just one candidate, Sam Lawrence in Hamilton East. 'Mitch' Hepburn's Liberals had won an easy victory.

'For the CCF, the 1934 election was a disaster,' one historian of the party, Gerald Caplan, writes. However, not for the first and certainly not for the last time a defeat was greeted as a 'moral victory.' The same was done in Saskatchewan in May, but there, at least, though soundly beaten by the Liberals, the CCF had become the Opposition. In Ontario insiders knew the claim to be hollow. That a great deal of organization and education remained to be done was the inescapable conclusion. No one knew it better than Spry. In order to provide the Ontario CCF with an official organ he set out to turn *The Farmer's Sun* into *The New Commonwealth*. With the LSR providing some financial aid the switch was completed in July. In this way Spry was able to reassert an editorial control that he had briefly lost earlier in the year; he became managing editor of the transformed publication.[18]

Finally, during the summer Graham Spry was nominated to be the CCF standard-bearer in Toronto East in a by-election called for 24 September. The first CCFer to contest a federal seat in Ontario, he campaigned furiously. 'The CCF's young man,' as *Saturday Night* dubbed him, knocked on doors whenever he had time and, in the warm evenings of late summer, spoke to any street-corner audience he could find. In the working-class districts there was evidence of support; some of his listeners were enthusiastic. More were sceptical, however, and the riding organization was weak and mostly untried. On election night Spry found that 16.3 per cent of the voters supported him. If this was a moral victory, perhaps the only person to enjoy real solace from it was the victorious Conservative candidate, T.L. Church. Had the CCF votes gone to the Liberals instead, he, too, would have been defeated in the mini-election of 1934.

Five seats had been at issue in Ontario, four of them straight fights between the Liberals and Conservatives. The Grits had taken these four for a net gain of one and increased their share of the vote in all five ridings. This confirmed what was already suspected from the results of five earlier by-elections held from October 1932 to April 1934, all of them won by the Liberals (the net gain was one). Then there was the demolition of three Conservative governments, in British Columbia, Saskatchewan, and Ontario, within a period of seven months. Barring something like a miracle, the Tories would fare very badly in a general election. But so would the CCF.

Canadian social democrats were discomfited by the Liberal forces on their right. At the same time they suffered annoyance from the smaller forces on their left. The year 1934 brought the first Communist approaches to the LSR. Until October the CPC was little interested in the league. Stewart Smith, chief theorist of the party by this time, had earlier in the year maligned the LSR intellectuals as constituting 'the direct contribution of "experts" by the bourgeoisie' to the 'social fascist' CCF. Their 'liberal capitalist theories,' however, were designed to do no more than make capitalism palatable to the masses, even as it continued to enslave them.[19] J.S. Woodsworth and other CCF leaders had been subjected to similar attacks for years; no one took them too seriously.

A change began to take place during 1934. Unpleasantly surprised by the fate of the German Communist party at the hands of Hitler's National Socialists and keenly aware of the Soviet Union's isolation in the world, the Communist International was led to reconsider its hostility to the 'social fascism' of democratic socialist parties. Soon Communist parties everywhere were instructed to mend their fences and seek co-operation with all anti-fascist groups, liberal, social democrat, or whatever, in building a 'popular front' against fascism. The new policy was confirmed at the Seventh Congress of the Comintern in 1935. Promotion of the idea of collective security through the League of Nations, which the Soviet Union had recently joined, was to be one function of the new policy; checking the spread of fascism was the other.

In Canada the policy inspired the formation of the Canadian League against War and Fascism (CLAWF). The first public meeting of this front organization took place in Toronto in October 1934. Not long afterwards E.A. Beder, an early LSR member who had become secretary of the CLAWF, invited the LSR through Frank Underhill 'to affiliate to the League officially ... We would be glad, too, if your branches would officially affiliate to the Local Councils wherever they exist.'[20] Local branches later received a similar invitation.

Initially there was a division of opinion. 'Personally I am dead against it,' Frank Scott informed Underhill: 'It seems to me that as we did not even affiliate with the CCF it would be rather curious now to tie ourselves up with this organization; our reason for keeping clear of these entanglements, viz. the necessity of our remaining a research and educational body rather than an active political one, is just as valid now as formerly.' Scott doubted, moreover, that the CLAWF would accomplish much in the pursuit of peace. The matter would have to await the next national convention. Underhill replied to Beder: 'I am personally in favour of affiliating with your organization, but we shall have to wait and see what the general opinion of the LSR is.'[21]

What that opinion might be was indicated at a meeting of the Toronto branch executive just before Christmas. Affiliation was turned down because the CLAWF was known to be 'powerfully influenced by the Communists.' No one wanted to run the risk of identifying the LSR with the Communist party. Not very surprisingly the 1935 national convention wasted little time in reaching the same decision. The CLAWF renewed its invitation at least twice, but these approaches were brushed off. 'Friendly contact' was permissible and individual LSR members were free to join the CLAWF; affiliation was, however, out of the question. Indeed, there was growing criticism within the LSR and CCF of individuals who would join a Communist-front organization. The not unreasonable suspicion lingered that the Communists meant the social-democratic movement no real good.[22]

The LSR's fourth national convention was held in Toronto on a bleak week-end in February 1935, bleak outside and bleak inside. The evidence of growing weakness was depressing. A number of branches had ceased to exist and membership was down to under five hundred. '[The convention] was a fairly gloomy affair, only one branch outside Montreal and Toronto being represented,' Frank Scott, the newly chosen national president, reported to Harry Cassidy in Victoria: 'Underhill was in his best pessimistic mood. As far as I can see there is only one real job ahead of us now and that is the completion of the book. If we cannot finish that, we may as well give up; if we do, our work will have been infinitely worthwhile.' Of course, Frank Underhill almost relished looking at the dark side. 'Whatever Frank Underhill's many excellencies,' the understanding Cassidy commented, 'he is not a person who inspires enthusiasm in those of uncertain faith.' Scott's faith was robust enough. All the same, he was surely putting better than the best possible face on things when, in the aftermath of the convention, he tried to cheer E.O. Hall, a down-hearted delegate from the London branch: 'There is no reason why we should feel at all discouraged at the results of our efforts over the past three years ... I believe that the LSR by direct and indirect methods has done a great deal to shift the whole current of political thinking in Canada.'[23] Precisely how he did not say. Since the book had not yet been published, however, he was thinking mainly of the work done in and for the CCF.

In fact, the book was nearing completion. Underhill, Joe Parkinson, and Irene Biss having failed to finish the editorial work during the summer of 1934, it had been taken in hand by Scott and Leonard Marsh, an economist at McGill University. Assisted by Eugene Forsey and Marsh's wife, Helen, the two men had worked steadily through the winter towards their goal.

Slightly built, with a bespectacled, narrow face, reminiscent sometimes of an eager schoolboy, Leonard Charles Marsh was coming to occupy a central position in the LSR. Combining ability with prodigious energy, he used his time with great effectiveness. Born in England in 1905, he had taken a degree in economics from the University of London and worked as a research assistant and lecturer at the London School of Economics before joining the McGill staff in 1930. The following year the university received a research grant of $110,000 from the Rockefeller Foundation and the young Englishman, who had been associated with Sir William Beveridge in the 'New Survey of London Life and Labour,' was appointed director of Social Research. Thus began an enterprise that spawned eleven pioneering works in Canadian economics, sociology, and education, from Marsh's own *Employment Research* (1935) to Everett Hughes's *French Canada in Transition* (1943), and including *Canadians In and Out of Work* (1940), in which Marsh grappled with the peculiarities of the class system of this country.

Leonard Marsh was already interested in socialism when he left England. The Depression and his research into unemployment and its effects in Montreal fanned his interest into fervour. He joined the LSR in 1932, but his modesty and the pressure of work kept him mostly on the sidelines during the first couple of years. The editorial experience he was gaining, however, and the bibliographical and secretarial skills of his Alberta-born wife (she had been a public librarian in Ottawa before she married him) made them peculiarly well qualified to push the LSR book to an end.

Push they did. The accumulated manuscripts were worked over, restructured, brought up to date when necessary. Some gaps had to be filled in. Everything had to be typed; then there were proofs to read and an index to be added. In late July 1935 it was over: a happy Leonard Marsh was able to inform Harry Cassidy that the task the latter had begun thirty months earlier was done at last.[24]

Social Planning for Canada was published in September 1935. In his foreword J.S. Woodsworth warmly welcomed the 528-page volume: it would be 'of great service in the formulation of the future policies of the CCF.' He urged CCF candidates and clubs to get a copy: 'Every CCF member ought to be able to give a reason for the faith that is in him.'

The preface by the research committee hit a scarcely less evangelical note. If 'greater equality and social justice among the mass of our population' were to be attained, a large number of changes would be necessary; they must be introduced 'by democratic and orderly means.' The book's purpose was, on factual grounds, to foster 'widespread public knowledge ... of the faults and deficiencies of our economic system, and of the constructive proposals to deal with them which spring from socialist ideals.' (Evidently the word *socialist* had ceased to be a bugbear.) But socialism must be understood to be more than a body of proposals:

> [It] crystallizes a protest – against gross inequality of income and economic power, against poverty and thwarted and repressed human lives, against waste and inefficiency, against the inhumanity and social stupidity of exploitation and war. Above all else, this protest has the right to be heard.
>
> Our book is an attempt to set out this protest and these proposals in specifically Canadian terms. It is not a series of doctrinaire generalizations, but an attempt to analyze and prescribe by a group who have tried to visualize a real and richer 'Canada for Canadians.' We do not pretend, of course, that a single volume can contain all the thinking required in this process. Parts of this book deal all too summarily with deep problems; sheer limits of space have compelled us to omit such vital subjects as, for instance, education and the position of women in the new society. But we are hopeful that the material gathered here will be of assistance not only to those who are already acquainted with socialist thought, but to all those with sincere interest in the future of Canada who want to examine its problems realistically.

Having no desire to limit its impact by seeming to speak only to present and prospective socialists, the LSR would not object if others borrowed its ideas.

Although a score of people had contributed to the volume, only seven members of the research committee signed their names to the preface and thus assumed responsibility for the book. They were Eugene Forsey, King Gordon, Leonard Marsh, J.F. Parkinson, Frank Scott, Graham Spry, and Frank Underhill. These thanked the others who had written chapters or memoranda, or had criticized or helped with the revision of the text. Some had asked to remain anonymous, such as Harry Cassidy, A.F.W. Plumptre, A.S. Whiteley, and a Nova Scotia physician, Dr Benge Atlee. Those thanked by name were Irene Biss, Alexander Brady, Humphrey Carver, G.M.A. Grube, Stuart Legge, Kenneth Taylor, Betty Ratz, a young bank economist in Toronto, and C.W. Topping, a professor of Social Work at the University of British Columbia.

The price, $3.75 in the stores and $3.00 to LSR members, was forbidding, the style rather less so. An unevenness betrays the multiple authorship, but the editors and revisers were generally successful. On the whole the book reads quite easily, and in places its prose is strikingly good. In spite of the price the initial printing of fifteen hundred copies sold briskly. The election campaign made it particularly topical; it also got some useful free advertising. Seven or eight weeks after the publication of *Social Planning*, a forty-page booklet criticizing it was published anonymously and distributed gratis to businessmen and newspapers around the country. Written by P.C. Armstrong, a public-relations officer with the Canadian Pacific Railway Company, the pamphlet described the book as a Marxist-inspired document in which misinformation and faulty logic were put to the service of a sermon preaching class hatred. Questioned were both the motives and the competence of the authors of the LSR book. Some of them, especially Frank Underhill, almost danced with rage. Frank Scott, however, seeking to calm his friend down, looked at the bright side: 'I am delighted that the incident has occurred. The vicious style of the document, its use of contempt for argument, its complete failure to answer the main thesis of our book, are admissions of great weakness. ... On the whole, our prestige – and our sales – should go up considerably.' Whatever the reasons, the first impression was virtually sold out by Christmas. A second printing of fifteen hundred copies moved well at first, but sales petered out before the end of 1936. Not until the war years did Thomas Nelson & Sons exhaust their stock.[25]

On the whole the LSR had reason to be pleased, not only by the sales but also by the attention given to the book. Not all notices were favourable, of course, but even a negative review was better than no review at all. At least the book had been noticed. Several of the reviews were almost fulsome in their praise. *Social Planning for Canada* 'fully justified its claim to be the first adequate treatise [on Canada] from a socialist point of view,' wrote an anonymous reviewer in the *CCF Research Review*, published in Regina: 'Buy it. If you cannot buy it, then borrow it. Read it.' Writing in *The New Outlook*, Salem Bland called it 'the most notable book that Canada has yet produced. Its influence, I believe, will be quite immeasurable.'[26]

Much less admiring was the review by Wallis Lefeaux, a Vancouver lawyer and Marxist who had come to the CCF through the SPC. 'To term the book a contribution to socialist literature is a misnomer,' he argued. In spite of their intentions and because of their ignorance of Marxism the authors had offered an apology for state capitalism. Lefeaux's review was soon, and not illogically, denounced by Robert Connell, leader of the British Columbia CCF, as constituting an attack on the Regina Manifesto! The review reinforced Connell's growing conviction that several of his nominal supporters were all too friendly to communism. As for the Communist view of the book, Tim Buck declared it to be interesting, but inadequate and naive.[27]

Other reviewers greeted the book's descriptions and prescriptions with scepticism and assigned to it mainly political importance. The political economist Harold Adams Innis, for example, deplored the book's reliance on British designs and its over-simplification of complex economic issues for political purposes. The journalist George V. Ferguson thought the authors were unrealistic to expect 'that, when the time comes, everyone will put his shoulder to the wheel for the common good.'

Too easily they ignored the possibility that their proposals for economic planning might produce 'a clogged, stupid, tyrannous and inefficient bureaucracy.' B.K. Sandwell, editor of *Saturday Night*, suggested that it was facile to suppose, as the LSR did, that socialism could be introduced gradually and by democratic means. A reviewer in the Toronto *Mail and Empire* held that all political parties would find useful ideas in the book, however, and R.A. MacKay, a political scientist at Dalhousie University, commented: 'If past experience in our politics is a guide to the future, we may expect many of the proposals of *Social Planning for Canada* to be quietly appropriated item by item by the traditional parties. The real function of minority parties in Canada is to provide the older parties with platforms.'[28]

During the last forty years one of the commonplaces of Canadian political analysis, of course, has been the notion that the CCF and its successor, the New Democratic Party, are idea-givers to the two major parties, and especially to the Liberals. In 1935 and 1936, however, these were not falling over themselves in a rush to borrow the LSR's ideas. As R.A. MacKay suggested, the process of appropriation would be quiet and slow. No one in the LSR wanted to wait for what the Liberals or Conservatives might do. The CCF embodied its hopes for the future.

IV

To the LSR one other event in 1935, the federal election, ranked in importance with the appearance of *Social Planning for Canada*. After all, by this time many members had already invested considerable physical and emotional energy in the CCF. 'Officially the LSR had no status in the party structure,' the anatomist of the party, Professor Walter Young, writes, 'yet it was more influential in shaping policy than constituency resolutions or the convention itself in the period 1932–40.'[29] The brain trust's work on the Regina Manifesto was only the beginning.

Frank Underhill's participation in the 1934 CCF convention in Winnipeg followed the precedent set in Regina. He had with him a draft by Escott Reid of a statement on foreign policy; amended by Underhill, it became the basis for the neutralist statement on peace in the Winnipeg immediate program. As he reported to Frank Scott, Underhill further 'got the National Council to agree to appoint ... four committees as permanent bodies, with academic people on them to do the work of drawing up memoranda, publishing leaflets, etc. and reporting to the next convention.' A committee on foreign policy would be chaired by E.J. Garland, with Underhill as secretary – 'and we shall co-opt you and Escott Reid.' William Irvine would chair finance, with J.F. Parkinson to help him. (In view of Irvine's attraction to Social Credit and Parkinson's antipathy to it, that promised to be an interesting committee.) With Eugene Forsey's assistance Angus MacInnis would convene the committee on labour and social services. Robert Gardiner, MP, had been given agriculture to convene; who should assist him Underhill was unable to decide. Finally, one more committee, on publicity, was established and placed in the capable if overworked hands of Graham Spry. 'So,' Underhill concluded, 'we now have a chance to go ahead and draft things and publish them if possible as at least semi-official documents.'[30]

Little actually resulted from this scheme. The assistance rendered by LSR members turned out to be more informal than Underhill had intended. Their agreement at the Winnipeg meetings notwithstanding, the MPs were not yet ready for the more effective organization that the historian desired. This did not stop him, however. He and Scott already advised J.S. Woodsworth on constitutional matters; this was made formal early in 1935, when the CCF leader served on a special parliamentary committee on the British North America Act. The national council of the CCF now adopted 'the general policy set forth by Prof. Scott in respect to the Canadian constitution.' Assisted by Underhill and Brooke Claxton – later in the year the latter was elected to the House of Commons as a Liberal – Scott drafted an amendment formula that assigned the right of ordinary amendment of the BNA Act to a majority of both Houses of Parliament assembled together and required the assent of all provincial governments only to amendments that affected minority rights.[31] A motion incorporating this formula was ultimately ratified by the CCF national convention of 1936.

By the summer of 1935, even in the absence of a formal tie, the LSR and CCF had grown very close. Parliament being in its fifth year, a fall election had become inevitable. The political stage was uncommonly crowded. Led by the irrepressible R.B. Bennett, the Conservatives had become more or less reluctant converts to a program of reform that the prime minister had announced in a series of six radio broadcasts early in the year. But Bennett had not been able to retain the loyalty of H.H. Stevens, who had left the cabinet and then launched his own political vessel, the Reconstruction party. Its program called for the reform of capitalism by means of increased regulation and social legislation and, not least, of the restoration of competition to those areas of the market from which it had vanished.

In Alberta and Saskatchewan, provinces where the CCF hoped to do well, the Social Credit movement was growing rapidly. Led by a persuasive high-school principal and radio evangelist named William Aberhart, Social Credit spoke of A + B, and promised 'just wages' and 'just prices' as well as a 'social dividend' of twenty-five dollars to be paid monthly to all adults. Also facing its first national test, the CCF was worried about the inroads Social Credit might make on its support, just as it was worried about the small Communist party and its attempts at electoral collaboration. Finally, looming very large was the pudgy figure of William Lyon Mackenzie King. Confident that the spectre of the Depression would defeat the Tories and that none of the other parties constituted a serious threat, the

Liberals stuck to the program of cautious reform adopted in 1933 and told the voters that the choice was 'King or chaos.'

To the LSR it was nothing of the kind. The Bennett 'New Deal' was regarded as either an election-year stunt or the sort of reform that a capitalist would like: marketing legislation that provided a measure of security to producers and processors at the expense of consumers and social legislation whereby the working class would be bought off with its own money. Harry Stevens meant well, but he sought to set the clock back on behalf, in Underhill's words, of 'a group of small manufacturers and retailers who are out to get Eaton's and Simpson's and the chain stores.'[32] Social Credit was economic nonsense: *Social Planning for Canada* devoted twelve pages to a demonstration of its 'futility.' To the same end the LSR had already published a leaflet, *Socialism or Social Credit?* It was distressing, therefore, to witness the sweeping victory of Social Credit in the Alberta election of 22 August 1935, the more so because the United Farmers' government was the victim. It had been beaten by the Depression and by scandal more than by Social Credit, but the defeat threatened further ill.

The Communist party fought for some of the same causes – civil liberties, the interests of the unemployed, and labour's right to organize, for example – that engaged the sympathies and energies of members of the LSR and CCF. But the CPC was also a confounded nuisance. The Popular Front was very much alive in 1935, and whether or not to join it was a subject of heated argument within the democratic left. Some LSR and CCF adherents had joined front organizations, notably the Canadian League against War and Fascism; others, resenting the Communist attacks of earlier years, objecting to the CPC's proletarian and revolutionary ethos, and distrusting its links with Moscow, steered well clear of joint action. They feared, furthermore, that co-operation would do the CCF electoral harm. The leadership of the movement held the CPC at arm's length; there it continued to be pesky.

Once a party of reform, the Liberals had for forty years been virtually indistinguishable from the Tories. King would win the election, but not because he deserved it. The victory, Underhill and others thought, might easily ring the knell of the federal Conservative party. The forces of reaction would flock to the Liberal banner or to that of a 'national government,' a Liberal-Tory coalition. Two years earlier Frank Underhill had anticipated the disappearance of the Liberal party in a repetition of the process that had taken place in Britain. His reading of *The New Republic* in 1934–35 led him to the view that the Conservatives, like the Republicans, would probably pass away as politics in North America divided along class lines. All truly progressive Canadians would turn to the CCF, thus making it the comprehensive farmer-labour party Canada needed. 'In future,' Underhill concluded in *Social Planning for Canada*, 'the electorate will have to choose not between two faithful servants of capitalism, but between a capitalist party and a socialist party. With all the mists raised by Social Credit parties, Reconstruction parties, and the rest, the fundamental issues are at last becoming clarified; and 'business' is faced with the horrid prospect that when the electorate tires, as it must, of the rule of the capitalist party, it will have no choice but to put the socialist in power.' Business would then have to submit, 'or abolish democracy.'[33]

Convinced by and large that the future belonged to the CCF, LSR members took an active part in the election campaign. Together with J.S. Woodsworth, Underhill drew up the party's election address; several LSR stalwarts offered themselves to the voters. Graham Spry ran in Toronto-Broadview, a new constituency that incorporated much of Toronto East, which he had contested in the previous year's by-election. King Gordon had been invited to run in Victoria, BC; George Mooney was running in Verdun, Quebec. In Toronto–St Paul's a recently returned Rhodes Scholar, E.B. Jolliffe, had entered the lists. In London, Ontario, Everett O. Hall, a high-school teacher who was a mainstay of the branch there, was seeking election.

What were the immediate prospects? Most LSR members permitted themselves a guarded optimism. Several large cities had elected CCF mayors in late 1934 and early 1935, among them Jimmy Simpson in sometime Tory Toronto. But against this stood the fact that little money was available for the campaign. Furthermore, east of the Ottawa River the CCF had nominated only three candidates, all in the area of Montreal. With fewer than half of the country's 245 constituencies contested by CCFers, the dizzying height of the party's ambition could only be to form the official Opposition.

Writing to his old mentor, J.W. Dafoe, Graham Spry in July did not know whether to be optimistic or pessimistic. In his own riding the Conservative incumbent had chosen to go with Bennett, and there would be a Reconstructionist in the field,

> two circumstances which, I think, definitely increase my chances, despite the removal of my best polling divisions into the next riding.
>
> We have twenty-seven CCF candidates now nominated. We will have forty to sixty in the province and they will be backed by a fair but inexperienced organization ... E.B. Jolliffe, formerly of the Canadian Press and another reprehensible Rhodes Scholar, is provincial organizer. I do not like to say how many seats we will get in Ontario; we might get none at all, but I think we will pick up a few. In all events, it will be an interesting election.[34]

To insiders an 'interesting election' is one with a lot of three- or even four-way fights in which their own party is not expected to do well. The CCF was to know a lot of those.

Few LSR members dared hope for much; all of them found the outcome of the election a dreadful disappointment. The Liberals swept into office with 173 seats although their share of the popular vote had scarcely increased; five Independent Liberals were also elected. The Conservatives were reduced to forty seats. Of the Reconstructionists only H.H. Stevens himself was returned, even though the party had gained 9 per cent of all votes. Although the CCF had polled only slightly fewer votes in a considerably smaller number of constituencies, that provided little consolation for the record of defeat. Only seven CCFers were elected. In spite of the best efforts of Ted Jolliffe and his assistants, none of the fifty candidates in Ontario was successful. Spry, E.O. Hall, and Jolliffe himself were among the many who lost their deposits. So was George Mooney in Verdun. One Labour-UFO candidate did get returned in Ontario, the redoubtable Agnes Macphail. Although she had left the CCF in 1934 when the United Farmers of Ontario did, her relations remained cordial with a number of people in the party she would eventually rejoin. Her re-election was the only bright spot in central Canada.

There were a few more in the West. J.S. Woodsworth and A.A. Heaps held their seats in Winnipeg; Angus MacInnis was also re-elected. The CCF gained two members in British Columbia, Grant MacNeil in Vancouver North and, in Nanaimo, against all expectations, an eccentric printer, 'Student of Occult Science,' and sometime member of the LSR's Vancouver branch, J.S. Taylor. Further south on Vancouver Island, in Victoria, King Gordon had run second in a close race.

From Saskatchewan came two new MPs with whom the LSR would get on well, the Regina teacher M.J. Coldwell (Rosetown-Biggar) and the young and fiery Baptist preacher T.C. Douglas (Weyburn). Elsewhere on the plains there was no cause for rejoicing. The advocates of Aberhartian Social Credit gained fifteen seats in Alberta and two in Saskatchewan, while every UFA–CCF incumbent went down to defeat. Among them were several who had taken a lively interest in the LSR, G.G. Coote, E.J. Garland, William Irvine, and especially Henry Spencer, who had served on the LSR's national executive in 1933–35. LSR leaders were profoundly sorry to hear of his loss and of those of the others. It was doubly distressing that they had been beaten by a bunch of 'Funny Money' fanatics.

Anybody who wished to claim a moral victory on the basis of the CCF's 800,000 votes was free to do so. Privately, at least, the national president of the LSR did not feel so inclined. Frank Scott had hoped for more. But the CCF's thunder had evidently been muted by the claims of other parties that they wanted to reform or restructure society. The Reconstruction party in particular, he guessed, had gained the support of many Canadians – farmers, white-collar workers, and small businessmen – who might otherwise have voted for the more radical CCF.

As a result of the study he and Harry Cassidy had done on the men's clothing industry two years earlier, Scott was acquainted with the national chairman of the Reconstruction party, the clothier Warren K. Cook. Scott now wrote to Cook to suggest that the possibility of establishing closer relations between the CCF and the Reconstructionists be considered. It would be a pity in the future to continue to split the protest vote. Cook responded with interest. He had recently read *Social Planning for Canada* and it struck him that 'there seems to be one difference between the CCF programme and our own and that is that you folks want to cross the river in one jump while we believe that we can cross the same river more quickly by using stepping stones.' Either this assessment was intended to be more polite than accurate or Cook had trouble understanding what he read. He did, however, undertake to meet Scott in Montreal on 7 November and promised that H.H. Stevens would also be there.[35] Nothing came of the meeting, however; Scott was already having second thoughts about the scheme and his chances of convincing others of its soundness. As for the Reconstruction party, it faded quickly from the political fabric.

Frank Underhill reacted to the set-back in a different fashion. His acquaintance Norman McLeod Rogers had been elected as a Liberal and was quickly taken into the cabinet by Mackenzie King. 'Now that Norman Rogers is in charge of the Department of Labour,' Underhill wrote to J.S. Woodsworth late in November,

> it should be possible to get something done there. Could you not press for adequate unemployment statistics, wider unemployment insurance and a properly staffed system of employment agencies? Also for a Dominion-wide system of health insurance ... The CCF should be pressing for particular measures of social reform. This seems to me the best way of preparing the Canadian mind for socialism, since the voting made it clear that there has to be a very big shift in opinion in favour of more state intervention before we can talk a complete socialist programme with any chance of success. This is, of course, reformism and it has its dangers. But we have to convince the middle classes that we have some interest in and capacity for details of administration as well as in general principles.[36]

Underhill did not see himself as a 'Liberal in a hurry.' For him, at this stage of his life, the point of the whole propagandistic and political exercise was the ultimate introduction of socialism, the socialism of *Social Planning in Canada*. He was typical of the LSR, however, and of social democrats generally in believing that half a loaf, or even a quarter, is a good deal better than none. With a bit of luck and a lot of hard work the rest of the loaf would sooner or later follow.

During its first four years the LSR, without underestimating the importance of political organization, had consistently overestimated the influence of political instruction. The outcome of the provincial and federal elections of 1934 and 1935 should have forced a reassessment of that estimate, should have led the LSR to re-examine the scope and merits of the educational approach. To do so, however, would have implied examination, possibly even acceptance, of the distasteful notion that, in politics at least, few people are persuaded by fact and logic. The LSR preferred to assume the underlying rationality and benevolence of mankind, just as it assumed that it was in command of the important facts. Some members came to challenge these assumptions or to believe that socialist ideas were mistaken: these then left the LSR. Others, the majority, concluded that the LSR and CCF were not doing enough to bring those ideas to the attention of the Canadian people. Clearly, renewed and redoubled efforts were in order.

5

In search of Canadian socialism

Never was the wish for a Canadian form of socialism stated more clearly than at Regina in 1933. Speaking to the founding convention of the CCF, J.S. Woodsworth told his enthusiastic listeners:

> Undoubtedly we should profit by the experience of other nations and other times, but personally I believe that we in Canada must work out our salvation in our own way. Socialism has so many variations that we hesitate to use the class name. Utopian Socialism and Christian Socialism, Marxian Socialism and Fabianism, the Latin type, the German type, the Russian type – why not a Canadian type?
>
> ... I am convinced that we may develop in Canada a distinctive type of socialism. I refuse to follow slavishly the British model or the American model or the Russian model. We in Canada will solve our problems along our own lines.[1]

In his audience were several members of the League for Social Reconstruction, already at work on a book that was intended to be of major assistance to the CCF. Theirs primarily became the task of formulating the distinctive Canadian socialism anticipated by their honorary president.

In the execution of this charge Woodsworth's influence was very important. Professor Norman Penner exaggerates but little in claiming that 'it was indeed Woodsworth who developed the main outlines of [the CCF] programme.' The 'prophet in politics' had a profound influence on the development of democratic socialism in Canada after the Great War. LSR members thought and still think of him with admiration and respect, even reverence. 'We all admired him for qualities we didn't have ourselves,' Frank Underhill recalled years later.[2]

It was Woodsworth's personal and political style, his devotion to principle and duty, his courage, honesty, integrity, and burning sense of justice, his 'largeness of spirit' that particularly impressed and influenced the LSR, his specific ideas on politics and economics less so. But his anti-capitalism and anti-imperialism and his desire for a unified Canada presaged and helped to shape the analyses and proposals of the LSR. Most important was his conviction that a Canadian socialist movement must not limit itself to the industrial working class but must reach out to the farmers and the petite bourgeoisie.

Throughout the 1920s Woodsworth had promoted the cause of his Canadian socialism. He had only limited success. The dominant strains of socialism in Canada were Marxist or derived from Marxism. There adherents were found in the Dominion and Canadian Labour parties as well as in the Socialist Party of Canada and the Communist party; they were often immigrants from the British Isles or from continental Europe. A self-congratulatory LSR pamphlet, *Canada and Socialism*, asserted in 1935 that before the Depression socialism in this country had been 'a European growth.' With the coming of the LSR and CCF this had changed, however: 'It is no longer a somewhat sickly immigrant; it is a vigorous infant, native to the soil.'[3] Socialism had become Canadian. More precisely put, it had become British North American.

Like its most obvious model the Fabian Society half a century earlier, the LSR was depression-born. Unlike the Fabian Society, the league was founded in a relatively recent colony of settlement, a huge, sparsely populated, northern country in which problems of transportation loomed large, export-oriented agriculture and the extractive industries were fundamentally important, and farming was carried out mainly by owners rather than tenants. In Canada, too, the federal system divided authority over economic development and social policy between the Dominion and the provinces. The nature of the country and its background as a colony, first of France and then of Great Britain, shaped the LSR's attempt to work out a Canadian socialism. *Social Planning for Canada* is the most imposing monument to that search and the only comprehensive statement of the ideas of the league.

'The End of a Century of Progress' is the title of the opening chapter. Although Harry Cassidy, Frank Underhill, Joe Parkinson, Leonard Marsh, and Frank Scott all tinkered with it, it was basically King Gordon's work. It is an indictment, couched in the language of moral censure, of Canada under monopoly capitalism. Most Canadians, according to the chapter, do not seem to see what is happening. Their faith in progress, in material and technical advance, is kept alive by the educational, political, and legal systems, and by a 'carefully controlled and manipulated press.' But Canada is no exception to the general rule of industrialized capitalistic countries:

> The same trends towards the greater and greater concentration of economic power are evident – the same maldistribution of wealth, the same shocking contrasts between luxury and indigence. Masses of official evidence point to the practice of exploitation and the

futility of governments' efforts to control or restrain ... Antagonisms of class become more and more apparent, and the period of capitalist decline serves but to intensify the resentment of the dispossessed towards the owning and the ruling classes. This inevitable conflict permeates every sphere of life, corrupting politics and the press, warping the true course of social justice, distorting the law to serve the interests of the defenders of the *status quo*, debasing the religious and cultural expression of the people. The way before the Canadian people is plain. A return to a more primitive society is obviously impossible, nor would it be desirable were it within the realm of possibility. An intelligent reconstruction of our economic life is not beyond the capacity of Canadians to achieve, nor are the obstacles in the form of the economic interests and privileges of favoured groups insurmountable. The time is fast arriving when special privileges at the expense of the welfare of the community will be considered as a luxury which no civilized nation can afford.[4]

A more detailed 'survey and analysis' of 'the present system' is provided in the next six chapters. Their titles are 'The Nature of the Canadian Economy,' 'The Structure of Canadian Industry,' 'The Mechanism of the Market,' 'Agriculture and the Farmer,' 'Government Intervention and Ownership: The Present Situation,' and, finally and most tellingly, 'The Inefficiency of the System.' These chapters were largely the work of Irene Biss, Eugene Forsey, and Parkinson, with contributions from several others – Stuart Legge, Wynne Plumptre, Betty Ratz, Kenneth Taylor, and A.S. Whiteley.

Basic to the first seven chapters is a handful of propositions or judgments. Capitalism is immoral and increasingly inefficient. The resulting social and economic evils have become acute in the era of monopoly capitalism. Half-hearted 'reforms' that do not get at the underlying inadequacy of capitalism will not improve the situation much. State intervention, whether through government ownership, regulation, or planning, whose purpose is to save capitalism will only perpetuate scarcity. However, 'capitalism has made planning possible'; it must be carried out in the interests of the overwhelming majority rather than the minority who now rule.

Its apotheosis of the profit motive and its attempt to attach a price tag to everything and everybody are at the core of the moral failure of capitalism: 'The great condemnation of our system is that it makes an interest in "things" the major interest to the almost complete exclusion of an interest in values. The basis of privilege is wealth, the creed of privilege is a belief in the making of money, the measure of human achievement is a monetary yardstick. This philosophy of acquisition renders impotent the finer impulses.'[5] The private ethics of capitalists are irrelevant within the higher immorality of a business civilization. The hunt for profits can ultimately justify any kind of behaviour, no matter how much it hurts human beings or despoils the land, water, and air that surrounds them.

One thing that could be said in favour of capitalism in its earlier, more competitive stage was that, working through the market, it allocated resources and rewards fairly efficiently. But this has become steadily less true. Even where it once did exist, the free market is no more. Working out its own inner logic, capitalism undermines competition. In the Canada described by the LSR the large corporations, often owned or controlled abroad, have become dominant. And within them the shots are called by a few magnates who themselves often own only a fraction of what they control, 'an irresponsible oligarchy [who] spread their tentacles over the whole of human life.'[6]

Even over those industries in which a measure of competition persists, agriculture, textiles, clothing, furniture, and so on, 'monopoly rules by remote control.' The money and labour markets are rigged; price and production policies in many industries are carefully managed in order to maintain prices, even in a slump. Monopoly capitalists are bound to protect earnings at any cost – to others. Those others are the great mass of the Canadian people, farmers and fishermen, industrial and clerical workers, small businessmen, and, always, the consumers.

Is the answer to try to restore competition? The authors of *Social Planning* think not. The growth of monopoly is inherent in modern industry and cannot be reversed, the wishes of H.H. Stevens notwithstanding.

What, then, of government intervention and regulation, the course of action counselled by Canadian and American reformers in the 1930s? *Social Planning* is sceptical. After all, Canada is not without experience in this field. There is a certain amount of social and labour legislation, and much more in the way of tariff protection, subsidies, some government regulation, and some outright ownership and operation. All too often, however, the intervention has consisted of business-oriented politicians shovelling money towards entrepreneurs. And yet some of the latter, 'fresh from enriching themselves at the public expense, ... denounce unemployment insurance as a "dole," and demand, with unconscious humour, that labour should "look after itself as business has done."' There is an echo here of R.H. Tawney's trenchant observation some years earlier: 'Few tricks of the unsophisticated intellect are more curious than the naïve psychology of the business man, who ascribes his achievements to his own unaided efforts, in bland unconsciousness of a social order without whose continuous support and vigilant protection he would be as a lamb bleating in the desert.'[7] Intervention means that businessmen get molly-coddled, even though they often seem not to realize it.

For this reason the LSR has no use for the principal features of the national policy. Protective tariffs in the Canadian experience are a form of legalized robbery; immigration has been largely a waste of effort, bringing more people to the country than it could absorb; railway policy has led to the formation of the Canadian National Railways, that 'monument to the insanity of capitalism.' Moreover, insofar as the primary purpose of the CNR's operations is to pay the interest on its indebtedness, it behaves no differently from privately owned corporations.

The characteristic behaviour of monopoly capitalists is restrictive; it is therefore 'unbelievably wasteful.' The trouble is that 'broadly speaking, the nearer anything gets to being a "free good" the less there is in it for the capitalist. This is just as true for the competitive capitalist as it is for the monopolist; but the competitive capitalist cannot restrict production and hold up price, while the monopolist can and does. This is why monopoly capitalism is essentially and inescapably a scarcity economy to a degree impossible to the competitive capitalism of earlier days.' In a world economy increasingly organized along national lines, few opportunities are now available for profits by expansion. Hence restriction is the order of the day, in National Socialist Germany, in Britain under the National Government, in the United States of the National Recovery Administration, in Canada, and elsewhere. 'It begins to look as if henceforth the best we can expect under capitalism, is successive temporary stabilizations on progressively lower levels, for everything but profits ...' In fact, the contradictions inherent in capitalism – *Social Planning* lists eight – are undermining the system. 'To reverse Adam Smith's phrase, "Each seeking only his own interest, is led by an Invisible Hand to promote the ruin of society."'[8]

The full meaning of government intervention in the Depression, as interpreted by the LSR, becomes plain. 'State capitalist planning' has as its 'avowed aim ... the preservation of profit and as far as possible of private ownership of industry. On this point Mr. Roosevelt, Mr. Bennett and Mr. Stevens are as clear and emphatic as Signor Mussolini. They believe it can be done without destroying political democracy. He does not.' The democratic and the fascist countries differ but little in their economic policies, for the needs of the corporations are paramount in both. 'As a witty American journalist puts it, "Fascism is just capitalism gone nudist."' The critical assessment of F.D. Roosevelt's New Deal explicit in *Social Planning* is at odds with the early enthusiastic reaction of LSR members, especially those who, like Harry Cassidy and Leonard Marsh, were keenly interested in welfare policy. By 1935, however, the conservative trend in Roosevelt's policies was clearer than it had initially been. The LSR's criticism matched that of left-wing intellectuals in the United States.[9]

State-capitalist planning in whatever form, complete or incomplete, whether accompanied by state control of banking or investment or not, is necessarily 'planning for scarcity.' Profits or plenty is now the choice. This is why political democracy is a stunted and endangered plant in the shade of monopoly capitalism. Rebellion seems likely as people come to realize that the economy and the state will not provide the standard of living they have the right to expect. Repression and possibly more fascist take-overs will result. Education will come under mounting attack as only too liable to produce unemployable agitators. The final threat is war, the danger of which increases as governments become more thoroughly identified with big business. 'After war, what? Certainly not capitalism as we know it. Perhaps communism, perhaps barbarism.'

And yet: a better future is possible. Technology is capable of providing plentifully for all. *Social Planning* concludes its critique of capitalism by saying that 'capitalist industry ... has provided the technique for socialism, but the effective use of the technique is impossible as long as the inequality of capitalist control survives.'[10] Political and economic democracy must be made real.

II

How accurate was the indictment then; how valid does it seem more than forty years later? The central question of the morality of capitalism is one to which men and women will provide different answers now as they did then. The profit motive has many defenders still, as does a free-market economy. The latter, like castor oil, is prescribed for others rather than for oneself, however: 'Any businessman who is honest will tell you that he would prefer to see increased competition among his suppliers and less competition for himself.'[11] The libertarianism of an Ayn Rand has relatively few adherents.

As for the operation of capitalism in Canada, the LSR's description is basically sound. Arguments about detail there may be, and disagreements as to whether its effects are inherent in the system or are the result of malfunctioning brought on, say, by excessive government intervention. But the great inequalities of wealth and income, the concentration of economic power in a few hands, the ability of corporations to rig markets and restrict production, their success in persuading governments to see things their way, capitalism's waste of natural resources, its inability to supply the economic needs of the poor: all these stand beyond reasonable question. 'The system is deeply wasteful of both people's talents and material resources; it is bureaucratic and inefficient; it is careless of the environment; in many ways it is still very unfair.'[12] Thus speaks a businessman.

Social Planning for Canada and left-wingers in the 1930s generally misjudged the recuperative powers of capitalism. They thought that the contradictions of capitalism would lead either to its replacement by socialism or communism or to the imposition of fascism, and that war would surely destroy it. Instead capitalism benefited greatly from the Second World War, from the lowering of trade barriers that followed, and from post-war military spending, especially in the United States. None of this the authors of *Social Planning* predicted. They did predict, however, that even non-socialist governments would increasingly intervene in the economy. In Western countries such intervention has sustained a rapidly growing number of state workers and has taken, through taxation, a share of the gross domestic product that would have seemed astronomical in 1935.

The authors of *Social Planning* did not anticipate that growing prosperity in the thirty years after the outbreak of war, and government transfer payments, would augment the real incomes of poor Canadians well beyond what they were in the inter-war years. The welfare state that has taken shape is not what the LSR had in mind. Too often social insurance, health care, and welfare payments have meant that the incomes of the very poor are augmented with money obtained from those just above them in the economic scale. Although its progressive features have increased during and since the Second World War, Canada's system of taxation still relies to a considerable extent (at least one-third) on indirect and user taxes, the incidence of which is usually regressive. Since the war, however, and especially during the last twenty years, the ability of the lower two-fifths of the population to consume goods and services has been enlarged by a capitalist-dominated state beyond the expectations of radicals of the 1930s.

Has capitalism then been proved not to be 'inevitably an economy of scarcity'? The answer in the late 1970s is bound to be cautious. The standard of living of many Canadians has ceased to rise. Indeed, unemployment in excess of 7 per cent and a rate of inflation that pushes 10 per cent are currently combining to force down the real incomes of many low- and middle-income earners. Meanwhile various restrictions in production and trade continue to cost consumers dearly. What, after all, are the price increases in petroleum imposed by the Organization of Petroleum Exporting Countries if not the consequences of a gigantic combination in restraint of trade? The ability of capitalism to deliver the goods is in greater doubt than at any time since the 1930s. And just as in those years, we are treated to the unedifying spectacle of men with sixty-inch waists lecturing the underweight on the virtue and necessity of dieting, the rich telling the others that they must be satisfied with less.

On scarcity the evidence is still debatable. On the relationship between capitalism and fascism in the 1930s the record is now reasonably complete. As the historian Martin Kitchen has recently shown, fascism was more than capitalism gone nudist, 'the mere implementation of the policies of a group or groups of monopolists.' The large corporations did not suffer under fascism, but support for the movement in Germany, for example, came mainly from 'small merchants, craftsmen and farmers of the old middle class' as well as civil servants, all of whom were strongly attached to the economic protectionism and hierarchical organization of Imperial Germany, who had never come to accept the democracy of the Weimar Republic, and who feared the modernizing present. Analogous groups in

Canada accepted political democracy and a relatively open, individualistic society, although less so in French than in English Canada. There was therefore very little support for a domestic, would-be fascist leader such as Quebec's Adrien Arcand, and even less for William Whittaker of Winnipeg. The protest vote of the small businessmen and farmers in Canada was in 1935 split among the Reconstruction party, Social Credit, and the CCF. The contemporary Marxist interpretation of fascism that the LSR employed did not describe even the European scene accurately, and it was largely irrelevant to Canada.[13]

This is not to say that Canada is safe from some domestic brand of fascism in the future. Once the middle class feels really threatened, who can predict how and where its members will jump? If big business should feel threatened at the same time and if widely accepted patriotic objectives should be in danger, an authoritarian movement of the political right could easily appear.

III

Criticizing is one thing; it is something else again to propose a superior alternative. Influenced in its moral condemnation of capitalism by Christian socialism and in its analysis of the failures and contradictions of the capitalist system by British and Marxist socialism and western agrarian radicalism, the LSR's indictment of the operation of the system had great force. But the LSR knew that its critics, in turn, would stand ready to attack its proposals as unworkable. The authors and editors of *Social Planning* therefore took great pains over the second and longer part of their book, 'What Socialist Planning Really Means.'

Once again most of the writing was done by the economists, Irene Biss, Eugene Forsey, and J.F. Parkinson, assisted by Alexander Brady and Kenneth Taylor. Harry Cassidy wrote the chapters on 'A Code for Labour' and 'Health and Welfare Services,' but Leonard Marsh also worked on them. The latter chapter benefited from the advice of the social-work expert, C.W. Topping, and that of Dr Benge Atlee. Humphrey Carver took care of the chapter on housing. Concluding the book are a chapter on political parties, mainly Frank Underhill's work, one on Parliament and the constitution, partly written by Underhill and partly by Frank Scott, and one on foreign policy, originally drafted by Escott Reid but ultimately updated and rewritten by Underhill.

Neither the title of the book nor that of this section was chosen by chance. '"Planning" was the seminal idea of the 1930's ...,' L.P. Carpenter, the biographer of the British socialist G.D.H. Cole, writes: 'It was the growing edge of socialism, the new departure and the new slogan with which many ventured to experiment.' Cole's own *Principles of Economic Planning* also appeared in 1935; a knowledgeable reviewer like A.F.W. Plumptre saw similarities between his work and that of the LSR.[14] Like many left-wingers in the Western world, moreover, members of the LSR were greatly impressed by the results of economic planning in the Soviet Union.

No fewer than five of the signatories of *Social Planning* visited the Soviet Union in the early and mid-1930s, Forsey, Gordon, Marsh, Scott, and Graham Spry. They were particularly taken by the evidence of comradeship and co-operation in the execution of the Five Year Plan. These and the benefits of planning outweighed the unhappy absence of political democracy and civil liberties. Frank Underhill wrote an uncritical review of *Soviet Communism: A New Civilization* (1935) by Sidney and Beatrice Webb, a book not noted for its clear-eyed view of Russia under Stalin. It was a 'Fabian *Nunc Dimittis*,' Underhill suggested: having seen the future the Webbs could now depart in peace. But most LSR members were no more than 'fellow-travellers of the fellow-travellers,' to use George Orwell's phrase. The Moscow trials later in the decade led to grave misgivings. The authors of the LSR's second book, *Democracy Needs Socialism* (1938), warned that the retention of political dictatorship in the Soviet Union jeopardized 'the real gains of the past twenty years.'[15]

Planning is necessary, *Social Planning* argues: even capitalist-dominated governments are introducing aspects of it, though for the wrong reason. What Canada needs now is 'true social planning which shall put the interests of the mass of the population first.' The 'organs of expert direction' must be grafted 'on to our present democratic machinery (which must itself be made more democratic in effect).' Planning must be continuous:

> Planning in a socialized economy means, not an omnipotent blueprint set out once and for all, but that technicians of every type required in the modern economic system are brought into organized relation both with the *organs* and the *aims* of government. This deliberate control over economic development is represented centrally by a National Planning Commission: it is undertaken because only thus can industry be organized to serve the interests of the many, as both producers and consumers, rather than the interests of the few.[16]

Throughout its life the LSR, though it tended strongly to intellectual elitism, identified itself with the interests of the many.

In the new polity of the co-operative commonwealth Parliament will define ends and appoint the planning commissioners; the cabinet will continue to administer the country. But the centrally important task of co-ordinating local proposals and producing a comprehensive plan will belong to the National Planning Commission. It will act as architect to its client, Parliament. The latter must approve the plan and has the right to reject it. However, conflict between the elected representatives of the people and the experts they have nominated is expected to be rare.

Their confidence in expertise and social engineering the authors of *Social Planning* shared with the Fabians. Consciously Fabian, for example, had been Frank Underhill's call in 1932 for 'a new Benthamism, adapted to the changed environment of the twentieth century, which will combine with the wider social vision, which we have presumably acquired in the last hundred years, that passion for maximizing the happiness of individuals which Jeremy Bentham contributed to his generation.'[17] However, *Social Planning* tempers its faith in experts with an expression of confidence in the people: 'Every man, woman, and child must play a part so that it is everybody's plan, and enthusiastic participation of the whole community is essential if it is to work well.' The influence of the ideas of Guild socialism, with their concern for the decentralization of power, may be present in the assertion that the plan must come from 'the collective advice, co-ordinated by the Commission, of the numerous bodies which are directing the economic life of the state' – co-operatives, trade unions, work councils, and the like.

> Socialism is not an inelastic method of running business through government departments administered from Ottawa by politicians and hidebound civil servants. It implies simply public ownership, production for the general good instead of for private profit, and the placing of ultimate authority in the hands of the State instead of in the hands of private shareholders. This is all compatible with local and individual initiative in industry, and a considerable amount of independence in operation. It is also compatible with various types of organization according to the needs of particular trades, ranging from farmers' co-operatives to joint-stock companies.

Social Planning is not unconscious of the dangers of bureaucratization in the new state. One valuable aspect of unions is held to be that they 'would represent a powerful force to counteract any tendency to dictatorial methods which might develop in the state "bureaucracy." '[18]

If planning is to work and the co-operative commonwealth eventually to become a reality, the hold over the economy of a handful of businessmen must be broken. After the election of the socialist party, steps must immediately be taken to socialize 'certain key functions and basic industries which are of strategic importance in the operations of the economy as a whole.'[19] Foremost among these are banking and investment; so are transportation and the other utilities. Other industries to be socialized during the 'period of transition' are those that are operated under conditions of monopoly, that are seriously inefficient, or that control important natural resources. The exception to this will be farmland already alienated from the Crown.

Compensation will be paid to those who are expropriated, but in such a way as to make the wealthy among them sitting ducks for the tax-man. Thus the grosser inequalities of wealth and income should fairly quickly disappear. This, of course, is confiscation, though gradual and given another name. Should strong opposition not be expected?

If it comes, the LSR is unafraid. Some dislocation will be unavoidable during the period of transition, but should there be attempts at sabotage a socialist government will have to take 'bold and comprehensive steps.' The mandate for change it has received is not to be denied. 'If selfish and privileged groups attempt to resist by violence the popular will thus expressed,' the authors of *Democracy Needs Socialism* elaborate, 'they will be compelled to obey the law by all the forces at the command of the state.'[20]

These are brave words. It may be just as well that they never needed to be tested in action. After all, is it self-evident that these forces, as well as the courts and the civil service, could have been relied on by a socialist government that wanted to undertake a reconstruction of Canadian society? *Social Planning* calls for 'the abolition of our superfluous militia and naval service ..., and the reduction of the RCMP to its pre-depression level.'[21] In view of what it might have assumed to be the natural reaction to such remarks, the LSR should not have assumed quite as blithely as it did that socialists would have the full co-operation of the forces of law and order. It would have been realistic, moreover, to assume that many members of the Bench would have felt a strong attachment to the *status quo ante*.

Social Planning suggests that the foreign investor will have to be treated more gingerly than his domestic counterpart, but it does not expect trouble from abroad, more particularly from the United States. Yet the investors of that country are the natural allies of those Canadians who would have most to fear from the introduction of a socialist commonwealth. Again, it is perhaps just as well that Canadian socialists in the 1930s never got beyond impassioned words. During that decade and since, the experience of many countries has been that those whose wealth or power are threatened by change are usually willing if not always able to defend themselves and their privileges, and that they can generally count on help from abroad. The capitalist lion, or the communist for that matter, does not turn unprotestingly into something like a lamb.

That it would do so without too much resistance is an assessment linked to the LSR's belief in parliamentary democracy and constitutional action. Socialism can be introduced gradually by means of education, the ballot box, and step-by-step legislation. The adoption of this Fabian approach and its explicit rejection of the revolutionary path exposed the LSR to criticism from the left. Too tender a regard for constitutional niceties, some said, would only benefit the defenders of the *status quo*, some of whom would not hesitate to stage a fascist coup. An early LSR dropout, Lorne T. Morgan, in 1938 argued that the LSR and CCF, like European social democratic parties, by putting their faith in parliamentary democracy and attacking those on their left who saw through the hollowness of the parliamentary game merely played into the hands of reactionaries and fascists. Deprecating revolution, social democrats failed to see 'that what they really want can only be obtained by means which they abhor and so repudiate.'[22]

Possibly. Criticism of this kind, however, did not make much impression on members of the LSR. Canada did not seem – indeed, it was not – a likely setting for a revolution. Moreover, the danger of reaction would grow if socialists talked irresponsibly. Most of all, means and ends must not be separated: insofar as a revolution was undemocratic it ought to be abhorred. If democracy needs socialism, socialism also needs democracy.

Administration in a socialized state will see new relationships between government departments and the various regulatory agencies; it will also require an undiluted merit system in the public service. A vital aspect of economic administration is the price system, 'the determination of profits, prices and costs.' For some purposes prices will serve the function of indicating financial costs. Most markets are not now free, however, and it may be undesirable, even were it possible, to try to liberate many of them. With the elimination of private monopolies some prices will become more sensitive to supply and demand, but others will have to be administered by the Planning Commission. 'The control of prices amounts to deliberate arbitration between different groups in the community as to how much of the national income they are to receive. Such power cannot be left to the hazards of unequal bargaining or to the discretion of private sectional interests.'[23] A new 'social' accounting system will be used to promote 'socially desirable undertakings' that by the old profit-and-loss method do not pay their way.

While groups such as farmers and small retailers will continue to get their earnings in the conventional way, those profits that are 'the chief sources of unequal wealth' will gradually disappear. Ultimately,

> the two main fundamental objectives would be attained. Income would be obtainable only by productive effort (except in the case of children, the aged or infirm) and not by ownership alone, or speculation, or financial manipulation. Further, economic power would be vested not in the hands of a small group of wealthy property owners, exerting willy-nilly an ulterior control over our economic and political activities, distorting social habits and values, and making democratic government a fiction; but in the hands of the agents of the public endowed with recognized functional authority and, in the last analysis, subject to democratic control.

The biblical bias in favour of honest work – 'If any would not work, neither should he eat' – is fully in evidence here.[24]

A biblical bias runs through the book, though it is usually subtle. After all, the LSR had no religious ties. 'We are ... a secular organization dealing with temporal matters,' S.B. Watson wrote in late 1936 on behalf of the Toronto branch executive to a member unhappy about the absence of a religious service at the Pickering Conference that year. 'While our members have a common ethical and philosophical background, it would be dangerous to assume any uniformity of religious outlook, although all of us acknowledge the great debt that the movement owes to those who are guided by spiritual motives.' Usually they belonged to the Fellowship for a Christian Social Order. Two of its leading members, King Gordon and Eugene Forsey, were co-authors of *Social Planning for Canada*; Gordon was a minister in the United Church. They and others like them in the LSR took a dim view of 'the general tendency of modern Christianity, and especially its Protestant branch, to succumb to the spirit of an acquisitive society.' But *Social Planning* also draws attention to 'prophetic voices [that] have been raised in the name of a high ethical religion against some of the more flagrant forms of social injustice' and surmises that 'it is not an impossibility that radical Christian thought and action may play an important part in the coming period of social reconstruction.'[25]

That some members of the LSR also belonged to the FCSO, that several were either ministers or sons of the manse, that the works of British and American Christian radicals, John Lewis, John MacMurray, Reinhold Niebuhr, Karl Polanyi, Harry Ward, and others, were well known in league circles: all these help to explain the moralistic tone of *Social Planning for Canada*, its judgment that the exploitation of man by man is wrong and the capitalist system corrupt, and its conception of what the co-operative commonwealth would be like. The religious background of those who had ceased to practise a religion must not, at the same time, be ignored. The biographer of R.H. Tawney, the eminent British socialist scholar, writes: 'Many socialist figures of Tawney's generation, some the offspring of clergy, distilled residual religious conviction into strong political conviction.'[26] This was true in Canada as well. One thinks of Frank Scott, the son of a clergyman; there were others. Secular in their outlook and expression, they owed their categories of good and evil largely to the Christian religion. In much the same way, though the subject matter of *Social Planning* is secular, the values it expresses are often those of radicalized Protestantism.

This is not apparent throughout the book. The chapter on 'Money, Banking and Investment,' for example, owes more to J.M. Keynes than Jesus Christ. Sober and technical, the chapter becomes slightly agitated only in its discussion of 'the futility of Social Credit.' The authors favour the use of the recently established central bank, the Bank of Canada, and of monetary policy in general in the interests of maintaining 'an approximately stable level of prices.' Violent fluctuations must be avoided. Whether now, in the period of transition, or under socialism, 'there is the same need for a stable or "honest" dollar.' The dollar should also be maintained 'at a stable value in terms of foreign currencies' whenever possible, though the maintenance of a stable internal price level takes precedence. The LSR's views were, of course, strongly influenced by the highly inexpedient, even disastrous, deflation of the early 1930s; they agreed implicitly with Keynes's opinion: 'The regulation of the standard of value [must] be the subject of *deliberate decision*.'[27]

The chartered banks are to be socialized because that way it will be easier to use them in economic planning, as part of a national investment policy. This will be the responsibility of the National Investment Board, which will exercise unified control over the whole area of finance and investment. Partly regulatory and partly positive in its operations during the period of transition, the Investment Board will gradually expand its positive activities in collaboration with the Planning Commission and the Bank of Canada. Thus Canada's resources will be intelligently and efficiently allocated, and 'those socially desirable but "non-paying" enterprises' financed that now inevitably go short of funds: 'slum-clearance, re-housing, social services, conservation of natural resources and the like.' (Even rich market societies underallocate resources to these areas because their citizens regard the taxes needed to supply them as an exaction in a way that the prices charged by business firms are not.)[28]

It is almost an axiom that the citizen wants more or better public services than he is willing to pay for in his taxes. Yet in their chapter on taxation and fiscal policy the authors of *Social Planning* insist that 'in the fully socialized economy there will be no problem of public finance as such.' In the period of transition there will be plenty of problems, however, as a socialist government struggles to finance the socialization of industry, emergency public works, social insurance, and the national debt. Conscious that the British Labour government of 1929–31 had come to grief over public finance, the LSR expected that, given a chance in office, a Canadian socialist government would do better. The Labourites had made the mistake of leaving capitalism in being: 'it was not their socialism which destroyed them, but their lack of it.' Certainly the LSR did not draw from the British experience the lesson some British socialists did, that the parliamentary process is a snare and a delusion.[29]

One way or another the national debt must be reduced while direct taxes are raised to pay for the programs deemed to be most necessary. Of course, 'only a fully socialized economy can provide a proper standard of living and adequate social services ... To demand from the transitional economy what can only be secured when the transition has been completed is to ask the impossible.' All the same, the Canadian worker, the poor and insecure victim of social injustice, has a right to early relief. The aim of the LSR's full program 'is to provide for working people (1) an adequate and secure scale of living, (2) healthy and decent conditions of work, and (3) genuine democracy in the conduct of industry.'[30] A socialist government will draw up an appropriate 'Code for Labour' and work towards its achievement with all possible speed.

As *Social Planning* sees the future, wages and salaries will be determined through a combination of collective bargaining and state wage regulation. The latter will be carried on by wage boards reporting to the Dominion Wage Board. Ultimately, the National Planning Commission must oversee and control the process to ensure that the proportion of the national income going to wages will not interfere with the urgent needs of social services and capital development. Everyone, however, is to get enough to live on, in accordance with the four principles of wage regulation: 'the basic needs of the workers, industry's capacity to pay, the maintenance of fair differentials, and family allowances.' Differentials will recognize the greater value 'to industry and therefore to the community' of the more skilled, able, and efficient. A range in earnings from $1,200 to $10,000 per annum seems sensible. (For most Canadians even the lower figure would have been an improvement.)[31]

It may not be feasible, especially in the period of transition, to set minimum wages high enough to provide for the needs of a family. The variation of earnings with a view to family responsibilities, using a system of industry-wide funds to which all workers will contribute and from which family allowances will be paid, will have the highly beneficial result of protecting family life. Mothers working at home as well as children will thus constitute a social responsibility.

This makes good sense. Whether the discussion of wage regulation as a whole does so is highly arguable, however. The potential for conflict would be immense, particularly because the power of trade unions would be much expanded. Represented on joint industrial and work councils as well as on wage boards and on various committees dealing with social insurance and the like, workers would be able to co-determine all matters that concerned them. The psychic satisfaction that this would bring and the benefits of the labour code generally would presumably prevent most strikes. However, it seems naïve to have assumed that the unions would without serious resistance submit to the wage levels and differentials authorized by the Planning Commission. Canadian radicals of the 1930s were able to feel kindly and romantic about unions, then few and weak, in a manner that is difficult to recapture today. The LSR also had faith in the willingness of Canadians, including unionists, to co-operate in the building and maintenance of the socialist commonwealth.

Social Planning goes on to predict that, in the new society, the economic security of Canadians will be complemented by improved health and social services. At present the system of health care, medical and dental, presents 'the familiar paradox of capitalism: ... men, women and children urgently needing services while the industry that is equipped to provide them cannot sell its goods.' Health insurance is necessary; preventive and curative medical and dental services must be readily available to all. 'The provinces should continue to assume major responsibility in this field ...,' but the Dominion must exercise a supervisory role in order to ensure some uniformity and must continue its work with Indians, immigrants, war veterans, and others who are its special responsibility.[32]

Haphazard and degrading, unemployment relief will disappear in the period of transition. Its place will be taken by a system of unemployment insurance. There will be a continued need for social workers: not only must the 'casualties of the present depression' be rehabilitated, but even under socialism certain forms of human distress will persist. There will be weak or unfortunate people 'who cannot solve their own problems of existence, and who will require special assistance from the community before they can stand upon their own feet.'[33] Children are one important example. An upgrading of services dealing with juvenile offenders is necessary; recreational facilities must be improved. In these areas as in health the provinces will be responsible, with the Dominion providing advice, supervision, and money in order to ensure that there is a reasonable minimum of services across the country.

Still disconcertingly relevant today, the chapter on 'A Housing Programme' proposes comprehensive town planning and the establishment of a federal housing authority. Its task will be to provide adequate housing for low-income earners. This is the only way slums will be eliminated; the 'social benefits' will be worth the cost: 'If devoting some part of the budget to subsidized housing "pays" in healthier and happier living conditions for many of the country's workers, in less repressive environments for their children, in reduced burdens of infantile mortality, tuberculosis, juvenile delinquency, contagious diseases, this is "profitable" expenditure in the best sense of the word.' That the operations of the open market did not and could not provide affordable good housing to many Canadians was recognized in 1934 by the Liberal premier of Nova Scotia, Angus L. Macdonald, and the Tory lieutenant-governor of Ontario, Dr H.A. Bruce. The first recommendation of a committee chaired by the latter – Harry Cassidy was its research director – was that, since private enterprise cannot provide 'poorer people' with 'good low-cost dwellings,' the three levels of government must take the lead.[34] The LSR's recommendations in this area sound a good deal less radical than they do in some others. But they nevertheless still run well ahead of the willingness of governments to spend.

Perhaps no chapter in *Social Planning* is more intriguing than that on 'The Rehabilitation of Agriculture.' It constitutes the sharpest variation from British and to a lesser extent European socialism. Agriculture in Canada, as in large parts of the United States, was very differently organized from agriculture in the Old World. The farmer working his own freehold property with machinery and possibly one hired hand was very common here. In the 1930s three in ten Canadians still derived their living from the farm, and among them, especially in the three prairie provinces, there was a lively tradition of criticism focused on the operations of 'Eastern big business.' Many farmers seemed to be natural allies for Canadian industrial workers.

Karl Marx had little use for farmers, believing the peasantry to be basically reactionary and, like small businessmen, due to be superseded by large-scale enterprises. Before the Great War, most European socialist parties demanded the nationalization of land and made no serious attempt to attract any group of agriculturalists other than farm labourers. But these policies along with other aspects of Marxist orthodoxy began to be questioned before 1910 by the German revisionists Eduard Bernstein, Eduard David, and their followers. In the aftermath of the war, when socialists and communists had split, 'of all the parties belonging to the Second [Labour and Socialist] International, the British Labour Party alone continued to demand the nationalization of the land as an essential condition for any agrarian reform.'[35]

In Canada this made no sense except to some unreconstructed, die-hard Marxists. The Communist party side-stepped the issue. In Saskatchewan the Farmer-Labour party for a while subscribed to the 'use-lease' scheme of provincial land ownership but abandoned it by 1936. Certainly nationalization made no sense to the authors of *Social Planning for Canada*. One informed English reviewer, Sir Stafford Cripps, shrewdly described the book as 'an attempt to devise a working Socialist policy for a country which is primarily agricultural, and whose agriculture is mainly in the hands of individual farmers employing but little hired labour ... There emerges a form of Socialism which, despite an occasional use of Marxian or class-war phrases, is essentially moderate and evolutionary.'[36] It owed this character in part to the desire to attract farmers into the fold.

Social Planning describes a political and economic context for the situation of the Canadian farmer. Beset by the world-wide collapse of agricultural commodity prices, forced to sell his products in markets where they face tariff and other discrimination, forced also to buy producer and consumer goods that are tariff-protected or subject to tariff duties, unable to match the monopolistic power of the processors and distributors of his products, burdened with debt: how is the farmer to be helped? 'An intelligent agricultural policy for Canada must be based, first, not upon a belief that free trade will bring an end to our troubles, but upon the recognition that economic nationalism in respect to foreign trade has come to stay, and that it is the part of wisdom for Canada to seek to discover, within this international framework, secure and stable markets for her specialized products.'

The growth of restrictions in world trade are the result of the breakdown of the competitive capitalist system in all countries. As consumer the farmer will benefit when the most costly forms of protection have been wiped out; as exporter the farmer 'will benefit by the expansion of international exchange which a socialist plan of import and export control will be able to foster.'[37]

Taking its lead from the opposition of many farmers to the operations of the open market and from attempts to replace it with co-operative marketing, *Social Planning* counsels the extension of co-operation and of the principle of 'orderly marketing,' to be embodied in the new federal Wheat Board. Farm debts must be written down and refinanced under government auspices so that they can be reduced in proportion to the reduction in farm incomes. Not only wheat growing but all kinds of agriculture must be carefully planned by 'a series of planning agencies – in the fields of research, marketing, processing, land utilization and settlement, transportation, exporting, etc. – all co-ordinated under the Agricultural Branch of the Planning Commission.' The burden of low commodity prices, now and in the future, must by various methods be spread over the entire community. All the agencies for processing and marketing must be publicly owned. Speculation in land values will have to be eliminated. The cultural and recreational facilities of rural Canada will be improved. 'To avoid misunderstanding,' the chapter concludes, 'we wish to emphasize again that the public ownership of the agencies of distribution which we propose does not interfere in any way with the full ownership of the land by the farmer. We do not at all recommend the nationalization of land now held by individual owners.'[38]

If the chapter on agriculture is in part explained by the wish to attract the farm vote, that on 'The Distributive Services' owes something to the desire not to alienate small businessmen. Retailing and marketing are declared to be in a mess. Where competition prevails it is often wasteful; where monopoly has taken over it is invariably accompanied by unduly high prices for consumers or by lower quality. (The investigations of the Royal Commission on Price Spreads had offered ample evidence of both.) As for advertising, the LSR's attitude towards it is unreservedly hostile.

Are large units of distribution more economic than small? 'It ain't necessarily so.' Small shops can be both useful and economic; small enterprises tend to treat their employees better. Methods need to be devised 'whereby the small-scale business can be operated as efficiently as the big corporation. That the small business, in many fields, can be operated as efficiently under intelligent management has been proved many times over.'[39] Co-operative purchasing by shopkeepers and the standardization of consumer goods are among the methods by which it can be operated efficiently. Necessary too are the supervisory activities of a commissioner of Internal Trade.

Not surprisingly *Social Planning* favours the establishment and encouragement of consumers' co-operatives. Indeed, in 1936 several members of the Montreal branch, among them Frank Aykroyd, Leonard Marsh, and Frank Scott, formed a committee called the 'Montreal Survey on Co-operation' and secured George Mooney as research director. The book the committee published two years later, *Co-operatives Today and Tomorrow: A Canadian Survey*, was enthusiastic about consumers' co-operation. How small retailers might react to it is a question that *Social Planning* conveniently ignores. In view of the hostility usually shown to consumers' co-operatives by small retailers, a hostility that matches their dislike of supermarkets and department stores, the matter should have been addressed.

That this was not done may have resulted either from a failure to perceive the potential conflict or from a desire to downplay anything that could interfere with the attempt to gain *petit bourgeois* support for the brand of socialism promoted by the LSR and CCF. Although small retailers, like farmers, are capitalists of a sort, they do not enjoy monopoly power. Accordingly, provided they learn to co-operate and are properly supervised by agencies of planning, *Social Planning* wants to let them carry on much as before. 'In such cases ... the productive property is being directly used by the owner: profits, rent and interest of this type are on a very different footing from the profits, rents and dividends of large concerns employing thousands of hands.'[40] This comment was heartfelt; it was also supposed to make clear to farmers and shopkeepers that they had nothing to fear and a good deal to gain from socialism, that they had a community of interest with the mass of working-class Canadians.

Few farmers seemed to believe it, except in Saskatchewan, and even fewer shopkeepers. In 1935 many working-class Canadians were also sceptical. 'That Canadians as yet are far from realizing the need for such social changes as are advocated in this book is obvious,' Frank Underhill wrote in the chapter on political parties. A serious problem of public education lies ahead: 'No system of socialism will work without the support of a determined and instructed public behind it, and this work of public education is the more necessary in a democratic movement which does not contemplate a violent or forcible transition to the new order.' The political means of securing the transition is expected to be the new socialist party, the CCF. Underhill has no patience with the anti-party tradition of Progressivism as it was still championed by the Ontario farmer politician, W.C. Good. The CCF is beginning to gain support from workers and farmers, but also from 'middle class groups, which elsewhere have too often proved a main strength of rising fascist movements.' The CCF is still badly organized, however – a favourite Underhillian theme emerges – and must pull up its socks:

A mere mass democratic upheaval, deriving its strength from the emotional appeals which are so easy in a period of depression, will sooner or later disintegrate or be captured by the spurious cries of 'easy money' cranks, superficial reformers, fascist demagogues and the rest. Only a disciplined socialist political movement, based solidly on the occupational economic organizations of the classes which suffer most from the present chaos of monopoly capitalism, offers any real hope to the Canadian people.[41]

Blessed are the disciplined, for they shall inherit the country.

Calls for a 'national government' of all parties are dismissed: that would mean 'a C.P.R. government, ... government by big business even more completely than in the past,' as well as 'slashing cuts in relief and social services.' No, the only way out of Canada's troubles is pointed by the LSR and CCF. But does that way not lead to 'the dangers of bureaucratic dictatorship,' as Liberal critics have charged? This is a red herring, comes the answer from the authors of the chapter on Parliament and the constitution, Underhill and Scott. The growing power of the cabinet and civil service and the increased use of boards and commissions has over several decades greatly limited the role of the legislature. The LSR's 'proposals for economic reconstruction' will continue this process.

Is there anything essentially undemocratic in this? Those who affirm that there is, are confusing the general principle of democracy with the particular machinery which was developed in the nineteenth century for giving effect to popular sovereignty. If democracy cannot equip itself with new agencies for fulfilling its purposes, then democratic government will be superseded by some form of government based on force. In an age when rapid technological changes are daily shifting the whole material basis of our civilization, our political democracy must trust itself more and more to technical experts and must develop a leadership which is experimental in temper and capable of quick decisions.[42]

Parliament, however, will retain the essentials, its hold over the cabinet, its right to lay down the main principles of policy and legislation, and its role as the chief national forum of discussion. It will do so without the Senate, however, that 'bulwark of property interests.' The Senate must be abolished. Minority rights can be protected more effectively in the British North America Act.

Well aware that not only the abolition of the Senate but also a number of the league's other proposals would require amendment of the British North America Act, the authors of *Social Planning* discuss the Canadian constitution in some detail. This, as well as the league's views about Canadian federalism and the question of Quebec, will be more conveniently dealt with in a separate chapter.

IV

More than anything else, what holds the programmatic chapters of *Social Planning for Canada* together is the optimism of its authors concerning human nature. They believe that man is essentially co-operative rather than competitive; they have faith in his ultimate rationality and goodness. At one point they write that the planned economy 'must invite the allegiance' of every educated individual 'who has, in addition, a sense of social justice and has not soured in his hopes of human nature.' It is because they have not soured in their hopes that they look forward with confidence to the socialist, co-operative commonwealth.

> The population of a socialist Canada will not be angels, but neither will they be demons. They will be ordinary men and women, rather above the general human average in physique and education. They will live and work in a society which will give them every encouragement to behave decently instead of offering premiums for 'putting one over' their neighbours; a society which will no longer preach honesty to its children in church and schoolroom only to 'send them out to be salesmen.' There will be no great corporations ... to debauch governments and parliaments and public servants ...
>
> To those who object that capitalism is 'rooted in human nature,' we answer: Possibly, but so was cannibalism. We no longer eat each other. A civilization is within our reach in which we shall no longer exploit each other. It calls for no more honesty and ability than are readily available in Canada. We *have* the men. The pioneer spirit is not dead, but the frontier which it must conquer has shifted from the physical to the intellectual and spiritual.[43]

Adjust the social and economic environment, and the human material will not show itself wanting.

The conviction that man is a co-operative animal, that he will embrace 'mutuality,' – that is, 'the ethic of the cooperative community' (the phrases are from the FCSO book, *Towards the Christian Revolution*) – leads the LSR to minimize the potential for conflict after the election of a socialist government. Industrial workers and farmers will *want* to co-operate with each other and with small businessmen as well as the urban intelligentsia. Local decision-making *will* mesh with effective central planning; an expanded bureaucracy will *not* arrogate to itself the excessive power now wielded by monopoly capitalists; liberty and equality *can* coexist with efficiency; the individual *will* have full scope to pursue all his legitimate aspirations, those that do not harm others. Men and women will share the magnificent opportunity, in the words of *Democracy Needs Socialism*, to 'co-operate in the greatest adventure of mankind – the building of a free society where science and the arts will flourish, and poverty and war will be banished.' All this requires is 'an ethical revolution – from the acquisitive and individualistic values which dominate our present economic society to the more humane, just, and equitable standards of a co-operative commonwealth.'[44]

Sceptics will entertain the suspicion that the LSR's hopes rested on far too kindly a view of human nature, that they were at bottom an attempt by intellectuals to have their libertarian cake and collectively to eat it, too. Their optimism runs counter to the disillusionment of the German ex-socialist Robert Michels: 'A realistic view of the mental condition of the masses shows beyond question that even if we admit the possibility of moral improvement in mankind, the human materials with whose use politicians and philosophers cannot dispense in their plans of social reconstruction are not of a character to justify excessive optimism.' Michels's statement early in the twentieth century of the 'Iron Law of Oligarchy,' the development of bureaucratic organization and oligarchic control even in democratic-socialist parties, has become well known. If the authors of *Social Planning* knew about it, however, they did not heed it. They thought better of socialists and of mankind. Not that LSR members were proof against disillusionment about human nature: one former member told me without prompting that he left the league because he had become convinced that it took too rosy a view of humankind.[45]

That the human race is basically co-operative, that our ability to co-operate and work in groups is why we have been 'so successful as an evolving species' can scarcely be denied. What is not so clear is that the co-operation of a hunting and food-gathering society or that of the agricultural village can be successfully adapted to an industrialized and international order. And if co-operation is possible within and among large groups, will not massive regimentation be necessary, regimentation on a scale and of a kind that would have been anything but acceptable to the surviving liberal sensibilities of LSR members?[46]

These are open questions. They are also enormously important: on the answer to them now rests the very future of humankind. If in answering them the authors of *Social Planning for Canada* were too optimistic, if they clung to a facile environmentalism, they were and are not alone. Eliminate the social and economic conditions that set man against man in the struggle for survival and the new world of mutuality, of free co-operation, would become possible. In the eyes of the LSR, the interdependence of human beings, their need to work together, is too evident to allow room for the notion that human beings will freely pursue their own advantage at the expense of others. Such activity is perverse; it is the result of a society that rewards the wrong activities. Adam Smith's Invisible Hand is worse than a fiction; it is destructive. It must be rendered harmless.

Upbringing, temperament, experience: these were responsible for the LSR's optimism, nobly expressed in Frank Scott's poem, 'Creed':

> The world is my country
> The human race is my race
> The spirit of man is my God
> The future of man is my heaven.

There will perhaps always be sceptics who believe such optimism to be foolish and mistaken, possibly even pernicious. The sceptics may be right. All the same, it is churlish to speak ill of those who would think well of us, who in any case think better of us than we believe ourselves to be.

V

How Canadian, how socialist, was all this? Were the ideas not mostly derived, mainly from British sources? Were the authors of *Social Planning for Canada* anything more than 'liberals in a hurry'?

Reviewing the book, H.A. Innis questioned its applicability to Canada. As usual he was critical of the use of economic theories developed in older countries to explain the phenomena of a new country. The LSR had borrowed many clothes from abroad, he complained, while ignoring some 'extremely valuable pieces of homespun clothing.' (He did not specify which.)

> The result may not appeal to fastidious tastes, and careful scrutiny will show many ill-fitting pieces, many pieces designed for one purpose and used for another, and many ill-secured pieces, which will certainly fall off if the subjects move about unduly or if the winds blow. The tailors have not agreed as to the design; but they have been apprenticed in London and Oxford, and it may appeal to more exclusive tastes insistent on imported styles.[47]

Those with more sensible tastes, however, would reject it.

His failure to discuss specifics blunted the point of Innis's criticism. A perusal of the footnotes in *Social Planning* alone, however, suggests that the LSR was eclectic at the very least. Among the British authors cited are H.N. Brailsford, R. Palme Dutt, J.M. Keynes, Harold Laski, John Strachey, R.H. Tawney, Sidney and Beatrice Webb, and Barbara Wootton. They range from a liberal would-be saviour of capitalism, Keynes, to a theorist of the British Communist party, Dutt. Of course, neither references to works nor their absence settles the question of intellectual influence. Intellectual debts may be incurred without the debtor's awareness of them, or they may seem to exist where they do not. Certain responses to capitalism and its apparent collapse in the early 1930s may have been so common as to make the question of who influenced whom unanswerable and even meaningless.

The matter is all the more problematic because the men and women of the LSR read the works not only of British but also of American leftists. The two weeklies, *The Nation* and *The New Republic*, were read by Frank Underhill and others; both of them were disenchanted with liberal reform in the early thirties and had come to look to some 'indigenous form of socialism.' Several league members were personally acquainted with the American socialist leader Norman Thomas and with the executive director of the League for Industrial Democracy, Harry Laidler. The publications of this organization were read in Canada. Stuart Chase and George Soule, 'American-style socialists' who rejected capitalism more because it was wasteful and inefficient than because it was exploitative, were cited several times in *Social Planning*. The book's analysis of monopoly capitalism owes something to them as well as to the study by A.A. Berle and Gardiner Means, *The Modern Corporation and Private Property* (1932). The economic interpretation of history as employed by the Progressive historian Charles Beard made a great impression on Underhill, who linked the American's ideas to those of Western populist radicals in his own interpretation of Canadian political history. The recognition that American influence was strong should be tempered, however, by the possibility that American radicals owed a good deal to some of the same British writers who were read so avidly in Canada. As more than one historian has pointed out, American Progressives were never loath to borrow ideas from their British cousins.[48]

As for the Canadian radicals of the LSR, although they attacked British imperialism and insisted that Canada must become fully sovereign in international affairs, they could not shake off being British. They came by it honestly enough. Some were recent immigrants from the United Kingdom; others received part of their education there. The native-born among them attended school during a period, from the last years of the nineteenth century into the early 1920s, when English Canada and its educational systems were steeped in a tradition that held that to be Canadian was to be British, and children were taught to be proud of both. For many Canadians, Britain was in the 1930s still the most obvious point of reference. Thus the authors of *Social Planning* were almost bound to take what they found useful in the work of British writers and try to adapt it to Canadian purposes. Even Frank Underhill's insistence on the essentially North American nature of Canada and his ready adaptation of the ideas of the American Progressive historians did not keep him from using British political models and drawing on ideas propounded by British writers. He was a devoted reader of the *New Statesman*, to which he occasionally contributed. In a sense he was himself a British intellectual, as were others in the LSR.

To seek to establish a clear distinction between Canadian and British socialism in the 1930s is a fruitless task. The main differences are obvious: on such subjects as agriculture and the operation of socialism in a federal state the writings of British socialists were of very little help. The two countries seemed to have enough in common, however, that diagnoses and remedies that seemed suitable in Britain often seemed suitable here as well. It was to this that Harold Innis objected, but his criticism was too general to be of use. And although he was no doubt right in asserting that *Social Planning* tried to adapt some British notions that were inappropriate here, neither that nor the derivative quality of much of the book made its socialism un-Canadian.

Fascinating as they are to the intellectual historian, questions about the derivation of ideas can distract him from recognizing that similar people are likely under similar conditions to make similar responses, whether they have or have not read something relevant to their concerns. Moreover, no piece of analysis or criticism, no proposal for change, will be much used unless the potential users see it to be applicable to their own experience and situation. They may, of course, be mistaken in their assessment. Finally, the derivative is not necessarily inferior. As the composer and musicologist Ned Rorem has said: 'Genius doesn't lie in not being derivative, but in making right choices instead of wrong ones.'[49] Not only in music is that the case.

Is the thought of the LSR socialist? Not to those who measure it against some standard of Marxist orthodoxy. The LSR was not ignorant of the work of Karl Marx. Most of its members were not well acquainted with it, however, and they saw no need to improve the acquaintance. In a conversation in 1967 Frank Underhill claimed of the voluminous writings of Marx to have read only the Communist Manifesto. The poet Earle Birney recalls that Harry Cassidy once told him that it was not necessary to read Marx and recommended G.D.H. Cole's *What Marx Really Meant* instead. Eugene Forsey, on the other hand, in his contribution to *Towards the Christian Revolution*, acknowledged a conscious debt to Marx, while David Lewis insisted in 1936 that 'Marxism is a method of approach to social history, behaviour, and struggle which the intelligent citizen disregards only through prejudice.' However, while there are in *Social Planning for Canada* three references to Lenin and one to Friedrich Engels, there is not a single reference to the author of *Das Kapital*. One reviewer, A.F.W. Plumptre, concluded: 'Neither the text nor the index suggests that the authors have read Marx.'[50]

Against this stands Professor Donald Creighton's accusation that the LSR popularized the Marxist interpretation of history in Canada in the 1930s and Professor Norman Penner's assertion that 'Underhill and his colleagues in the LSR [brought] a Marxist interpretation to bear on problems of Canadian history and economy.' If they did so, they were scarcely conscious of it. But that is quite possible. As the American historian Stanley Pierson has recently shown, a more or less well-understood Marxism was part of the British socialist tradition in which the LSR shared. The Fabians were influenced by Marxism even as they altered it and discarded some of its important elements.[51]

In the Depression of the early 1930s certain Marxist notions – monopoly capitalism as inevitably an economy of scarcity, the decay of capitalism, the contradiction between the forces of production and the relations of production – had wide currency among radical British intellectuals, Harold Laski and the Marxist John Strachey at their head. In the United States, too, they passed for good coin among radicals. Given how closely the LSR followed currents of thought in Britain and the United States, it would have been astonishing indeed had these Marxist ideas not turned up in *Social Planning for Canada*. And turn up they did.

At the same time, *Social Planning* was far from being Marxist, as were the LSR and CCF in general, in its evolutionary approach to socialism, its adoption of the route of education, permeation, and parliamentary action pioneered by the Fabians half a century earlier. It was not only in rejecting the revolutionary method that the LSR diverged from Marxism, moreover. The long-time Canadian Communist leader, Tim Buck, mistakenly suggested in his reminiscences that 'the big arguments' between the Communists and the LSR/CCF were over 'how.' Not just the means, but also the goals were at issue.[52] Neither the socialization of all the means of production nor the dictatorship of the proletariat were among the objectives of Canadian democratic socialists.

In view of this, several neo-Marxist and leftist scholars, among them R.T. Naylor, Gary Teeple, and Peter Sinclair, have refused to describe the program of the LSR and CCF as socialist, calling it 'liberal reformist' and 'populist' instead. By contrast, the ex-Communist Norman Penner, citing approvingly O.D. Skelton's definition of socialism as an indictment and analysis of capitalism, a panacea, and a campaign against it – 'socialism is intelligible only as the antithesis of the competitive system' – has no difficulty in attaching the socialist label to the ideas of the LSR. And these are certainly socialist by Robert Heilbroner's standards: there must be a 'predominance of some form of planning,' an ideology that intends the creation of 'an egalitarian society in which no class may gain the strategic position conferred by the ownership of society's productive assets,' and, eventually, 'a wholly new kind of society, free of invidious striving and built on motives of cooperation and confraternity.'[53]

Reference to rival definitions cannot settle this debate. For example, readers of Professor Kenneth R. Minogue's witty and provocative book, *The Liberal Mind*, will have no difficulty in placing the authors of *Social Planning for Canada* as 'salvationist liberals.' To Minogue, modern twentieth-century liberalism, 'enlarged and somewhat refurbished ... provides a moral and political consensus which unites virtually all of us, excepting only a few palpable eccentrics on the right and communists on the left.'[54] Thus democratic socialists, concerned with efficiency and social harmony, are by definition liberals.

It is useful to be reminded that British socialism was born in part of liberalism and was influenced by the reformist liberalism of John Stuart Mill, J.A. Hobson, and L.T. Hobhouse, and later of William Beveridge and J.M. Keynes. It is also worth remembering that both Marx and Mill believed in progress through the application of science and technology. All the same, Professor Minogue overstates the inclusiveness of liberalism, something that was no doubt easier to do in the early 1960s than in the 1930s, or today. The LSR very largely rejected the market economy and the capitalist mode of production: liberals did not. To call the authors of *Social Planning for Canada* 'liberals in a hurry' is ultimately to assert that they were not serious in their quest for the co-operative commonwealth.

My remarks will not mollify those who measure socialist purity against the standards of Marx, Lenin, Stalin, Trotsky, or Mao. True believers are notoriously jealous in their worship. Those who lay claim to orthodoxy often attach a special quality to certain words, and socialism is one of them. These people are like Parson Thwackum, the churchman in Henry Fielding's *Tom Jones*, who

> doubted not but that all the infidels and hereticks in the world would, if they could, confine honour to their own absurd errors and damnable deceptions; 'but honour,' says he, 'is not therefore manifold, because there are many absurd opinions about it; nor is religion manifold, because there are various sects and heresies in the world. When I mention religion I mean the Christian religion; and not only the Christian religion, but the Protestant religion; and not only the Protestant religion, but the Church of England. And when I mention honour, I mean that mode of Divine grace which is not only consistent with, but dependent upon, this religion; and is consistent with and dependent upon no other ...'

Except to fundamentalists, socialism is no more capable of precise definition than Christianity, nor is socialist honour limited to Marxists. By 1935 the LSR and the authors of its book had come to call their organization and ideas socialist. On the evidence there is no good reason for the historian or social scientist to do otherwise.

6

'Canada – one or nine?'

Most socialists in the Western world troubled themselves little about problems of federalism. They lived in more or less unitary states in which ultimate economic and fiscal authority rested with a central government. In Canada it was otherwise. And yet in socialist principle it was highly desirable, even necessary, that one sovereign authority be able to plan for the entire economy. For a planned economy to become possible in this country there would have to be some changes made.

The problem of sovereignty in the modern state did not greatly interest the authors of *Social Planning for Canada*. A rudimentary theory can be deduced, however. The people ought to be sovereign; Parliament, the cabinet, the agencies of government, and, in the planned economy, the National Planning Commission: all ought to work to realize the popular will, as reflected in elections as well as in the economic directives reaching the Planning Commission from local bodies. Certain minority rights, however, 'matters of race, language, religion, and education,' ought to be guarded against the operation of popular sovereignty. One could not always trust the Canadian majority.

Four fundamental conditions are assumed in *Social Planning* to be necessary to the planned state:

1. The ultimate responsibility of a modified but democratic parliamentary system to public opinion.
2. The conferring of adequate powers upon the federal government to render its control of economic policy full and effective.
3. The development of organs of economic planning for the formulation of economic policy, and the necessary modification of the procedure and structure of parliament to ensure that full advantage is taken of expert knowledge.
4. The reorganization of finance, commerce and industry to ensure the effective administration of national economic planning.[1]

Given these conditions it should be possible to control economic policy intelligently. No longer will powerful corporations enjoy the opportunity of using Canada's divided jurisdiction in economic matters for their own ends.

Leftist dissatisfaction with the constitution as it had evolved since 1867 antedated the founding of the LSR. J.S. Woodsworth, for example, during the post-war depression expressed concern that divided jurisdiction served both employed and unemployed working men badly. At the meetings of the Canadian Political Science Association in the summer of 1931, Frank Scott exclaimed: 'Just at the very time when the exigencies of the economic situation call for drastic action, for increased international co-operation and for a planned internal social order, we find ourselves with cumbrous legislative machinery and outworn constitutional doctrines.' The failure to deal coherently with unemployment Scott held to be a particularly dismal result of divided constitutional competence.[2]

As professor of Constitutional Law at McGill University, Scott very naturally became the LSR's expert on the British North America Act. In 1934 the league sponsored publication of a pamphlet prepared by him. Entitled *Social Reconstruction and the B.N.A. Act*, its argument is that most of the redistribution of powers necessary to build the new society can take place within the terms of the act. The Dominion residuary clause is the key. According to the opening words of Section 91 of the BNA Act, the Dominion is entitled to make laws 'for the Peace, Order, and good Government of Canada, in relation to all Matters not coming within the Classes of Subjects by this Act assigned exclusively to the Legislatures of the Provinces.' Over time this had come to be interpreted by the courts as a power employable during occasions of war or national emergency only. But, Scott wrote: 'The present emergency [in the administration of unemployment relief] would seem to be as great as that which justified controlling newsprint in 1919 ... A national crisis, if severe enough, will automatically increase Dominion legislative powers.'[3] A further possibility is legislation giving effect to treaties and international conventions to which Canada is a party. The Dominion government has so far failed to act on the conventions of the International Labour Organization (ILO) because they deal with matters that are believed to be within provincial jurisdiction. However, Ottawa can probably use the treaty-making power under Section 132 of the act in order to implement the ILO conventions now that the pro-Dominion decisions of the Judicial Committee of the Privy Council in the Radio Broadcasting and Aeronautics cases (1932) are available as precedents for the expansion of the power of the central government.

In reviewing the pamphlet the Queen's University political scientist Norman McLeod Rogers, though himself a centralist, expressed the view that Scott, the LSR, and the CCF underestimated the far-reaching amendments in the act that would be necessary in order to transfer control over property and civil rights to the

Dominion. More important, the Canadian people seemed scarcely ready for such a transfer. If that were so, responded Frank Underhill, it was because the people were backward and timid: 'We shall never get anywhere in this country until our people have emancipated themselves from the ancestral parochialism which still makes them such persistent fundamentalist worshippers in the sectarian chapels of "provincial rights."'[4] The trouble with democracy and popular sovereignty is that people may persist in wanting what, from the reformer's point of view, is bad for them. It is this apparently perverse persistence, of course, that political education is supposed to correct.

Frank Scott was mainly responsible for the section on the British North America Act in *Social Planning for Canada*. Its thesis is that the BNA Act does not impose any particular economic system on the country; it is 'a mere political framework' within which Canadians are free to work out their destiny: 'All the economic changes necessary for the creation of a cooperative commonwealth in Canada could be effected by adjustments in the distribution of powers without involving any change in the essential qualities of the federal scheme such as responsible government, federalism or minority rights.' The act already gives the Dominion government greater power to legislate for the economy than is often appreciated; concurrent legislation with the provinces is a further possibility. Some amendments will nevertheless be necessary to bring the act into the modern industrial age. Most urgent are changes that will permit the passage of social legislation by Ottawa because that can currently be done, if at all, only by virtue of the treaty-making power.

Earlier Scott had suggested that Section 132 of the act, empowering the Parliament and government of Canada to perform the obligations of Canada or of any province to foreign countries arising out of British Empire treaties, be used to implement various ILO conventions. But in *Social Planning* he wrote that R.B. Bennett's use of that power to justify elements of his 'New Deal' legislation of early 1935, 'though probably sound, is somewhat uncertain; in any case there is no reason why Canada should be tied in these matters to the snail's pace of the other capitalist powers.'[5] Further amendments would permit the centralization of control over companies, the rationalization of the fiscal system, the adoption and execution of a national economic plan, and the abolition of the Senate.

How should these amendments be secured? The way they were in the past, by action of the Dominion Parliament. The 'compact theory' of Confederation, which contends that all provinces must assent to an amendment, makes no historical sense. 'Parliament alone represents all provinces, speaks for every Canadian, and should properly be held responsible for a matter of such national importance.' Dismissing the extreme claims of provincial rights does not have to involve a threat to minority rights. Five years earlier Scott had noted that the provinces have done more damage to minority rights than the Dominion ever has. (One has only to think of the Manitoba School Question or anti-Oriental actions in British Columbia.) Now he proposed that certain sections of the BNA Act, 51 and 51A, 92(1) and (12), 93 and 133, and the new amendment formula, be entrenched. 'Provincial powers over economic matters and social legislation ... are not in this group. Quebec's right to tolerate sweatshops whose existence holds down living standards in other provinces, is not a minority right.' Civil liberties ought to be protected, however, by means of an entrenched Bill of Rights clause in the act.[6]

The essence of the proposed amendment formula resides in four points:

1. The power of amendment to rest within Canada.
2. Ordinary amendments to be by majority vote of the Dominion Parliament, assembled in joint session of the two Houses.
3. Amendments affecting minority rights to require, in addition to Dominion approval, the assent of all the provincial legislatures.
4. Any province not dissenting within one year to be presumed to have given its assent.[7]

This was the outline of the amendment formula that Scott had suggested in his evidence before the Special Parliamentary Committee on Revision of the Constitution early in 1935. It would be our last request to the imperial Parliament, he said. The formula would reflect the 'particularly unified form of federalism' that we were intended by the Fathers of Confederation to enjoy.

Finally, *Social Planning* sketches a few ways in which the Senate may be abolished, without being too optimistic about the potential success of any of them. Should they fail, new appointments could be used to change the composition of the Senate. Aware that this would take time, Scott ended the discussion a bit lamely: 'In the face of determined public opinion the second chamber might well hesitate to become the last bulwark of reaction.'[8] It cannot be said that the LSR habitually overestimated the opposition some of its proposals might have aroused had a socialist party ever had the opportunity to try to put them into practice.

A few weeks after *Social Planning* was published, a Liberal administration replaced the government of R.B. Bennett. The new prime minister, cautious Mackenzie King, referred the social and marketing legislation of the 'Bennett New Deal' to the courts for an opinion on the constitutionality of the various measures. Frank Scott especially believed this to be a crucial test case. Sackcloth and ashes were not enough, therefore, when the ultimate opinions were handed down by the Privy Council in 1937. 'The most exaggerated doctrines of provincial rights have been accorded full recognition,' Scott lamented, 'and the national sovereignty of

Canada in the international field has been destroyed.'[9] He was referring to Lord Atkin's statement that the Dominion government could not use the treaty power to legislate for matters that, under Section 92 of the BNA Act, are a provincial responsibility. The broader interpretation indicated by the Radio and Aeronautics cases had apparently been reversed. Scott was distressed, too, by the difficulties that the Privy Council had put in the way of concurrent legislation. The total effect was to make Canada even less able than it had been in 1929 to deal with economic crises since these did not justify the invocation of the Dominion residuary clause.

What was to be done? The amendment formula had become even more centrally important than before. The responsibility for social legislation had to be rearranged; so, too, the financial relations between the provinces and the Dominion. Last but not least, appeals to the Privy Council must end.

Initially there was disagreement in LSR circles as to how seriously the new Royal Commission on Dominion-Provincial Relations ought to be taken. Its members, especially the economist H.F. Angus from the University of British Columbia, the dean of English Canadian newspapermen, J.W. Dafoe, and R.A. MacKay, the political scientist from Dalhousie University, were men who had earned the LSR's respect, if not confidence. But was not this royal commission simply a device to postpone action in the hope that the problem would disappear of itself? Still, an LSR brief was obviously in order.

Canada – One or Nine? The Purpose of Confederation, was the full title of the document that Leonard Marsh and Frank Scott presented to the commission one chilly January day in 1938. What, it asked, were the purposes of Confederation in 1867? First, 'the union of British North America in a single federal state'; second, 'the preservation of the parliamentary system of government after the model of the British constitution'; third, 'the protection of minority rights'; fourth, 'the creation of a national government fully empowered to deal with essentially national problems and possessing a residue of power over matters of common concern to all the provinces'; and finally, 'a progressive development toward the legislative unity of Canada in matters of property and civil rights, in all the provinces except Quebec.' These purposes, the LSR argued, are still valid. 'Confusion and uncertainty now exist in Dominion-Provincial relations, but they are not due to weaknesses in the constitutional principles originally adopted.'[10] The Fathers of Confederation drew up a good design.

What has gone wrong since then? Not surprisingly, given what had recently happened, the Privy Council is singled out for blame. Over the years it has substituted 'a theoretical, inefficient and loose English concept of federalism for the practical, balanced and unified Canadian concept.' After seventy years of judicial interpretation the Dominion Parliament has lost its residuary powers except in an emergency greater than the Depression, as well as much of its power to regulate trade and commerce and to make treaties. It has become 'almost totally incapable of providing for the masses of the Canadian population that protection against the national evils of unemployment, fluctuating wage and price levels, and social insecurity which is being increasingly demanded today.'[11] As a result people now look to the provinces for help. Alas, most of the provinces do not have the financial means.

A further obstacle to the achievement of the purposes of the Fathers has been 'the decline in authority of the central government consequent upon the reduction of its legal powers, which has been followed by a great revival of sectional feeling in Canada.' (This was a mistaking of cause and effect: it is now generally accepted that the provincial attack on the Dominion's powers, led by the Ontario Liberal government of Oliver Mowat, did not result from but rather provided the occasion for the process of judicial review that undermined the constitution of 1867.[12]) The divisive impact of provincialism has become particularly noticeable in the 1930s. 'Today, for considerable sections of the Canadian people Ottawa has become almost the seat of a foreign power – a Geneva amongst a group of sovereign states.' While this was coming about, however, 'the economy has been moving steadily in the direction of monopoly control.' The economic power of the corporations now rivals, if it does not exceed, that of government. Bay and St James Streets, the corporate centres of Toronto and Montreal, have become a tail that can wag ten dogs. Monopoly capitalism has also brought a great maldistribution of wealth and a new 'industrial feudalism,' which only a strong central government will be able to check.[13]

Of the original five purposes of Confederation only two, the union of British North America and the safeguarding of minority rights, have been somewhat imperfectly accomplished, though the latter gives rise to continued debate. 'The preservation of parliamentary institutions has also been achieved, but democracy as a way of life has deteriorated in many respects in Canada.'[14] This is the consequence of the growing power of small monied cliques, which has given increasing importance to the accident of birth, and of the great disparity in bargaining power between capital and labour. As for the two remaining purposes, the achievement of a strong central government has been largely blocked, and the unification of the law in the common-law provinces has been completely ignored.

This is a sad record. But Canadians now want more than the original five objectives. They desire 'the provision of a basic minimum of social security for every citizen' and – most important to the LSR if not to Canadians – the assumption of that measure of control and planning of the economy that is 'necessary to maintain economic stability, to eliminate unfair competition and waste, and to see that natural resources are developed in the best and most efficient manner.'[15] Here are new purposes and responsibilities for the central government. Pass the requisite constitutional amendments and it will become possible to ease the fiscal difficulties faced by provincial and municipal governments, equalize the burdens and benefits of life in Canada, redistribute income and wealth equitably among individuals and regions, and foster the growth of a comprehensive patriotism at the expense of provincial loyalties.

There is no intention to reduce the provincial governments to a municipal status. 'Their exclusive powers over local matters will remain; it will only be their present power to deal with matters of national concern which will be taken from them.' No doubt some provincial premiers will scream, but in the interest of the common good they should be ignored. In any case the provinces will retain important administrative functions even when the ultimate economic powers have been centralized. The brief concludes with the words of Thomas D'Arcy McGee, spoken during the Confederation Debates: 'The principle [of federalism] itself seems to me to be capable of being so adapted as to promote internal peace and external security, and to call into action a genuine, enduring and heroic patriotism.' Frank Scott recalls that, by and large, the brief was well received.[16]

Fundamental to the LSR's understanding of Canada was that its real problems are those not of federalism but of capitalism. 'Only the CCF dare recognize this,' Frank Underhill asserted in *Social Planning for Canada*, 'and accordingly only the CCF can reconcile the apparent conflict of regional economic interests, and attain nation-wide unity.' However, even the CCF was not free of regional differences of opinion, and on occasion someone noted that nation-wide unity was not much in demand. Underhill observed in 1938 that most Canadians had responded to the Depression by intensifying their parochial loyalties. 'As one looks back now on the years since 1932 when the CCF started its campaign,' he told his audience at the Couchiching Conference in August, 'one can see that the chief reason for its seeming lack of success was not its socialism but its nationalism.' This was highly debatable: there is no evidence that socialism was any more popular than centralism. Also debatable was his assessment that nationalism was on the rise and that the next election would turn on efforts 'to capture the reviving national feeling ... and to exploit it' for partisan purposes.[17]

Echoing the assertion in *Canada – One or Nine?* that 'the identification between local autonomy and democracy is largely out of date,' Underhill ridiculed the views of those who, like Ontario's Premier Mitchell Hepburn, seemed to believe

> that the provincial government in some mystic way is in more direct touch with the individual citizen and represents him more truly than the federal government ... In the horse and buggy days of the nineteenth century there was a good deal of foundation for this belief

of most democrats and liberals that local governments were more truly representative and much safer than central governments. But the conditions which gave validity to such beliefs have mostly passed away in our day.[18]

To be sure, 'there is a real danger in the accumulation of power at the centre.' The effective check against this, however, Underhill found not in the provincial governments but in the organization of trade unions, co-operatives, and so forth. After all, well-organized groups of businessmen were well able to play one level of government against another. Canada must pass beyond that game.

Centralization came soon enough. However, it did not come in the way that Underhill and other LSR members wanted. After war broke out in Europe in September 1939 and Canada joined in, the Dominion government quickly assumed wide-ranging emergency powers that were scarcely checked at all. Under the circumstances the moderately centralizing recommendations of the report of the Commission on Dominion-Provincial Relations were something of an anticlimax. Ottawa was to assume greater responsibilities in the economic and social fields. Various new fiscal arrangements would ensure that the provinces could afford the functions they would exercise. The poorer provinces would obtain transfer payments ultimately provided by the taxpayers of the wealthier provinces.

The LSR's response to the report was one of qualified approval. The commission might have done better; it might also have done worse. Frank Scott reportedly maintained at the Couchiching Conference in August 1940 'that the commission failed to do the job it might have done by a consideration of the whole economic structure of the nation with a view to proposing basic changes leading to a better economic and political order.' Commentators in the pages of *The Canadian Forum*, since 1936 an LSR organ, agreed. Nevertheless, they said more for the report than they said against it; it represented at least a step or two in the right direction.[19]

Had it survived, the LSR might three or four years later have accepted the report more readily. By 1943 Scott, Underhill, and company were backing away from the centralism of the 1930s, assigning more responsibility to the provincial governments than they earlier had been prepared to grant.[20] The main reason is not hard to find. In 1943 the CCF became the official Opposition in Ontario. The following year hopes for a provincial victory were rewarded in Saskatchewan. Bright also was the future in British Columbia, where the CCF had become the Opposition in 1941. These events encouraged interest in the role that provincial governments might play in the coming of the co-operative commonwealth. That interest was not new, but in the war years it reached its zenith. Power in Ottawa was still seen as the key to ultimate socialist success, but power in the provinces had come to assume greater importance to socialists than at any time in the 1930s.

II

Quebec, to the LSR, was one of nine provinces, but one not quite *comme les autres*. For historical reasons it did not have the common law and was officially bilingual in its courts and legislature. In the 1930s it also seemed to be uncommonly reactionary and even readier than other provinces to tolerate political corruption. No admirer of Quebec's ways, Frank Underhill in 1931 quipped that 'The only province which has not been subject to [the] regular alternation between short periods of comparatively good government and long periods of decay is Quebec. In Quebec they enjoy bad government all the time.'[21] In Quebec, too, the population seemed during those years to be peculiarly impervious to the attractions of the socialist and centralist message as purveyed by the LSR and CCF.

The LSR found unacceptable, could not take seriously, traditional Quebec nationalism focused on the provincial territory and the French language, and to some extent on the Roman Catholic religion. Men like Frank Scott and Graham Spry were proponents of a bicultural concept of Canada. They believed fervently that the linguistic and cultural rights of French Canadians outside Quebec deserved better protection than these had yet received. Spry spoke of biculturalism as early as 1929; Scott told the delegates to the CCF founding convention in Regina that their movement was 'likely to encourage the learning of French. There is no reason why we might not come out with a bilingual currency.'[22] Hand in hand with other Canadians, French-speaking Quebeckers would work to build the co-operative commonwealth.

Doggedly but very largely in vain, the LSR sought to attract French Canadian members and to gain supporters for the CCF in Quebec. In attempting these thankless tasks, they argued that an extension of the Dominion's power to regulate the economy need not be inconsistent with Quebec's cultural autonomy. The ramifications of the latter interested the LSR less than the problems centralization was designed to cure. A *Canadian Forum* editorial, presumably by Spry, explained in 1936 that the problems of Quebec were at bottom the same as those of the rest of the country. 'The cure lies in correcting the conditions that make the French Canadian the victim of English Canadian business domination. This is not a race question, but an economic and social problem.' Business domination is the villain, and if the attempt to render it harmless should require some drastic measures, Quebec is not to worry. The abolition of the Senate, *Social Planning for Canada* assured its readers, is not intended to weaken or undermine

> the security of the provinces in our federal system, and especially the position of the French province [sic] of Quebec. It is not the position of Quebec that is being attacked, but only the position of that part of it which is located in the neighbourhood of St. James St., Montreal.

> The real safeguards for racial and religious minority rights in the Canadian constitution lie in two things: the numerical and hence political strength of the minority ...; and certain special sections of the B.N.A. Act which Dominion legislation cannot invade without being declared *ultra vires* by the courts.

After these sections have been entrenched as the LSR proposes, 'racial and religious minority rights would in fact be safer than at present.'[23] This ought to satisfy French Canadians. That these might not care to see themselves as a 'minority' seems not to have crossed LSR minds.

French Canadians could be a confounded nuisance. Civil liberties, nowhere safe in Canada, were perhaps most endangered in Quebec after the Tory-dominated Union Nationale government of Maurice Duplessis took office in 1936. People like Frank Scott and Eugene Forsey considered the Padlock Act of 1937 to be a milestone along Quebec's road to fascism. Entitled 'An Act respecting Communistic Propaganda,' the act gave extensive powers to padlock (lock up) any premises used for the dissemination of 'Communism or Bolshevism.' Neither of these terms was defined; the task of definition was left to the attorney general (Duplessis himself), or to his designates. That the Dominion government refused either to disallow the act or to refer it to the Supreme Court for an opinion on its constitutionality – it appeared to deal with the criminal law – was interpreted by the LSR as 'political cowardice.' The act had the open support of the Roman Catholic hierarchy and the press, including the two English-language newspapers in Montreal, and the tacit support of the business community. This distinguished it from some Alberta banking and press-control statutes, disallowed in 1937 and 1938, which had been profoundly offensive to the banks and to the press. The disallowance of these statutes signalled a revival of Dominion control over the provinces, Forsey wrote. However, the concurrent failure of Ottawa to strike down or refer the Padlock Act suggested that 'the Dominion Government will be on the side of the big battalions.'[24] This augured ill for civil liberties, especially in Quebec.

More than any other institution in Quebec, the Church fostered social conservatism while seeming also to encourage a nationalism based on race and language. The ownership of most major business enterprises by English-speaking people made it understandable that English Canadians generally, *les Anglais*, had become objects of resentment. French Canadian nationalism, however, was muddling the opposition to monopoly capitalism in the province. To the authors of *Democracy Needs Socialism* (1938) the conclusion was 'inescapable': nationalist and racist slogans were being used in order to prevent French Canadians from considering the economic issues on their merits. Only the large business corporations stood to benefit from this, for they had nothing to fear from the fascism that racial nationalism tended to encourage.[25]

French Canadian nationalism, whether of the conservative Catholic variety favoured by Abbé Lionel Groulx or the more liberal kind professed by Paul Gouin and the *Action Libérale Nationale*, by concentrating on French-speaking Quebec was an obstacle to the achievement of a more comprehensive national feeling. It menaced the possibility of effective action by the central government on economic matters; it was irrelevant to the basic economic needs of French Canadians. To exalt racial loyalties above those needs seemed romantic at best, reactionary at worst, and in either case parochial.

Not much sympathy for Roman Catholicism was inherent in the overwhelmingly Protestant background of LSR members. Tolerance for the nationalism of French Canadians was little more likely given the pan-Canadian sentiments of the English-speaking intelligentsia of Ontario and Quebec in the early decades of the twentieth century. From the opposite point of view, the centralizing ideas of the LSR struck French Canadian intellectuals as outlandish. On the whole, Professor Michael Oliver writes, 'French Canadian nationalism during both the 1920s and 1930s focussed narrowly on Quebec ... The main concern ... was the *État national*, whether in loose affiliation with, or separated from, the rest of Canada.'[26] Nationalists had learned the 'lessons' of the hanging of Louis Riel, of anti-French school legislation in Manitoba and Ontario, of conscription for overseas military service during the Great War: French Canadians were not safe in the larger Canada. Trying to convince them that they were wrong was to no avail. No amount of assurance about the future of 'minority rights' was going to change their minds.

While the centralism of the LSR and CCF was deeply suspect, their socialism was, if anything, even more so. The denunciations by Roman Catholic churchmen of the alleged materialism, godlessness, and hostility to private property of socialism carried great weight. Mgr Georges Gauthier, Archbishop of Montreal, declared in 1934 that the 'errors' of the CCF 'rendered it unacceptable for a Catholic.' Even more distressing was Cardinal Villeneuve's condemnation of the CCF in late 1938.[27] The mass of the population heeded these warnings. Even in English-speaking Canada the hostility of the Church meant that the movement had little influence among Roman Catholics.[28]

Only on the subject of neutrality in a war overseas did the views of the LSR and French Canadian intellectuals largely coincide. French Canadians were also regarded as natural allies in the process of achieving complete independence from Great Britain. However, these matters, to which we shall return, were not enough to produce an alliance between even radical English and French Canadian intellectuals.[29]

In trying to attract French Canadians, Scott and other LSR members were Sirens singing to the companions of Odysseus. The ears of French Canadian intellectuals were closed with a wax compounded of race, language, and religion, their memories dominated by past injustices, their hopes centred on future autonomy or even independence. These things the LSR could not appreciate.

III

For the LSR, the centralization of governmental power within Confederation was not an end in itself. It was a means, not without its drawbacks – 'there is a real danger in the accumulation of power at the centre,' Frank Underhill conceded – to worthwhile ends. These included the provision of minimum standards of social services in the poorer provinces, the establishment of socialist planning, and ultimately the introduction of the co-operative commonwealth. A socialist government in Ottawa, advised by the National Planning Commission, would have the power to act in the interests of the great mass of Canadians. The power of the corporations would have been broken. The national interest would no longer be defined by 'a few men seeking private profits' and by politicians indebted to them.[30]

The LSR considered its centralism to be a necessary part of its Canadian socialism. It was not a sufficient part. A number of Canadian intellectuals and politicians, many of them in no way socialists, were convinced in the Depression that the Dominion government should have the power to deal with economic problems that affected the entire country. Not a few believed that Ottawa had once enjoyed that power but had lost it in the course of judicial interpretation of the BNA Act. Others held that the process of interpretation, carried out with flexibility, would have extended that power to Ottawa even if the Dominion government had not originally possessed it.

The political scientist Alan Cairns has called the former group 'fundamentalists' and the latter 'constitutionalists' – the two overlapped – and has shown how in the 1930s these groups joined in vigorous criticism of the Privy Council. Both believed that in the perilous circumstances of the Depression the Dominion government should be dominant. As one of the constitutionalists, the lawyer Brooke Claxton, said in 1935 in discussing the Dominion residuary clause:

> Things being as they are, if the conditions of living and working of the people of the Dominion is [sic] not a 'matter of national concern' which has already attained 'such dimensions' as 'to justify the Canadian parliament in passing laws for their regulation,' then we should change our constitution or give up trying to have a country in Canada.
>
> ... It is a queer comment on our laws and on our Courts, but particularly on ourselves, that in the European War we found the constitutional power necessary to a united effort to

kill and defeat the enemy, while in the depression we have not the power to unite in building the foundations of peace.[31]

To the centralist this piece of irony was a commonplace worth repeating.

In the 1930s – and not in that decade only – those who were 'trying to have a country in Canada' were struggling against centrifugal forces that Professor Cairns suggests they did not fully understand. In this struggle the LSR found itself in good company. Professor Donald Creighton, otherwise no friend of the league, recalls that after he joined the research staff of the Royal Commission on Dominion-Provincial Relations in 1938, his 'interests, sympathies and beliefs' came closer to those of the LSR:

Indeed it could be said that the young men who worked for the Royal Commission and the young men who founded the League for Social Reconstruction shared a common concern for Canada in depression and a common hope for its better future. *Social Planning for Canada* ... offered a rigorously socialist programme. *The Report of the Royal Commission* was, of course, not nearly so radical in its recommendations; but it did lay down the bases of the interventionist and welfare state of the future. And both the book and the report assumed that the creation of the new Canada was a national enterprise which must be carried forward under the leadership of the federal government.[32]

In the light of this assumption, the interventions of those who challenged federal leadership were bound to appear disruptive. Unhappily for the LSR and the royal commission, the challengers included at least four provincial governments, led by 'Duff' Pattullo, William Aberhart, Mitchell Hepburn, and Maurice Duplessis.

Unlike the politicians and many of the people whom they represented, much of the Canadian intelligentsia during the inter-war years looked to Ottawa for leadership. As Professor Margaret Prang has shown, the 1920s witnessed the founding of an unprecedentedly large number of new national organizations. Among them were the Canadian Teachers' Federation, the Canadian Institute of International Affairs, the Canadian Federation of University Women's Clubs, and the Canadian Authors' Association. The United Church of Canada was created in 1925. 'All were in some measure an expression of the rising national sentiment.' One of the champions of that sentiment and the co-founder in 1930 of the Canadian Radio League, Graham Spry, comments: 'It was a period not of "nationalism" in any narrow sense but of "nationhood" ... There was simply the emotion and conviction to carry forward in every field the concept of Canada and of Confederation, not in opposition to or separation from others but in the realization of a national self.'[33] Among intellectuals like Spry the emotion and conviction were actually strengthened by the Depression: of this the LSR was an important manifestation.

Unfortunately for the hopes of nationalist intellectuals, the forces undermining Canadian unity and nationhood had been growing steadily stronger since the late nineteenth century. By 1930 they were very potent. Indeed, their strength is implicit in the difficulties one experiences when trying to define nationalism in Canada. 'What the vast literature on the subject adds up to,' Professor Prang notes, 'is that nationalism is where you find it.' More recently the historian Douglas L. Cole has written that the difficulties in definition result from the fact that 'Canada never became a nation, except in a political and constitutional sense.' Cole's preferred definition of nationalism is centred on ethnicity and language, and there neither was nor is a Canadian nation that is ethnically and linguistically homogeneous. As Eugene Forsey has said, 'Canada is both two nations and one.'[34]

Nationalism as the LSR embraced it consisted of support for the pursuit of unfettered Canadian independence and of the use of the state to achieve certain social and economic goals. According to the useful categorization by the political scientist Anthony Smith, the LSR's ideas constituted a form of 'nationalism without nation' of what he calls the 'territorial' type. As distinct from ethnic nationalisms, which start from a sociological nation, 'a pre-existent homogeneous entity, a recognisable cultural unit ..., "territorial" nationalisms start from an imposed political entity, and possess no common and distinctive cultural identity to protect.'[35] Alternatively, the projected nation may consist of one 'strategic' cultural group and a subgroup, or of two strategic groups. The nationalism that may result is of the 'mixed territorial' type: it must accommodate the sensibilities of both groups.

Certainly forms of nationalism that are based on a single ethnic group and language the LSR considered to be inappropriate in Canada. They could only be disruptive: of that no further sad proof was needed. In the effort to open up half a continent, develop its resources, and assimilate the many thousands of immigrants who were arriving from continental Europe, English Canadians had asserted the essentially British and English-speaking nature of Canada. In the process the position of the French language outside Quebec had been consistently downgraded. This could only have the result of fanning the *nationaliste* fire in Quebec, a fire that had been burning with varying brightness since the early nineteenth century. Conflict between English and French Canadian nationalisms had been particularly intense during the Great War, when the heat produced by school regulations concerning the language of instruction in Ontario and Manitoba was further raised by the issue of conscription.

The debate over that issue also highlighted the existence of mounting dissatisfactions of class and region. Industrialization and urbanization had yielded by the time of the war as one by-product an urban proletariat unhappy with the distribution of the riches and comforts of the country and turning increasingly to political as well as industrial organization. At the same time the countryside felt left behind and disgruntled. Governmental policies aimed at economic growth had fostered strong regional resentments. These were strongest in the agricultural hinterlands of Ontario and the West, but they were not absent from the Atlantic provinces and rural Quebec. The Canadian Pacific Railway, the terms on which it gained its contract, the conditions of its construction, and its operating practices, created dissatisfaction also. That unhappiness, shared by the prairie West and the business community of Toronto, abated only in part with the construction of new transcontinental lines during the Laurier years. And these soon brought their own problems and resentments. Dominion government control over the Crown Lands and resources of the three prairie provinces, not surrendered until 1930, was a further source of annoyance.

By the end of the war and throughout the 1920s dissatisfaction with the workings of government and suspicion of the motives of politicians, though not confined to the federal level, affected the Dominion government with great force. Burdened also with debt and the responsibility of paying war pensions, Ottawa's willingness if not ability to provide economic leadership had been seriously undermined. At the same time it was becoming clear that the east-west axis of the St Lawrence system and the fur trade, which the transcontinental railways had continued, had been undermined as well. Crucial were the development of new resource staples, notably metals and pulp and paper, and a new source of energy, hydro-electric power. Markets were increasingly in the United States. A shift in patterns of investment had been accelerated by the war. Great Britain and Europe declined in importance as creditors; the United States triumphantly took their place.

The new pattern was reinforced by the media, the glossy periodicals, often made with Canadian paper, the films and radio, and by the availability of the automobile to growing numbers of Canadians. Registration of passenger vehicles exceeded one million in 1931, and many roads ran to the border. Construction on the first controlled-access highway in Canada began in 1931: the Queen Elizabeth Way was to run for 145 kilometres from Toronto to Fort Erie and Buffalo. It was opened by Their Majesties at St Catharines in June 1939; not until 1962 was the Trans-Canada Highway as an all-season route to be completed. Air travel also early reflected the pull from north to south: the inaugural flight made by the new Trans-Canada Air Lines on 1 September 1937 was from Vancouver to Seattle!

The attraction of the south, while it was making the mass of Canadians more American in taste if not yet in outlook, reinforced local loyalties that had existed since before Confederation. So did the responsibility that the provincial and municipal governments had for social services and education, increasingly important in an urbanizing country. To some extent this was counteracted, at least in

English Canada, by the need to make the educational system serve the purpose of Canadianizing the children of immigrants. (This may go far to explain the sympathy for centralization among the English Canadian intelligentsia; they are exposed to education much longer than anyone else.) In any case, the Canada of the 1930s of which the LSR was so critical was one in which regional patriotism still counted for much, in the poor as well as the rich provinces.

LSR writers both belittled this regionalism, because it distracted Canadians from recognizing the primacy of social class, and insisted that the final responsibility for social services must be shifted to the central government because this would promote equity among regions. A few spokesmen, like the Toronto schoolteacher and later member of Parliament Joseph W. Noseworthy, believed that the responsibility for education should be shifted for the same reason.[36] No doubt it was easier for English-speaking intellectuals living in Toronto and Montreal than for Canadians elsewhere to think that the important differences in Canada are those not of region, race, or language, but of class. But were their attitudes to regionalism not unduly insensitive, their views about equity among the provinces and regions not ill advised?

As to the latter question, H.A. Innis, in reviewing the report of the Royal Commission on Dominion-Provincial Relations, asked:

> Are the provinces to be regarded as static institutions – the sacred kine of the federal structure and supported to resist economic adjustments? Are we to have a new constitutional Procrustean bed? Provincial equity may imply a rigid framework checking economic adjustments. Vast differences in economic and political strength and efficiency, historical background and tradition, and political structure suggest that proposals to make provinces equal *de facto* as well as *de jure* may involve serious handicaps.[37]

Innis was temperamentally more inclined to look for difficulties than most LSR writers, and he was much less ready to propose solutions. His questions were well put, however. It is not unfair to the LSR's intellectuals to say that they never confronted these questions squarely, although they did agree with Innis that the tariff, largely ignored by the royal commissioners, was the source of some of the grosser inequities among regions.

In trying, by its socialist lights, to prescribe for the common good, the LSR was unable to give much credit to provincial and local loyalties or to Quebec nationalism. It is hard to imagine a group of English-speaking intellectuals from central Canada in the 1930s doing so, however. To attach primacy to nation-wide economic problems and their solutions meant looking to Ottawa for salvation, not to nine provincial capitals.

Today (1980) the economy is in serious trouble. The centrifugal tendencies are at least as strong as they have ever been. Several provinces, led by Alberta and Quebec, are determined to bolster their claims to economic autonomy. A government is now in office in Quebec that is in principle committed to separation and something called sovereignty-association with the rest of Canada.

The menace to Canada is clear. Confederation is already highly decentralized; whether it can undergo further decentralization and survive remains to be seen. What a decline in the present powers of the federal government will do to the poorer regions is somewhat conjectural: the very identity of those regions will be in doubt. However, provincial equalization will almost certainly disappear. The rich will get richer, the poor, poorer.

Should one call for the centralization of economic power as the men and women of the LSR did? They were rowing against the stream; today one would be rowing against the rapids. The LSR's vision of a united socialist Canada was far from ignoble, but it seemed irrelevant to most Canadians then. A similar vision may seem even more irrelevant to Canadians today. Since 1940 the undermining of the east-west axis has continued, disguised as it was during the war years and for some time afterwards by the emergency powers Ottawa exercised. The Americanization of Canada has accelerated, powerfully assisted since the early 1950s by the medium of television. Efforts to counteract the Americanizing influences have not been lacking; their success has not been great.

If socialism is ever introduced on the northern half of this continent, it will very probably be in some new political entity not yet known. The country that the LSR loved will have taken on some new form.

7

Spreading the word

Canadian socialists necessarily live between disappointment and hope as the setbacks of yesterday are set against the possibilities of tomorrow. With the Dominion election of 1935 and the disappointing performance of the CCF receding in memory the spirits of LSR members began to rise once more. At the LSR convention of 1936, held at the Royal York Hotel in Toronto in February, the national president, Frank Scott, pointed the league's way to the future. 'The publication of *Social Planning for Canada* marked the end of the first period of LSR research,' he told the delegates:

> It crystallized the first important body of Canadian socialist thought. Development must now proceed from that point, toward a filling in of the gaps in the book, and toward a greater clarification of specific parts of the programme. The public will accept socialism provided they are told just what steps they must take to reach it. Vague generalizations must give way to practical details, and while the LSR cannot draft Acts of Parliament, it must get nearer to that process than it has yet done. In particular it should make Canada 'consumer-conscious,' and promote co-operative enterprises. Slogans are all very well in the political field, but the LSR tries to convince people by the sheer force of its logic and the accuracy of its analysis.
>
> Capitalism ... has been granted a new lease of life. But the socialist can draw as many arguments from 'prosperity' as he can from depression. In both, injustice is rampant. During prosperity, the increased national income goes to profits rather than wages; increased production does not mean elimination of unemployment; private monopoly grows apace; the distribution of wealth grows more unequal. And all this leads to war and new depressions. The LSR must keep people conscious of where they are going during this 'recovery.' The public mind is more open to new ideas than it has ever been before. The LSR must supply them through all the means at its command.[1]

These were inspiring words. They were reinforced by the report of the national vice-president and treasurer, G.M.A. Grube, who noted that, because 'the authors of *Social Planning for Canada* had very generously signed away their royalties in favour of the LSR,' the league's financial position was strong: there was 'a cash balance of $925.89.'

The outgoing national secretary, Graham Spry, presented a report that dwelt on accomplishments, not failures. LSR members had been active as candidates and organizers in the recent election; the LSR book had already sold over fifteen hundred copies. Membership stood at approximately five hundred. Most of these were in Toronto and Montreal, but there were branches in London, St Catharines, Kingston (Queen's University), and Dauphin, Manitoba, and 'loosely organized groups' in Barrie, Belleville, Hamilton, Oshawa, and Sault Ste Marie. Reports on branch activities were heard from S.B. Watson for Toronto, Frank Aykroyd for Montreal, E.O. Hall for London, Kay Montagu for St Catharines, and J. Lavine for Kingston. At least in central Canada the league was still active.

What of the future? An ultimately inconclusive discussion on membership in the LSR pitted those who wanted a campaign for more members against those who desired only a gradual increase in the membership. 'Socialism in Canada must be made respectable,' the advocates of expansion argued; 'otherwise the problem of the middle classes and their class prejudices could not be solved. A political party [would] not attract the middle classes, but they would respond to an LSR campaign.' Others, opposing this line, argued that 'the chief job of the LSR must continue to be research,' and that for this 'a small but active membership,' like that of the Fabian Society some decades earlier, would be enough.

That there was room for improvement in the LSR's activities was clear. Frank Underhill said that a lot of the league's educational work was wasted, especially during the election, in preaching to small groups of the converted. He stressed 'the need in socialist education and propaganda of more specific proposals.' Dr Harry W. Laidler, executive director of the League for Industrial Democracy in the United States, who was present as a guest, discussed the work of his organization and the means by which one could most effectively reach people. He singled out 'the radio, the dramatization of strike situations, the organization of students, and the holding of economic seminars.'

Among the resolutions passed one was to be distributed immediately to the press. It expressed protest 'against the action of the police at Regina on the night of July 1st, 1935,'[2] urged that all charges arising out of that violent termination of the On-to-Ottawa Trek be dropped, and reaffirmed the LSR's opposition to Section 98 of the Criminal Code. Other resolutions to be publicized in due time concerned LSR opposition to cadet training in schools and universities, and protest against the disenfranchisement of relief recipients.

Four members of Parliament attended the LSR meetings: they readily agreed that a closed gathering between the CCF MPs and the LSR executive was very much in order. The parliamentarians set the agenda for it, and all seven of them travelled to Montreal the following month. The eccentric printer J.S. Taylor was there and the two Scottish Canadians, also from British Columbia, Angus MacInnis and Grant MacNeil. From Saskatchewan came another Scot, the boyish, eloquent, and far from dour Baptist preacher T.C. 'Tommy' Douglas, and the more restrained former school principal M.J. Coldwell. Sitting for Winnipeg constituencies were the English-born upholsterer A.A. Heaps, distrustful of the LSR intellectuals 'whose pleasant, academic isolation was a long way from the labour battlefields,'[3] and J.S. Woodsworth, far from distrustful and still honorary national president of the LSR. His daughter Grace, a schoolteacher who had married MacInnis in 1932, was the secretary of the parliamentary group; she was also on the LSR executive.

Other members of the executive who attended the meetings were the president, Frank Scott, the new vice-president, Graham Spry, his successor as national secretary, Helen Marsh, and seven members-at-large. Carlton 'Bill' McNaught and Frank Underhill had come from Toronto and David Lewis from Ottawa – he had returned from Oxford in 1935 and was now articling with the law firm of Biggar and Smart. Frank Aykroyd, Eugene Forsey, King Gordon, and Leonard Marsh were already in Montreal, since February the site of the LSR national office. Three others had been invited to attend, J.C. Hemmeon of the Department of Political Economy at McGill, George Mooney, a CCF candidate in the recent election, and R.B.Y. Scott of United Theological College.

As the small group met in March 1936, 1,300,000 Canadians were still on relief, down only 200,000 from the spring of 1933, when economic recovery had begun. One suspects that these facts, or Adolf Hitler's recent demilitarization of the Rhineland and his subsequent vote of confidence from the German people, on that week-end captured the public imagination far less than the fate of Bruno Hauptmann. Convicted of the kidnap-murder of the Lindbergh child, the killer was waiting to hear the answer to his plea for pardon. Would he get it? On the front pages Premier William Aberhart's prediction that Alberta would be able to meet the bond interest due on 1 April paled into comparative insignificance.

To the politicians and intellectuals meeting in Montreal, Alberta's distress was much more important than Hauptmann's agony. (Aberhart's prophetic gifts failed him; Alberta had to default. Hauptmann did not get his pardon.) Provincial financial difficulties had prompted a proposal by C.A. Dunning, Dominion minister of Finance, for a provincial loan council. This was one of the topics the MPs wanted to discuss: should they support it? The proposal envisaged a Dominion guarantee of provincial loans, both principal and interest. However, 'the Council, which would include the federal Minister of Finance and the Provincial Treasurer, would have to authorize every loan.' Eugene Forsey observed that the council might be used by a

Dominion government to harmstring a future CCF provincial government; Frank Scott 'advocated calling for a Royal Commission to make a thorough survey of the whole problem.' There was a consensus 'that the CCF should oppose this bill on the basis that it is a half-hearted attempt to deal with the question without adequate preparation.'[4]

Other matters on which the MPs wanted advice were alternative budgetary proposals (J.C. Hemmeon undertook to prepare a brief on the impact of raising various kinds of direct taxation), debt reduction, the railway problem, amendment of the BNA Act and the Bank of Canada Act, and the newly appointed National Employment Commission. The details of what was said are less important than the evident interest with which the parliamentarians listened to the intellectuals, and their willingness to take counsel.

This extended to the discussion of the next national convention of the CCF and the future of the movement. Debate centred on the stand that should be taken on the matter of the 'united front' clamoured for by the CPC as well as by some CCFers. On this subject the MPs had more to say than their advisers: there should be no affiliation with the Canadian League against War and Fascism, whether at the national, provincial, or local level. However, it would be unwise to avoid collaboration with communists in the 'daily struggle' for civil liberties and the rights of labour. Whether it was wise to allow individual members of the CCF to join the CLAWF was a knotty question best left knotted.

Nothing definitive was said about the final topic, a CCF provincial program. Frank Scott assumed responsibility for preparing a brief on this subject to be presented to a further meeting scheduled for Ottawa during the Victoria Day week-end.

That meeting opened on Sunday morning, 24 May 1936. The site for this second conference was the Centre Block of the Parliament buildings. Winter was now a memory; the flowers of late spring were blooming around Parliament Hill. Of the MPs whose home territory this was only Abraham Heaps was absent. The LSR contingent was a bit thinner than in Montreal: Frank Scott, Helen and Leonard Marsh, Eugene Forsey, David Lewis, Grace MacInnis, and, from Kingston, Gregory Vlastos. E.J. Garland, though a member of the LSR executive, attended the first session only, primarily in his capacity as national organizer of the CCF. Soon to be the party's national treasurer, A.M. Nicholson was there, as was H.N. Dalton, who assisted M.J. Coldwell in running the embryonic national office of the CCF. There were others who drifted in and out of the sessions, among them J.S. Allen of the Montreal LSR branch, W.H. Alexander, a classics professor and LSR member from Edmonton, Harold Winch, member of the Legislative Assembly in British Columbia, and Mrs Lucy Woodsworth.

The first major item of business was the prospect of the CCF across the country, with Garland presenting a sobering report of some strength but also of considerable weakness, especially in Ontario. He warned that 'the movement was turning in on itself ...' and identified a trend to provincial bureaucratization, notably in Saskatchewan. 'Officials in every province tend to withhold cooperation on the national field.' Professor Alexander optimistically predicted the early breakup of Social Credit in Alberta; already it was dividing into 'Aberhartists and Douglasites.'[5] That was good news; bad news was that in Ontario there was renewed trouble concerning collaboration with the Communists. There was a serious dispute between factions within the CCF over participation in May Day marches.

Discussion in the second session turned to the national convention of the CCF, to be held in July. Frank Underhill had sent along drafts of convention resolutions on 'Foreign Policy and World Peace,' 'Unemployment and Housing,' and 'Finance, Debt and Taxation.' All these required further work; Scott, Lewis, and Leonard Marsh were among those assigned to alter the drafts.

At the third and final session the fiery twenty-nine-year-old Harold Winch discussed the prospects of the CCF in British Columbia. A victory in the next provincial election seemed likely, and he thought it important to establish just how far a socialist provincial government could go. He then read a draft policy for such a government. It was subjected to careful criticism, especially by Frank Scott. Winch was impressed. Upon his request, Scott shortly supplied him with some draft proposals for inclusion in the election program of the British Columbia CCF. They had been prepared by Scott and Leonard Marsh; the constitutional lawyer emphasized again that 'a CCF government in a province must necessarily work within the limits imposed upon it by the BNA Act in its present form. It cannot of itself introduce a fully planned and socialized economy.'[6] Winch himself had said as much at the May meeting; perhaps Scott suspected that some British Columbians would be less sensible.

Any suspicions he might have had soon proved themselves to be justified. The election platform adopted by the British Columbia CCF at its convention in July 1936 showed considerable similarity to the document that Scott had submitted to Winch. There was one crucial difference, however, and it provided the occasion for a split in the provincial movement later in the year. The convention adopted a clause that demanded the provincial socialization of finance and credit. Proposed by Dr Lyle Telford, a popular physician and leader of the CCF clubs, it was inspired by Social Credit theory. The clause was opposed by the provincial leader, Robert Connell, the leading Marxist in the party, Wallis Lefeaux, and the three MPs, Angus MacInnis, Grant MacNeil, and J.S. Taylor. Nevertheless, it got the decisive approval of the group that supported Ernest Winch and his son Harold.

Of course the latter knew from Frank Scott that the clause was unconstitutional. The personal antagonism that existed between the two Winches and Connell was apparently strong enough, however, to lead the former to support Telford's proposal. Connell refused to accept the clause on socialized finance; he repudiated it publicly and suggested also that Ernest Winch was pro-communist. In August 1936 Connell and three other MLAS were expelled from the CCF for having broken party discipline. The deposed leader did not go quietly. As a matter of course he had in June received from Scott a copy of the letter to Harold Winch and of the draft proposals. To the annoyance and embarrassment of Winch *père et fils* Connell was soon using these documents to back up his claim that he was right in opposing the Telford clause.[7] All Scott could do was commiserate with an unhappy Harold Winch; privately he thought the British Columbians had made a mess of things.

Not long after their expulsion the dissident MLAS were followed by J.S. Taylor, MP for Nanaimo, who left the CCF caucus to sit as an Independent. Like Robert Connell, he had been an early member of the LSR on the west coast. Harking back to those more innocent days, the two men now joined others in forming the Social Constructive Party of British Columbia. Very difficult to distinguish from the CCF, lacking an effective organization, the new party fared very badly in the provincial election of June 1937 and quickly disappeared. Connell went back to church work and part-time journalism; Taylor soon joined the Liberal caucus. He did not contest his seat in the general election of 1940.[8]

For Frank Scott and the LSR there was an ironic aftermath to the affair. The election did not produce the CCF victory that Harold Winch had expected. On the contrary, although the party again elected seven MLAS, it lost its status of official Opposition to the resurgent Tories. A chastened Winch Junior shortly afterwards wrote to Scott of the need in BC for 'men and women of technical and legal ability and knowledge. If only you and Marsh and Forsay [sic] could attend us in BC I am certain that we could go over the top ... Failing your arrival, however, I must continue to hope that you will carry on as our BC unofficial brain trust.' Half a year later, in February 1938, Scott reported to the LSR executive that he had received another request from Winch: the CCF MLAS wanted help in a study of the problems that would face a CCF government in BC. (The financial clause had already been abandoned.) If anyone commented on the unhappy events of the summer and fall of 1936 he was not quoted in the minutes of the meeting. Scott was authorized to render the requested assistance.[9]

After May 1936 there were no further joint CCF-LSR meetings. They were unnecessary; the organizations were becoming closely intertwined. Whereas the pattern in the early years had been for some of the parliamentarians to serve on the LSR executive, this was reversing itself by 1936. By invitation and increasingly by right, the LSR's founders were attending meetings of the CCF's national hierarchy. At the same time they continued to draft policy statements for the movement. For example, the important resolution on foreign policy adopted by the 1938 national convention in Edmonton, calling for neutrality legislation of the kind recently adopted in the Union of South Africa, was drafted by Frank Scott and Frank Underhill.

The intertwining of the LSR and CCF coincided with an increasing centralization of control in the national party. When M.J. Coldwell, national secretary from 1934 to 1935, was elected to the House of Commons, it made sense to move the national office to Ottawa in early 1936. For two more years the office was staffed by part-timers. This was less than satisfactory. Eugene Forsey had ample reason in March 1937 to complain about the slapdash work of some CCF officers. Graham Spry, on the CCF provincial executive in Ontario just as Forsey was in Quebec, expressed his annoyance more than once. 'We should organize some inner group,' he wrote to David Lewis in the spring of 1937, '... which submits itself to national order and discipline, so that we have more machinery than just provincial councils which naturally and notoriously take a provincial point of view.' These comments reflected a general sense of weakness in the CCF, a debilitating malaise that improved organization might cure.[10]

Spry and Forsey were sharing their concerns with a highly sympathetic reader and one who was soon able to do something about them. David Lewis was appointed national secretary on a part-time basis in August 1936. Two years later, after the wealthy LSR and CCF member Alan Plaunt had made a confidential guarantee of five thousand dollars per year to the CCF's leaders, Lewis became the movement's first full-time national secretary. The appointment was made in spite of J.S. Woodsworth's initial opposition; he feared that the CCF would become too centralized and lose its spontaneity. But the centralizers were now assuming power: Coldwell, national chairman from the Winnipeg convention in 1937 until 1942, Lewis, and Frank Scott, who joined the national executive in 1938 and succeeded Coldwell as chairman in 1942. 'Continuous, intensive organization work directed firmly and intelligently from the centre' is the movement's greatest need at this time, Lewis told the delegates to the CCF convention in 1938. Writing about the convention in *The Canadian Forum*, Scott fervently agreed with his former student.[11]

Professor Walter Young in his history of the national CCF has amply discussed the key role in the party played by Lewis after 1937. Lewis organized the CCF more effectively, greatly strengthened its ties with organized labour, and completed the shift of control within the party from the West to central Canada. In these developments, especially the first and third of them, his influence reinforced and focused that of the LSR. This is less than surprising. An intellectual, David Lewis was a founding father of the league. He stayed in touch with its leaders while he was reading law at Oxford, rejoined it upon his return from England, and was elected to the national executive in February 1936. Several other LSR stalwarts preceded or followed him in taking positions in the party hierarchy, among them King Gordon, G.M.A. Grube, and, of course, Frank Scott.

Gordon, who in 1936 was national vice-president of the CCF, almost made it into Parliament that year. The constituency of Victoria had become vacant through the death of the incumbent soon after the election, and Gordon was chosen to contest the by-election. He did not rate his chances highly; although he had trailed the Conservative victor by little over one thousand votes in October, he now faced a former Tory provincial premier, Dr Simon Fraser Tolmie. The CCF had a good local organization, however, and the final result was much closer than expected. Tolmie finished a mere ninety votes ahead of Gordon, with the Liberal candidate a close third. Tolmie's death the following year made necessary a further by-election but, Gordon recalls, 'by this time the Liberal surge across the country was in full swell and our Victoria group was shaken by ideological dissension. I ran a bad third, a good three thousand votes behind my Liberal opponent.'[12] It was the third loss in three years; Gordon was not to run again.

Many LSR members became involved in the CCF clubs and in party organization at the local level. Occasionally they were elected to legislative bodies. Thus began a long career in municipal politics for the remedial-speech teacher William Dennison when, in 1937, he was elected to the Board of Education in Toronto. Local CCF work was, in fact, the main reason for the high mortality rate among the small LSR branches. It distracted members of the larger branches, too. 'Last year it was bad enough to have to choose between the meetings of the LSR and of the Garland CCF Club,' one member complained to J.C. Risk, a lawyer who was secretary of the Toronto branch in 1936–37: 'This year, being secretary, I shall have to be at the Garland Club on third Tuesdays. So many members of this club are also LSR originals that the conflict must surely have come to the attention of LSR executives [sic].'[13] When the combined claims on their time came to seem excessive, members tended to mind the CCF's business more than the league's. The practical demands of politics were more pressing than those of research, discussion, and education. This was especially true in the branches outside Toronto and Montreal, for the main work of research and education was done in the two metropolitan centres. Since people who were not at least CCF sympathizers rarely joined the LSR or soon left it again, the drift into the CCF was bound to undermine the independent existence of the league. But in the later 1930s the party clearly needed all the help it could get. That help the LSR gave gladly.

II

George Grube reported to the 1936 convention of the LSR that the organization, thanks to royalties obtained from the sale of *Social Planning for Canada*, was in better financial shape than it had ever been before. This happy fact helped the LSR a few months later to take over *The Canadian Forum*. That periodical had almost become a Depression casualty: the league saved it.

From 1927 to 1934 the *Forum* was owned by the publishing house of J.M. Dent & Sons, which paid its managing editor a small stipend and made good its annual losses. The firm allowed the managing board complete editorial freedom. Since the managing editor in the early 1930s, J.F. White, and his chief collaborator at this time, Frank Underhill, had come to call themselves socialists, this meant that by the autumn of 1932 the *Forum*'s tone was decidedly leftist.

A bit worried that this might affect the operations of his publishing house, Hugh R. Dent expressed his concern to Underhill. The periodical was intended to be a forum for all points of view; it seemed regrettable 'that "The Forum" has published almost entirely the progressive view of politics, and that ... very little if anything has appeared from the opposite side.' Underhill responded that this was unavoidable given the history of the *Forum*, the kind of readership it enjoyed, and its inability to pay contributors. The result was that it 'must appeal for material to writers who write chiefly because they sympathize with the paper and its outlook on life ... Broadly speaking, most of our contributors on the political side are men in academic life, they being the only class in Canada who are interested enough or foolish enough to write articles on public affairs without seeking any pecuniary or political reward.' Of the sort of people who had been writing for the *Forum* since its founding in 1920, not a few were by now highly critical of the status quo.[14]

Satisfied with Underhill's explanation, Hugh Dent extended his firm's financial support for another six months. A further year was then added. However, in order to avoid losses which had become heavier and more burdensome as the Depression deepened, J.M. Dent & Sons disposed of the *Forum* in the late winter of 1934.

The new owner and editor was Steven Cartwright, a young Liberal of progressive views. His tenure was brief; after a year he abandoned the hopeless task of making the *Forum* pay for itself and sold it to Graham Spry for one dollar. 'The Forum has no capital,' Spry informed J.W. Dafoe, 'but, if we can maintain a circulation of over 1000, we can meet our printing costs ... Keeping the publication alive will be a struggle. We have, however, our own printing press, the Stafford Printers.'[15]

Another one of Spry's many ventures, the press was named after Sir Stafford Cripps, who had contributed five pounds in aid of the project. The LSR had put up one hundred dollars, and various individuals had pledged enough money to enable Spry to purchase a second-hand press. *The New Commonwealth* and the *Forum* were the chief customers, but work was also done for the Ontario CCF and for a number of CCF candidates in the Dominion election of 1935. Unfortunately, many of these jobs were never paid for. Cash flow was always a problem, Morden

Lazarus recalls. A recent graduate in pharmacy from the University of Toronto, he became unemployed in 1934. He joined the LSR, met Spry, and was persuaded by him to take charge of Stafford Printers. There he was assisted by his future wife, Margaret Sedgewick, a graduate student in English who was the only one capable of operating the exceedingly balky folding machine. The two did not earn much, but then neither did Spry.[16]

In 1935 Graham Spry restored to the editorial columns of the *Forum* the socialist tone that they had lost the year before. Several of his LSR associates joined the board of contributing editors, among them Humphrey Carver, Eugene Forsey, King Gordon, George Grube, Frank Scott, and Frank Underhill. They worked without pay, as did contributors. But Spry soon found that, in the absence of advertisers, one thousand subscribers could not possibly balance the books. The journal lacked the resources necessary to seek to expand its circulation. It was losing money by the hundreds; only its ability to run up a debt at Stafford Printers kept it going. And that could scarcely last for long.

What was to be done? No one associated with the *Forum* was willing to see it die, least of all the executive of the LSR. No other Canadian publication of its kind was friendly to socialism; it was important that the *Forum* survive and grow. At a meeting of the national executive on 1 May 1936 the decision was made to assume control of the monthly, provided Spry would sell his shares for the dollar he had paid for them and a settlement could be reached with Stafford Printers, the *Forum*'s biggest creditor. Spry agreed; the printer had little choice but to make the best deal it could.[17]

The LSR executive intended to put at least two hundred dollars into the venture, but it could scarcely have acted without the promise of one thousand dollars from Bill McNaught. His conditions were that part of the money be used to pay a business manager, that the LSR control the *Forum* and take responsibility for increasing its circulation, and that Underhill 'continue to write for the magazine and participate in its editorial direction as in the past.' The advertising man attached great importance to the purchase: 'I feel that The Canadian Forum is pre-eminently a publication that should stand for and help propagate LSR ideas, and that both financial and other support for The Forum might very well constitute one of the LSR's major efforts. If this were done, it would be only natural that the LSR should have control of the policies of the paper.' Arrangements were made to pay two hundred dollars to Stafford Printers and to transfer the remainder of the debt to the LSR in the names of George Grube and Frank Scott. As the league was not an incorporated body, the shares of the *Forum* were distributed among members of the national executive and those members and sympathizers who put money into the periodical. Helen Marsh, the national secretary, proudly wrote in a postscript to the minutes of the 1936 national convention: 'The Forum, an excellent monthly to which all LSR members should be subscribers, is now the official organ of the LSR, and as such will consistently express its views.'[18]

For the next half-dozen years the *Forum* was the LSR's chief means of reaching Canadians. Around the enterprise a good deal of the social life of the Toronto branch came to revolve. 'The committee would meet on Sunday evenings at Frank Underhill's home,' one of the contributing editors, Humphrey Carver, remembers: 'Ruth Underhill kept us going with tea and cake and glasses of beer, while Frank's devastating and witty commentary on the current political scene would provide the background for the upcoming issues of the *Forum*.'[19] In addition to the Underhill home on Walmer Road, the McNaught home on Blythwood Road became a popular gathering place for those who worked on the monthly.

Among those who joined it in 1936 were Eleanor Godfrey, a young arts graduate of the University of Toronto, and Mark Farrell, a recent graduate in commerce from the same university. The former put in two terms as managing editor, in 1936–37 and from 1939 on; the latter was the business manager Bill McNaught had insisted on. After qualifying as a chartered accountant in 1937 Farrell served as managing editor until March of 1938. He brought to the *Forum* a financial *savoir faire* which it had never enjoyed before.

The *Forum* needed all of it and more. Of most immediate concern was circulation. It was found that the number of paid subscribers in May 1936 was only 897, the total having 'greatly declined' in the two years since Dent & Sons had sold the magazine. The cash flow was quite inadequate, particularly during the summer when few subscriptions came up for renewal. Very quickly the $1,200 supplied by the LSR and McNaught melted away. By December Mark Farrell told the national secretary: 'The Forum steadily proceeds towards its doom.'[20] Circulation gradually rose during 1937, but in late October of that year the LSR executive had to face four unpleasant facts. The *Forum* was still two hundred short of the fifteen hundred subscribers that McNaught had in 1936 estimated would be necessary in order to break even. Secondly, it had already soaked up two thousand dollars, McNaught's thousand and five hundred each from a Toronto physician, Dr Jacob Markowitz, and from the LSR itself. Thirdly, it owed seven hundred dollars to Stafford Printers, which could not handle another issue without getting at least some money on account. Finally, the *Forum* was quite, quite broke, with no hope of financial relief in sight.

What now? There was only $150 in the LSR treasury, the national president, Leonard Marsh, reported to Frank Underhill. Either a special appeal must be made to members and readers, or the *Forum* would perish. Perhaps it should be allowed to die, the historian replied: 'In all the years I have been connected with it I have never seen any scheme for boosting its circulation which really worked ... We might last till sometime in the spring with a little help, and then there will be another crisis. The LSR doesn't seem likely to have enough financial resources to keep the Forum going out of its own ordinary revenue, and unless a sugar daddy is lurking in Montreal there doesn't seem much hope for us.'[21] Most members of the executive recoiled from this view. With $250 obtained from the Montreal and $150 from the Toronto branch, and with the money from Christmas renewals, the *Forum* limped through the winter. Switching the printing contract from Stafford Printers to a still cheaper shop also helped, though it gravely injured Stafford Printers. Then in March 1938 came reorganization and a bright new idea, the Canadian Forum Sustaining Fund.

The idea seems to have been Eric Havelock's. The classicist was an unlikely financial wizard, but in March he became the *Forum*'s treasurer and set up the Sustaining Fund. Its purpose was to obtain, primarily from subscribers, modest sums of money that together would cover the deficits so long as they might persist. Havelock chaired the fund; Lou Morris, bibliophile and the journal's new circulation manager, was its treasurer. The other members were McNaught, Dr Markowitz, and D.V. LePan, a young teacher of English at University College. Meanwhile, George Grube replaced Mark Farrell as managing editor, thereby saving the cost of his meagre stipend.

The new arrangement saved the *Forum*. An average of $850 a year was collected during the fund's first four years. Losses during this period averaged slightly more than one thousand dollars annually, but at least twice Alan Plaunt made up the difference.[22] From the spring of 1938 on the *Forum*'s finances gradually became less worrisome, while its circulation kept growing.

After the middle of 1935, when Graham Spry bought the *Forum* from Steven Cartwright, its pages offered members of the LSR more opportunity than ever before to publish their views. Especially frequent were the contributions of Frank Underhill, but the names of Eugene Forsey, G.M.A. Grube, and Frank Scott also appeared often. The *Forum* concentrated on current affairs. Its columns contained the LSR's assessment of the politics of the later 1930s, of the early efforts of the Congress of Industrial Organizations (CIO) in Canada, of the Padlock Act and the increase in the appropriations for defence, of the Abyssinian crisis, the Spanish Civil War, the Munich agreement, and the seemingly inexorable approach of general war in Europe, and of a whole range of other matters, domestic and international. The monthly also continued the coverage of the arts and literature that had distinguished it from the start. It was fortunate in 1937 to obtain Earle Birney, the poet and teacher of English, as literary editor and to have Pegi Nicol's advice on art. The book-review section, the responsibility alternatively of Grube and Underhill, was lively and attracted the contributions of many of Canada's leading intellectuals.

The country was recovering fitfully from the Depression; the *Forum* recovered with it. Probably no contribution sums up this period better than the architect Humphrey Carver's wistful piece in April 1937 marking the resumption of construction on what was to become the Park Plaza Hotel in Toronto. For seven years a skeleton had stood on the northwest corner of Avenue Road and Bloor Street. 'For seven lonely years the starveling skyscraper stuck itself up like a scarecrow in the heart of the metropolis, an awful reminder of the anti-climax to a period of reckless ambition.' In 1937 it was being completed at last.

III

Even as the first copies of *Social Planning for Canada* were reaching the bookstores, S.B. Watson of Thomas Nelson & Sons, the publishers, saw the need for a cheaper, abridged version. Within the year Eugene Forsey, Leonard Marsh, and Frank Scott were at work on one. Other projects in the mid- and late 1930s included the financing of the publication of *Jungle Tales Retold*, prepared by Grace MacInnis and her brother, Charles Woodsworth. This pamphlet was based on material from the report of the Royal Commission on Price Spreads. The LSR also reprinted two thousand copies of a pamphlet, *Co-operative Buying Clubs*, that had been first produced by the Extension Department of St Francis Xavier University in Antigonish, NS, a pioneer in the co-operative movement. The league itself produced a mimeographed pamphlet with the title 'So You're Going To Study Co-operation.' At the 1937 national convention the secretary reported a brisk demand for these pamphlets, 'due to the widespread interest in consumer's co-operation.'[23]

That interest resulted the following year in a book written by George Mooney, *Co-operatives Today and Tomorrow: A Canadian Survey*. The LSR had collaborated in this project: Frank Aykroyd, Leonard Marsh, Frank Scott, and R.B.Y. Scott were members of the survey committee that sponsored it, and Marsh assisted with the volume. In the later 1930s Frank Scott, national president from 1935 to 1937, and Marsh, who served in the same capacity from 1937 to 1939, were ubiquitous. George Mooney was very busy himself: formerly with the YMCA, he was by 1938 executive director of the Canadian Federation of Mayors and Municipalities. His book examined sympathetically the growth and practices of consumers' and producers' co-operatives in Europe and North America and concluded with the rhetorical question: 'Is it too much to say that the practice of Co-operation provides us with a yardstick by which to measure the quality of our civilization?'[24]

Two pamphlets by Eugene Forsey saw the light in 1937. *Does Canada Need Immigrants?* asked the first. Not at present, whatever the Big Business proponents of immigration might say, was the answer. In response to the question posed in the title of the second pamphlet, *Recovery – for Whom?*, Forsey wrote that 'the capitalist class is getting the lion's share of the new "prosperity."' A third pamphlet, *Guide to LSR Activities*, was prepared by Helen Marsh for the guidance of branch executives and the information of new members.

These three pamphlets fell far short of the twelve asked for by the national convention of 1937. Given the demands on the time of many LSR members, however, the group's written output was impressive. Virtually everyone had a full-time job; then there were speaking engagements, working on the *Forum* or for the CCF, participating in other organizations, and so on, To read the 1930s scrapbooks of Leonard Marsh, for example, is a humbling experience. He served as an adviser to the Canadian Federation of Mayors and Municipalities and the Dominion Bureau of Statistics, presented briefs to various bodies such as the National Employment Commission chaired by Arthur B. Purvis and the Royal Commission on Dominion-Provincial Relations, conducted a 'social interpretation tour,' which in July and August of 1936 took its participants through Denmark, Sweden, Finland, and the Soviet Union, and was actively involved in adult education through the YMCA, the McGill Department of Extension, the Workers' Educational Association of Canada, and, later, the Canadian Association for Adult Education. He was an indefatigable public lecturer. All this was on top of his teaching and his work as director of Social Research at McGill University. In addition he co-authored the two books of the LSR while publishing two substantial books in his own right, including the magisterial *Canadians In and Out of Work* (1940), and collaborating on a third. Everything was done without the benefit of a sabbatical year, then still an uncommon phenomenon in the Canadian university. It was a full life, and yet it was not atypical.

What this sort of work load meant from week to week is perhaps hard to imagine. Whether their interests were widely dispersed or narrowly focused, the leaders of the LSR were forever short of time. Highly illuminating is a letter written by Eugene Forsey in 1937 in response to some gentle criticism from a student at Mt Allison University of the league's failure to reach beyond the intelligentsia to the working class. We are doing our best, but both money and people are in short supply, Forsey replied:

> At present, most of the burden falls on the shoulders of an incredibly few. I shall cite my own case, not because it's unique, or because I've done more than others, but because I know most about it. During all of last fall, winter and spring, I had from thirteen to sixteen hours a week of university lecturing (and as you doubtless know, one lecture may mean hours of preparation). I had fortnightly meetings of the National Executive of the LSR, fortnightly meetings (or more) of the provincial council of the CCF, (of which I am president), two or three speeches a week at the least, frequent meetings of the Civil Liberties Committee (of which, during most of the time, I was chairman), occasional meetings of the Spanish Aid Committee, an average of five letters a day at least (quite apart from my personal corre-

spondence), two press statements for the CCF to help draft, two meetings of the CCF National Council to attend, a CCF pamphlet to help draft, the National Conventions of the LSR and FCSO to attend (a dinner speech at one of them), memoranda on the 'defence' estimates for nine organizations, a chapter of a new LSR book (done over a week-end – 5,000 words – in the midst of all these other things), a good deal of editing work on this book with Frank Scott, an average of 5,000 words a month for the Forum, and telephone calls galore on every conceivable and inconceivable subject ... (I did nearly all of these things simply because if I hadn't, they wouldn't have got done, or not at the right time.) This is all I can remember at the moment, but it is by no means all I had to turn my hand to. Obviously no reasonable person can expect first class propaganda from this sort of background.[25]

Even when allowance is made for some pardonable exaggeration, it appears that Forsey's working week must have run to seventy hours at the very least.

Members who were active in the Toronto branch were likely, too, to be working hard on the *Forum*. Frank Underhill, for one, often contributed four or more editorials and articles and as many book reviews to a single issue. Frank Scott was at this time writing a book for the Canadian Institute of International Affairs; it appeared under the title *Canada Today* in 1938. Simultaneously he was working with Marsh and Forsey on the new LSR book. It is said that busy people waste no time.

Democracy Needs Socialism was published by Thomas Nelson & Sons in February 1938. At 150 pages and $1.25 it was expected to have a wider appeal than the longer and costlier volume from which it was derived. But the new work was no mere abridgment. Unlike *Social Planning for Canada*, it devoted a meaty chapter to the question of women's rights. It also tried to come to terms with three developments that had become much clearer since its predecessor had been sent to the publishers: the economic recovery, the challenge of fascism to democratic and parliamentary institutions, and the continued drift towards a major war. 'The world depression is over,' the preface to the new book begins: 'Recovery – an insecure and patchy recovery – has arrived. Capitalism has been given a temporary reprieve by the trade cycle.' But for many Canadians the Depression is not over, and 'we are headed straight for another and worse economic crisis at this very moment, more surely even than we are headed for war.' The preface was written in the late summer or early autumn of 1937; by the time the volume appeared the economy had already taken a turn for the worse. Ironically – the irony had been foreseen in *Social Planning for Canada* – it was the war that brought recovery and full employment at last.

An increased concern with fascism was due in part to the growing strength of Nazi Germany and the Italian invasion of Abyssinia; however, it owed rather more to the Spanish Civil War. In the summer of 1936 elements of the Spanish Army, led by General Francisco Franco and widely regarded as fascist, challenged the republic. Of all the conflicts of the 1930s none more fully captured the imagination of leftists around the world and in Canada. 'Every socialist, every liberal, we would almost say every man of any decent feeling, can only hope that the government will prevail,' stated an editorial in *The Canadian Forum*. Graham Spry soon established the Spanish Medical Aid Committee; its chief accomplishment was to finance the passage of Dr Norman Bethune to Spain, where he formed the Canadian Blood Transfusion Service. Spry's committee and a similar one in Montreal, in which several LSR people were active, were not long afterwards merged into the Committee To Aid Spanish Democracy. Although this organization came to be controlled by Communists, it enjoyed the active support of many other Canadians. Among them were Dr Salem Bland, honorary chairman of the committee, Spry, who was one of its vice-chairmen, and S.B. Watson, who sat on its executive council.[26]

Canadian and especially Quebec reaction to the civil war alerted the LSR to the potential dangers of fascism in this country. French Canadians very largely favoured the insurgents. The republic was regarded, not without reason, as hostile to the interests of the Church; that was enough to condemn it. Friends of the republic were deeply distressed when a meeting in Montreal planned for 23 October 1936, at which representatives of the Spanish government were scheduled to speak, was cancelled by municipal order. There had been Roman Catholic protest against the meeting, and students at the University of Montreal had threatened to break it up. Fearing a disturbance, and scarcely well-disposed to the cause of the republic, the executive committee of Montreal gave orders to prevent the meeting from taking place.

The Montreal branch of the LSR, which had co-sponsored the meeting, took the cancellation badly. Frank Aykroyd, the local president, roused the membership. Eugene Forsey's reaction was not atypical; he interpreted the incident to David Lewis as part of a growing body of evidence that fascism was a threat at home as well as abroad. Frank Scott, in advising J.S. Woodsworth early in 1937 on the recently introduced Foreign Enlistment Act, described it as a concession to 'the Quebec fascist crowd.' By seeming to be neutral, the Canadian government implicitly recognized the rebels as belligerents 'of equal moral standing with the people's elected representatives.' Scott later helped Lewis draft a resolution on Spain for the 1937 national convention of the CCF. It expressed support for the republic and criticized the Western democracies, Canada among them, for their ambiguous attitude towards the combatants.[27]

Misgivings about Quebec attitudes were strengthened by the warm cordiality that was seen to exist between the Roman Catholic hierarchy and the new government of Maurice Duplessis, whose Conservative-dominated Union Nationale in

1936 ended forty years of Liberal rule in Quebec. Both the hierarchy and the business community were hostile to the CIO, the militant labour organization that started to show itself in Canada during 1936; LSR eyes early discerned the same hostility in the Union Nationale. The Padlock Act nevertheless came as a nasty surprise. 'Just see Mr. Duplessis' St. Patrick's Day present to us,' an outraged Eugene Forsey wrote to Graham Spry: '... Obviously the bill as it stands may if it goes through (and I fear it's certain to), mean a reign of terror for anyone the hierarchy and Duplessis don't like.' Forsey suspected that the act was part of a wider attack, also involving Ontario's Mitchell Hepburn, on the CIO.[28]

The organization drive of the CIO in the early months of 1937 rivalled the Spanish Civil War in the imagination of Canadian radicals. 'Whatever its crudities, the CIO is the most hopeful phenomenon that has appeared on this continent for many years,' Frank Underhill asserted at the Couchiching conference that August. In March the LSR national convention had expressed sympathy for the sit-down strikers at the Holmes Foundry in Sarnia, Ontario, and demanded a public inquiry into the beating they had received at the hands of an angry mob. Several leading LSR members gave active support to the striking workers at the General Motors plant in Oshawa: George Grube and Eric Havelock addressed a mass meeting of strikers. During this strike Premier Hepburn's loathing for the CIO became abundantly clear; was he in collusion with Premier Duplessis in an attempt to crush the new industrial unions? The LSR feared the worst.[29]

Several LSR members therefore joined in the founding in April 1937 of a Civil Liberties Committee, which became the Canadian Civil Liberties Union (CCLU). Convinced that the Padlock Act was an unconstitutional invasion by Quebec of the field of criminal law, the LSR executive decided to petition the Dominion government either to disallow the act or to refer it to the Supreme Court for an opinion. Eugene Forsey and another LSR member, Hubert Desaulniers, also helped draft the CCLU's petition. But the minister of Justice, Ernest Lapointe, declined to adopt either of the courses proposed to him. He was unconvinced that the act invaded the federal jurisdiction and advised those who felt injured by it to trust to the courts. Writing in the *Forum*, Forsey denounced this as 'political cowardice': Ottawa was evidently afraid to offend Quebec.[30]

Especially in Quebec the political weather was inclement. Frank Scott argued to David Lewis that the best policy for the Quebec CCF would be to form a 'united front,' not with the Communists but 'with the nascent liberal group' in order 'to stop corporatism and fascism.' For an unsigned article that appeared in the prestigious American journal *Foreign Affairs* Scott chose the title 'Embryo Fascism in Quebec.' The National Social Christian Party of Adrien Arcand seemed only the most extreme manifestation of a general trend to right-wing authoritarianism.[31]

Canadian fears were further fed by British and Amercan writers. British radicals of the kind associated with the Left Book Club worried in the later 1930s about the possibility of a domestic form of fascism.[32] The alarmist novel by Sinclair Lewis, *It Can't Happen Here* (1935), which purported to show that a fascist take-over could happen in the United States, found its way into the footnotes of the second LSR book.

The authors of *Democracy Needs Socialism* describe fascism as one of four 'blind alleys,' each promising at its entrance 'that we can solve our economic problems within the framework of capitalism.' The other three traps are liberalism, reformist conservatism, and Social Credit. But liberalism in Canada, wedded to business interests, has become conservative. Reformist conservatism in the manner of H.H. Stevens, R.B. Bennett, and Bennett's brother-in-law, W.D. Herridge – he provided the immediate inspiration for much of the 'Bennett New Deal' – speaks of a controlled capitalism, which meant, to the LSR, that 'the state controls the economic system, but capitalism controls the state.' Social Credit promises 'the simplicity and apparent mathematical exactness of "A + B"' and more money to everyone. It is quite out of touch with economic reality.[33]

Fascism is identified in *Democracy Needs Socialism* as a form of 'controlled capitalism.' But it is more than that. The present era is one of widespread poverty and distress experienced by people who have been educated to expect better. Their general dissatisfaction 'is the cause of all the "isms."' Fear of that dissatisfaction may lead the ruling class to suppress democracy. However, 'the threat to democracy comes even through democracy itself.' Desperately looking for relief from defeat, humiliation, and economic distress, a large part of the German people 'accepted the Nazi party as the means of salvation and Adolf Hitler as their saviour.' Fearful and unsophisticated people are prone to respond to chauvinistic slogans: 'It is a matter of serious concern to remember that fascism depends for its strength not only on the character of the dictator and the military support he can muster, but on at least the temporary support of a large section of the people.' Fascism's popularity in Europe was initially aided by its apparent radicalism but even more by its xenophobia. Of these two, the radicalism has proved to be a sham.

> Once fascism establishes itself, it is quite apparent that it stands for the fusion of the economic power and the political power in the capitalist state, accompanied by the suppression of all the rights usually enjoyed by a free citizen. In Italy and Germany trade unions, co-operatives, and other workers' organizations have disappeared, press censorship is complete, military organization dominates the national scene. In one respect at least fascism fulfils its promise. It promises to destroy democracy, and it does.[34]

To its neighbours the fascist state is often a menace; it is even more so to ethnic minorities within, especially to Jews.

The corporatism, racial nationalism, anti-Semitism, and strident anti-communism of French-speaking Quebec invite comparison with Europe: 'Civil liberties and the rights of labour are the principal elements of democracy which have gone down to the dust under fascism. There is good reason for being apprehensive ... at the developments in Quebec.' In the rest of Canada, too, lovers of democracy need to be vigilant. Above all, the failure of the would-be saviours of capitalism to alleviate the poverty and insecurity of a large part of the people makes more urgent the need for social reconstruction. Recovery is benefiting the holders of securities rather than the farmers and workers. Only socialism can change this. 'Socialism is the democratic *alternative* to revolution, and to the reactionary dictatorship which futile attempts at unorganized revolt would surely bring to pass.'[35] Socialism will checkmate capitalism and fascism.

By this time the LSR had none of its hesitation of five years earlier about using the term *socialism*. It was still circumspect when referring to the CCF, however. After reading a draft chapter of *Democracy Needs Socialism* the vice-president, Joe Parkinson, objected to statements as to what the CCF would do upon coming to office. 'This ... is unwise,' he wrote to the national secretary for 1937–38, C.M. Lapointe, 'because (a) we cannot speak for the CCF, and (b) we are not officially affiliated with the CCF and write only as socialists ... I may say that Underhill, Havelock and Grube agree with me on this.' Out came the offending passages. A postscript to the book states that, although many league members are active in the CCF, the LSR is not affiliated with any party, and 'membership in the LSR is open to all. Individual members of every political party will find the educational work of the League helpful and stimulating on all national issues.' The league was trying to work both sides of the street. In sending David Lewis a copy of the new volume C.M. Lapointe wrote: 'The LSR hopes that the CCF movement will find this book a useful implement in socialist education.'[36] This sentiment was heartfelt.

IV

It was difficult in the later 1930s for LSR members to take much solace from the present. Frank Scott, although he remained hopeful about the future, posited to David Lewis in July 1937 that 'the CCF is far too far left for most Canadians.' In fact, the interest in socialist proposals, never great, was waning. The reasons for this are far from clear, but it was reflected in the sense of weakness that pervaded the CCF. King Gordon, writing to Scott about the 1937 convention of the party, commented on 'obvious symptoms of decline.' Two months later, appalled by the disarray in the Ontario CCF just before the provincial election, he wrote: 'I shall be glad when it is all over and only hope that we have a plausible post-mortem verdict prepared in advance. The bald statistics are going to look sorry enough.' He was right. With candidates in thirty-nine out of ninety constituencies, the CCF received only 5.3 per cent of the popular vote. Its only sitting member, Sam Lawrence in Hamilton East, went down to defeat: indeed, no CCF candidate even came second.[37]

The crushing defeat of the Ontario CCF was only the most disconcerting in a series of setbacks. Early in 1936 James Simpson lost his bid for re-election as mayor of Toronto. In 1937 the CCF in British Columbia ceased to be the official Opposition. The Saskatchewan CCF did manage to retain that status in the provincial election of 1938, but the following year the remnants of the United Farmers of Alberta pulled out of the CCF. Only in isolated pockets, notably in Winnipeg and Vancouver, did the party have much working-class support. East of the Ottawa River the CCF scarcely existed, except in Montreal and the Cape Breton peninsula.

LSR members tended to take the disappointments of the CCF personally. They could, after all, be taken as evidence that the league was not performing its task of education. There was no sign, moreover, that either of the traditional parties was adopting LSR ideas. Some members came to believe, no doubt, that there was something wrong with the LSR's analysis of Canadian society or its approach to social and economic change. Such people often dropped out, their interest and enthusiasm exhausted or redirected. After 1935 it was increasingly less likely that their places would be filled by new recruits.

This raised the danger of cliquishness. As early as 1936 a member of the Toronto executive, J.C. Risk, worried that the LSR would 'develop into a polite debating society, for the intellectual entertainment of a small number of thoroughly converted members.' It was admittedly congenial regularly to meet others who shared one's convictions or outrage, but what difference did this make if the LSR as a whole was losing strength? The national secretary tried to paint a cheerful picture at the 1937 national convention, but she could not disguise that only five branches, Montreal, Toronto, St Catharines, London, and Dauphin, were still active. Still, she found no cause for self-recrimination as she viewed the year just past. The LSR had been active in a multitude of ways; it had also entertained Walter Nash, the minister of Finance from New Zealand, when he visited Canada. A valuable contact with the social-democratic movement in the Antipodes had thus been made, and literature was now being received. A number of French socialist pamphlets had been received from Paris, moreover; these were being examined with a view to their usefulness in Quebec.[38]

The convention expressed its confidence in the future by instructing the national executive to prepare a revision of the leaflet containing the manifesto, 'including changes in the manifesto if thought advisable.' What began as minor surgery quickly became a major operation. The ten clauses of the existing document were transformed in a new draft into eight 'essential first steps' and ten 'more ultimate steps in the creation of a socialized society.' The eight first steps were reforms, methods of coping with pressing problems within the context of an economy still capitalist. The first two clauses dealt with the needs of workers for union recognition and certain kinds of welfare legislation; further clauses referred to the constitution, foreign policy, immigration, taxation, research policy, and health and medical care.

Among the ten 'more ultimate steps' were the creation of the National Planning Commission, the socialization of banking, insurance, and investment, the public ownership of utilities and industries in or approaching a condition of monopoly, the development of co-operatives, and the establishment of import and export boards. New were clauses dealing with public control of agriculture, the public ownership of resource industries, penal reform, student aid, and 'equality of political, social and economic rights for all persons irrespective of race, colour, sex or creed.'

In distinguishing between measures of reform and measures of socialism the new document varied from the undifferentiated approach of the 1932 manifesto. It differed also in more freely using the terms *socialized* and *socialization* and even, once, the weighty word *socialist*. The stress on a number of immediate steps was 'practical politics,' comments Professor Leonard Marsh – he was national president at the time: 'Doctrinaire goals which do not spell out first steps are not much use.'[39] The goals were not inherent in those steps, however. At least some of the reforms proposed by the LSR have been introduced by the federal government and various provincial governments during the past forty years without bringing Canada conspicuously closer to being a co-operative commonwealth. Bits and pieces of social legislation may, indeed, forestall demands for more basic changes.

Perhaps this is why the draft manifesto was rejected. The minutes of the 1938 national convention were never distributed, and no record of it survives. The arguments for and against the draft have very largely escaped from the memories of those who attended the meeting. It is known that the convention referred the fate of the document to the executive. The following year 'it was reported that the Executive had decided to retain the original form.'[40] Neither a justification nor an explanation is available.

The weakness of social democracy in the later 1930s can easily be expressed in electoral terms. Of more immediate relevance to the LSR was the departure from Canada in 1937 of two of its most valuable members, King Gordon and Graham Spry. After losing the Victoria by-election of 1937 Gordon was called to New York in order to help edit the autobiography of his recently deceased father. He then decided to accept the offer of an editorial position with the firm that was publishing the book. A few years later he became managing editor of *The Nation*, one of the foremost left-wing weeklies in the United States. In him the LSR, CCF, and FCSO had lost an indefatigable worker.

Another such was lost when Graham Spry went. The immediate occasion for his leaving was a quarrel in the Ontario CCF, which resulted in Spry's failure to gain re-election as chairman. Blunt and outspoken, he had annoyed too many people with his complaints about the organizational weakness of the movement and its chronic shortage of funds. He expected much of his co-workers, perhaps too much. But Spry, who had since early 1933 devoted his entire life to the cause of Canadian socialism, had for some time been plagued by second thoughts. He was growing tired of his hand-to-mouth existence. Until March 1936 he had been largely dependent on what could be raised by the LSR on his behalf, and that was never more than six hundred dollars a year, as a fund-raising letter sent out early in 1936 made clear. *The New Commonwealth* could not support him, and the Ontario CCF, to which he looked for funds in 1936–37, was impecunious. Writing to David Lewis in the spring of 1937 about labour organization in Ontario – 'everywhere the CCF is almost totally ineffective' – an exasperated Spry added: 'It looks as if inevitably I would have to drop out. I simply cannot carry on any longer; every cent I manage to scrape up goes into the CCF – for the radio, the New Comm[onwealth], the Stafford Printers – and I am up against it ... Margaret Sedgewick feels as I do – as long as we are ready to go on like this, nothing will be done to correct the situation.'[41]

In early June he quit. He intended to take a holiday, he informed his parents: 'I will then look about me for the largest salary I can find.' He did not like doing this, but 'as long as I am ready to sacrifice myself ... the CCF will allow me to do so and do nothing to maintain me.' He was rapidly approaching forty years of age and he was in love: it was time to look to his own future. Nothing being open to him in Canada – he was told his socialism counted heavily against him – he left for New York and then for London, where he took an executive position with an oil company. Irene Biss followed him in 1938; the two were married in June.[42]

Good people were leaving. The LSR was still attracting new members, however. In 1937–38, for example, two relative newcomers were convening study groups in the Toronto branch. C. Brough Macpherson, who had recently joined the Department of Political Economy at the university, led a group in examining 'The Fundamentals of Socialism.' W. Jarvis McCurdy of the Department of Philosophy led another group in studying a book by members of the FCSO, *Towards the Christian Revolution*. Monthly branch meetings continued to draw a hundred or more, and social gatherings were as popular as ever. The Montreal branch continued to be similarly active, with monthly meetings, parties, and occasionally a special event. Late in 1938 the British socialist scholar Harold Laski, with whom Frank Scott was acquainted, spoke about the 'Prospects of Democracy' to an LSR-sponsored meeting. Usually the branches found their speakers closer to home.

As a result of the efforts of J.S. Woodsworth the branch in Winnipeg was revived in 1937; the following year it published a booklet. *Pioneers in Poverty* described the hardships suffered by western farmers during the preceding eight years. Winnipeg was not the only branch to become active for a second time. The London branch had before the 1937 national convention disaffiliated itself because it was thought the capitation fees exacted by the national office could be better spent at home. Nine months later one man managed to persuade a majority of the branch members that they should instead affiliate with the Canadian League against War and Fascism. This split the branch. Several thought the move a great mistake: led by E.O. Hall, high-school teacher and CCF candidate, and R.E.K. Pemberton, a classicist at the University of Western Ontario, they managed to disband the branch. A short hiatus followed. Then, early in 1938, the branch was re-established without the main champion of the united front. Affiliation with the national office was secured, and a full program was planned for 1938–39. The branch had only fifteen members, however.[43] It remained to be seen how long it and the other small branches, at Dauphin, St Catharines, and Winnipeg, could maintain themselves in the face of other claims on their members' time.

The year 1938 was the last full year of peace. For the LSR it was a tolerably good year. Its branches were now few, and membership had dropped to around four hundred. However, the word was still being spread. The league's submission to the Royal Commission on Dominion-Provincial Relations had been well-received and had been published as a pamphlet. With the Sustaining Fund now attracting funds the *Forum*'s future looked unexpectedly bright. *Democracy Needs Socialism* was selling at a modest but satisfactory rate. Over all this activity, however, loured the thunderclouds of war. The storm broke in September 1939. Long before it ended the LSR would become one of its many casualties.

8

Peace or war?

Wars and rumours of war disfigured the 1930s. Not long after the beginning of the decade Japan invaded Manchuria; not long before it ended, the second major war in a quarter century broke out in Europe.

What the LSR had to say about Canada's external relations was powerfully influenced by the ever-present spectre of war, which reinforced the ghosts of the Great War. Approximately sixty thousand young Canadians had died in 1914–18, most of them in the fields of Flanders and northern France. There was a strong desire to prevent that from ever happening again, a desire, too, to avoid a recurrence of the quarrel over conscription and the expense and economic disruption that attended war. These desires eventually led most members of the LSR, like many other Canadians, to seek Canada's salvation in neutrality and North American isolation. But this search, understandable as it was and is, mistook two ineluctable realities. The first was that of the relations and confrontations of power in an interdependent world. The second and more immediately decisive was that of English Canadian sentiment towards Great Britain and the Empire–Commonwealth.

The LSR was opposed to imperialism. Its leading spokesmen inveighed against the economic, political, and cultural dominance of an imperial metropolis over its dependencies, the more so because imperialism in the modern era was held to be prompted by the capitalists' need for natural resources and captive markets for their products. The LSR also deplored what was believed to be the lingering constitutional subordination of Canada to Britain.

As a result of the First World War and the policies followed by the government of Sir Robert Borden, Canada had become a signatory at Versailles and a member of the League of Nations. Subsequently the process of defining the status of the dominions had resulted in 1931 in the Statute of Westminster. This did not, however, settle to everyone's satisfaction the precise nature of Canada's relationship to Great Britain and the Empire, particularly when and if Britain should go to war. Did the statute in that case guarantee the Dominion's right to neutrality?

Few Canadians were much interested in the debate that centred on this question. Whatever they personally thought about war, most no doubt assumed that, as in 1914, should Britain be at war, Canada would be too. Certainly many English Canadians still identified Canada's international interests and stature with that of the Empire–Commonwealth. Few French Canadians did so; however, for them it was the path of realism to recognize that, in a crisis, the English-speaking majority would have its way. Indeed, this recognition fed nationalist sentiment in Quebec.

To the LSR, there was all too much evidence of a colonialist sentiment that had survived from pre-war days. Worried about the threat of war and convinced that the Statute of Westminster did not assure Canada's right to neutrality, the league's spokesmen demanded that Canadian sovereignty in world affairs be unequivocally affirmed by Ottawa and secured by legislation. This was, in effect, a demand that there be a formal breach of the British connection.

It suited governments to ignore this demand. The Conservatives felt strongly tied to Britain; and though some Liberals shared the LSR's frame of mind, William Lyon Mackenzie King knew that the British connection was too strong to be broken. Nor did he wish to be responsible for breaking it. If Britain should be attacked by a European foe, Canada would stand by Britain's side. In King's view there was nothing to be gained and probably much to be lost, especially in Quebec, by clarifying the issues or by asserting a theoretical right to neutrality. This could only lead to quarrels between French and English Canadians and impair a precarious national unity, to say nothing of the unity of the federal Liberal party.[1]

The anti-imperalism of the LSR had both English and Canadian antecedents. J.A. Hobson's classic *Imperialism* was well known. Goldwin Smith, the English-born man of letters who favoured Canadian separation from the Empire and in 1891 predicted Canada's union with the United States, was one of Frank Underhill's intellectual heroes. So was John S. Ewart, the Ottawa lawyer whose *Kingdom Papers* and *Independence Papers* made the case for Canadian sovereignty. In 1932 Underhill told the older man: 'I have been spending some of my time ... reading over your earlier pre-war series and have been very much struck with the acuteness of your analysis and the prophetic insight which it is clear now that you displayed. I had never realized before just how completely we have been working out all the ideas which you were expounding twenty years ago.' Even allowing for the demands of courtesy there is no question that Underhill meant this.[2]

Among those influenced by Ewart was John Wesley Dafoe, the editor of the *Manitoba* (later *Winnipeg*) *Free Press*. Graham Spry had worked for his newspaper in the early 1920s and in 1932 described himself as 'a disciple formed politically by the policies of the *Free Press*.' Escott Reid corresponded with Dafoe about international relations; Dafoe was a founder of the Canadian Institute of International Affairs, for which Reid worked as national secretary from 1932 to 1939. Underhill, like Reid and Spry, admired Dafoe's commitment to Canadian independence, although eventually they all became critical of his attachment to the League of Nations.[3]

Professor Douglas Cole points out that J.S. Ewart is 'particularly helpful' in allowing us to understand the term *nationalism* as it was used by Canadian 'constitutionalists' before the Second World War. Ewart, and the LSR after him, saw the Canadian nation as a constitutionally and politically but not ethnically or linguistically circumscribed entity that ought to take its place among the sovereign nations of the world. By doing so Canada would complete that movement towards full self-government that had begun in the 1830s.[4]

J.S. Woodsworth was as convinced an independentist as any; his influence on the LSR was, of course, considerable. He was also a pacifist. At least one of the leading figures in the LSR, G.M.A. Grube, shared his conviction. Grube had performed military service during the war; so had Underhill and Carlton McNaught. At least one of them carried from the experience a near-obsession. 'The stupidity of GHQ and the terrible sacrifice of so many of the best men among my contemporaries sickened me for good of a society, national or international, run by the British governing classes,' Underhill wrote many years later.[5] That all those Canadians had died ultimately to no very good purpose was a view that many other members of the LSR shared. The wish to avoid another war or, at least, Canadian involvement in it grew steadily after 1933, the year of the Nazi seizure of power in Germany and the failure of the World Disarmament Conference at Geneva.

Initially the LSR took an internationalist position. Its manifesto called for 'a foreign policy designed to obtain international economic cooperation and to promote disarmament and world peace.' Escott Reid asserted in a piece drafted in 1933 (for the book that eventually became *Social Planning for Canada*) that 'the true internationalist must be a socialist, just as the true socialist must be an internationalist.' Only socialist governments can effectively pursue the search for peace, he argued. The economic rivalry among capitalists of different countries, each group aided by its government, inevitably produces war. In its current form, therefore, the League of Nations as a league of capitalist powers is imperfect. Nevertheless, even a socialist government in Canada ought to support it: 'It [is] our only hope for maintaining peace long enough for socialist governments to be established in the majority of the countries of the world.'

Support ought not to extend to participation in military sanctions against aggressors, however. Nor should Canada's membership in the British Commonwealth be allowed to drag us into a war overseas. 'To the establishment of [the] world society Canada can contribute, in the first place by setting her own house in order, that is by establishing a planned economy in Canada; and secondly, by accepting control by the world society of many matters which are now considered to be of purely domestic concern, such as tariffs, immigration and raw materials.' Even this was too ambitious for some of Reid's friends on the editorial board. Three told him that it would be unwise to cede control over Canadian resources, trade, and immigration to foreign, capitalist-dominated governments. National economic planning was the main goal to which Canadian socialists could aspire at this time.[6]

Scepticism about the limits of the possible in the dog-eat-dog world of capitalism is manifest in *Social Planning*'s discussion of international trade. In principle the authors favour the removal of tariff protection:

> The principle of non-discrimination is, of course, very far from being the whole socialist policy for foreign trade. Indeed it is no more essentially a socialist principle than is cleanliness. An intelligent socialist community will practise both as a matter of course, as indispensable conditions of progress. But just as capitalism may make cleanliness practically unattainable for many people, so it may lead to the adoption of foreign trade policies which, from the point of view of the community, are foolish to the verge of incredibility.

Canada must trade; economic nationalism is therefore folly. Why make expensively at home what can be bought cheaply abroad, especially when the latter will encourage other nations to buy our goods? The reply that protection provides jobs is unconvincing. Too often those jobs are badly paid and do not, on balance, compensate for the injury done to Canadian consumers. For example, 'in the woollen cloth industry ... salaries and wages of 3,900 employees in 1930 amounted to $3,400,000. Professor [K.W.] Taylor of McMaster University estimates that "the total excess cost to Canadian consumers (calculated at manufacturers' or import prices) of their supply of woollen cloth was at least $7,000,000 or more than double the amount of all salaries and wages."' The average annual income of workers in this industry was $870, well below the poverty line for all but single people.[7]

And yet, *Social Planning* conceded, in the short run there may be sound reasons for developing certain branches of production beyond the point indicated by the principle of non-discrimination. This would be part of a policy of '*effective control* in the interests of the community'; it is to be pursued until that time when a socialist world order makes effective international control possible. Before then, a non-discriminating Canada will simply find itself a sheep among protectionist wolves. Economic nationalism may be folly, but, like all folly, it will not be easy to overcome.

The chapter on foreign policy in *Social Planning for Canada* was largely Frank

Underhill's work, but it must have expressed the view of most LSR members at mid-decade. According to it, Canadian membership in the British Commonwealth offered the greater likelihood of entanglement in war, our membership in the League of Nations the lesser. A thumbnail history of Canada's relations with Britain casts Sir Wilfrid Laurier as the nationalist hero who nevertheless 'was not able to keep out of imperialist entanglements altogether.' Against his will he had to send troops to South Africa. A different kind of nationalist, Sir Robert Borden, believed that 'Canadian nationalism would attain its full growth only when we played our part in the making of imperial policy.' But policy continued to be made at the centre, as British statesmen endeavoured 'to get us to help in making the world safe for British capitalism.' The Chanak crisis of 1922 marked the turning point: Canada refused to support Britain in its near-Eastern policy. The process of constitutional clarification that resulted in the Balfour declaration of 1926 and the Statute of Westminster five years later meant that 'the British Commonwealth ceased to be a single entity and dissolved into a loose entente of sovereign nation-states ... It seemed the final triumph of Laurier.'[8]

Was it?

Unhappily, no. In the 1930s 'the world is once again drifting towards war as it was in the days of Laurier.' British statesmen are beckoning Canada once again. The nationalist position will have to be restated with precision and emphasis: 'Canadian nationalism is an achievement of no significance if Canadian policy is in the end always to be determined by the *faits accomplis* of the British Foreign Office.' English Canadians are in danger of being swept off their feet for a third time, as in 1899 and 1914:

> Mere nationalist aloofness and mere pacifist spirit ... will not be enough to keep us out of the next European war ... An effective policy for keeping us out of war must be based upon an understanding by the Canadian people of what wars are really about. Until we grasp the fact that war is an inherent institution in our present capitalist civilization and that it can only be eliminated by a world-wide reconstruction of our social and economic institutions, we shall always be liable to storms of irrelevant emotion; and we shall be unable to resist when we are invited to fight for democracy or freedom or parliamentary institutions or international law or collective sanctions. If we wish to realize Laurier's dream of a peaceful people living in a peaceful continent, we shall have to concentrate upon this work of reconstruction within our own country.[9]

Like charity, reconstruction begins at home.

What of the League of Nations? Canada went into it not because of 'any profound international spirit among her people ... [but] because it provided a proof that we were now accepted among the older nations of the world.' We then promptly took a lead in trying to weaken the provisions for sanctions in the League Covenant. We did so not because of a recognition that a league of capitalist powers was unlikely to remove the causes of war, but because 'no Canadian government has ever been so naïve as to fail to perceive behind the imposing façade of internationalism at Geneva the hard reality of European power politics.' Current efforts to beef up sanctions are simply intended to maintain the Anglo-French domination of Europe, which was secured in the Treaty of Versailles. 'But even in [the] uninspiring role as a society of retired burglars defending the principle of property the League is now failing to function.' Collective security is a noble idea; unhappily, 'it is incompatible with the capitalist imperialism of the great powers.'[10]

As an exporting country, Canada has a strong interest in European stability and prosperity. But Europeans will have to work these out for themselves. 'We should therefore make clear to London and to Geneva that we intend to fertilize no more crops of poppies blooming in Flanders fields.' A policy of neutrality will not be easy; we none the less ought to adopt neutrality legislation of the kind proposed to the United States Senate by the Nye Committee on Armaments. Serious economic dislocation will be the price of neutrality; the price of war will be much higher yet.[11]

Social Planning foresees one more danger. Only American intervention can halt Japanese aggression in China, and although many Americans have no interest in a Far Eastern war, capitalists seeking to maintain the 'Open Door' may force the issue. 'The Canadian people as a whole have no more interest in this American imperialism than they have in British imperialism'; we must keep out of any Asian adventures.[12]

To keep out of war and to do what little we can to promote the coming of a true international community: these are the proper aims of Canadian foreign policy. The gradual creation of this international community will involve the modification of Canadian policies with respect to tariffs, raw materials, the treatment of Oriental settlers, and so forth: 'Canadians who look forward to a League of socialist commonwealths should be doing their best now to educate public opinion in favour of such modifications. But the best contribution we can make in such a direction is to establish a socialist commonwealth within our own borders.'[13] These, the concluding sentences of *Social Planning for Canada*, neatly capture the frustrated internationalism of most LSR members. Since the international action they believed to be necessary seemed impossible, they threw up their hands and prayed for peace in their time, or at least in their country.

Scepticism about the League of Nations was confirmed by the Abyssinian crisis in the late summer and autumn of 1935. Sanctions alone could not deter Italy from aggression, Escott Reid wrote; they should be linked to economic concessions. He noted that fifteen years earlier the Canadian delegation to the league had opposed an Italian motion aimed at promoting a more equitable distribution of raw materials among the nations of the world. The assumption that poverty breeds thievery was thus shifted from the personal to the international plane.[14]

Neither Reid nor Underhill thought it wise for Canada to participate in any action that might result in war. Support for sanctions at this point, the latter argued sophistically, was in reality support for Great Britain 'in her present anti-Italian policy.' Thus champions of the League of Nations such as J.W. Dafoe and N.W. Rowell were in effect preparing us to line up 'behind Britain in any future crisis.' This went too far for some LSR members. Soon Eric Havelock criticized 'certain socialists who in everything that the League now proposes or undertakes discover the bogey of capitalist imperialism.' After all, the Soviet Union had recently become a member of the League of Nations and was a strong proponent of collective security. Havelock became very critical of the neutralist position, but he was in a small minority until September 1939 or even later.[15]

The neutralists were reinforced in their stand by reading what American isolationists and British critics of the League of Nations wrote. *The New Republic* and *The Nation* were read closely and the views of men such as Bruce Bliven, Walter Millis, and Charles Beard carefully noted. Bliven was the editor of *The New Republic*. Millis was a journalist whose *Road to War* (1935), a best-selling account of American entry into the Great War, represented that conflict as 'an inevitable result of the "ceaseless, intricate, and insane game of European diplomacy" and deprived it of moral content.'[16] Charles Beard, the distinguished Progressive historian, in 1934 published an isolationist polemic, *The Open Door at Home*, which strongly influenced Frank Underhill. Professor Richard Hofstadter has said of Beard that he 'evaded the central dilemma of international politics: that the quest for security involves hazardous competitive confrontations of *power*, and is not simply a pursuit of competing interests of trade and empire.'[17] Of Underhill and others in the LSR the same can be said.

Two books by John Maynard Keynes, *The Economic Consequences of the Peace* and *A Revision of the Treaty*, were read and reread with interest. They pictured the Treaty of Versailles as a badly botched job that on economic grounds alone was indefensible. British left-wing criticism of British foreign policy also found eager readers in Canada. Articles by Sir Stafford Cripps and H.N. Brailsford appeared in *The Canadian Forum* in 1936–37; they were not designed to weaken the neutralist opinions of many of their readers.[18]

Those opinions hardened as war drew closer. When Marvin Gelber, a young business executive, accused Underhill and Escott Reid of being 'liberals with a Versailles complex' who closed their eyes to the menace of German national socialism, Underhill responded: 'Mr. Gelber wants to take sides in Europe because he can see nothing there but Hitler ... Having myself taken part in a fairly recent war for the elimination of Kaiserism from Europe, a war which eliminated Kaiserism only to replace it by Hitlerism, I have lost my faith in the effectiveness of the policy of burying more Canadians in that continent – whether we profess to bury them for the sake of liberalism or democracy or socialism or communism.'[19] Least of all did Underhill want to see them buried there in support of Britain's foreign policy. And yet he must have been melancholically aware that this was the most likely reason for the creation of any future Canadian expeditionary force.

During the four years between Mackenzie King's return to office and the outbreak of war the LSR was very eager to secure a clear statement of Canada's right to neutrality in a British war. Nothing had been expected from the Conservatives under R.B. Bennett, but King's heart was believed to be in the right place. King eschewed clear statements; his foreign policy was as non-committal as he could make it. As Escott Reid pointed out after a year, the maintenance of national unity was the guiding principle of King's policy. To this end Canada would carefully tend its relations with Britain and the United States, minimize its commitments at Geneva as at London, leave Parliament or the people of Canada in the future to decide questions of belligerency, and promote a multilateral reduction of tariffs. 'You have the matter well sized up,' J.W. Dafoe commented, upon receiving an advance copy of Reid's paper. Dafoe also believed that King wanted to have nothing to do with war but that the fear of English Canadian reaction kept him from saying so. 'I must congratulate you on your article. It is much the best analysis of this tangled problem I have read.'[20]

But the LSR wanted more than analyses; it sought firm assurances. 'What will parliament decide,' Frank Scott impatiently asked J.S. Woodsworth:

> To back out of a war in which [Canada] is already committed on the side of Great Britain? Or merely how many troops to send? ... It is at present constitutionally impossible for parliament to decide to remain neutral in a British war until the first steps have been taken, as in South Africa, to secure Canadian control of the documents evidencing the Crown's intentions. Canada has never yet declared war or peace in her life and could not do so as matters now stand.

For this reason Scott could discern some merit in the Foreign Enlistment Act. 'There is nothing in the bill about Spain in particular,' he wrote Angus MacInnis: 'When enacted ... it will tend to assist Canada in maintaining her neutrality whenever she may want to maintain it.' The CCF MPs should seek to oppose the wording of one objectionable section, but in the last resort they should support the act and then seek to oppose its application to Spain.[21]

'Keep Canada out of War': this was the title of an article by Frank Underhill in

Maclean's magazine in May of 1937; it was also the message that the LSR preached incessantly during the last years and months of a precarious peace. Canada 'must pursue a positive foreign policy designed to protect her neutrality,' the authors of *Democracy Needs Socialism* wrote: 'The time to avoid commitments is now, not at some future time when the war fever has been aroused.' Canadians are isolated by geography from conflict – 'we are guarded by Generals Atlantic and Pacific,' as Underhill put in – and have 'an opportunity to put their own house in order ... The fight against fascism and dictatorship should begin at home.' Some are trying to make profits by selling war materials abroad; others are tempted to embroil the country in war in order to distract the attention of Canadians from domestic problems. The government has started to increase the defence estimates. However, 'Canada's real need for defence is not against foreign invasion, which is nowhere threatening, but against the social disintegration which economic insecurity and injustice produce.'[22] Since home defence requires no additional expenditure, the government must be laying the basis for participation in a war overseas. To this the LSR and CCF were strongly opposed.

Left-wingers were not alone in seeking a clear statement of Canada's right to neutrality. In the winter of 1939 a public statement appeared in the form of a twelve-page pamphlet with the title *Canadian Unity in War and Peace*. It demanded 'the immediate declaration by Parliament of Canada's right to decide issues of War and Peace.' The seventy-five signatories, some of them French but most English Canadian, were drawn from the worlds of law, medicine, religion, education, business, farming, and journalism. Of the seventy-five no more than half a dozen were ever active in the LSR; of those prominent in the LSR only one, Frank Scott, signed the document. He had also helped to draft it.[23]

In his book *Canada Today* (1938), prepared for the Canadian Institute of International Affairs, Scott claimed 'that a considerable majority of the people of Canada believe either that the Dominion has or that it should have the right to remain neutral whenever it so desires.' He further asserted that 'fully half the population' was isolationist and that 'many in the other half will turn isolationist if British policy continues during the next few years to be what it has been since 1931.'[24] But it did not escape him that the isolationist moiety, consisting mainly of French Canadians and European immigrants, was much the less influential half. He realized how strong were the proponents of the British tie and how well situated. When war came, they would almost certainly carry the day.

In attacking the British connection, Scott, Underhill, and company were flogging a horse that was showing signs of age. But there was life in the old nag yet. Not only did many Canadians still believe in the value of common foreign and defence policies for the Empire-Commonwealth, but British leaders had not abandoned all hope that such policies could be devised. Prime Minister Mackenzie

King spent a good deal of time at the Commonwealth Conference of 1937 turning down proposals for common action. He did not brag about this in Canada. To King the prospect of a European war in which Britain would be a participant was chilling. It seemed only too likely to tear his party and Canada asunder. Yet he knew, as did his French Canadian ministers, which way the country as a whole would go should such a war break out. During the Czechoslovakian crisis of 1938 the cabinet agreed that Canada would stand by Britain.[25] Dreaded war was drawing nigh.

Much of this was hidden from the LSR. It wanted public statements. King ought to confront the issue squarely even though it might cost him votes. National unity would be better served by frankness than by obfuscation.

King did not see it this way. He was shying at shadows, perhaps, but to him they were substantial. By leaving things vague he also saved himself potential trouble. In supporting the British policy of appeasement he hoped that, with luck, the problems of Canadian participation in war would never have to be squarely and publicly faced. For their part, the LSR's members were, with few exceptions, dead set against Canadian participation, but they also deplored appeasement. G.M.A. Grube charged in the spring of 1938 that Prime Minister Neville Chamberlain was willing to indulge Hitler, Mussolini, and Franco because he thought the alternative to them was communism. Appeasement, however, was 'a weak and almost suicidal policy' that would only feed the Hitlerian appetite for conquest. *The Canadian Forum* judged the concessions made at Munich to be a monumental blunder. Sooner or later Britain would have to fight to protect herself and her imperial interests. The terms on which that war would be fought became less favourable with each compromise.[26]

The pusillanimity of Canada's political leaders was nowhere clearer than in their attitude to refugees from Europe, especially Jews from Germany and Austria. 'The failure to solve the refugee problem is but blatant proof of capitalism's complete inability to marshal natural wealth and manpower into beneficial channels,' the *Forum* editorialized in January 1939. Canada's record in this instance is distressing: we seem to be altogether inactive. 'The arguments against admitting refugees are mostly economic,' the *Forum* noted in March, 'but racial and national prejudice, though less vocal, is probably the more powerful factor. It seems to us less important to preserve the preponderance of British (or French) blood, than to preserve the spirit of liberty and democracy, and few better helpers in that struggle could be found than the victims of despotism. Racial exclusiveness is no less stupid in Canada than it is in Germany and Italy.' Since the refugees have skills and are ready to use them, the economic arguments against admitting them are fallacious: 'If the struggle against fascism is a reality, let us then provide for the relief of casualties, as we do in war.' And let Canada for a change take the lead in doing so. Alas, no lead of this kind was to come from Mackenzie King's Ottawa. Without a strong current of public opinion in favour of the admission of refugees, the government did next to nothing.[27]

II

Among foreign countries the United States loomed largest by far in LSR eyes as in those of Canadians generally. 'In actual fact,' Frank Scott once asserted, 'the United States is not regarded as a foreign country at all. When the Canadians talk about the "foreigners" in the population, they are not thinking of American settlers.' Frank Underhill over the years emphasized the similarities between the two North American countries. 'It was not the Declaration of Independence which made the Americans a separate people,' he wrote in 1929: 'It was the Atlantic Ocean; and Canada is on the same side of the Atlantic.' Not long afterwards he described Canada as a backward United States: 'We are likely to trail along behind our neighbours in political developments as in everything else.'[28]

The rise of the CCF led the historian to change this tune. Early in 1933 he surmised that socialism might well triumph in Canada first. Thirty months later, the CCF's star having dimmed, he reverted to his earlier position. 'A genuine upheaval' would take place first in the United States, he told a largely American audience in 1935: 'We shall trail along behind you.' Frank Scott quickly contradicted his associate. Farmer-labour co-operation had in Canada advanced 'to a point that is not immediately likely in the American political scene.' Furthermore, the absence of a 'due process' clause from the Canadian constitution meant that the legal barrier against socialist innovation was much less forbidding in Canada.[29]

Canadian-American relations did not, to LSR writers, constitute a controversial subject. Stoically they accepted the fact that the American presence would always to some extent limit Canadian international and even internal freedom of action. 'History and geography,' Scott noted in 1932, 'have combined to place Canada in such a position *vis-à-vis* the United States that no weapons save moral ones are of any use in the last resort to protect Canadian independence.' But how could Canada best reduce the limitations on its freedom to the minimum? An isolationist policy might not serve Canada well, Escott Reid pointed out in the *Forum*. Turning our backs on Britain and Europe would increase our economic and military reliance on the United States to a degree so high that we might, in fact if not in law, become part of it.[30]

In his 1933 draft chapter for the LSR book Reid had suggested that the role of mediator between the United States and Great Britain best suited Canada; by finding a balance in our relations between the two giants we would gain the greatest freedom available to us. In Underhill's final version of the chapter on foreign policy in *Social Planning for Canada*, however, Canadian-American relations had almost dropped from sight. 'We may here neglect purely North American questions. It is safe to take for granted that Canada's relations with the United States are on such a basis that any questions arising between the two countries can be dealt with amicably.'[31] This is facile. When an elephant and a mouse settle their differences amicably, who gets his way? More to the point: if Canada should turn to socialism, what would the response of a capitalist United States be, given that American citizens own a sizeable portion of Canadian industry?

In its discussion of capital investment *Social Planning for Canada* recognizes the problem. It is *not* that of the nationality of the owners: 'That foreigners control this or that *particular* industry will trouble none but those earnest patriots who, in defiance of all the evidence, persist in believing that the Canadian capitalist is a different kind of being from the foreign, that the one is a philanthropist, the other a robber and a cheat. For the rest of us, the real importance of foreign investment in Canada is something quite different.'[32] How, even when industry is socialized, can the dividends and interest paid abroad be eliminated? The domestic investor is an easy target, but what of the foreign, and especially the American investor?

The answer is sobering: 'Unless the United States goes socialist when we do, or before, or has its hands very full with industrial and political unrest (likely enough eventualities all), even a socialist Canada will probably have to give preferential treatment to the foreign investor.' The possibilities of economic or commercial retaliation are too great if American investors feel cheated. (The possibility of military intervention is ignored.) But Canada need not be over-cautious. 'A government making a forthright endeavour to eliminate the wastes of capitalism has no reason to fear that its credit will be ruined.' In any case, with so much unused capacity in industry, capital imports are unlikely to prove a pressing exigency for some time to come. As a result, there is no call to be too solicitous about the feelings of American investors.[33]

Socialization of industry was in the 1930s a hypothetical consideration. The threat of war in Europe was real. It is not surprising that some leading members of the LSR, Underhill in particular, argued that American isolationism should be a model for Canadians. But even he did not want Canada to lean too heavily on the United States; that would be as dangerous as too close a tie with Britain. 'If we are to perform that function so dear to our sentimental after-dinner speakers of interpreting the Americans and the British to each other,' he stated at the 1937 Couchiching Conference, 'we must be genuinely independent of both ... This delicate art of balance requires a Machiavellian clearness of head as well as long experience before it can be acquired. It is high time that we came to understand in Canada that even the first elementary steps in the art cannot be learnt by colonials.'[34] And yet the art needed so urgently to be learnt.

On the whole the British connection was thought to be a greater danger to Canada, at least in the short run, than the American presence. But the latter had evident dangers, too. For example, Graham Spry explained in 1935 that the slogan 'the state or the United States' had carried a special meaning to the radicals in the Canadian Radio League. The Americanization of broadcasting involved its control by 'great business organizations,' many of them American. Little concern for the expression of the views of 'socialist groups, trade unions, and farm associations' was expected from big business. Thus the cultural threat to Canada was really a capitalist threat.[35]

Spry was joined by Underhill in this view. 'Our big businessmen are our chief American influences,' the historian once wrote, 'and the tendency of their activities is not one whit altered by the vigour with which some of them wave the old flag. If they prevail indefinitely Canada will become only a geographical expression.'[36] Capitalists would sell or invest where there was money to be made. In the process they were gradually integrating the continent. But socialists might do no less.

In spite of occasional insight into the difficulties that the presence of the United States created for Canada and Canadian socialists, the LSR's view of the republic was mostly calm to the point of complacency. Relations with individual Americans were so cordial that it was hard to conjure up an American menace, Anti-Americanism 'has declined in recent years,' Frank Scott suggested in 1938, '... and the decline is an indication that Canadians have matured to the point where they no longer fear the loss of their identity on the American continent.' Three years later he acquiesced in the view that the increasingly intimate relationship with the United States that came with the war would ultimately lead to the loss of Canadian independence. The logic of the historical development of the two countries would lead both to democratic socialism. National independence was not the highest good but only a stepping stone to the 'higher federalism' of the nations of the world. 'A small power may move in the orbit of a larger power without thereby losing its identity. Any union in the future is less likely to come through outright annexation than through joint merging in some supranational organization.' This was not a statement of LSR views. However, it was consistent with that concern for international co-operation that the league had a decade earlier called for in its manifesto.[37]

III

National independence was a means, not an end. The immediate end was the creation of the co-operative commonwealth. War would interfere with this. The

LSR therefore opposed everything that, like the connection with Britain, threatened to take Canada into war.

Nazism and Italian fascism were noxious, no doubt. German military aggression should be stopped. But most LSR members believed that participation in war would strengthen domestic fascists; and what could we really do about the European species? The antifascist governments in Europe would have to get together to deal with them; there was little of value we could add to their endeavours, and the attempt to do so might tear the country apart.

The LSR misjudged the relative potency of the military forces in Europe, but it could scarcely be blamed for that. Nor can it be faulted for failing to foresee the Nazi-Soviet Pact of August 1939. And other Canadians shared the desire of league members for neutrality. No less a person than O.D. Skelton, under-secretary of state for External Affairs, counselled Mackenzie King in 1938–39 that Canada should stay neutral even if Britain went to war over German aggression in eastern Europe. He was not alone in his department in taking this line.[38]

With the aid of hindsight it is not hard to identify the weaknesses in the neutralist position. We know now how close Germany came to conquering all of Europe, North Africa, and the Middle East. We also know, far better than anyone outside the Nazi inner circle then knew, the full extent of Nazi *Schrecklichkeit* and its ambitions. The LSR was wrong in thinking that German aggression was only of limited concern to Canadians. However, of the MPs who voted for war in September 1939 and of the men who enlisted, not many did so primarily because they felt strongly about the German invasion of Poland or passionately disapproved of Nazism. Few Canadians wanted war; fewer still wanted to go to war over a boundary dispute in central Europe. Prime Minister Chamberlain's success at Munich in averting war over another such dispute had been greeted with joyous relief not only by Mackenzie King but by many of his countrymen as well. No, in 1939 'Canada went to war because Britain went to war. Not for democracy, not to stop Hitler, not to save Poland. Canada decided to fight ... only because Prime Minister Neville Chamberlain felt himself unable to escape the commitments Great Britain had made to Poland six months earlier.'[39] Thus writes J.L. Granatstein. 'By Britain's side, whate'er betide': most English Canadians followed the path of loyalty and filial duty. Other Canadians followed.

For years this sort of automatic response had been feared in LSR circles. Men like Scott and Underhill had hoped in vain to forestall it, to have the issue of participation in an overseas war decided on its merits and in the light of logic and common sense. The decision might then conceivably be against war, they thought. Like themselves, Canadians generally might prefer to tend their own gardens and leave European quarrels to Europeans.

The LSR's basic preference for international solutions to world problems was consistent with its desire for national solutions to nation-wide problems. It made sense to try to cope with difficulties at the level that offered most hope for their solution. While squalls of provincial self-assertion did not budge the LSR from its centralist course, however, the approaching storm of war did induce it to seek shelter in a neutralist, even isolationist harbour. It was far better to work towards the achievement of socialism at home than to help safeguard the fruits of British 'capitalist imperialism' overseas.[40]

This explains the stress on independence from Britain; it also explains the comparatively weak concern about the American threat to Canadian self-determination. The emotional ties of many English Canadians to Britain and the Empire-Commonwealth were strong; it made sense to counter them with an appeal to the geographical separateness of Canada. This was all the more necessary because of the presence of large groups that felt no strong link with Britain. War could only be disruptive. Yet it drew ever closer. It is not surprising to find that the enterprises in which the LSR was engaged just before war broke out were mostly directed to the doomed objective of keeping Canada neutral.

9

The war years

When Canadians woke up on 1 September 1939, their radios told them the momentous news: for some hours the German armed forces had been assaulting Poland. In Toronto, listening to the news reports, Eric Havelock calculated what they would mean for Canada. Surely Britain and France would stand by Poland? That would bring a major European war, and Canada would enter it. Like other members of the LSR, Havelock, its national vice-president, dreaded this war. Unlike many of them, however, he believed that Canada ought to intervene. A couple of conversations during the day confirmed his suspicion that other members of the national executive still disagreed. The following day, therefore, he wrote to the national president, Louise Parkin, in Montreal, outlining the situation as he saw it.

Canada, Havelock assumed, would be at war.

1) Isolationism is a *possible* attitude to maintain throughout the war ... But it cannot be put forward as *LSR* policy (or as CCF): working class sentiment is I should guess predominantly interventionist.
2) This leaves us nothing much to say on foreign policy as such now. We can only concentrate on *manner* of conducting war ...
3) ... [To] ask our government to stress war is to frustrate Nazi machine not German people: this may be good propaganda, but we happen to believe in it and should try to make our governments live up to this policy when and if peace comes. My view is that *left wing* collaboration in conduct of war is only way to ensure some control over its conclusion.[1]

Havelock stood ready to confront Nazi Germany.

Others saw the matter differently. Indeed, during the ten days that passed from Germany's attack on Poland through the British and French declarations of war on 3 September to the Canadian entry on 10 September, most LSR members tried to stick close to their pre-war stand. Canada might not enjoy the right to neutrality, but intervention was not in the country's best interests. Canadian participation should be strictly limited. Even after 10 September this view stayed alive.

Not until the spring of 1940 was this attitude shattered, along with the Allied armies in Belgium and northern France. From then on the war effort and the improving fortunes in wartime of the CCF increasingly claimed the time of LSR members. Two years later the league ceased to exist.

The LSR had entered the year 1939 aggressively in pursuit of new members. Two leaflets were issued, *We Want Membership Groups* and *Why Social Reconstruction?* The national executive also approached a number of people – members-at-large, CCF MPS, and so on – in the hope of founding new branches or revivifying old ones. Scant success rewarded the campaign. 'The Branch here has not met for two years,' Robert Liddle wrote to the national secretary from Sault Ste Marie, 'and at the present time there is little chance of reviving it; we are busy organizing the CCF in this constituency.'[2] From other places a similar message came: the most likely recruits were already active in the CCF or in other groups, such as the Civil Liberties Union.

The London branch carried on an active program in the winter of 1938–39, but it ceased to meet the following autumn. The last local secretary, Gordon Jack, reported that some members had simply dropped out, while others had become wrapped up in the activities of the CCF. Kay Montagu reported from St Catharines in the spring of 1939 that the branch there had failed for the same reason.[3]

As a result of a quarrel in the Alberta CCF a new branch was formed in Calgary. Having been expelled on organizational grounds, the Calgary CCF Club applied for recognition as a branch of the LSR. Unacquainted with what had happened, the national executive warmly welcomed the new affiliate, only to be taken to task by the executive of the Alberta CCF: 'Our members in Calgary are very much opposed to providing any opportunity for these people to do through a group that is looked on as being allied to the CCF what they have been deprived of doing through the CCF itself.' Nonplussed by this, the LSR executive referred the matter to M.J. Coldwell, national chairman of the CCF, for adjudication. He did not respond, and at the national convention held in Montreal in June 1940 the national secretary happily acknowledged a 'thriving new Calgary branch.' Only three other branches were left, Toronto, Montreal, and Winnipeg.[4]

Next to invigorating the league's membership, increasing *The Canadian Forum*'s subscription list was the project closest to LSR hearts. At the 1939 convention George Grube claimed that five hundred additional subscribers, bringing the total to 2,700, would allow the monthly to pay its way, provided the editor worked without salary. A further seven hundred subscribers, he guessed, would support a paid editor as well. The delegates decided to help by approving a scheme whereby a joint LSR membership and *Forum* subscription would be available at reduced cost. But the Toronto branch balked; the financial arrangements seemed too bothersome. Besides, the branch president, Jarvis McCurdy, wrote: 'We felt very dubious about the wisdom of the policy of thus identifying the Forum as a "club paper," when it has to be sold to a public by no means identified with the LSR in opinion.' Since the *Forum* had been a club paper for the last three years, the argument was obtuse. Possibly it reflected the caution that had infected some LSR members with the coming of the war. Whatever the case, Helen Howes, the national secretary, was unimpressed. She pointed out that in Montreal the new arrangement had resulted in thirty to thirty-five new subscribers as well as five new members for the LSR.[5]

Professor Kenneth McNaught has stated that the league 'was dissolved at the beginning of the Second World War.' This is mistaken; however, the war did serve as a major distraction. Initially it was a source of dissension. Disagreement about the course of Canadian foreign policy had been mounting since the Munich Agreement if not earlier. Although opinion was predominantly neutralist, a minority favoured Canadian intervention in a war against Nazi Germany. Prominent among the latter were Eric Havelock and Joe Parkinson in Toronto and R.E.K. Pemberton in London. It was clearly no coincidence that all three had been born and raised in England.[6]

Until September of 1939 the difference of opinion stayed mostly in the background. There was no discussion of foreign affairs at the last pre-war convention, which met in Strathcona Hall on Sherbrooke Avenue and in the Grove Hotel, an historic inn in Beaconsfield, on 20–21 May. The tone of the convention was quite cheerful. The Montreal branch had reversed a trend by increasing its paid-up membership from 100 to 140. Although the bankruptcy of Stafford Printers had left the LSR holding one hundred now virtually worthless shares, the league's balance sheet had improved as a result of royalties received from the sales of *Democracy Needs Socialism*. At the same time 'the Forum was in a better financial position than it had ever been.' On the whole the mood was positive as the delegates listened to the guest speaker, Professor Charles W. Lightbody of St Lawrence University, speak about 'Leadership and Democracy.'

As new national president the delegates elected the only non-academic and woman ever to hold that position, Louise Parkin of Montreal. A handsome housewife of broad intellectual and artistic interests, forceful and charming, she had joined the LSR through the influence of Frank Scott. Born into an old English family in 1900, she was educated at Berkhamstead Girls' Grammar School. She had first come to Canada in 1925 to visit her banker uncle; two years later she married Raleigh Parkin, only son of Sir George Parkin, late secretary of the Rhodes Trust. Her relations by marriage thus came to include the three Parkin daughters and their talented husbands, W.L. Grant, principal of Upper Canada College until 1935, J.M. Macdonnell, general manager of the National Trust Company and later a Conservative MP, and Vincent Massey, wealthy scion of a family of farm-machinery manufacturers, Liberal chieftain, and, after 1935, Canadian high commissioner to Britain. As her brother, Claud Cockburn, the brilliant journalist and founder-editor of *The Week*, was a leading English communist intellectual, Louise Parkin's near relations spanned the entire political spectrum. She herself at length joined the CCF. Her husband, who worked as an investment counsellor for Sun Life, was dubious about her political involvement but did not interfere.

Differing views of the war and what Canada's role in it should be came quickly to the fore on 1 September. At that very time Louise Parkin was wondering what to do with a letter from the Toronto branch asking the national executive to take 'all possible steps to demand a plebiscite on the question of Canada's participation in the forthcoming war.' Two years earlier the Toronto group, which contained such fervent neutralists as Escott Reid, G.M.A. Grube, and Frank Underhill, had tried to convince the national executive to sponsor a 'peace ballot' for Canada. An affirmative reply would have demanded the cessation of Canadian rearmament, legislation to take all profits out of the sale of 'war munitions and materials,' and strict neutrality in any future war overseas. The idea had been rejected: the expense of putting such a ballot before the people was far too great for the LSR. In 1939 the German invasion of Poland quickly settled the matter. It was too late for plebiscites now.[7]

By the time the LSR national executive met in Montreal on Tuesday, 5 September, Great Britain was already at war. For the moment Canada's status was somewhat in doubt. Frank Scott believed that the country was technically at war, and in some ways its government was behaving as if it were. A special session of Parliament was to meet later in the week, however, and Canada's declaration of war was a foregone conclusion. In spite of Eric Havelock's heated arguments the LSR executive decided that they could not support intervention beyond economic aid and opposed an expeditionary force. The LSR would promote the preservation of democratic rights and civil liberties while pointing the way to a better post-war Canada. Louise Parkin accordingly sent a letter to the prime minister setting forth the league's view that 'foreign policy is the projection of domestic policy into international affairs' and warning that the war would be fought to little purpose unless civil liberties were preserved and the conditions for a peaceful post-war order established. Mackenzie King's answer was characteristically courteous but evasive.[8]

Grube, Scott, Underhill, and, after the first day, Eugene Forsey attended the emergency meeting of the CCF national council in Ottawa on 6–8 September. The front pages of the newspapers were completely dominated by the war. Conflicting news came from both the eastern front and Germany's western frontier, but it was nonetheless clear that the Poles, though resisting gallantly, were taking a dreadful beating. The Canadian armed forces had begun to mobilize on 1 September, and everywhere men were flocking to the colours: five hundred recruits per day in Toronto alone, *The Globe and Mail* reported on 7 September. On the previous day King had taken the widely respected Colonel James L. Ralston into the cabinet as minister of Finance; King's close associate Norman Rogers was promoted to the Defence portfolio. Everything pointed to Canadian entry into the war.

That much the CCF council could agree on. Beyond this it was split. J.S. Woodsworth argued passionately against the CCF's involvement in the war effort. He opposed the war on socialist as well as Christian grounds. The 'last war settled nothing'; Canada had no business in this one. The LSR people, Frank Scott at their head, largely agreed with Woodsworth. Canadian participation would be a grave threat to democracy at home; the CCF ought to guard against this and not add to it by throwing itself into the war effort.

George Williams, leader of the Saskatchewan CCF, made the most fervent case for full participation. An ardent interventionist, he had in 1937 refused to appear on a platform with King Gordon, then national vice-chairman of the CCF, because of apprehensions that Gordon would speak about 'pacifism and neutrality.'[9] Now Williams argued that, inasmuch as this was a war against fascism and dictatorship, the CCF could not hold back. A Nazi victory in Europe would destroy democracy even here.

The majority of those present were neutralist to a lesser or greater degree. However, the fact of war loomed large. A compromise took shape. It was first enunciated by Angus MacInnis, reporting the views of the British Columbia CCF. The party should oppose conscription of manpower and a Canadian expeditionary force, and support the maintenance of civil liberties and the rendering of economic assistance to Britain on a non-profit basis. The government would be urged to assume operation or control of munitions factories and other war industries.[10] Woodsworth's motion that 'this council will refuse to support any measure which will put Canada into war' was side-stepped. On the morning of 7 September the council voted thirteen to nine – this later became fifteen to seven – to adopt a statement incorporating the main elements of MacInnis's proposal.

An official statement, *Canada and the War: The CCF Position*, was written by a group that included the LSR representatives. The latter were also asked 'to evolve a policy of peace for the CCF.' George Williams, for one, thought they had all too much influence. 'The thing that boils me up about the "Intelligentsia" group in the East,' he complained to Angus MacInnis some months later, 'is their continuous attempt to foist upon the CCF an Isolationist policy and to explain the decision of the National Council from the Isolationist point of view.' The grievance pin-points a quarrel in the party that persisted into the spring of 1940. Although Williams chose to ignore the fact, there were others besides the LSR intellectuals who opposed anything more than economic participation.[11]

Not all league members felt this way, of course. Eric Havelock resigned as treasurer of the *Forum* because he did not want to be identified with its editorial policy of limited commitment. He also offered to resign the vice-presidency of the LSR. 'I have no intention of resigning ordinary membership,' he told Louise Parkin, '... believing in common with Mr. Woodsworth at the other extreme of opinion that our ranks must remain closed despite differences of attitude.' Havelock's offer was not accepted, and he served out his term. At least one member, J.F. Parkinson, believes that 'a fair number of members resigned' in protest against the league's equivocal attitude to the war.[12]

During the so-called Phoney War or *Sitzkrieg*, the LSR clung to its neo-neutralism. For the time being it focused its attention on profiteering, war aims, and especially civil liberties. Then, in April 1940 the war took a dramatically new turn: Germany invaded Denmark and Norway. The following month the Netherlands, Belgium, and France crumpled under a full-scale German offensive in the west. As the magnitude of the disaster became clear the LSR turned to full support of the war effort. Even so, other goals were not lost from sight. At the 1940 national convention, held in Montreal a few days after the evacuation of Dunkirk, delegates insisted that the league should retain its critical perspective and its opposition to conscription. 'Our job is to do what no other organization will do and not to work up a fervor of war.'[13]

Some members, notably Frank Underhill, were more reluctant than others to say farewell to their neutralism. In an obituary for Dr O.D. Skelton written early in 1941 the historian reaffirmed his belief that the non-committal policy counselled by the under-secretary of state for External Affairs during the 1930s had under the circumstances been wise. Frank Scott, however, said less than a year later that Canada's quasi-isolationist policy between the wars had been a mistake. In the post-war world this country must support the creation of a new and improved League of Nations.[14]

II

In September 1939 the future of *The Canadian Forum* became a matter of concern. It was by no means clear that the journal would not soon be proscribed if it continued to express hostility to full Canadian participation in the war. More realistic was the fear that its editors might face persecution of some kind. George Grube and Frank Underhill had been denounced in the Ontario legislature some months earlier for their 'disloyalty' to the British Empire. 'The danger to me and F.H.U. would not come from the censor, but from Queen's Park,' Grube wrote, explaining to Louise Parkin why the two of them wished to remove their names from the *Forum* mast-head: neither could afford to lose his teaching post. Eleanor Godfrey, who was about to get married to W.H. Graham, became managing editor for a second time. Henceforth only her name and that of the business manager, Lou Morris, would appear.[15]

Behind the cover of anonymity, Underhill and Grube carried out their editorial duties. The former resumed the political editorship, surrendering the editing of book reviews to Grube. Earle Birney carried on as literary editor until he took leave from the University of Toronto in 1940 to join the army.

In spite of the early fears, the *Forum* experienced no interference from the authorities. Once, in late 1940, the RCMP searched its premises in vain for Communist literature – the CPC had been banned by order-in-council in June – but there was no trouble with either the censors or Queen's Park. Eleanor Godfrey was managing editor for the duration of the war; meanwhile the pens of LSR members filled the *Forum's* pages under their own or assumed names – Carlton McNaught used 'Fergus Glenn' and 'R.W. Tolbridge' – or, in Underhill's case above all, anonymously.

Efforts to raise the circulation did not cease. In 1940, for example, all LSR members were asked to procure at least one new subscription each while supplying the *Forum* with the names of five prospects. Campaigns of this kind had some effect: by August 1940 there were 2,600 subscribers. However, the goal of a balanced budget receded even as circulation rose. 'It is a pity the Forum is such a money sponge,' Eleanor Godfrey commented. Continued strong LSR support for the monthly was essential, McNaught (since September 1939 the *Forum* treasurer) told Jarvis McCurdy in October 1940. Alan Plaunt was approached for money once again in 1941. 'The problem of financing the Forum is becoming more acute,' McNaught wrote. Both the LSR and Plaunt responded with cash.[16]

Then, just as the league itself was quietly expiring, the *Forum's* condition improved. 'With the aid of the sustaining fund and an expanded circulation due partly to subscriptions for armed services centres, as well as some wartime advertising in which all publications shared, the financial problem was somewhat lightened.'[17] The increasing interest in socialism and the CCF after 1941 had its effect on the *Forum*'s mailing list as well. In 1942 the number of paid subscriptions passed three thousand and the magazine had, in Alan Creighton and Lou Morris, two paid employees.

III

Did the LSR have an important purpose in wartime? Some members quickly decided that deeds now mattered more than words or research. Why not suspend the LSR's educational efforts for the duration?

Such notions were rejected by the national executive. 'We feel,' Helen Howes told an inquirer, 'that since the machinery of civilization has broken down, it is all the more imperative to find out the reason and to study and discuss how best the structure of our economic system can be changed in order to make such a thing impossible in the future.' The commitment to public education was unchanged. But was it enough? 'I am bothered by the last year of the LSR,' Louise Parkin revealed to Frank Underhill in March 1940: 'Some of the stagnation is due to the effects of the war on us as on other groups. I think we are clearer now as to what we should do in the way of group work, pamphlets, etc. if only we can raise the groups or individuals to do them, and the cash to publish them. We have got terribly inbred. If it were not for the Forum we would have nothing to show for ourselves.' Is the educational philosophy of the LSR outdated? the agenda for the 1940 national convention asked. 'Is it possible to teach people things in which they are not interested?' Had the LSR been trying to approach Canadians through subjects 'they SHOULD be interested in' rather than those 'in which they ARE interested?'[18] For reformers as for intellectuals, these, if taken seriously, are devastating questions. They imply nothing less than the notion that ideas and policies are products that must be adjusted to suit the market or else abandoned. This is a blow struck at the very heart of socialism.

The convention at which the questions were to be considered opened in Strathcona Hall, McGill University, on Saturday, 8 June 1940. Overcast skies and scattered thundershowers dimly mirrored the military situation in northern France. There German forces were crossing the Somme and Aisne rivers in force: before the week-end ended motorized units had reached Rouen and pushed within fifty kilometres of Paris. Italy was poised to enter the war on Germany's side. Norway had ceased hostilities and Allied forces were being withdrawn from the area of Narvik. Even censorship could not hide the truth that the war was going very badly indeed. Of interest to the LSR, too, was that the Canadian government had on 5 June reacted to the mounting crisis in Europe by outlawing sixteen organizations, both left and right wing, that were judged to be disloyal.

The turn-out for the convention was good in contrast with that of the previous year. Thirty-eight people showed up, including six CCF MPs. Old friends Angus MacInnis and M.J. Coldwell were there as well as recently elected newcomers G.H. Castleden (Yorkton), Clarence Gillis (Cape Breton South), A.M. Nicholson (Mackenzie), and P.E. Wright (Melville). Two defeated candidates from the Montreal area, Dr Stanley Allen and R.L. Calder, KC, also attended.

Discussion was very lively, not least because differences concering the war effort remained. Eric Havelock assiduously promoted a degree of participation that still went too far for most of his listeners. Typical was Underhill's response: 'the role of the LSR [is] to point the way continually to an extension of civil liberties since there are enough people who will "get on the bandwagon."' Havelock did not get the approval he wanted to publish his views in a series of articles in the *Forum*.

A statement on civil liberties passed with three dissenting votes. It indicated qualified support for the policy of outlawing 'Nazi, Fascist or Communist' activities if these were clearly intended to undermine democracy or aid the enemy. Due process must be observed, however, and activities by self-appointed vigilantes suppressed. Essential liberties must be safeguarded, 'in particular free criticism of governmental policy and the rights of labour.'

Overwhelmingly rejected was a suggestion that the LSR be merged with the CCF. Mark Farrell, by then living in Montreal, thought it inadvisable 'for the sake of the Canadian Forum'; others argued that an autonomous educational role still existed. Some doubted that it was being played effectively, however. A Toronto delegate, J.W. Noseworthy, 'raised the question of the LSR supplying the CCF with educational material and mentioned the difficulty in Ontario during the last election in getting suitable material, particularly for agriculturalists and middle classes.' (That election, held in March, had been a further disappointment. Only eight CCFers had been elected, none in central Canada. A.A. Heaps and Grant MacNeil had gone down to defeat. But those who looked at the bright side noted that the party, while contesting only 96 constituencies out of 245, had gained 8.5 per cent of the popular vote.) David Lewis, now firmly ensconced as national secretary of the CCF, urged the LSR to continue to help the party with getting 'the facts of the situation over to the people ... We must teach the proletariat first and organize them afterward.'

More publications were planned. Harriet Forsey was already at work on a pictorial essay illustrating the maldistribution of wealth and income in Canada; it was published the following spring as a pamphlet, *Poor Man Rich Man*. Suggestions for further publications emerged from a discussion of the recently published report of the Royal Commission on Dominion-Provincial Relations that took place after dinner at the McGill Faculty Club. George Grube chaired the session, in which Frank Scott surveyed the constitutional and Eugene Forsey the economic implications of the report. In the subsequent discussion period 'It was pointed out that there will be considerable objection, especially in Ontario, to the Dominion Government spreading opportunity equally across the Dominion. We must impress upon the people that it is only certain people, the upper class, who will be affected [adversely], not the people as a whole. In other words, it is a class levelling rather than a provincial levelling.'[19] The LSR decided to give qualified support to the moderately centralist recommendations of the report. A summary appeared in the *Forum* in December and was later published as a four-page leaflet, *What the Sirois Report Proposes*.

Elected national president at the 1940 convention was William Jarvis McCurdy, the first Torontonian to hold the position since 1935. Lanky and rugged, deliberate in his speech, he had an aura of the rustic. Not a particularly perceptive observer of the current scene, he got the job because he was hard-working and thorough and because no one else could be found. As Louise Parkin had discovered the year before, being president of the LSR was not so much a kudos as a lot of work. The one who got the job was the one most reluctant to refuse it.

Born in Richmond, Quebec, in 1904, Jarvis McCurdy was the son of a Presbyterian clergyman who served several rural churches in Quebec, Ontario, and the Atlantic provinces. After graduating from Dalhousie University in 1926, McCurdy had gone to Harvard to study divinity. He soon switched to philosophy and completed his doctorate in 1932. Two years later he managed to land a teaching position at the University of Toronto; soon afterwards he joined both the LSR and the Fellowship for a Christian Social Order. He recalls that while he lived in Boston the Sacco-Vanzetti case greatly affected him. When the Depression came, McCurdy, a man of strong feelings, 'just naturally turned to Socialism.'

On the face of it the LSR was still healthy. Especially the Toronto and Montreal groups were active, the national secretary reported to the convention, and branches in Winnipeg and Calgary also carried on programs. A gloomier note was sounded by the treasurer, C.E. French. Capitation fees from the branches were often in arrears, and royalties from the sale of *Democracy Needs Socialism* had virtually dried up during the past year. The LSR was losing its ability to perform good deeds. When he informed a benefactor that paid-up LSR membership had dropped to just over two hundred by the end of the summer, Carlton McNaught was emphasizing the point that little more financial help for the *Forum* could be expected from the league.[20]

That the Sirois Report should be the focus of LRS research had been decided by the convention. Jarvis McCurdy informed the branch secretaries that local groups should study it carefully 'with a view to preparing a "Social Planning for Canada" on a provincial basis ... To say that this is no time for study is mere defeatism.' Alas, lack of response from the branches doomed this project. Nor did the LSR get down to a proposal made by David Lewis. Noting the dearth of literature about the effects of the war on Canada, he asked the national secretary, Eileen Troop, whether the LSR could not put a book together. 'Those of us who are continually engaged in the work of organization cannot possibly find the time to do any part of the job, even though I, for one, would very much like to try it.'[21] He would have to: the idea was the genesis of *Make This YOUR Canada*, a book he co-authored with Frank Scott and published in 1943.

The Montreal branch, in arrears with its capitation fees since 1939, during 1940–41 virtually limited its activities to four discussion groups. 'The fringe of membership seems to lie dormant and few new members are added to our list,' the branch secretary reported in April 1941. Monthly meetings of the Toronto branch continued to be well attended, due in part to an innovation called a 'membership supper.' The 1940 convention was told that 'this was a buffet affair held at the home of one of the older members, prior to each monthly meeting, where the members got to know each other, their hostess and the speaker of the evening.'[22] In Toronto as in Montreal, however, membership continued slowly to decline.

The tenth and last national convention met in Toronto on Saturday, 14 June 1941. It was pleasantly warm; in Europe the war was hot and getting hotter. Newspaper rumour had it that conflict was imminent between Germany and the Soviet Union (the invasion of Russia began on 23 June). Canada's contribution to the war effort was signalled by the graduation on Saturday of the first class of Royal Air Force observers from the Bombing and Gunnery School at Picton, Ontario. The day before, Lionel 'the Big Train' Conacher, MPP, had gathered together three of the greatest forward lines in hockey for a Victory Loan show in Toronto. Making the pitch to Canadians were Charlie Conacher, Joe Primeau, and Harvey 'Busher' Jackson of the Toronto Maple Leafs, Frank Boucher, Bill Cook, and Fred 'Bunny' Cook, the 'Kid Line' of the New York Rangers, and Milt Schmidt, Bobby Bauer, and Woody Dumart of the Boston Bruins. In other times the last three were known as the 'Kraut Line'; it is most unlikely Lionel Conacher used this nickname during the show. Meanwhile, in Ottawa, 'in a final impassioned battle just before Parliament adjourns, Conservatives … struck at Canada's war effort and what J.G. Diefenbaker termed the "deadening torpor of complacency" which had seized the Government.'[23] The freshman MP from Saskatchewan was already demonstrating his way with words.

Complacency was in short supply at the LSR convention. The national secretary reported that the branches in Calgary and Winnipeg had not communicated with the national office for months. Efforts to found new branches in Edmonton, Windsor, and Sackville, NB, had come to nothing. The treasurer, a teacher named E.D. MacInnes, reported that cash on hand was a measly $1.32. 'Are we tired radicals?' Eileen Troop wondered, and called for a revival of the old zeal tempered by realism: 'The LSR is always destined to be a small group and it should regard itself as such and stop getting depressed about itself, stop talking about our failures and get to work on research which is there waiting to be done.'[24]

There was some pre-convention opinion that the LSR had outlived its usefulness. 'The thing is having practically no effect on our community,' Eugene Forsey, the national vice-president, wrote to Frank Underhill: 'What I'm afraid of is that the LSR will either drag out a useless, semi-comatose existence, merely consuming energy better spent elsewhere, or that it will be grabbed and used by the C.P.' He feared that Jarvis McCurdy was insufficiently alert to the Communist threat. Underhill, setting forth his own views, noted that the older members now had little time to do more than keep the *Forum* going, and that few new members had joined lately.[25]

However, most of the delegates at the sparsely attended convention were not yet ready to call it quits. Instead they elected George Grube as president; Forsey allowed himself to be re-elected to the vice-presidency. McCurdy became national secretary and Ellet MacInnes stayed on as treasurer. Anyone looking for a symbol may find it in the re-election of J.S. Woodsworth as honorary president. He had suffered a stroke in May 1940; a second stroke in October 1941 peremptorily ended his attempt to resume public life. Five months later the 'prophet in politics' was dead.

The LSR, whose advent Woodsworth had hailed a decade earlier, did not long outlive him. Evidence of dwindling interest mounted after the 1941 convention: even Montreal and Toronto branches were by then losing members rapidly. In November the national executive, represented by Grube, McCurdy, MacInnes, and Underhill, met with three members of the Toronto branch executive, Geoffrey Andrew, Brock King, and J.W. Noseworthy, to discuss a motion by Underhill to disband the league. After a long debate it was defeated. The LSR would continue: 'Another earnest attempt should be made to organize its members into research groups and to bring in new blood.' But it was too late for transfusions. The last LSR open meeting of which there is a record took place in Montreal in March 1942. The speakers were David Lewis and Joe Noseworthy; the latter had the previous month delighted every CCFer, and possibly every Liberal too, by defeating the Conservative leader, Arthur Meighen, in a by-election in York South.[26]

Noseworthy's victory was particularly gratifying to the LSR because he was one of its own. The campaign did lead to a quarrel within the organization, however. Eugene Forsey, who enjoyed good personal relations with Meighen, took issue with an attack on the Tory leader written by Underhill and carried anonymously in the *Forum*. Forsey's complaints about Underhill's unfairness were overshadowed by the jubilation over Noseworthy's triumph. The CCF was on the move. However, the incident did nothing to pull the LSR out of its slough.[27]

The branch in Toronto arranged a program of occasional meetings in 1941–42. The last capitation fees ever, fourteen dollars, were paid by this branch in June 1941. An advertisement inviting readers to join the LSR appeared in the *Forum* until October 1942. The rest is silence.

IV

In late January 1942 *Saturday Night* carried an article by Frank Scott with the title 'Ten Years of the League for Social Reconstruction.' Scott adopted the elegiac mode: 'There has been a dispersal of leaders, and the actualities of politics, particularly since the new advances of the CCF, seem more attractive today than the pursuit of theoretical truth. This is perhaps a pity.' Canadians needed to think systematically about their society and its future, he continued; in doing this the LSR had during the 1930s made an important contribution. Now, in wartime, some of its ideas, especially those on planning, were being adopted by a government intent on running the war effort efficiently. 'The only thing wrong with the LSR idea, it seems, was that we did not adopt it.'[28]

There *had* been an exodus of leaders. Harry Cassidy left in 1934, Graham Spry and King Gordon in 1937. The following year Irene Biss followed Spry to England. Escott Reid joined the Department of External Affairs in 1939; in 1941 J.F. Parkinson and Leonard Marsh took leave from their university positions in order to take posts in the wartime bureaucracy in Ottawa.

For some members the *Forum* became the chief concern. Others decided that the FCSO, which was very active during the war years, best satisfied their interests. Others again were caught up in the work of the Civil Liberties Union, which after the outbreak of war had more than enough work to do. Under the War Measures Act and the Defence of Canada regulations – they came into effect on 1 and 3 September 1939 – the civil liberties of dissenters and labour leaders often got short shrift. The *Forum* soon began to carry a column exposing abuses of the civil liberties of groups and individuals and describing the activities of the CCLU. These activities were stepped up after the order-in-council of 5 June 1940 banned organizations such as the Communist party.[29]

The war itself was a diversion. Some members resigned in 1939 in protest against the LSR's stand on participation. Others joined the armed forces or became otherwise involved in the war effort. The federal bureaucracy drew in a handful of members.

Above all other reasons for the LSR's decline and disappearance stands the CCF. The party and its obvious need for workers seemed to render the LSR redundant. Even before the war some members had reached the conclusion that the league was not political enough. After 1940 the CCF became the focus of democratic socialist activity as never before. It was feared in September 1939 that the party might undergo proscription; instead the war took it, as it took Canada, out of the stagnation of the late 1930s. 'Although few in the party saw the war as an opportunity to advance,' Walter Young writes, 'it would not be far short of the truth to argue that the immediate result of the war was that it helped to save the CCF.' The movement had needed a new cause: 'The war provided a new panoply of evils against which the forces of democratic socialism could be arrayed.'[30] As the war grew older the CCF picked up steam.

Very tentatively the federal election of 1940 pointed the way. Disappointing as the results were, in every province other than Ontario, where the number of candidates was half what it had been in 1935, the CCF popular vote increased. In 1941 the party captured a plurality of votes in British Columbia and regained the status of official Opposition. Joe Noseworthy's electrifying by-election victory seemed the harbinger of further triumphs to come. 'The Canadian people are at long last on the march,' the *Forum* exulted.[31] More than ever the practical tasks of organization loomed large.

During the next two years these tasks proved amply rewarding. In 1943 the CCF took 34 seats to become the Opposition in Ontario. The following year the party came to power in Saskatchewan. By the time the CCF's bubble burst in June 1945 – it lost 26 seats in the Ontario election and managed to take only 28 constituencies, all but one west of the Lakehead, in the federal election one week later – the LSR was a receding memory. An attempt in the post-war period to revive the reality would fail.

Although it is true that the LSR ceased to exist as an organization in 1942, that statement is misleading. The league's demise was not total. Education and research did not cease when the LSR dropped from sight. *The Canadian Forum* became its living monument. Furthermore, some LSR members continued to do within the CCF the kind of work they had earlier done in the league. Both *Make This YOUR Canada*, the Lewis and Scott bestseller of 1943, and *Planning for Freedom*, a book of essays published by the Ontario CCF in 1944, were prepared by people who had been active in the LSR.

When the league was founded, there was no political party in which leftist intellectuals could feel at home. Shortly afterwards the CCF began to take shape, and though the LSR rejected formal affiliation it hastened to make itself useful. By the time the organization quietly disappeared amidst the alarums of war, the intellectuals had made the party their own. In 1942, the very year the LSR met for the last time, one of its former presidents, Frank Scott, was elected national chairman of the CCF. In the party the league lived on.

EPILOGUE

The Second World War and the organizational needs of the CCF had led to the demise of the LSR. After the war the absence of such an organization was sometimes seen as one reason why few young intellectuals were drawn into doing socialist research. As early as 1945 David Lewis mentioned to H.D. Hughes, acting general secretary of the Fabian Society, that there was talk of reviving the LSR. Nothing seems to have come of this. Three years later, however, Lewis stressed to Frank Scott the importance of calling the league back to life as a research organization. There was, he wrote, 'a great need for the kind of thinking which the LSR used to do. The LSR would also be an obviously useful instrument through which to tie to the work of the party the new generation of professional and technical people who at the moment have no definite place in that work.' A revived league should not be allowed to grow too large, however: 'I believe that one of the reasons why the old LSR died ... is that we attempted to make it a mass organization as well as a research instrument.' Scott noted in his reply that 'the old LSR was a semi-political party, since it ante-dated the CCF.' The second time around it would not need to be a quasi-party: 'We should keep numbers down and specialize in research and writing.'[32]

In spite of this agreement between the national chairman and secretary of the CCF, it did not prove easy to revivify the league. After more than two years of occasional discussion, however, and a study by the party's research director, Donald C. MacDonald, a 'Committee on Social Research' was founded in Kingston, Ontario, in June 1950. Among the members of this small group were Paul Fox and Kenneth McNaught, the latter a son of an LSR stalwart, Carlton McNaught. According to Professors Fox and McNaught, the new group did not have the energy of the old LSR and did not survive for long.[33]

More significant, though further removed in time and possibly in outlook from the LSR, have been the initiatives of the 1960s and 1970s. The publication of *Social Purpose for Canada* in 1961 brought to its editor's mind a comparison with the LSR's major book. 'We could not have escaped the influence of the democratic socialists who wrote *Social Planning for Canada* if we had wanted to,' Dr Michael Oliver wrote, 'and in spite of striking differences sometimes between the remedies (and to a lesser extent the diagnoses) proposed in the two books, their common purpose is unmistakable.'[34] In contributing to the later volume Frank Scott provided a personal link with the earlier; other contributors to *Social Purpose for Canada* included Kenneth McNaught and a writer who would later become prime minister of Canada, Pierre Elliott Trudeau.

The younger McNaught was also part of an organization that took shape at the University of Toronto in 1962, the University League for Social Reform (ULSR). In part it owed its inspiration to an address in Toronto by Frank Scott drawing attention to the work done by the LSR a generation earlier. The ULSR decided to remain aloof from party politics, however. Professor Abraham Rotstein, editor of the group's first volume of essays, *The Prospect of Change* (1965), explained that the ULSR preferred to take a non-partisan, 'broad left-of-centre' approach to the issues of the day.[35] It also limited itself almost entirely to practising academics. Links with the past were demonstrated by asking Frank Underhill, long since converted back to reformist liberalism, to write the foreword to the ULSR's second book, *Nationalism in Canada* (1966), and having Frank Scott do the same for the fourth volume, *Agenda 1970: Proposals for a Creative Politics* (1968).[36]

With the appearance in 1970 of *Close the 49th Parallel etc.: The Americanization of Canada* the ULSR's tone was clearly becoming more radical. The membership, if such it can be called, had spread beyond the confines of the University of Toronto. Indeed, whereas nine of the thirteen contributors to *Agenda 1970* were at the University of Toronto, only one of the twelve contributors to *Thinking about Change* (1974) was. Moreover, the influence of Karl Marx was significantly stronger in this, the seventh, than in the earlier volumes.[37]

Marxist influence was even more pronounced in *Capitalism and the National Question in Canada*, published in 1972 for the Studies in the Political Economy of Canada (SPEC) group. It was founded by former members of the ULSR who were committed to the achievement of 'socialist independence' in Canada. The contributors to its second volume, *The Canadian State: Political Economy and Political Power* (1977), were drawn from across Canada, though a special debt was acknowledged to the 'interdisciplinary faculty-student "Seminar on Contemporary Socialist Problems"' at Carleton University.[38] As in the ULSR, participation in SPEC is very largely limited to academics.

Neither the ULSR nor SPEC much resembles the old LSR. Among the most notable differences are the narrow constituency of the newer groups and their unwillingness to co-operate with a political party. One result is that they tend to consist of people who are speaking and writing mainly to and for each other. Yet the lively interest in research and education is very similar to that of the LSR. Though the socialisms vary considerably, the historian can nevertheless draw intellectual connections. However, neither of the more recent groups has so far matched the political influence of the LSR in the 1930s and 1940s.

10

Professors in the public eye

'Will radical leadership emerge from Canadian universities?' the University of Alberta classicist W.H. Alexander asked rhetorically in 1934. His answer was no. 'The "successful" way of life in our universities may be equated with the life of conformity both to doctrine and authority.' Five years later, writing from the University of California, the former LSR and CCF member added: 'Our people as a whole and fundamentally have little use for universities except as purveyors to their material comfort, and none at all for academic heretics.' Most academics knew their small place in society and kept to it. To be a trouble-maker was unrewarding.[1]

Into the decade of the 1970s Canadian professors have not been noted for their active involvement in politics or public controversy. In his *Vertical Mosaic*, published in 1965, the sociologist John Porter wrote of Canada: 'It would probably be difficult to find another modern political system with such a paucity of participation from its scholars.' Two political scientists noted in 1967: 'Ideological contributions of intellectuals to any party have been slim, certainly since the League for Social Reconstruction helped the young CCF draft the Regina Manifesto.' Another political scientist complained in 1970 that Canadian academics 'have become [sic] intellectually conservative and loath to engage in controversy that has not been sanctioned by their professional norms.'[2] If these and other observers are to be credited, Canadian professors have on the whole been reticent, uncontroversial souls, and the LSR was a startling exception to the rule.

Should we assume from this, however, that the academic freedom of the individual professor has been severely circumscribed at Canadian universities? Murray G. Ross, a recent anatomist of universities in England, Canada, and the United States, thinks not: 'On the whole it can be said that up to 1960 there was a healthy degree of freedom in Canadian universities but that there did not seem to be many professors in Canada who were inclined to test the degree that would be tolerated.'[3] The fault, if fault there were, presumably lay in academics themselves. Dr Ross cites the formation of the LSR and its support of the CCF as evidence of the substantial degree of freedom available to Canadian academics. He also notes the best-known attempt to dismiss a professor for his controversial activities, the case of Frank Underhill in 1940–41. That it was resolved in the historian's favour Ross takes as further evidence of the healthiness of academic freedom in Canada.

Neither the role played in the LSR and the CCF by some academics, however, nor the Underhill incident provides the clear evidence Ross seeks. And what, indeed, is a 'healthy degree' of academic freedom for the individual? Did it exist in all or most institutions? Why were so many professors apparently disinclined to put it to the test?

An attempt to answer these questions using the experiences of academics associated with the LSR and the CCF as the main source of evidence suggests that during the inter-war years the academic freedom of professors at many Canadian institutions was subject to significant if unwritten limitations. These were imposed by outside agencies as well as by academics themselves.

II

Poverty and financial dependence, especially if involuntary, are not conditions in which candour flourishes. In the inter-war years none of the approximately twenty-five Canadian universities was really wealthy, though a few were better off than the rest. Endowments were mostly small; so was the revenue derived from them. Thus Professor Robin Harris writes that in 1921:

> The combined endowment of Acadia, Dalhousie, King's, Mount Allison, and St. Francis Xavier, which together enrolled about 1,700 students, was substantially less than that of any *one* of three New England colleges, Amherst, Bowdoin, and Williams, none of which enrolled more than 500 students. Furthermore, where Amherst, Bowdoin, and Williams concentrated on the liberal arts, the Maritime colleges also offered courses in professional subjects.

The endowments of *all* Canadian institutions totalled $28.3 million in 1921, $48.5 million in 1931, and $57.1 million in 1939. Only in Quebec, with McGill University as the best-endowed institution in the country, was the revenue from endowments the single most important source of income. The universities in the four western provinces had virtually no endowment at all.[4]

While not ignoring potential donors universities looked mainly to two other sources of income, tuition fees and provincial government grants. The former loomed large in the affairs of the Atlantic colleges; the latter were easily the main source of income in Ontario and the West. The central place occupied by grants in the finances especially of the western universities had dire consequences during the Depression. In Saskatchewan, for example, the grant dropped by 41 per cent from 1930–31 to 1933–34; in British Columbia it fell by 60 per cent from 1929–30 to 1932–33. In the latter province a businessmen's group, the Kidd Commission, issued a report in 1932 that recommended that the university grant be ended altogether![5]

Increased tuition fees could not compensate fully for the declines in government aid. Budgets were trimmed at many institutions, especially in the West. Among other things this meant cuts in faculty salaries and a virtual halt to promotions involving increases in salary. Since the cost of living decreased by almost a quarter from 1929 to 1933 and rose only gradually from that year until 1940, the effects of cuts were mitigated somewhat. Like the universities, however, the professoriate became steadily more impecunious. Salaries had scarcely been munificent to begin with! Only the more senior faculty at the better-financed institutions, notably Toronto and McGill, were still reasonably well off.[6]

In 1931 there were 2,843 full-time and 2,224 part-time teachers. In spite of an increase in full-time enrolments of only 11 per cent (from 34,119 in 1930–31 to 37,866 in the last pre-war academic year), faculty numbers rose steadily during the decade. By 1939 the full-time faculty totalled 3,412 and the part-time 2,435, an overall increase of more than 15 per cent.[7] Since revenues generally stayed level or declined, we may surmise not only that there were few dismissals on budgetary grounds but also that young academics were being taken in at low salaries. Average and median compensation both fell. Yet to many of the men and women who taught in the universities even a badly paid position was easily preferable to none. Their options were few indeed.

The 1920s was not a decade in which the universities were showered with money, though one institution, McGill, managed to raise five million dollars during the period and saw its income double from 1920 to 1933.[8] It was only in retrospect, during the Depression, that the twenties came to seem almost a golden age. Even at the best of times, however, the universities had to struggle and beg for funds, to scrimp and save in order to make ends meet. The constant worry about money and the understandable desire not to offend existing and potential providers probably goes a long way to explain why Canadian academics were so little involved in politics and public debate.

But there is more to the explanation than that. Put simply, political participation by academics was neither expected nor much appreciated. Anti-intellectualism was not as strong here as in the United States; the traditions of both French Canadian Catholicism and Scottish Canadian Presbyterianism gave honoured places to men of learning. Much as in the United States, however, contributions to public life by scholars and scientists were much more warmly welcomed when the contributors were acting as practical experts than when they came as preachers or 'ideologues.'[9]

Probably typical was the attitude of Howard Ferguson, for most of the 1920s the Conservative premier of Ontario and minister of Education. He did not approve of academics who meddled in politics. Once he confessed himself to the Rev. H.J. Cody, then chairman of the Board of Governors of the University of Toronto, 'tempted to tick off a number of salaries of some men who seem to take more interest in interfering in matters of public policy and public controversy than they do in the work for which they are paid.'[10] Among the men who disturbed Ferguson's equanimity at one time or another were the political economists C.R. Fay, H.A. Innis, and E.J. Urwick, and the historian F.H. Underhill. Any professorial remark, whether within its author's professional competence or not, that offended Ferguson or aroused critical comment among the voters he was apt to regard as unwarranted.

Instructive, too, is the attitude expressed in 1929 by a member of the University of Toronto Board of Governors. Professors should stay out of politics, Angus MacMurchy told a reporter for the student newspaper, *The Varsity*: 'After all, your university professor is in the same position as the school teacher, is he not? Doesn't his salary come out of the taxes? People paying the taxes send their children to schools and they don't want politics preached to them.'[11] He conceded that professors in Britain were free to participate in politics, but 'we are not as far developed along these lines.' Nor, presumably, should Canada be.

Perhaps most important was that the self-image of many Canadian academics precluded political or controversial activity. They saw the university pre-eminently as a 'sanctuary of truth,' to use Howard Adelman's phrase, an ivory tower necessarily remote from the world of affairs. This was not unrelated to the image of a beleaguered garrison, a cultural fortress constantly threatened by a world that had to be propitiated. It is not for nothing that Professor Northrop Frye has identified the 'garrison mentality' as characteristic of the Canadian imagination as reflected in our literature.[12] Most scholars were content to leave the world to its own devices. They pursued their work, adhered more or less to the church of things-as-they-appeared to-be, and regarded with misgiving those of their colleagues – there were not many – who sought to play a more conspicuous part on the world's stage.

Before the twentieth century the academic as social critic was disposed to see himself as a moral tutor to a society too easily tempted into materialistic paths. He usually professed the humanities; his philosophical outlook was idealist. If he was barely heard when he spoke, this was primarily the result of his prudent or principled self-imposed exclusion from the hurly-burly of life. Academics mostly addressed themselves to their fellows. Only a few subscribed to non-controversial reform causes; most remained aloof.

Early in the century the social scientist emerged, committed to an empirical method. Readier to act as adviser to government and business, he might as a consequence attract considerable public attention. Scornful on occasion of the persistence of 'outworn' doctrines and policies, he was rarely outspoken in his criticism of the social order. The powerful of the land, churchmen, businessmen, and politicians, had scant reason to regard him as a threat to their interests.[13]

Socialism hardly touched Canadian academics before the Depression; communism did not do so even during the 1930s. The Conservative and Liberal parties sufficed those few who desired a political affiliation. Left-wing parties were proletarian and, except in a few isolated regions and cities, weak. They were not likely to attract support from *petit bourgeois* professors. In French Canadian universities, still dominated by the Roman Catholic Church, socialism was too easily equated with atheism; in English Canadian universities it was simply bad form. Socialists and socialism were not respectable; Communists were beyond the pale of employment. Even less-radical movements for change found few academic supporters except in the Methodist colleges, strongly influenced by the Social Gospel. However, enthusiasm was tempered by the dismissal of Salem Bland from Wesley College, Winnipeg, in 1917. Although his dismissal was justified on budgetary grounds, suspicion lingered that his outspoken Christian socialism was at least a contributory cause.[14]

Because professorial involvement in politics and public debate was rare, the meaning of academic freedom for the professor did not in Canada become the controversial question that it was in the United States. In 1922, however, a definition was attempted by Sir Robert Falconer, for a quarter-century president of the University of Toronto and at the time Canada's leading educationist. In an address delivered under the auspices of the Alumni Association Sir Robert asserted the freedom of the professor to teach and carry on his research without let or hindrance. In order to enjoy freedom within the academy, however, the professor must use discretion without. In teaching the young he assumed a grave responsibility. 'He is a citizen with a right to all the privileges of a citzen, but at the same time like a judge or a great civil servant he has high functions the exercise of which may make it wise for him not to perform all the offices of the ordinary citizen. Especially is this the case in a State University.'[15] It was 'expedient' that someone teaching in a state university should neither be active in 'party-politics' nor express himself on 'burning political questions.' Injudiciousness in these matters might redound to the harm of the offender's institution and his colleagues.

Sir Robert doubtless recalled that early in the century provincial politicians had still meddled in the making of appointments at the University of Toronto. It was common prudence to prevent a situation in which they might again be tempted to interfere in the university's affairs. Academic freedom even in its narrow sense, limited to classroom, library, laboratory, and study, was not free from threat.

Professors ought not to provoke criticism or attack by seeking to expand their freedom. Fortunately, prudence came easily to academics.

What Sir Robert championed in his 1922 address was essentially the *Lehrfreiheit* of nineteenth-century German universities. But he must have known that this was not the most controversial aspect of the issue of academic freedom. In the United States, where the German principle had for decades been accepted by the major institutions, the debate from the 1890s into the 1920s centred precisely on those rights that Falconer sought to limit, the rights of the professor as citizen. To what extent, if at all, should the professor be free to express his views in public, on matters in which he was professionally competent and on those in which he was not? Should he enjoy a latitude not generally enjoyed by employees to make possibly controversial statements about economics, politics, religion, or ethics without fear of discipline, particularly when those statements might be held against the institution that employed him?

In Great Britain, where universities had a high degree of faculty self-government, the 'freedom to follow and express political and social views in opposition to government or convention' was not in serious doubt.[16] Matters stood differently in the United States (and Canada). Executive heads of universities and their governing boards tended to take a dim view of anything that might adversely affect the income or reputation of their institutions. In some a single benefactor might wield great power and use it to rid the university of the heterodox; in others state legislatures might intervene to force the dismissal of men with unpopular views.

Levels of toleration varied among universities and from occasion to occasion. Out of the struggles to establish the rights of academic freedom in both its narrow and broad senses and out of the wish of some academics to be part of a self-governing profession emerged in 1915 the American Association of University Professors. The AAUP sought to define academic tenure and academic freedom in such a way as to provide academics with the widest possible protection against discipline or dismissal. Success was uneven.[17]

Nothing like the AAUP would develop in Canada until after the Second World War. When it did it was in response to the deteriorating economic position of the professoriate in the 1940s rather than to any perceived threat to academic freedom.[18] In the 1910s and 1920s professorial self-censorship added to informal institutional controls meant that there was nothing in Canada like the celebrated cases involving academic freedom south of the border. It is unlikely, then, that Falconer had any member of his own teaching staff in mind when he circumscribed academic freedom in phrases that might have come from the lips of a president of an American state university. Probably he regarded his address as a strong defence of academic freedom within the university against those people who would interfere with it even there. The notion that professors ought to inculcate approved ideas only was by no means dead.

Before the Depression no professor at a provincial university seems to have acted as if the Falconer doctrine was mistaken. At some of the private institutions, notably McGill and Queen's, academics exercised a wider freedom. Thus the McGill political economist Stephen Leacock was active in the Conservative interest in the federal election of 1911. The Liberal preferences of the Queen's political scientist O.D. Skelton were evident long before he left academe in 1925 in order to become under-secretary of state for External Affairs. The role ostensibly played by the *Queen's Quarterly* in bringing professorial intelligence to bear on political matters was praised by the Toronto *Globe* as it commented on Falconer's address on academic freedom. Sir Robert, the *Globe* suggested, was going too far in his restrictions on the political activities of professors.[19]

Nine years later the *Globe* was in the vanguard of those who told a group of professors at the University of Toronto to 'stick to their knitting.' The occasion was the widely publicized open letter of January 1931, signed by sixty-eight members of the teaching staff, that protested against police interference with allegedly communistic meetings. Not a few people took the letter as evidence of 'red' sympathies among the professors and argued that this damaged the university in the public mind.

That the connection between the signatories and the university was so easily made was a source of concern to both President Falconer and members of the Board. One of the latter, the millionaire businessman and philanthropist Sir Joseph Flavelle, wrote to George Wrong, emeritus professor of history, that the professors should have taken care not hastily 'to put themselves at variance with other representative bodies in [the] community.' He thought that the sixty-eight had needlessly stirred up press and public and feared that this might have unfortunate consequences for the university. After all, it 'must carry public opinion whereby it can be adequately housed and maintained.' Sir Joseph did not believe that the university's exigency should silence professors completely; he did want them to be very cautious.[20]

Ultimately, after weeks of discussion and an assurance from the president that his staff would behave more circumspectly in the future, the governors took no action other than to dissociate themselves formally from the letter of the sixty-eight. Premier George Henry was satisfied with this.[21] For his part President Falconer had been confirmed in the views he had stated in 1922. Controversy was dangerous to the university.

In June 1931 Falconer reprimanded Frank Underhill for having written critically of Prime Minister R.B. Bennett in the *New Statesman*. The article had elicited criticism from the Conservative Toronto morning paper, the *Mail and Empire*.

This, Sir Robert thought, was precisely the sort of publicity the university could do without.[22]

Underhill, who had been one of the initiators of the letter of the sixty-eight, defended himself by pointing out that in Britain and the United States professors could participate in public debate. He continued: 'If professors at Toronto must keep their mouths shut in order to preserve the autonomy of the University then that autonomy is already lost. A freedom that cannot be exercised without danger of disastrous consequences is not a real freedom at all. In the midst of all the intolerance which is rampant in the world at present a University plays a sorry part if it does not raise up its voice for freedom of speech.'[23]

Falconer was unpersuaded. 'The practice in British Universities or in the privately endowed Universities of the United States cannot be adduced in justification of what may be done in the University of Toronto,' he told Underhill. Professors ought to be satisfied with their freedom to teach and carry on research. The institution depended heavily on the goodwill of the legislature; it was therefore 'not only inexpedient but dangerous to the well-being of the University' if professors participated in 'party matters.'[24]

It seems likely that some other Canadian university presidents also thought this way. In general the issue of political participation had scarcely arisen, however. Apparently there was nothing like a formal policy against such participation. Academic self-censorship made such a policy all but superfluous.

As for academic support for radical movements, even in the second year of the Depression it was still unheard of. George Wrong was surely right when he assured Sir Joseph Flavelle in early 1931: 'In the main the universities of the Western world are strongholds of conservative thought and a steadying influence in our society. This is not less true of McGill and Toronto than of Oxford and Cambridge.'[25] It was even more true of Laval and the University of Montreal. Yet even as Wrong was writing some faculty members at English Canadian institutions were beginning to stir.

III

The LSR first came to public notice in April 1932 when R.B. Bennett drew attention to it during a speech in the House of Commons. That he made the mistake of ascribing the LSR manifesto to the hand of Vincent Massey, former Canadian minister to Washington and president of the National Liberal Federation, suggests not only that the prime minister was badly informed but also that the league had so far avoided identification with other radical groups.

Although Premier Henry of Ontario took somewhat apprehensive notice of the new organization during the summer of 1932, he exerted no pressure on the

University of Toronto to discourage faculty members from joining it. However, when late in the year some of its professorial adherents became active in the new CCF, there was a strong sense in influential circles that the bounds of propriety had been crossed. Canon H.J. Cody, who in 1933 would surrender his chairmanship of the Board of Governors to succeed Falconer as president, told a complainant that 'Professor Underhill has already been warned on account of certain actions in the past, and will be dealt with in the future.' The historian was told to get off the executive of the provincial CCF clubs. So was Eric Havelock; the authorities at Victoria College thought he was going too far in his political activities. (Havelock was in trouble again in 1937 when he addressed the General Motors strikers in Oshawa. He 'got carried away': in a fiery speech he allegedly insulted both Premier Mitchell Hepburn and the president of General Motors of Canada, Colonel Samuel McLaughlin. The classicist was instructed to apologize to the targets of his scorn and not to repeat this sort of indiscretion.)[26]

Underhill did not go without protest. From Norman Thomas, the American socialist leader, he obtained the names of academics active in American politics. At the same time he wrote a former student, then studying in England, asking him to gather similar information about British professors. His correspondent in turn approached Harold Laski of the London School of Economics. 'I told Laski that it was you who wanted this information,' S.D. Clark wrote Underhill: 'He told me to tell you that if there should be trouble at Toronto to let him know and "his gang" would do what they could about it.' Ironically, a year later Laski himself was in some trouble at the LSE because of his political activities.[27]

Predictably, Underhill was again unable to convince President Falconer of the justice of his case. He had no real choice but to resign from the clubs' executive.

Others also drew in their horns. In the autumn of 1933 Harry Cassidy went so far as to resign from the St Paul's CCF Club: 'For a variety of reasons I think that I can, for the present at least, be more useful if I am free of connection with a political party.' At the same time he wrote to D.M. LeBourdais, secretary of the Association of CCF Clubs, asking that his name be removed from the list of speakers that the central office had sent to the clubs. 'It would be easier for me to meet criticisms if my name did not appear on your official list of speakers,' Cassidy explained. That these criticisms were real is suggested by some comments that Cassidy, upon resigning his position at the University of Toronto in 1934, addressed to President Cody: 'I know that the trials of the President of a great university are numerous, and that I might have contributed to them on occasion. I can assure you that I appreciate very much your tolerance of faculty members such as myself expressing unorthodox ideas and of our being given genuine freedom in the University of Toronto to discover and express the truth as we see it – even if we may be wrong.' The gratitude seems a bit exaggerated: it should probably be interpreted with reference to Cassidy's expressed hope that he might some day return to teach at the University of Toronto.[28] However, it does seem that under Cody's presidency a measure of freedom was tolerated that went beyond that sanctioned by Falconer.

Instructive is J.F. Parkinson's response to a request by M.J. Coldwell in 1935 that he serve on a CCF committee appointed 'to interpret the financial plank of the CCF in the simplest possible language.' The economist declined the invitation: 'Up to now I have refrained from becoming an official of the CCF in any capacity whatsoever in view of (a) the fact that this step would put a weapon in the hands of opponents who take different views from ourselves as to the rights of a professor in a state-university; (b) the fact that I cannot manage to give any time to active political work in view of my heavy job of teaching etc.' Parkinson's readiness to give unofficial help suggests that the first point loomed larger in his mind than the second.[29]

In Montreal an LSR founder lost his teaching position. The Board of United Theological College, acting on a church decision to economize, in the spring of 1933 abolished King Gordon's chair of Christian Ethics and Religious Education. The decision was unpopular. Very quickly the student organization by a large majority passed a resolution 'asking the Governors of the College to reconsider the question ... and offering themselves to supply a portion of the salary connected with the College chair.' The Montreal *Gazette* reported that some of Gordon's colleagues were ready 'to assist financially as well.' The sum of $1,500 was raised, and Gordon was kept on for another year.[30]

Some of Gordon's friends early suspected that a need for economy was not the only reason for the board's action. During his two years at the college Gordon had more than once got into the newspapers because of his outspoken Christian socialism and his support for the CCF. Was it not possible that the board, dominated by conservative businessmen and scarcely less conservative clergymen, was using financial exigency as a cloak for ridding the college of an undesirable radical?

This suspicion gained strength in 1934. Despite a willingness by interested parties to endow Gordon's chair for another year, the board declined the offer. His dismissal became a *cause célèbre* within the United Church. Gordon had plenty of support. The editor of the weekly church paper, *The New Outlook*, was Rev. William B. Creighton, a member of the LSR's Toronto branch. The paper was evidently unhappy with both the behaviour of the governors and the 'inadequate and unsatisfactory' explanation issued by the church's General Council. It seemed more than possible that Gordon had fallen victim to those who opposed his views.[31]

Less inclined to pull punches was Gordon's friend Graham Spry. In an article written for *The New Commonwealth* he identified the important Montreal businessmen on the board, told the story of Gordon's relations with them, and concluded that the young minister had lost his position as the result 'of a deliberate and determined effort on the part of the reactionary members of the Board.'[32] Calls for Gordon's reinstatement were unavailing, however. From 1934 to 1937 he was travelling secretary of the Fellowship for a Christian Social Order, maintained by funds that friends and well-wishers raised for him; then he left for the United States. Not until well after the war did he again teach at a Canadian university.

At McGill University the attitude of administrators and many academics was one of annoyed tolerance. Eugene Forsey reported to Underhill in March 1933: 'I hear [Sir Arthur] Currie is much "worried" by my recent political speeches, or rather (I fancy) by the impertinent comments of busy-bodies who plague him on the subject.' But Forsey was reappointed. He was for twelve years a sessional lecturer; four recommendations by the head of his department that he be promoted were turned down. Senator Forsey recalls that at least one dean of Arts told him his public statements were 'injudicious.' But he does not think that his socialism was more than a contributory cause of his non-renewal in 1941. Had McGill wished to let him go for that reason it would have done so much earlier.[33]

Professor Frank Scott notes that McGill was far from friendly to socialism. He was well connected: his grandfather had been a professor of Medicine at McGill and his father, Archdeacon F.G. Scott, was widely loved and respected. But many people in the university disapproved of the notoriety gained by the younger Scott, a notoriety due chiefly to his activities in the CCF. An abortive attempt was made in 1942 to prevent him from serving as national chairman of the party. But, although the normal progress of Scott's university career was slowed, his teaching position was never in danger.[34]

What might have happend to his career had he been a Communist may be inferred from a letter which Colonel Wilfrid Bovey, Principal Currie's Man Friday, sent to the commissioner of the RCMP in December 1932. General J.H. MacBrien had inquired concerning the political views of a few men; Bovey replied at some length. He explained that King Gordon was not employed by McGill, and that in any case he was a '"Ramsay Macdonald [sic] socialist", in other words, he disapproves the existing economic arrangements, but desires their change by parliamentary action, not by revolutionary action.' Scott was put in the same camp. Forsey was dismissed as incapable of exercising 'influence over anyone who knew him, least of all over the students.' Whatever the students really thought, there was no doubt about Bovey's opinion. 'If you have any questions concerning any other people here whom I might know,' he added, 'you can count on me to help you out any way I can. The above information is all given you on Sir Arthur's suggestion.'

A letter from Commissioner MacBrien to Sir Arthur Currie two months later said in part: 'Since receiving Col. Bovey's letter dated December 17th, and having had a conversation with you when you were good enough to call to see me, I am quite satisfied that you are doing all that is possible at McGill to assist in the control of Communism.' The apprehensions that McBrien had entertained concerning Forsey and Scott had been allayed. Indeed, there had been 'no actual trouble' at the University of Toronto or McGill: the implication was that MacBrien did not worry about the young CCF.[35]

Professor Leonard Marsh noticed little hostility to and experienced no interference with his political involvements. He attributes this to his being much less active in the CCF than in the LSR. The latter occasionally aroused concern among the mighty but far less so than the former.[36]

At Queen's University as at McGill more freedom for the individual professor existed than at Toronto. Appointed in 1936 to the Department of Philosophy at Queen's, Martyn Estall never felt inhibited from being active in the CCF or LSR. 'I served under six principals,' he comments, 'and had no cause to feel constrained politically by any of them.' His older colleague Gregory Vlastos, who taught at Queen's in the 1930s and 1940s, says: 'The administration maintained a correct attitude.' No pressure was ever applied to him to cease his work in the left-wing organizations in which he was active; no one ever suggested to him that his activities might endanger the finances of the university.[37]

Two incidents in the 1930s are worth noting although they did not involve members of the LSR. In 1933 no less a person than R.B. Bennett proposed that the Liberal-leaning political scientist R.A. MacKay be dismissed from Dalhousie University for showing political partisanship. The reason was an article in *Maclean's* about the aftermath of the Beauharnois Scandal. President Carleton Stanley and the board rejected the suggestion, however, and MacKay did not hear of the incident until afterwards and then only unofficially. Not long after this incident, the historian Arthur Lower offended many by saying that he could never be loyal to Britain, only to Canada. In 1934 this was a damaging admission indeed. There were demands that he be fired from the staff of Wesley College. Not only were they rejected, however, but the principal publicly claimed for Lower the right of free speech.[38]

At the provincial institutions in the West the pattern was different. In 1935 the Board of Governors at the University of Alberta passed a resolution forbidding staff members from running for the House of Commons. The target was the classicist William Hardy Alexander, who had been nominated by the CCF in the constituency of Edmonton West. Three years later an isolationist speech by Carlyle King, an LSR member and English professor at the University of Saskatchewan, led to a command from the president that he cease discussing international affairs in public. King felt he had no choice but to comply.[39]

The latter two incidents, added to what we know about the University of Toronto, are perhaps too few to permit a strongly held theory about the difference between public and private institutions with regard to academic freedom. Their rarity may suggest, however, that especially at the western public universities professors tended to keep their mouths shut and to avoid organizations deemed to be controversial. Thus Grace MacInnis reported from Vancouver in 1939 that 'the LSR is closely identified in people's minds with the CCF and we find that the academic people here are fearful of the connection.'[40] Little was to be expected from them in the attempted re-establishment of an LSR branch. Like the public universities of the three prairie provinces, the University of British Columbia provided the LSR with next to no adherents.

The situation was not greatly different elsewhere. The league gained early and kept the reputation of a band mainly of professors. This owed more to their prominence in the LSR than to their numerical presence in it, however. Of the six national presidents of the League in its ten-year existence only one, Louise Parkin, was not an academic; of the six national vice-presidents only two were not (see appendix three). Academics were also heavily over-represented on the executive committees of the two main branches, Toronto and Montreal, though in neither did they constitute more than a tenth of the membership. Even in university towns where very few professors joined the LSR, as in Kingston or London, they assumed positions of leadership.

Outside Montreal and Toronto, however, only a handful of academics joined the league: Martyn Estall and Gregory Vlastos at Queen's, K.W. Taylor at McMaster University, R.E.K. Pemberton and one or two others at the University of Western Ontario, no more than five or six at all the western universities combined, a couple of sympathizers in the Maritimes (B.S. Keirstead at the University of New Brunswick and C.P. Wright at Acadia University) and in the French Canadian universities none at all – a little more than a dozen altogether. From coast to coast probably no more than fifty professors ever belonged to the LSR. Well over 90 per cent of the members and a fair number of the national executive and council, more than half by the later 1930s, were not university teachers. Yet as a group of academic 'brain trusters' the league was and is regarded nevertheless. That reputation is mainly a tribute to the educational work done by the LSR, for it was with that work that the academics were most closely associated.

IV

Of the criticism levelled against professors who entered the public arena and expressed controversial opinions much was directed at Frank Underhill. The historian's provocative commentary on current events landed him in the boiling cauldron more than once. The difficulties he experienced probably reinforced the habit of timidity among many of his colleagues. Freedom of speech for professors employed in publicly supported institutions was an uncertain thing: this was recognized within the academy and without. From his diplomatic post Hugh L. Keenleyside wrote to Underhill in 1933: 'There are a great many of us [civil servants] who appreciate and admire the courage with which you have been carrying on your campaign for a realistic and honest approach to the problems that are facing the country. The fact that we understand something of the handicaps under which you must work increases that admiration.'[41]

Underhill's manner of stating his views gave quite as much offence as what he actually said. Like the waspish schoolmaster Dunstable Ramsay of Robertson Davies's *Fifth Business*, the historian could not resist 'getting off "good ones" that went far beyond any necessary self-defence and were likely to wound.' His facility for finding an incisive phrase, admired by some, doubled his offence to others. 'You attack leaders by name in terms not gentle nor courteous,' George Wrong in 1933 reproved his former student and protegé: 'I do not regard your opinions as "deplorable" though I should have such a word in mind, I fear, if I were discussing your mode of expressing them.' Demands for Underhill's dismissal would mount, Wrong had a few days earlier warned, if he continued to engage in unseemly political wrangling at the expense of his scholarship.[42]

Like Dunstable Ramsay, too, Underhill occasionally had reason to regret his own sharpness. Periodically he was called to account by President Falconer and his successor, Canon Cody. As often as not it was less what he had said than the way he had said it that got him in trouble. One such occasion, the most distressing up to that point, took place in June 1937. Underhill had fallen foul of the new *Globe and Mail*.

The previous autumn a gold-mining magnate, William H. Wright, had purchased the two Toronto morning papers and merged them into one. In charge of the newspaper was Wright's confidant, George McCullagh, a dynamic bond salesman and mining stockbroker who had risen from humble origins to become a millionaire at thirty. He had 'a completely free hand' at *The Globe and Mail*, but there was nothing in the paper's editorial policy, 'protection for the mining industry and loyalty to the British tradition,' that Wright would have wanted to alter.[43]

Underhill probably knew little about the internal operations of *The Globe and Mail*, but he disliked what he read. And soon he had an opportunity to say so. In late May he joined G.V. Ferguson of the *Winnipeg Free Press* in a radio debate over 'Freedom of the Press'; in its course the historian quipped: 'At present in Toronto I have no alternative to reading at my breakfast table ... whatever a couple of gold-mining millionaires may think is good for the people of Ontario.'[44]

The newspaper responded sharply. The Canadian Broadcasting Corporation had no business allowing socialists like Underhill to pollute the air waves:

> If it cannot find men free of bitter political partisanship and class hatreds to fill in the time, it had better close down.
>
> The same thing should be said of the University of Toronto, and especially Victoria College, where socialism is seething ... Many a parent hesitates to send his son to these institutions because of the subversive doctrines in which he is likely to be 'educated.' 'One finds a widespread suspicion,' said Professor Underhill, 'that all that is accomplished by our elaborate educational machinery is to turn out masses of sheep who are just literate enough to become the victims of newspaper propaganda.' The sheep would fare better if certain professors, like Mr. Underhill, were turned out en masse and the public purse was relieved of the burden of supporting the kind of 'education' they promote.
>
> It is beyond comprehension that the public should pay to have members of the League for Social Reconstruction instruct the youth of the country.[45]

President Cody was bound to be upset by this. Not only was George McCullagh on the Board of Governors, but he was also known to be one of Premier Mitchell Hepburn's closest associates. (It was not widely known that he placed speculative investments for the premier.) Not for the first time Underhill was called in to explain himself to the president.

The historian found this meeting worrisome. 'The President is very anxious that I don't cause any more trouble in the near future,' he wrote to a friend, 'and since he has treated me pretty decently I don't want to make trouble for him.' As one consequence an article about the growth of the CIO in Ontario, written by Underhill for *Current History*, appeared there under Graham Spry's by-line instead.[46] Hepburn and McCullagh were both known to be sensitive on the subject. Now aware that his job was definitely in danger Underhill promised Cody that he would censor himself and moderate his public utterances in the future.

He tried to live up to this promise even though it was soon clear that a number of leading newspapers took issue with *The Globe and Mail*. Among them were the *Winnipeg Free Press*, the *Toronto Star*, *The Ottawa Journal*, and *Saturday Night*. Underhill was realistic, however: it was not their editors but Cody and the Board of Governors who disposed of his position. Even before the incident he had become circumspect about signing his name to pieces of journalism. During the next two years he contributed fifty-four articles and editorials to *The Canadian Forum*; only three of these appeared over his name.

Should professors be socialists, or socialists professors? The publication of *Social Planning for Canada* prompted Sir Edward Beatty, president of the Canadian Pacific Railway, to suggest to a convocation audience at the University of Western Ontario that socialism was surely an inappropriate doctrine for a university man to embrace. B.K. Sandwell, the editor of *Saturday Night*, demurred. Socialism was not a discredited theory, he wrote, and academics were entitled to their opinions. Moreover, since none of the signers of the LSR book had indicated a university affiliation, nothing improper had occurred. However, 'if Sir Edward had confined himself to the general question of university men using their academic prestige to further unacademic ends, he would have made an important and much neglected point.'[47] The point is still worth making today.

It was made in the Ontario legislature in March 1936. George Henry, now the leader of the Opposition, had asked the minister of Education what he intended to do about an unnamed academic – it was probably Underhill – 'who goes around the province making radical speeches and styling himself as a professor of the University of Toronto.' Members of the government asked for specifics and wondered if the Tories wished to limit freedom of speech. Then Leopold Macaulay spoke. The prominent Toronto lawyer and former Conservative cabinet member confessed:

> I can't for the life of me get excited at what some professor says. Anyhow, they're wrong nine times out of ten. They're entitled to express opinions. I object only when they plaster it all over the Province, when they are making these speeches, that they are professors of this and that. I'm a member of the Board of Governors of Victoria University, and I get plenty of criticism for my opinion on this matter. But in my mind, a professor is just the same as [a] coal-heaver at the University.[48]

Possibly the unflattering candour owed something to the lateness of the hour: Macaulay's tolerance was tinged with contempt. However, his attitude obviously pointed to a greater degree of freedom for academics.

Persons who, like Sir Edward Beatty, took professors more seriously than Macaulay did were bound to take a different line. In a convocation address at Queen's University in 1937 the president of the CPR again cautioned academics against espousing radical ideas. They might mislead impressionable students as well as the uninformed public. (There was, in fact, very little evidence that either students or the general public were much impressed by what radical academics had to say.) 'A sense of responsibility must be brought into play,' Sir Edward said, 'even if it prevents the turning of a striking phrase or the gaining of a little passing and useless publicity.'[49]

Beatty did not propose that anyone be dismissed. But at least one LSR member was 'tired of being blackguarded and slandered': the criticism had clearly been directed against the league. The CPR president should be asked to name some names and back up his insinuations, Eugene Forsey suggested to Underhill. However, the Montrealer was not optimistic about 'getting action out of the academic crowd in general.' Their main response to the likes of Sir Edward was sycophancy, and Forsey would not 'take the rap alone.'[50]

Forsey was already too much in evidence, not least because of his spirited opposition to Quebec's recently introduced Padlock Act. In 1938 Jean-François Pouliot, the Liberal MP for Temiscouata and a supporter of the act, suggested to Mackenzie King that 'the RCMP should investigate such socialists as Frank Scott and Eugene Forsey because of their subversive ideas.' Representative of this frame of mind also was an editorial attacking Scott by name and challenging his competence, and that of others like him, to teach in a university at all. Their opinions were too far out of line with that of the great majority of Canadian parents; and how could these opinions fail to affect their teaching?[51]

This statement questioned academic freedom even within the narrow boundaries of classroom, laboratory, and study. Those boundaries were in the inter-war years not yet secure. That education can, even should, be a subversive activity in itself, corroding ideas, beliefs, and values, was not a notion that commanded general assent. On the contrary, some people insisted that one function of education ought to be the reinforcement of sound principles and constituted authority, that one duty of professors is to uphold established verities, especially in times of danger.

Such a time was the early spring of 1939. Seemingly averted at Munich six months earlier, war in Europe threatened once again. In March German troops had occupied Bohemia and Moravia and entered Prague; Britain had responded by offering a guarantee to Poland, now most immediately menaced by Hitler's territorial ambitions.

Canadian defence spending had been increased in 1937; further substantial increases were proposed in early 1939. The LSR and CCF were critical of rearmament, and at a CCF convention the pacifist G.M.A. Grube expressed himself vigorously on the subject. When his comments were drawn to the attention of the Ontario legislature, Premier Hepburn and the leader of the Opposition, George Drew, agreed that Grube should be disciplined. 'Usually when we find communistic activities, we find among them leading spokesmen who are associated with our universities,' Hepburn noted with regret. It was time the University of Toronto took appropriate action.[52]

Probably with a sigh of relief President Cody pointed out to the press that Grube taught at Trinity College; not a penny of his salary came from the provincial grant and he was beyond the jurisdiction of the university's Board of Governors. In that case, the premier blustered, either Trinity could discipline 'this foreigner, Grube' – he had been born in Belgium – or the federation of the college with the university might be revoked or adjusted in some way harmful to the Anglican institution.

At this point George Drew brought Frank Underhill's name into the discussion; the university *could* do something about *him*. Drew quoted from a paper the historian had written some years before. Underhill was to be condemned by his own words: 'We must therefore make it clear to the world, and especially to Great Britain, that the poppies blooming in Flanders fields have no further interest for us. We must fortify ourselves against the allurements of a British war for democracy and freedom and parliamentary institutions.'[53] This sort of disloyal talk could weaken the commitment of students to the Empire and to British democratic institutions, Drew charged. Yet these students might soon have to go to war to defend them. Hepburn agreed with Drew that Underhill should be silenced and promised to investigate whether the provincial grant to the university could not be used as a lever to accomplish that end.

President Cody called in Underhill once again. The latter regretted that he had expressed himself so provocatively but pointed out that he was being attacked for something he had written four years earlier. Moreover, he had himself fought and been wounded in Flanders fields; he had certainly meant no disrespect of those who had died there. For two years he had observed his promise of 1937 to 'try to avoid undesirable publicity,' he subsequently wrote to Cody; the tone of this letter was one of hurt innocence mixed with supplication. The historian could not guarantee that someone would not again find some far-fetched excuse to denounce him 'as being offensive or disloyal.' However, he could be trusted to 'do [his] best in future to behave as reasonable men would expect a professor to behave.'[54]

Cody was apparently satisfied with this. The problem with the assurance, however, was that it was by no means clear who these reasonable men were and what they *did* expect. The balance of newspaper opinion ran against Hepburn and Drew. Alan Plaunt reported to Frank Scott that Grube and Underhill had been defended by the *Toronto Star*, the *Winnipeg Free Press*, *The Ottawa Journal*, *Ottawa Citizen*, and *Le Devoir* among others; their editors upheld the right of academics to speak out on questions of public policy, however controversial. From the University of New Brunswick an agitated B.S. Keirstead wrote to Underhill: 'Now that [Hepburn] has raised the issue of academic freedom I hope that the University of Toronto will stand behind you and fight the issue out with him. If Toronto can't do it, I don't believe it can be done by any institution in Canada.' Perhaps he meant: 'provincial institution.'[55]

Undoubtedly the matter looked very different to President Cody than it did to Keirstead or the editor of the *Toronto Star*. Quite aside from what he personally thought of Underhill's opinions and political ties – he was a conservative in more than one sense – Cody had to deal with unhappy politicians, board members, and alumni. 'University authorities often find themselves in a difficult situation,' the *Forum* commented, 'and although professors are always told that they have the full right of free speech, it has often been made plain to them that they should exercise that right in silence.' In his 'Letter to a young man contemplating an academic career' W.H. Alexander added: 'You must never forget that our universities are themselves products of the capitalist system ... They are too respectable either to fight or to tolerate within themselves a fighter.'[56] A dismal and exaggerated assessment, perhaps, but one that Underhill was also coming to believe.

If the historian was ever more reluctant to speak his mind in public one reason may have been a letter that his friend and steadfast defender, Alan Plaunt, had received from George Drew. Plaunt had charged Drew with attempting to suppress free speech. 'No question of free speech is involved at all,' the Tory politician replied: 'Canada is a British country and those of us who believe that Canada should remain British have a right to say that in our great institutions of learning anti-British doctrines shall not be taught.' It was simply unacceptable that 'our youth are instructed by parlour pinks who preach Empire disunity from the cloistered protection of jobs which give them all too much free time ... It is the duty of those charged with the education of our young people to play their part in making sure that Canada will remain British.'[57] There is no reason to believe that Drew was alone in his opinion.

Sixteen months passed, months during which Underhill stayed out of the public eye. Profoundly disturbing events were taking place in Europe. By the third week of August 1940, when academics, clergymen, journalists, businessmen, and others gathered for the annual YMCA conference at Lake Couchiching, the war was almost one year old and going very badly. France had surrendered two months earlier; an air battle was raging over Britain. Whether Hitler would try to invade England before the autumn was still unclear, the outcome of the war very much in doubt.

Sensitive to the changed realities of power in Europe, President Franklin Roosevelt and Prime Minister Mackenzie King met at Ogdensburg, NY, on 17 August and agreed to a Permanent Joint Board on Defence. That the United States was willing to sign 'what amounted to a joint defence pact with a belligerent ... had to count as a gain for the hard-pressed Allies,' Professor J.L. Granatstein writes. With Britain in danger, furthermore, it seemed to King 'prudent and wise to safeguard the Dominion by accepting the protection of the United States. No Canadian government could have done otherwise.'[58]

So it seemed to Frank Underhill when he spoke at Lake Couchiching on 23 August. In what was intended as a scholarly talk, but one that probably had its share of Underhillian quips and asides, he sketched for his listeners what seemed to him to be the implications and deeper meaning of Ogdensburg. Canada had gone to war primarily to emphasize our connection with Britain; the effect of the war so far had been to emphasize our geographical location on the North American continent. In defence matters Canadians now had 'two loyalties, the old one to the British connection ... and the new one to North America involving common action with the United States.' And in the long run our ties with Britain seemed bound to weaken while those with the Americans gained strength.[59]

Today Underhill's remarks sound trite. It was otherwise in 1940. There was a war on; Britain was fighting for survival. To predict a weakening of the British connection, of the Mother Country herself: was that not treason? And did Underhill not contemplate the trend with a certain satisfaction? There are truths we do not care to hear, lips we do not wish to hear them from.

At Couchiching, where Underhill's address was heard in context, no one got particularly excited. But newspaper reports let loose a hurricane of protest. A former prime minister, Senator Arthur Meighen, urged the minister of Justice to intern Underhill if he should have been reported correctly; his disloyalty could hinder the war effort.[60] This suggestion had no effect. Far more dangerous to the historian than Meighen's rather wild suggestion were demands, led by the Toronto *Telegram*, that he be fired.

Underhill had not expected this reaction. Deeply worried, he promised President Cody that he would refrain from making any speeches outside the university for one year. But this was no longer enough. A majority of board members had finally reached the view that Underhill was an incorrigible trouble-maker whose presence on the faculty harmed the university. (Some of them had reached this conclusion years earlier.) Canon Cody, who for years had shielded the black sheep while upbraiding him, was at last prepared to recommend his dismissal.[61]

Some months after his speech at Geneva Park, when Underhill had already begun to breathe a little easier, he was suddenly summoned to appear before an *ad hoc* committee of the Board of Governors. The date and time were Thursday, 2 January 1941 at 3:30 P.M.; the place was the Board Room in Simcoe Hall, that temple to the god of university administration on the Front Campus. Facing Underhill on that frosty day were the chairman of the board, Rev. D. Bruce Macdonald, the chancellor, Sir William Mulock, and Leighton McCarthy, KC. The two younger men – Macdonald and McCarthy were both around seventy – yielded to Mulock the right to state the board's case against Underhill. Within weeks of his ninety-seventh birthday, a man of great forcefulness and some wealth, a cabinet minister under Sir Wilfrid Laurier and more recently chief justice of Ontario, Sir William still dominated his environment.

The snowy-bearded patriarch explained that it would be best for all concerned if Underhill resigned quietly. The university would otherwise have to dismiss him: 'public opinion as expressed in the newspapers and elsewhere' was against the historian. Sir William urged Underhill to think carefully on the matter and discuss it with his friends before letting the board know what he intended to do before its next meeting on 9 January. The governors might be generous with respect to severance pay and pension rights if only this unpleasantness could be concluded with a minimum of damage to Underhill and the university.

A shocked Underhill asked some questions; Macdonald and McCarthy tried to answer but added little to what Mulock had said. 'It was a case of mutual incompatibility,' McCarthy said: 'the simple, sensible solution was separation.'[62] The alliteration did not, for Underhill, sweeten a very bitter pill. He left Simcoe Hall shortly after 4:00 feeling very much afraid. Resignation or dismissal: it was Hobson's choice! What university would hire him? He had been in hot water repeatedly; who would want a known trouble-maker on their staff? At just over fifty years of age he thought his teaching career was over.

After consulting with some friends and colleagues, however, Underhill decided against resignation. Instead he demanded a hearing so that he might defend himself against whatever charges might be brought against him. This hearing never took place. President Cody and a majority of board members altered their intention to rid themselves of Underhill. That he was not dismissed was due in part to interventions on his behalf by groups of students and alumni and by a deputation of senior faculty members. Two members of the Board of Governors, J.M. Macdonnell of the National Trust Company and J.S. McLean of Canada Packers, also defended him vigorously. Both had known him for years; both took a wide view of academic freedom.

Probably most important proved to be Underhill's friends in Ottawa, notably Alan Plaunt and Hugh L. Keenleyside. The latter, secretary of the Canadian Division of the Permanent Joint Board on Defence, kept high personages, among them the prime minister himself, *au courant*; he also personally urged Cody to consider the harmful consequences that Underhill's dismissal might have for the course of Canadian-American relations. After all, it would be tied to his address at Couchiching the previous summer. In the dark days of early 1941 such a consideration was bound to carry weight. The evidence that Underhill had strong political support was probably decisive. In any event, the board reversed itself with a minimal loss of face: it had never even made the ultimatum to Underhill public!

The historian kept his job. But this victory, if such it can be called, was less a victory for the principle of academic freedom than one for the influence of Underhill's supporters. His close brush with unemployment shook him, and he voluntarily extended the censorship he had increasingly imposed on himself since 1937. Although he did not cease to comment on public affairs in the *Forum* and elsewhere, he did so cloaked in an anonymity that was for several years virtually complete.

Underhill's well-publicized adventures sparked a good deal of debate. Educated people were far from being at one on the meaning and scope of academic freedom. Each incident showed that there were influential Canadians who expected professors to be complaisant, politically and in other ways, to be, in fact, much like the 'three ... most presentable professors' of Stephen Leacock's *Arcadian Adventures with the Idle Rich*, 'cultivated men who were able to sit in a first class club and drink whiskey and soda and talk as well as any businessman present.' At the very least academics should keep their views to themselves unless they had something 'useful' and 'constructive' to contribute.

The *petit bourgeois* background of many professors predisposed them to acquiesce in these expectations. So did the financial weakness of the institutions in which they served, the conviction that the ivory tower ought to be removed from the world, and the awareness that controversial outspokenness earned few or no rewards inside the academy or out. Indeed, punishment was more likely.

It is perhaps less surprising, then, that so small a proportion (between 1 and 2 per cent) of Canadian academics joined the LSR than that approximately a score were very active in it. No doubt the unsettling impact of the Depression played a part in leading some to become involved. But personal variables were also important. Exposure to the English educational system was one of these: most of the league's leading figures had obtained all or part of their university education in Britain. Several of them, including Eugene Forsey, King Gordon, and Frank Scott, had been Rhodes Scholars in the 1920s; Frank Underhill was a Flavelle Scholar at Balliol College, Oxford, just before the Great War. Particularly at Oxford and Cambridge the intellectual atmosphere was more heady and permissive than was the case in Canada.

Another variable was religious background or conviction. Not only were several LSR leaders sons of the manse or of strongly Protestant homes, but half a dozen or so were active in the Fellowship for a Christian Social Order. Among them were Forsey, Gordon, Eric Havelock, Jarvis McCurdy, and Gregory Vlastos.

A third variable was incomplete socialization into the professorial role at the time the Depression struck. The academics who joined the LSR were typically young, in their late twenties and early thirties; most got their first university appointments in the late 1920s. Underhill was an exception: he was in his forties and except for war service had been teaching since 1914. But among the men and women of the LSR Underhill was particularly concerned to claim for professors some of the rights of a self-governing profession as well as its prestige. Besides, perhaps there was something to Harold Adams Innis's belief that to have survived the trenches marked a man like Underhill for life, that it left him subject to a curious recklessness.[63]

Strong moral conviction is not limited to young people, nor is the courage to act on it. But courage is often in part a result of youth and inexperience. So, one hostile critic of the LSR observed in 1935, is conceit concerning one's own abilities. In attacking *Social Planning for Canada* P.C. Armstrong referred to men 'often immature and poorly trained, who have obtained teaching posts in our universities during the period when these institutions were expanding very rapidly.' Sentimental and inclined to overestimate their own abilities, they assumed 'that they are both bound and able to undertake the reform of society overnight.'[64]

Though not devoid of truth, this *was* malicious. Neither intelligence nor wisdom is the exclusive property of middle or old age. And whatever one may think of their proposals for change or explanations of domestic or international politics, of the ability of the LSR's academics there can be no doubt. Some were already in the 1930s making distinguished contributions to scholarship and public life quite apart from their work in the LSR; more have done so since, in Canada and abroad.

V

No era of sharply increased involvement of academics in politics, especially radical politics, was ushered in by the LSR. For several decades the professor in the public eye continued to be the exception to the rule. Since the demise of the league in 1942 and even before that, the relatively few who have gone into politics have usually opted for 'pragmatic' accomplishments rather than ideological contributions. Not the least obvious example is the current prime minister, Pierre Elliott Trudeau.

The nature of the institutions, the background of those who taught in them, natural caution, and professional preoccupation have all contributed to the political quiescence of the Canadian professoriate. This account would be incomplete, however, without a discussion of the views of a political economist whose influence on his colleagues lasted into the 1960s, Harold Adams Innis, and of his dispute with Frank Underhill about the role of the social scientist in society.

Professor John Porter was disposed to assign considerable importance to Innis in explaining the reluctance of Canadian academics to participate in politics. In the interest of their scholarly integrity, Innis believed, social scientists should stay aloof from politics. This was not for the sake of preserving an Ivory Tower where unsullied Truth was worshipped, but for the sake of preventing the development of scholarly disciplines from being thrown off course by the demands of political necessity. To use Howard Adelman's terminology again, Innis adhered not to the Sanctuary of Truth but to the Sanctuary of Method.[65]

At a very early stage Innis took an interest in the LSR. Graham Spry recalls that the economist attended a meeting of the research committee in the late fall of 1932.

When the league in 1933 became involved with the CCF, however, Innis withdrew in dismay. He soon took a dim view of the closer relations that seemed to be developing between politicians and academics, especially economists. The best the economist could do was to give his tentative advice and leave the politician to adapt it as he might, Innis told the Conservative Summer Conference at Newmarket, Ontario, in 1933. The responsible economist, that is; without naming LSR names he took a swipe at those who had presumed to compete with demagogues and had 'become demagogues themselves in the competitive process.'[66]

Innis's skill in identifying problems was marked. His reluctance to prescribe solutions – his sense of the limits of knowledge was very strong – did not go uncriticized, however. At the meeting of the Canadian Political Science Association in 1935 Frank Underhill, in referring to a book Innis had co-edited, *The Canadian Economy and Its Problems* (1934), deplored its failure to discuss ends and goals. This was typical of Canadian intellectuals generally, Underhill asserted. The chief contribution of intellectuals to public life since the demise of the Canada First movement in the 1870s had been to justify, explicitly or implicitly, the purposes and policies of the ruling cliques of lawyers and businessmen. Economists had been 'happy in their unambitious way as the intellectual garage mechanics of Canadian capitalism'; historians had helped 'to sell the system to the public with a slick line of talk about responsible government and national autonomy.' At this time of crisis, Underhill said, the social scientist had either to 'accept the ends and values in our present social system or ... [make] up his mind to the best of his ability as to what our social objectives ought to be and to publish his conclusions to the world for the criticism of his fellows.' Innis's attempt to escape from this choice represented 'a retirement to the ivory tower.'[67]

Innis picked up the gauntlet immediately. His main counter-attack came not long afterwards in a review of *Social Planning for Canada*. He used strong language. He referred to 'footloose adventurers in universities [who] turn in some cases to business and its profits during booms, and in others to political activity and popular acclaim during depressions'; he deplored 'external activities, even to the point of writing party-platforms and bank-letters'; he judged that 'elections in a depression are not conducive to high standards [of scholarship] in the discussion of complex problems of the social sciences in volumes written for political purposes.' According to his biographer, Innis believed that the appearance of the CCF was accompanied in the work of the LSR by a serious and seductive threat to the autonomy of the social sciences. This explains the bitterness of his review.[68]

Underhill soon replied in kind. He noted that the intrusion of professors into politics was common in Britain and was not unknown even in Canada. The rub seemed to be that recently some Canadian academics had become active on the radical side. Could it be that the hostile reaction of Innis and others was prompted by outraged respectability? 'All Canadian economists are divided into two classes; there are ... those who have already served on Royal Commissions; and there are ... those who are still hoping to do so. Now to serve on a Royal Commission one must have achieved a reputation for respectability. But for any reader who is familiar with the inside of our Canadian universities there is no need to develop this point further.'[69] This was as unworthy as anything Innis had said; it was also silly. After all, several of the LSR's leading lights were economists!

At this point the public quarrel ended; the private argument between the two men went on for some years. Nevertheless Innis helped to defend Underhill in January 1941. He joined the deputation of senior academics who went to see President Cody and afterwards wrote to him that he was prepared to risk losing his own position in order to save Underhill. To Innis 'the fraternalism of war' – both men had served overseas; both had been wounded – far outweighed the differences between him and the other man.[70]

Both Innis and Underhill had made telling points without convincing each other or, one suspects, many witnesses to their debate. Innis's disapproval of academic involvement in politics matched the mood of most professors; it did not create that mood. Underhill's influence was by no means strong enough to lead many academics into the realm of public controversy. Indeed, his experiences probably scared some off!

Academic tenure was still too frail a reed. It was typically held during the pleasure of the governing board on the advice of the executive head of the institution. That, as Underhill found when in January 1941 he asked Leopold Macaulay for an opinion, was the case at the University of Toronto.[71] Formal hearings of dismissal at which charges had to be laid and substantiated were not yet features of the Canadian academic landscape. Underhill asked for one, but the university was under no obligation to grant his request.

It must be added that dismissals were rare. Innis observed in 1936: 'There is sufficient truth in the statement that it is impossible to leave a Canadian university except by death or resignation, to evoke general recognition of its accuracy.'[72] King Gordon was very much an exception. But it required only one exception of that kind to remind academics of their basic vulnerability.

VI

In the 1980s the freedom of Canadian professors to speak their minds is generally well established. As it has developed in the last twenty years tenure offers wide security against reprisal from governments, administrators, or colleagues. Yet in 1972, at a time when the influence and prestige of Canadian academics was at or near its historical zenith, Professor David Braybrooke of Dalhousie University wrote: 'The most serious complaint that the public has against professors in the matter of tenure is not that professors should not have it, but that having it they should not use their special freedom more frequently and more vigorously.'[73] Now as in the 1930s, it seems, most academics seek peace and quiet.

The writing of the history of Canadian universities is still incomplete, and the history of academic freedom in Canada has only recently become an object of study. Hence even Canadian academics know little about either. We lack books such as those written by Frederick Rudolph and Laurence Veysey about the American college and university; we have nothing like the two volumes in which more than twenty years ago Richard Hofstadter, Walter P. Metzger, and R.M. MacIver traced the vicissitudes of academic freedom in the United States from colonial times into the McCarthy years.

The excesses of that time and the comparative paucity of scholarly literature about Canadian universities may have led to a smug belief that academic and intellectual freedom has been safer here than in the United States. Such a belief remains to be carefully tested.[74] That there was no witch-hunt in the Canadian universities during the early years of the Cold War, however, may not be evidence of a greater degree of tolerance for heterodoxy among our intellectuals so much as of historical differences between the two countries. Smugness on that score may be compared to a bachelor's self-congratulation because he is not a wife-beater.

First, as S.M. Lipset has shown, Canadians defer more to élites than do Americans; hence the anti-élitist aspects of the post-war anticommunist campaign in the United States had little relevance in Canada. Second, insofar as that campaign was anti-intellectual, its counterpart in Canada as described by scholars such as Gerald Caplan and Walter Young was rather pale in comparison and not so long sustained.[75]

Third, in the later 1940s and early 1950s many Americans were reacting against F.D. Roosevelt, the New Deal, and the growth of 'Big Government.' Canadians, whose cast of mind is more favourable to the exercise of governmental power – the political scientist David Bell has called us 'cratophiles' – did not react to the expansion of government and of welfare-state measures in the same way. Indeed, Canadians generally welcomed the expansion of social-welfare policies in the late war years; this approval helped re-elect the federal Liberals in 1945.[76]

Fourth, many Americans came to resent the vastly increased involvement of their country in world affairs and the necessity to exercise international leadership after the Second World War. Canadians, however, had no opportunity either to resent or to accept the latter, and they may have welcomed the former as proof of Canada's increased stature. Fifth, unlike many Americans, Canadians were little concerned about the 'loss of China' and had no pressing need to find a scapegoat for it or for the frustrations of the Korean War.[77]

This does not mean that Canadians were comparatively 'soft on communism.' On the basis of the evidence the opposite may be true. Canadians were strongly anticommunist. The Communist Party of Canada, technically illegal from 1931 to 1936, was officially proscribed in 1940, went underground, and did not emerge again until 1943, thinly disguised as the Labour Progressive party. The Gouzenko spy affair just after the war confirmed many Canadians in the opinion that Soviet Russia was not to be trusted and that Canadian Communists were likely to be traitors. In the labour movement there were determined attempts to purge them. As Irving Abella and others have shown, Canadian Communists concentrated their interest in the labour unions; this led in the 1940s to bitter battles between Communists and supporters of the CCF.[78]

However, and here is yet another contrast with the situation in the United States, there was among Canadian intellectuals and more particularly in Canadian universities a near-absence of witches to be hunted. The National Film Board, under attack for alleged bias in Russia's favour, had to dismiss a few employees after the war. Worth a special note is the historian and diplomat Herbert Norman, hounded to his death in 1957 mainly by American anticommunists. Norman was a comparative rarity because he had actually been a member of the Communist party in the 1930s. Among professors there were none such.[79] A few sympathizers there may have been, but they kept their opinions private.

The LSR and CCF, not fully respectable but not at most universities beyond the pale, were organizations as radical as academics dared to join. Few of them did. Those who joined did not eventually become victims of some McCarthyite persecution; indeed, some of them have gained the highest honours Canada can bestow. At the time many of them had their troubles, however. Most of it was little more than petty harassment; some of it was genuinely menacing. It was noticeable and it took courage to face. It is evidence that the degree of academic freedom available to professors was at a number of Canadian universities subject to fairly narrow limits. Any future history of these universities and of academic freedom in Canada must assign an important place to King Gordon, Frank Underhill, and the other academics in the LSR.

11

Conclusion: the LSR in Canadian history

Conceived in the Depression year of 1931 and born in the following winter, the League for Social Reconstruction was active for almost a decade. By 1941 its energy had been spent, and within another year, amidst the alarms of war, it quietly disappeared. Not without a trace, however: its campaign for socialist reform, for a more genuine and complete democracy, did not come to an end. It continued under the banner of the Co-operative Commonwealth Federation, the new political party with which the LSR had after 1933 largely identified itself.

Begun with the purpose of increasing public awareness of social and economic problems and thus, it was hoped, helping to create the conditions for reconstruction, the league initially adopted a non-partisan stance. (It found none of the then-existing parties attractive.) That stance was never completely abandoned: the LSR's membership was never limited to members or supporters of the CCF or to those who considered themselves to be socialists. By the mid-1930s, however, those who did not at least think kindly of the CCF and its prospects were likely to feel uncomfortable within the league.

The LSR's ideas show Fabian, Marxist, Guild, and Christian socialist and reformist liberal influences as well as insights gained from domestic sources, especially the agrarian radicals of the prairie West. The same eclecticism is evident in the LSR's prescriptions for change. The best statements of the league's thought are its two published books, *Social Planning for Canada* (1935) and *Democracy Needs Socialism* (1938). Another important source, particularly for LSR views on domestic and international politics, is *The Canadian Forum*. For much of the 1930s the monthly was under LSR control; indeed, in 1936 the league purchased the *Forum* and managed with difficulty to save it from extinction.

The LSR's critique of monopoly capitalism focused on the power of the modern corporation, on its subversion of political democracy while denying economic equality. The league proposed to overturn this power by means of an ethical revolution that would create the conditions for the establishment of the co-operative commonwealth. In this society 'the basic principles regulating production, distribution and service will be the common good rather than private profit.' The commonwealth would take shape gradually, during a period of transition in which the state expanded its control over the economy while it socialized key industries and the living conditions and incomes of Canadians steadily improved and became more equal. Private fortunes would be taxed away, and ordinary workers would get an effective voice in the economic as well as the political realm.

Social and economic planning, carried out centrally by experts, would somehow mesh with the willing and effective participation by ordinary people in the making of decisions. The National Planning Commission would report to cabinet and Parliament but only after it had assessed and incorporated the submissions of local bodies, co-operatives, unions, joint management-worker councils, and the like. Through these and through their elected representatives at all levels, Canadians would share in the shaping of their country. Thus popular sovereignty and democracy would become realities.

LSR writers believed that human beings were at least potentially enlightened and beneficent enough to build a society both free and communal. All legitimate desires for individual freedom would find expression in the co-operative commonwealth. Those desires that contradicted the practice of co-operation were by definition illegitimate and would eventually disappear, the remnant possibly to be treated as a form of illness. Elitist at least in intellectual concerns, the LSR had nothing against the recognition of special merit and accomplishments. But these should not confer extraordinary privilege or power.

Some of the league's proposals were designed for introduction into a society still predominantly capitalistic. These were measures of social welfare and labour legislation that would reduce the inequalities of wealth and power in Canada and make the society more humane. Such reforms, however, were seen as no more than interim objectives along the road to the new society.

In their discussion of politics the LSR's intellectuals expressed confidence in the available electoral and parliamentary machinery. Fearing the chaos that revolution would bring, they professed to believe that socialist change could be accomplished and maintained by constitutional means. Some alterations would be necessary, such as the abolition of the Senate. Political democracy would work to satisfaction, however, once the mass of Canadians came to understand that socialism was in their own best interests. Thus the LSR held that farmers and small businessmen had a natural community of interest with industrial workers that outweighed their differences. All of these groups should support the Canadian socialist party, the CCF. Characteristic of this attitude was a chapter heading in *Make This YOUR Canada*, written in 1943 by two of the original founders of the LSR, David Lewis and Frank Scott, 'Political Action for the 99 Percent.'

The LSR's main primarily political goal was the unquestioned realization of

Canadian sovereignty *vis-à-vis* both Great Britain and the provinces. With respect to the latter the LSR held to a centralizing federalism. Minority rights, notably those of French Canadians, were to be safeguarded, but the Dominion government had to have the capacity not only to cope with the nation-wide economic problems of the Depression but also to bring the corporations to heel and nationalize them if necessary. Insofar as French Canadian nationalism hindered these objectives it was an obstacle to progress. Since disregard for civil liberties was even more pronounced in Quebec than elsewhere in the country, LSR writers like Eugene Forsey feared the rise of a domestic fascism here. The only important points of agreement between most LSR members and the bulk of French Canadians were that our relations with Britain were still too close and that neutrality in a future European war would be more than desirable.

The desire for neutrality led the LSR to see the British connection as potentially harmful to Canada and to insist that all official strands of the connection be cut. At the same time the LSR was generally complacent about Canada's relations with the United States. The isolationism of that country was an attractive model during the later 1930s. However, the desire of most LSR members for neutrality, which also led them to denigrate the League of Nations, overlay a frustrated internationalism that reasserted itself during the war. Internationalism was implicit in the LSR's socialism, and had been from the beginning.

II

Whatever one makes of the LSR's ideas, its significance in one respect is clear. It marked the first time in Canadian history that a group of intellectuals had become active in politics under the socialist banner.

A limited precedent existed, as Kenneth McNaught suggests in his biography of J.S. Woodsworth. The Canada First movement of the 1870s had been founded by intellectuals who were disgruntled by the crass materialism of the new nation and hoped to lift the minds of Canadians to higher concerns. Both groups proposed new national goals and policies. Both initially assumed a non-partisan role but quickly drew close to a political party that was sympathetic to their aims. Both took shape in the midst of an economic depression that helped to create an audience for social criticism. Both could boast among their number the most incisive political critic in the country: Goldwin Smith in the 1870s, Frank Underhill in the 1930s. The latter admired the former and tended to overestimate the part he had played in Canada First. Some aspects of Smith's thought emerged in the LSR, notably his insistence on the North American destiny of Canada (though not his annexationist conclusion) and her need for complete independence from Britain.

The contrasts between the two organizations are at least as marked as the similarities, however. The men of Canada First were akin to the American Mugwump of the late nineteenth century, 'a conservative in his economic and political views,' as Richard Hofstadter notes. The strain of social criticism in Canada First was in no way socialist: like the Mugwumps' criticism it tended to look backwards and proved most acceptable to later Conservative intellectuals such as Principal George M. Grant of Queen's University, Sir George Parkin, and the McGill economist Stephen Leacock. Aspects of the Mugwump sensibility were perhaps not completely absent from the ideas of the LSR, but on the whole these looked steadfastly to the socialist commonwealth of the future.[1]

An organization of 'utopian' intellectuals in Karl Mannheim's sense,[2] the LSR hovered between liberal humanitarianism and socialism. However, during its ten-year life it shifted perceptibly from the former to the latter. It served some hundreds of the Canadian intelligentsia as an agency of economic, social, and political criticism. Its efforts were sometimes most unwelcome. Several of the more visible of its members felt pressure at one time or another that was intended to intimidate and silence them. The efforts of Frank Underhill to resist such pressures while adapting to them constitute a fascinating chapter in the history of academic and intellectual freedom in Canada.

Canadians expected their intellectuals to be 'useful' or 'constructive' in an auxiliary capacity, or else decorative and possibly entertaining. They did not expect them to be critical or radical. Before the 1930s whatever criticism Canadian intellectuals had directed against their society had been muted, had rarely been radical, and had not led to the formation of a movement seeking social change. As the first such organization, the LSR desired a more central place for intellectuals than they had hiterto enjoyed, desired to claim for them the role of economic and social experts, of guides to a political party that would introduce the new social order. Although the league established close relations with the CCF, that party did not have an opportunity anywhere to put its ideas into effect until it was elected in Saskatchewan in 1944. That was its only major success. But although the LSR's hopes for major change and reconstruction at the national level grew dim, Canadian society as it developed from the 1930s into the 1970s *did* witness a steady increase in the power and influence of the intelligentsia. The most important agency of this process was not the political party system but the civil-service bureaucracy, especially that of Ottawa. The ideological bias of what was happening was far from radical. The process was associated with pragmatic accomplishments directed towards the growth of a welfare state, a necessary response to the changed realities of an urban and industrial Canada. As part of the growth of that state intellectuals have become less peripheral in Canadian society than they once were, but in general they have been neither willing nor able to use their increased influence in order to try to secure a radical reconstruction of society.

The LSR, as the first organization of socialist intellectuals in Canada, was an intellectual by-product of the Great Depression. Its existence owed much, however, to the character and concerns of the men and women who founded and sustained it and, indeed, to the man who more than any other inspired them, J.S. Woodsworth. Those who joined the LSR were mostly young, with a strong sense of social responsibility that in a number of cases was rooted in religious conviction. They were also interested in the arts and sciences and were founders and mainstays of many voluntary organizations. *The Canadian Forum* served them as a mouthpiece, but they took seriously its commitment to foster literature and the performing and graphic arts in Canada. Their rescue of the *Forum* in 1936 entitles them to the continuing gratitude of Canadians concerned about our cultural life.

Through the presentation and interpretation of what it held to be factual material the LSR hoped to give readers and listeners a clear appreciation of what was happening and to encourage them to vote and otherwise act in Canada's best interests. The league propagandized mainly at the level where most of its members felt at ease, that of the educated middle-income groups or 'middle class.' Though there was a recognition that these groups were generally hostile to proposals of thorough-going change – this in part explains the LSR's initial avoidance of the term *socialism* – there was also the hope than an exposure to 'the facts' would alter this. Men were basically rational; the truth would set them free.

Never did the LSR realistically assess what it was up against. 'Attempts at changing attitudes or social prejudices experimentally by the dissemination of information or factual argument have been notably unrewarding,' say two social psychologists, Mustafer and Carolyn Sherif. A psychiatrist, J.A.C. Brown, comments:

> There are, perhaps, three main reasons for this: (1) deep-seated attitudes tend to be part of an integrated pattern of associated beliefs within the individual which cannot be changed item by item ...; (2) peripheral attitudes are a function of the group rather than of the isolated individual and can only be changed by altering group attitudes collectively; (3) to try to alter an individual's attitudes by direct instruction is to imply that he is wrong and this is interpreted, consciously or unconsciously, as an attack, of which [Gordon] Allport says: 'It is an axiom that people cannot be taught who feel that they are at the same time being attacked.'

Brown also writes: 'Political propaganda is much less effective than has often been thought ... and in particular, the mass media play only a small part in changing people's attitudes.' They reinforce existing attitudes rather than alter them.[3]

In western countries those attitudes, whether they incline people to support one party or another, are among the middle classes generally favourable to capitalism, the market system, and the privileged position of and concessions to business. All citizens are subjected to a steady stream of information that upholds the primacy of business. As the economist Charles E. Lindblom has recently noted, much of the propaganda that reaches people, particularly through the educational system and the media, associates private enterprise with political democracy. Businessmen also 'use their disproportionate influence to try to create a dominant opinion that will remove grand issues from politics.' These grand issues are 'private enterprise, a high degree of corporate autonomy, protection of the status quo on distribution of income and wealth, close consultation between business and government, and restriction of union demands to those consistent with business profitability, among others.' The issue of central planning of the economy is another one. No homogeneity of opinion is secured in this way, but that is not necessary. 'Values are more confused than conservative, and the confusion is sufficient to keep a range of grand issues quiescent.'[4] Thus few people challenge basic institutions or pay attention when someone else challenges them. Such voices are in any case hard to hear; newspapers and broadcasting stations are, at least in North America, almost all owned and operated by business firms. The few that are not rely on advertising or more direct corporate support, or on the support of governments that have nothing to gain from making the position of business a matter of public controversy.

Although the prestige of businessmen dropped in the early 1930s as a result of their failure to halt the economic decline, the basic outlines of the private-enterprise market economy were still accepted by the mass of Canadians, certainly by middle-income Canadians. The LSR challenged some of the basic features of the economic system; most people ignored the challenge. Reformist propaganda, Gordon Allport notes, has most effect on people who, for whatever reason, are 'on the fence.'[5] Many Canadians may have been frightened during the Depression without therefore becoming favourably disposed to new ideas or new ways of doing things. On the contrary, especially among middle-class people the great hope was that life would soon return to normal. There were enough economic casualties among small businessmen, professional people, and white-collar workers for the level of anxiety to be high.[6] That anxiety did not lend itself to an imaginative restructuring of society; it led most people to rock no boats. There was no advantage to being known as a radical.

Few, at the same time, listened to the LSR's messages about sovereignty and the need for neutrality. The regional loyalties of many Canadians were strengthened by the Depression; defenders of provincial rights were not hard to find. If the league's centralist proposals were largely ignored, however, its views about the

British connection did get some attention. This is because they were held to be offensive. When Frank Underhill came close to being dismissed from the University of Toronto in 1940–41 it was less his socialism than his 'anti-Britishism' that was at issue. Many English Canadians still treasured the links with Britain. They felt the natural ties of affection and tradition; they also knew that the world was a dangerous place and the Old Country a protector. And not a few derived from the assertion that Canada was British a comforting reminder of their own supposed superiority over French Canadians and foreigners. The extent of non-British immigration in the 1920s worried some Canadians. Emphasizing the imperial tie was a way of coping with the unease.[7]

Fearful, career-conscious, believing the capitalist system to be generally beneficial, the middle classes and the intelligentsia stayed well clear of the LSR and its proposals. Like the founders of Canada First sixty years earlier, the founders of the LSR misapprehended the readiness of educated Canadians to strike out in new directions.

III

What *was* the influence of the LSR? What impact did it have on the thought or society of Canada? What is its place in Canadian history?

Most obvious is the LSR's influence on the CCF. Starting with the Regina Manifesto, the party's program, policy statements, and organization were powerfully influenced by the intellectuals of the LSR. When CCF politicians spoke, they frequently had reference to ideas worked out by the LSR.

Journalists such as G.V. Ferguson and Wilfrid Eggleston early called the league a 'brain trust' for the CCF. In 1934 the Communist theoretician Stewart Smith gave the term an unflattering twist. In *Socialism and the CCF* he wrote that the LSR had assumed 'the task of the "scientific" leadership of the workers and the farmers. The CCF "brain trust" is the direct contribution of "experts" by the bourgeoisie to the new party, which is designed to hold the masses under capitalist influence.'[8] Ten years later no less importance was attached to the LSR by the anti-socialist propagandist Burdrick A. 'Bert' Trestrail. He was the author of a widely distributed paperback, *Stand Up and Be Counted (Or Sit Still and Get Soaked)*, which was part of the wave of anti-CCF propaganda that flooded Canada during the last two years of the war. Trestrail identified a menace, socialism, concocted by a conspiracy, the LSR. The CCF's legislative leaders he dismissed as puppets; the really dangerous men worked behind the scenes. The 'socialist baby' was 'the brainchild of a few college boys,' the 'professional social students' of the League for Social Reconstruction. They pulled the strings.

Trestrail identified only two of them: Frank Scott, a law professor with too much spare time, and David Lewis, 'a Jewish immigrant boy' who had somehow managed to stay out of the armed forces. 'These boys, with a few cronies, ... make the balls for Coldwell, Jolliffe, Winch and the others to fire.'[9] Should the CCF gain power, Trestrail warned, the LSR masterminds would be in charge. 'Make This MY Canada' should have been the title of the Scott and Lewis book.

It is not clear whether Trestrail's description owed more to a realization that identifying the CCF with intellectuals would help to discredit the party or to a belief that they really ran the show. The LSR, of course, had ceased to exist by the time that he wrote. But its influence, though not as strong as in Trestrail's imagination, lingered. Its main symbol was the elevation in 1942 of Frank Scott to the national chairmanship of the CCF. (It is ironic that, ten years earlier, Scott had opposed Frank Underhill's wish to affiliate the LSR with the party. In the 1940s, while the former served the CCF as chairman, the latter became gradually more disillusioned with it and soon after 1950 left it altogether.) David Lewis had become the CCF's full-time national secretary in 1938.

Comparisons between the LSR and the Fabian Society have come easily to chroniclers of the left in Canada. 'A Canadian version of the Fabian Society,' Walter Young has called the league. The LSR was, in fact, much more important to the CCF than the Fabian Society ever was to the Labour party. According to the historian A.M. McBriar the most ambitious claim for the influence of the Fabians upon Labour before the First World War that can be substantiated is that the policy of the Labour party 'was *in general* cautious, non-revolutionary and collectivist, and was therefore *in general* similar to that policy which the Fabian Society had recommended many years before the Labour Party came into existence.' With the acceptance by Labour in 1918 of the new constitution and the manifesto *Labour and the New Social Order*, both drafted by Sidney Webb, Fabian influence increased. However, another historian of the society, Margaret Cole, makes no sweeping claims for Fabian influence even in the 1920s, and of the 1930s she writes: 'The story of the Fabian Society proper, during these years, can be very briefly told, for it is one of inertia amounting almost to complete stagnation.'[10] The contrast with the LSR in that decade is startling.

By helping to give the CCF's program a clarity that it otherwise might have lacked, leading members of the LSR were trying to ensure that the new movement would not compromise itself out of existence in the way the Progressive party had done. The Regina Manifesto was not rigidly doctrinaire. Like the LSR's own manifesto, it was born of mutual accommodation among people who did not always agree. However, both documents counselled economic planning, looked to a centralization of important government functions, anticipated the nationalization of many enterprises, and sought to establish a basis for politics in social class; both challenged the profit motive and the power of business corporations. The Regina

Manifesto and the policies derived from it meant that the CCF stood clearly apart from other political parties.

This was its strength and its handicap. Its supporters and opponents both knew where the party stood. There were far more of the latter than of the former, however. 'Most Canadians were unwilling to see business, profits, and competition as evils,' Walter Young comments. They would not abandon their own hopes for wealth or 'support a party that was not identified with the status to which they aspired.' B.K. Sandwell, for many years the editor of *Saturday Night*, once said that 'the average North American is too good at thinking of himself as a boss to hate bosses as a class.' Then there were the engrained regionalism of Canadians in general and the inability of French Canadians and many of the relatively recent immigrants from Europe to identify with a party that was largely British and Protestant in its intellectual antecedents and the background of its leaders. 'The CCF is ... no menace for future elections,' J.L. Ilsley, Liberal MP and later cabinet minister, told the Montreal Reform Club in 1933; the vast majority of Canadians opposed the increased interference with the private ownership of productive property that the new party promised. 'The main issue in elections of the future will continue to be fought between the two old parties.'[11] Ilsley did not say it, but his prediction was favoured by the electoral system of single-member constituencies, which discriminates against third parties seeking to attract nation-wide support and reinforces regionally based parties.[12]

Ilsley's prediction was very nearly accurate. Only briefly, during the Second World War, did the national CCF represent a threat to the older parties. This was due more to its being recognizably different from them than to the exact contents of its program. (Of course, it *was* different partly *because* of its program.) 'It made little difference what the CCF said, how its pamphlets looked, or what program emerged from its conventions,' Professor Young writes; 'There is no evidence that the popularity of the CCF in 1943 and 1944 was due to what it was saying in 1942 any more than its rapid fall from public favour in 1945 resulted from its program.'[13] Support for the CCF indicated lack of confidence in the Liberals and Conservatives.

And yet the CCF gained support because it was the party that best expressed protest against the horrors of the Depression. Many Canadians feared a return to the unemployment, poverty, and anxiety of the 1930s; they desired 'a reformed post-war society characterized by increased personal security from want.'[14] This non-ideological desire was not limited to Canada; Britain experienced something very similar and in 1945 elected a Labour government as a result.[15]

In Canada the CCF had much less success. By late 1943 the massive anti-socialist campaign got under way, while the two major parties, especially the Liberals, adopted new policies to try to meet the democratic demands for change.

Support for the CCF declined; the elections of 1945 indicated that the socialist menace, if it had ever existed, had all but vanished.

All the same, almost sixteen of every hundred voters in Canada supported the CCF in 1945, most of them in Ontario, British Columbia, Saskatchewan, and Manitoba. Neither in the doldrums of the later 1930s nor in the post-war years did the CCF dwindle into obscurity and complete insignificance. The government elected in Saskatchewan in 1944 stayed in office for twenty years. And it is at least arguable that the CCF everywhere was sustained by a program that into the 1950s struck a sizeable minority of Canadians as worth working and voting for. In shaping the CCF's program the LSR could not ensure the party's success, but they did ensure its survival for a quarter-century, eventually to turn into the New Democratic Party. The CCF was not without influence, moreover, as an idea-giver and agitator for change. The movement towards a welfare state in Canada owes something – how much is impossible to determine – to the efforts of the CCF and later the NDP.

Not only within and through the CCF did the LSR make an impact. The organization influenced an indeterminate number of Canadians who were in no sense socialists but who saw the need for some measure of reform, political, social, and economic. Although a firm Liberal and without mentioning specifics, J.W. Dafoe nevertheless wrote to Graham Spry in 1936: 'I think the contribution to political discussion which you and your group are making is very valuable – particularly in view of the almost complete disappearance, for the time being at least, of the Conservative party as an intellectual factor.'[16] Many of the LSR's ideas may have been unacceptable, but the organization did not work in isolation and it was not ignored by everyone. *The Canadian Forum* was read in other than radical circles. The league's members belonged to many voluntary associations, among them the Canadian Institute of International Affairs, the Canadian Political Science Association, and the Committee of the Canadian Institute on Economics and Politics, in which their views got a hearing. The friends and acquaintances of LSR members included politicians such as Brooke Claxton and Norman Rogers, businessmen such as J.M. Macdonnell and J.S. McLean, journalists such as J.W. Dafoe and G.V. Ferguson, and educators such as Carleton Stanley and Terry MacDermot. The list is far from complete. Furthermore, Eugene Forsey, King Gordon, Carlton McNaught, Louise Parkin, Escott Reid, Frank Scott, Graham Spry – these and other members had connections within that network of Canadians who dominated the worlds of religion, education, politics, and business. In a country in which background and connections mattered – and still matter – this may have given some weight to their words. It meant, in any event, that their words were at least likely to be heard.

At another level, the position of several of the LSR's leading members as university professors no doubt helped to spread their ideas among the younger generation. Without suggesting that they used their lecterns as pulpits for their views, one may surmise that their students did not remain ignorant of these. A few students actually joined the LSR or CCF; probably more were influenced in subtle ways to see Canada and the world in a different light from the one to which they had been accustomed.

To point to the connections of LSR members is one thing, to demonstrate an influence on the political process quite another. It can be conceded right away that the league's influence on foreign policy was negligible. Canada went to war in 1939, the LSR's wishes notwithstanding, and if at that time or subsequently Canada gained a greater measure of sovereignty this owed nothing to the advice of LSR spokesmen.

Similarly, in the realm of Dominion-provincial relations the league had no real influence on what happened. The centralization of power after September 1939 owed everything to the fact of war and the need to wage it effectively, and to the consequent increase in Ottawa's fiscal powers. A measure of economic planning by government was introduced, but only because it was necessary and most of it only for the duration.

With respect to welfare legislation matters look somewhat different. As the surviving signatories of *Social Planning for Canada* observed in 1975, 'many of the prescriptions of change presented in this book have only historic interest for the simple reason that they have been put into effect.' Examples are a wholly state-owned central bank, 'a fairly comprehensive system of provincially funded medical and hospital services,' and 'a widely developed system of social insurance and social welfare to alleviate the burdens imposed on people by unemployment, old age, and the like.'[17] To these features of the welfare state must be added a system of collective bargaining that, whatever its failings, serves the collective needs of blue- and, increasingly, white-collar workers better than anything available to them before the Second World War.

The book had no direct influence on these developments, Frank Scott and his co-signers of 1975 surmised, 'but there can be no question of the influence it exerted on the policies and platforms of the CCF and, indirectly, on those of the other parties.' In addition, 'the merits of government planning, the better distribution of incomes, deficit financing, and so on' were demonstrated to the Canadian people during the Second World War, and this lesson was not forgotten in the post-war world.[18] These developments were in line with what the LSR had proposed in the 1930s: their ideas were available to all.

What was accomplished, however, often looked very different from what the league's intellectuals had had in mind. As Professor Maurice Bruce has said of the analogous experience in Great Britain: 'The *influence* of the Webbs, for instance, like that of [Lord] Beveridge, has been immense upon ideas, but in practice severely limited.'[19]

The LSR and CCF had no monopoly on reformist notions. The federal Liberals, for example, moved no faster than they were pushed, but when they did move they had men within their ranks who, without wishing to eradicate private enterprise, had formed their own ideas on how to manage the economy and cope with the harsher consequences of industralization under capitalism. They might borrow from the LSR, but the counter-cyclical proposals of J.M. Keynes, which league members like J.F. Parkinson helped to spread, were also accessible. From the late 1930s on, bureaucrats and politicians in Ottawa increasingly made use of them.

Some businessmen, too, showed that they saw a need for reform. As a radical historian, Alvin Finkel, has recently pointed out, a significant number of them indicated when R.B. Bennett introduced his 'New Deal' in 1935 that they were in favour at least of expanded social insurance, provided this did not undercut investment or the predominance of business. One is reminded of Eric A. Havelock's warning in 1932: 'Today our capitalist society is perfectly capable of self-adjustment by developing into a form of industrial Fascism wherein the more crude forms of social injustice are veiled by doles and social services.'[20] The *forms* of political democracy can be preserved so long as its *substance* – 'the maximum participation of all citizens in order to create a community based upon the mutual and respectful interaction of all toward commonly agreed-upon goals'[21] – is nullified and both the state and industry are run from the top.

The welfare measures that have been introduced in Canada during the last forty years have not, by and large, seriously affected either the distribution of wealth and income in Canada or the favoured position of business. They *have* helped to augment somewhat the power of the senior members of the public service at the expense of politicians and businessmen. Are social-welfare measures therefore a sham? Should they be repudiated by those who, like the LSR, have struggled for a more equitable and humane society? Not so: Canadian society may be little more equitable than it was in 1940 – wartime taxation did accomplish *some* redistribution – but it is considerably more humane.

Haste was made slowly: the limitations upon the budget in a capitalist economy weighed heavily with policy-makers. Many of the recommendations of the *Report on Social Security for Canada*, prepared by Leonard Marsh for the Committee on Reconstruction in 1943, were excluded from the package of reforms introduced by Mackenzie King's government in 1944–45. But some, such as family allowances, were passed into law. *The White Paper on Employment and Income* (1945) drafted by Queen's University economist W.A. Mackintosh underscored the need for fiscal policies that would encourage the maintenance of full employment. The dominion government took this to heart.[22]

Popular demand was at the bottom of the movement for reform. The welfare state as it took shape in Canada did not, could not eliminate economic inequality, nor was it intended to do so, but it did meet the concern of large numbers of voters that poverty be less demeaning and that they have increased security from unemployment and want and better access to medical care and education. This was far from being everything the LSR had in mind, but it was a significant part. The co-operative commonwealth has not been built in Canada. Nevertheless the society is more generous to the unfortunate (and the shiftless) than it was forty to fifty years ago, and members of the lower- and middle-income groups enjoy as a right public services whose benefits to them are enormous.

The public expenditures and services were made possible by an expansion of the economy that the LSR completely failed to foresee. For approximately thirty years after the outbreak of war in 1939 there was a spectacular though not uninterrupted growth in the Canadian economy. It proved possible not only to meet the need of business for a favourable investment climate, for incentives and concessions that fuelled profits and capital accumulation, but also to satisfy demands for employment and improved public services that legitimized the state in the eyes of many Canadians. Real incomes rose: the proportion of the population living at or below the poverty line dropped from one-half in the 1930s to rather less than a quarter by 1971. The tax collector was taking a growing percentage of incomes, of course, while the number of state workers grew. However, since most taxpayers felt better off than ever before, resistance to rising taxes was muted. In any case, although the combined effect of taxes and government expenditures was a moderate redistribution of income from the well-to-do to the poor, the distribution of total income was much the same in 1971 as it had been twenty years earlier.[23] Wealth increased; inequality remained. And beyond the persistent inequality of income and wealth there remained something the LSR had found more disturbing yet, inequality of influence and power. How much had really changed in Canada?

IV

During the first twenty-five years after the Second World War the ideas of the LSR came to seem in part uncontroversial, in part impractical or irrelevant. The concerns of Canadians centred more on the tensions of the Cold War and the threats of nuclear destruction, environmental pollution, over-population, and the like than on the power of the corporations and the alleged inability of capitalism to keep on delivering the goods. Canadian radicals became distressed as never before by the expansion of foreign and especially American investment in Canada, and by what they held to be a concomitant subservience of Canadian foreign and defence policies to those of the United States. In the 1960s the question of Quebec assumed an importance it had rarely had earlier, certainly more than the LSR had ever granted it.

Since 1970, however, high rates of inflation and unemployment remind us regularly that the economy is in crisis once again, that we are experiencing structural problems that neither business nor government seems able to resolve. Demands have mounted, especially from businessmen and Conservative politicians, that government expenditures be frozen or reduced. The number and remuneration of public servants and other state workers are under attack. (Whether the jobs that are being lost in the public sector can be replaced by jobs in the private sector remains to be seen.) Wage and salary earners are asked to make do with less so that we may become more productive and business will be encouraged to invest. Labour unions have been widely criticized for their intransigence and greed. The prevailing wisdom is that 'there is no such thing as a free lunch,' heard often from the mouths of men with expense accounts.

Have Canadians wanted 'too much'? Have public services been expanded under popular pressure to the point where they are beyond our capacity to pay? Has enterprise been made unprofitable because of excessive union demands, government interference, and taxation? These and similar assertions have in some circles become commonplaces. Yet there is reason for scepticism of easy answers; it is more than possible, as Charles Lindblom suggests, that

> ... a market-oriented system may require for its success so great a disproportion of business influence, both through the privileged position of business and through business disproportion in electoral and interest-group activity, that even modest challenges to it are disruptive to economic stability and growth. Union power may be 'too much' for the survival of private enterprise long before it is great enough to match the privileged position of business. Similarly welfare state demands may be 'too much' long before they manifest a political equality in electoral and interest-group activity.[24]

When the democratic demands for increased economic security and a larger voice in the management of enterprises are judged to be beyond the capacity of the existing economic system to satisfy, people in high places think it natural that the demands be reduced rather than that the system be changed or superseded.

That this is implicit in the capitalist state the LSR's intellectuals half a century ago followed other socialists in pointing out. The privilege and irresponsible power of the few is incompatible with the rights of the many. Democracy needs socialism.

Damaging criticism can be raised against some of the LSR's ideas. Readers with a dark view of human nature will have no use for the league's optimism and for the proposals that flowed from it. Even sympathetic readers will not be able to escape the conclusion that a good deal of what the LSR had to say was naïve or plain wrong, or applicable to the 1930s but now of no continuing importance. But lots of good sense and shrewdness in analysis were also there, and some of the LSR's ideas have relevance today. Focused on the power of the modern corporation and its ability to subvert political democracy, these ideas are worth taking seriously. Also worth considering is the league's interpretation of Canadian federalism and its future, especially at a time when provincialism seems to be at least as strong as in the thirties.

All the same, the LSR's place in history does not depend on a demonstration of the current uses of some of its thought. It was the first organization of left-wing intellectuals in Canada; it enunciated the main principles of a Canadian socialism; it shaped and sustained the CCF; it kept alive *The Canadian Forum*; it helped to bring about the welfare state in Canada. None of these is of world-shaking importance, but in our history they do matter. Because of them the League for Social Reconstruction will not be forgotten.

APPENDICES

I

The LSR Manifesto

The League for Social Reconstruction is an association of men and women who are working for the establishment in Canada of a social order in which the basic principle regulating production, distribution and service will be the common good rather than private profit.

The present capitalist system has shown itself unjust and inhuman, economically wasteful, and a standing threat to peace and democratic government. Over the whole world it has led to a struggle for raw materials and markets and to a consequent international competition in armaments which were among the main causes of the last great war and which constantly threaten to bring on new wars. In the advanced industrial countries it has led to the concentration of wealth in the hands of a small irresponsible minority of bankers and industrialists whose economic power constantly threatens to nullify our political democracy. The result in Canada is a society in which the interests of farmers and of wage and salaried workers – the great majority of the population – are habitually sacrificed to those of this small minority. Despite our abundant natural resources the mass of the people have not been freed from poverty and insecurity. Unregulated competitive production condemns them to alternate periods of feverish prosperity, in which the main benefits go to speculators and profiteers, and of catastrophic depression, in which the common man's normal state of insecurity and hardship is accentuated.

We are convinced that these evils are inherent in any system in which private profit is the main stimulus to economic effort. We therefore look to the establishment in Canada of a new social order which will substitute a planned and socialized economy for the existing chaotic individualism and which, by achieving an approximate economic equality among all men in place of the present glaring inequalities, will eliminate the domination of one class by another.

Such measures as the following are among the essential first steps for the achievement of the new social order:

(1) The creation of a National Economic Planning Commission as the principal organization for directing and co-ordinating the operation of the whole economy in the public interest.

(2) Socialization of the machinery of banking and investment to make possible effective control of credit and prices and the direction of new capital into socially desirable channels.

(3) Public ownership (Dominion, provincial or municipal) of transport, communications, electric power and such other industries as are approaching a condition of monopoly, and their operation, under the general direction of the planning commission by competent managements divorced from immediate political control.

(4) The development of co-operative institutions in every sphere of economic life where they are appropriate, notably in agricultural production and marketing and in the distribution of necessities to consumers.

(5) The establishment of import and export boards for the regulation of foreign trade.

(6) Social legislation to secure to the worker adequate income and leisure, freedom of association, insurance against illness, accident, old age, and unemployment, and an effective voice in the management of his industry.

(7) Publicly organized health, hospital and medical services.

(8) An aggressive taxation policy designed not only to raise public revenues but also to lessen the glaring inequalities of income and to provide funds for the socialization of industry.

(9) The amendment of the Canadian constitution, without infringing upon legitimate provincial claims to autonomy, so as to give the Dominion Government adequate power to deal effectively with urgent economic problems which are essentially national.

(10) A foreign policy designed to obtain international economic co-operation and to promote disarmament and world peace.

The League will work for the realization of its ideal by organizing groups to study and report on particular problems and by issuing to the public in the form of pamphlets, articles, lectures, etc., the most accurate information obtainable about the nation's affairs in order to create that informed public opinion which is necessary for effective political action.

SOURCE: League for Social Reconstruction, *Handbook* [1933]

II

The LSR Constitution

1. *Definition*
The League for Social Reconstruction is an association of men and women who are working for the establishment in Canada of a social order in which the basic principle regulating production, distribution and service will be the common good rather than private profit.

2. *Purpose*
The League, through its publications and the work of its branches, aims to educate Canadian public opinion in the principles and proposals outlined in the Manifesto.

3. *Constitution*
The League consists of a national Executive, with headquarters at Toronto, and local branches established in various parts of the country.

National Executive
The National Executive consists of an Honorary President, a President, a Secretary-Treasurer, and a Committee. These officers are elected at the annual Convention. At any meeting of the Executive, if a member from any local branch be available, he may be co-opted to the Executive for that meeting.

The National Executive exercises a general control and supervision over the activities of the League as a whole. It has an absolute discretion in regard to publications put out under the name of the League or of any of its branches. It is entitled to fifty cents per member per annum from local branches for central expenses, and may impose additional per capita levies on branches from time to time as necessity demands.

National Convention
The supreme governing body of the League is the National Convention, which is called annually by the National Executive. At any time when a written demand is made by at least half of the branches, the National Executive shall call a special Convention.

The Convention consists of (i) members of the National Executive, and (ii) delegates from local branches, each branch being entitled to one voting delegate for every 25 full members, or fraction thereof. Other members of the League may attend the Convention, but without the right to vote. If a branch is unable to send its full quota of voting delegates, the delegation which does attend from the branch may cast the full number of votes to which the branch is entitled.

The Convention elects the members of the National Executive, and decides upon matters of policy affecting the League as a whole. It alone has the power to amend the Manifesto and this Constitution.

Local Branches

Local Branches may be organized wherever there are ten persons who can be found to accept the obligations of full membership in the League.

On any matter not dealt with in this constitution, the local Branches are left free to create their own organization and to work out their own programme of activities. It is desirable, however, that each Branch should have a President, a Secretary-Treasurer, and an Executive Committee. The Secretary-Treasurer should keep a roll of members, and forward the contribution of fifty cents per head to national headquarters. It is his duty to keep in touch with the National Secretary, and to secure the advice of the National Executive on the more important problems that may arise in the work of the Branch.

Membership in the Branches is of two sorts, full and associate. Full members subscribe to the declared aims of the League, and have the right to vote at meetings. Associate members are merely asked to express a general sympathy with the objects of the League, and have no vote. Both types of member receive League publications free.

The finances of the Branches may be arranged on any basis convenient to the Branch, with the exception of the fifty cents per head per annum due to the National Executive. There is also the obligation to meet the additional levies when made.

Students in any college or university may form a local Branch on the above conditions; or students may, if they wish, become members of the nearest local Branch. The fee due from student members to the National Executive shall not exceed twenty-five cents.

SOURCE: League for Social Reconstruction, *Handbook* [1933]

III

National Officers of the LSR

	President	Vice-president	Secretary	Treasurer
1932–33	F.H. Underhill (Toronto)	none	Isabel Thomas (Toronto)	Isabel Thomas
1933–34	F.H. Underhill	none	Isabel Thomas/ Graham Spry (Toronto and Ottawa)	Isabel Thomas
1934–35	F.H. Underhill	none	Graham Spry	George S. Hougham (Toronto)
1935–36	F.R. Scott (Montreal)	G.M.A. Grube (Toronto)	Graham Spry	G.M.A. Grube (acting)
1936–37	F.R. Scott	Graham Spry	Helen Marsh (Montreal)	Helen Marsh
1937–38	Leonard Marsh (Montreal)	J.F. Parkinson (Toronto)	C.M. Lapointe (Montreal)	J.A.R. Mason (Montreal)
1938–39	Leonard Marsh	E.O. Hall (London)	Helen C. Howes (Montreal)	C.E. French (Montreal)
1939–40	Louise Parkin (Montreal)	E.A. Havelock (Toronto)	Helen C. Howes	C.E. French
1940–41	W.J. McCurdy (Toronto)	E.A. Forsey (Montreal)	Eileen Troop (Toronto)	E.D. MacInnes (Toronto)
1941–42	G.M.A. Grube	E.A. Forsey	W.J. McCurdy	E.D. MacInnes

The Honorary President from 1932 to 1942 was J.S. Woodsworth (Winnipeg and Ottawa)

Notes

Where no place of publication is indicated it is Toronto.

Abbreviations: *CF* – *The Canadian Forum*; *DNS* – *Democracy Needs Socialism*; *SPC* – *Social Planning for Canada*.

CHAPTER I

1 See my article, 'The Great Depression: Past and Present,' *Journal of Canadian Studies* 11 (Feb. 1976), and the documentary history I have edited, *The Dirty Thirties: Canadians in the Great Depression* (1972).
2 Public Archives of Canada (PAC), Frank H. Underhill Papers, Underhill to Mrs W.B. Somerset, 30 Apr. 1933. The original of this letter and of the memento presented to Mrs Somerset are both in the Underhill Papers.
3 Gunnar Myrdal, *Beyond the Welfare State* (New York 1967 [1960]) 54.
4 W.L. Morton, 'The 1920s,' in *The Canadians 1867–1967*, ed. J.M.S. Careless and R. Craig Brown (1967) 229.
5 League for Social Reconstruction, Research Committee, *SPC* (1935) 15.
6 See A.E. Safarian, *The Canadian Economy in the Great Depression* (1970 [1959]).
7 See James Struthers, 'Prelude to Depression: The Federal Government and Unemployment, 1918–29,' *Canadian Historical Review* 58 (Sept. 1977).
8 Leonard C. Marsh, *Canadians In and Out of Work* (1940) 367–8, 371–2.
9 Norman Penner, *The Canadian Left: A Critical Analysis* (Scarborough, Ont. 1977) 177.
10 T.W.L. MacDermot, 'Radical Thinking in Canada,' *CF* 12 (Oct. 1931) 11.
11 See H. Blair Neatby, *The Politics of Chaos* (1972) 183–4.
12 Neal Wood, *Communism and British Intellectuals* (New York 1959) 37.
13 Frank A. Warren III, *Liberals and Communism* (Bloomington, Ind. 1966) 5.
14 See Gad Horowitz, *Canadian Labour in Politics* (1968) 29–44.
15 Frank Underhill, Foreword to *Nationalism in Canada*, ed. Peter Russell (1966) xvii.

CHAPTER 2

1 Public Archives of Canada (PAC), Frank H. Underhill Papers, Underhill to J.W. Dafoe, 30 Nov. 1930, copy.
2 Signed originals in Underhill Papers. See also J.F. White, 'Police Dictatorship,' *CF* 11 (Feb. 1931); Michiel Horn, '"Free Speech within the Law": The Letter of the Sixty-Eight Toronto Professors,' *Ontario History* 72 (March 1980).
3 Montreal *Gazette*, 4 and 5 Feb. 1931. PAC, J.S. Woodsworth Papers, F.R. Scott to Woodsworth, 13 and 16 Mar. 1931. See also E.A. Forsey, 'Montreal Is A Quiet City,' *CF* 11 (June 1931).
4 University of Toronto Archives (UTA), H.M. Cassidy Papers, Cassidy to Woodsworth, 2 May 1931, copy.
5 Underhill Papers, J.S. Woodsworth to Underhill, 26 Apr. 1929. See also Olive Ziegler, *Woodsworth: Social Pioneer* (1934) 188–9.
6 PAC, Brooke Claxton Papers, Claxton to Burton Hurd, 21 Feb. 1930, copy; also Claxton to Hurd, 26 Jan. 1931, copy. Underhill Papers, Terry MacDermot to Underhill, 16 Nov. 1930.
7 Underhill Papers, MacDermot to Underhill, 10 Sept. 1931.
8 Underhill Papers, Graham Spry to Underhill, 1 Oct. 1931.
9 Graham Spry Papers (privately held), Spry to George V. Ferguson, 3 Nov. 1931, copy. Claxton Papers, Spry to Claxton, 6 Jan. 1932.
10 F.R. Scott Papers (privately held), Underhill to Scott, 18 Dec. 1931, Underhill Papers, Scott to Underhill, n.d. [Dec. 1931].
11 Underhill Papers, Scott to Underhill, 6 Nov. 1931, 12 Feb. 1932.
12 F.R. Scott to the author, 19 Feb. 1975.
13 *Winnipeg Free Press*, 21 July 1933.
14 Claxton Papers, Claxton to G.R. McCall, 2 Mar. 1932, copy.
15 Claud Cockburn, *In Time of Trouble* (London 1956) 212.
16 Canada, House of Commons, *Debates*, 26 Apr. 1932, 2405. 'Youth the Stranger,' *Ottawa Evening Citizen*, 29 Apr. 1932. Scott Papers, Woodsworth to Scott, 29 Apr. 1932. See also [F.H. Underhill], 'L.S.R.,' *CF* 12 (June 1932).
17 Thomas Fisher Rare Books Library, University of Toronto, J.S. Woodsworth Memorial Collection, LSR Papers, Membership Book, Toronto branch. York University Archives, E.A. Beder Papers, 'Members and Associate Members of the Toronto Branch, the League for Social Reconstruction.'
18 Douglas Library Archives, Queen's University, G.M.A. Grube Papers, 'Report of the Toronto Branch to the LSR National Convention, 1934.'
19 Underhill Papers, 'Political Radicalism in the Thirties' (Unpublished address, Carleton University 1959) 3–4.

20 Hendrik de Man, *The Psychology of Socialism*, trans. Eden and Cedar Paul (New York 1974 [1928]) 224.
21 Ibid., 226–9 passim.
22 *SPC*, 473.
23 Scott Papers, *Handbook of the League for Social Reconstruction* (Feb. 1933) 8.
24 Ibid., 9.

CHAPTER 3

1 Scott Papers, Scott to C.E. French, 4 Apr. 1932, copy. F.H. Underhill, 'The League for Social Reconstruction,' *CF* 12 (Apr. 1932) 249.
2 Underhill Papers, Norman McL. Rogers to Underhill, 18 Jan. 1932. F.H.U., 'O Canada,' *CF* 10 (Jan. 1930) 116. See also 'O Canada,' *CF* 12 (Oct. 1931).
3 Kenneth McNaught claims that 'a few LSR people' had been called in. *A Prophet in Politics* (1959) 259. He is unable to recall where he got this information. There is no documentary evidence for the claim, and no one from the LSR with whom I have spoken remembers attending the meeting. The first academic historian of the CCF, L.T. Calvert, writing in 1941, makes no mention of LSR members at the meeting in Ottawa.
4 University of British Columbia, Archives, Angus MacInnis Papers, Francis J. McKenzie, 'The Cooperative Commonwealth Federation, Report written for the Vancouver Branch of the LSR, 22 Aug. 1932.'
5 Underhill Papers, Scott to Underhill, 7 and 30 Sept. 1932. Scott Papers, Underhill to Scott, 29 Sept. 1932.
6 Underhill Papers, Woodsworth to Underhill, 7 and 17 Oct. 1932; Scott to Underhill, 20 Oct. 1932.
7 Underhill Papers, Woodsworth to Underhill, 7 Oct. and 1 Nov. 1932. Scott Papers, Underhill to Scott, 1 Dec. 1932; Havelock to Scott, 20 Dec. 1932; Scott to Woodsworth, 3 Jan. 1933, copy. See also Gerald L. Caplan, *The Dilemma of Canadian Socialism: The CCF in Ontario* (1973) 14, 24–6.
8 LSR Papers, Minutes, Toronto branch, 11 Jan. 1933.
9 This and previous quotations are from the Scott Papers, *Handbook of the LSR*, 6–7.
10 Scott Papers, Isabel Thomas to Scott, 4 Apr. 1933. LSR Papers, Minutes, Toronto branch executive meeting, 14 Apr. 1933; Ellet MacInnes to Bert Robinson, 17 June 1933, copy. Underhill Papers, W.H. Fyfe to Underhill, 14 Mar. 1933.
11 MacInnis Papers, Wallis Lefeaux to MacInnis, 21 Apr. 1933; MacInnis to Lefeaux, 10 May 1933, copy.
12 Grube Papers, Cassidy to MacInnis, 28 Feb. 1933, copy; Cassidy to Woodsworth, 18 Apr. 1933, copy.
13 Underhill Papers, Woodsworth to Underhill, 4 May 1933.

14 Underhill Papers, Woodsworth to Underhill, 13 July 1933.
15 Grube Papers, Spry to Cassidy, 24 July 1933; Cassidy to K.W. Taylor, 26 July 1933, copy. George H. Williams, quoted in the *Toronto Daily Star*, 22 July 1933. Underhill Papers, Woodsworth to Underhill, 25 July 1933.
16 Eugene Forsey to the author [June 1968].
17 L. St G. Stubbs was the first candidate to be put forward by the CCF for a seat in the House of Commons: he was defeated in a by-election in Mackenzie (Saskatchewan) in October 1933. See also James H. Gray, *The Winter Years* (1966) 92–5.
18 M.J. Coldwell, quoted in Walter Young, *The Anatomy of a Party: The National CCF 1932–1961* (1969) 44n. For a fuller discussion of the Regina Manifesto, a reproduction of Underhill's Rosseau Lake draft, and a textually accurate version of the final document, see Michiel Horn, 'Frank Underhill's Early Drafts of the Regina Manifesto 1933,' *Canadian Historical Review* 54 (Dec. 1973). After that account was written Mlle Anne Moreau found two intermediate drafts in the Scott Papers, as well as a letter by Frank Underhill to Frank Scott, 26 Jan. 1951, which contains the former's recollections of the drafting of the manifesto. As a result of this new information I have amended my account in a couple of particulars. I am grateful to Mlle Moreau for drawing this additional material to my attention.
19 G.V.F., 'C.C.F. "Brain Trust,"' *Winnipeg Free Press*, 25 July 1933. Some months later another journalist, Wilfrid Eggleston, was referring to the LSR as 'Woodsworth's "brain trust."' 'Canada's Party on the Left,' *Current History* 39 (Jan. 1934).
20 Grube Papers, Spry to Cassidy, 24 July 1933. F.H. Underhill, 'The CCF Convention and After,' *CF* 14 (Sept. 1934) 463. G.V. Ferguson, letter to the editor in *CF* 15 (Oct. 1934) 17
21 LSR Papers, 'Third Annual Report of the League for Social Reconstruction, 1934.'
22 Woodsworth Papers, Underhill to Woodsworth, 2 May 1933. Underhill Papers, Woodsworth to Underhill, 4 May 1933. Escott Reid, 'The Effects of the Depression on Canadian Politics, 1929–1932,' *American Political Science Review* 27 (June 1933) 464. For a different assessment, see McNaught, *A Prophet in Politics*, 266–7.
23 LSR Papers, 'Third Annual Report ..., 1934.' See also Irving Brecher, *Monetary and Fiscal Thought and Policy in Canada 1919–1939* (1957) 99.
24 R.B. Bennett to H.H. Stevens, 18 May 1931, quoted in J.R.H. Wilbur, 'H.H. Stevens and the Reconstruction Party,' *Canadian Historical Review* 45 (March 1964) 5. J.R.H. Wilbur, ed., *The Bennett New Deal: Fraud or Portent* (1968) 20.
25 George Henry to R.B. Bennett, 15 Feb. 1934, quoted in Richard Wilbur, *H.H. Stevens 1878–1973* (1977) 117.
26 E.A. Havelock to the author, 7 Mar. 1968.
27 Underhill Papers, Graham Spry, 'Report on a Trip to Britain to Visit the Socialist League and Labour Party Offices'; Spry to Underhill, 12 July 1933.
28 Scott Papers, mimeographed letter to LSR members from the national president [Underhill], Oct. 1933.

29 Underhill Papers, Woodsworth to Underhill, 4 May 1933. Spry to Underhill, 24 May 1933, and attached 'Memorandum on the League for Social Reconstruction.'
30 Grube Papers, Spry to Cassidy, 24 July 1933. Cassidy to Scott, 23 Aug. 1933, copy.
31 Claxton Papers, Spry to Claxton, 29 Aug. 1933. Scott Papers, Minutes, national executive meeting, 16 Sept. 1933. Graham Spry to the author, 25 Oct. 1966.
32 Grube Papers, Underhill to branch secretaries, 16 Oct. 1933, copy.
33 Claxton Papers, Spry to Claxton, 13 Mar. 1934, 22 Feb. 1935. Graham Spry to the author, 23 May 1978, 28 June 1978.
34 Scott Papers, 'Report for the season 1933–34, Montreal Branch'; Grube Papers, S.E. Briard to Spry, 3 Jan. 1934.

CHAPTER 4

1 Underhill Papers, Scott to Underhill, 15 Oct. 1935.
2 Louise M. Parkin to the author, 1 Nov. 1977.
3 Conversation with Mr R.E.G. Davis, July 1978; Humphrey Carver, *The Compassionate Landscape* (1975) 55.
4 Underhill Papers, J.F. White to Underhill, 30 July 1932. LSR Papers, Minutes, Third Annual Convention, 1934; Third Annual Report of the LSR, Underhill Papers, Grace MacInnis to Isabel Thomas, 6 June 1933.
5 Underhill Papers, D.M. Baillie to Underhill, 12 Mar. 1934. LSR Papers, Elsie Matheson to Helen Marsh, 22 Apr. 1936. F.H. Underhill, 'Spade-Workers for a New Social Order,' *Saturday Night* (10 Mar. 1934).
6 Grube Papers, 'Report of the National Secretary, 1934.' The list in the E.A. Beder Papers of the 'Members and Associate Members of the Toronto Branch of the League for Social Reconstruction,' probably dating from early or mid-1934, contains 219 names, 45 of them out of town.
7 Woodsworth Papers, F.H. Underhill, 'Memorandum Based on Discussions at LSR Conference, February 1934.'
8 Underhill Papers, J.S. Woodsworth to Underhill, 27 Feb. 1934.
9 Scott Papers, Scott to Underhill, 9 July 1934, copy; Underhill to Scott, 23 July 1934. For the text of the 'Immediate Programme' see Horn, *The Dirty Thirties*, 445–7.
10 PAC, CCF Records, Underhill to Woodsworth, 24 July 1934.
11 Underhill, 'Revolt in Canadian Politics,' *The Nation*, 12 Dec. 1934. See also Underhill, 'The CCF Convention and After,' *CF* 14 (Sept. 1934).
12 Grube Papers, 'Report of the National Secretary, 1934.'
13 Stafford Cripps, 'Socialism in Canada,' *Political Quarterly* 5 (July 1934) 351.
14 J. King Gordon to the author, 2 Oct. 1972.
15 *The New Outlook*, 9 May 1934, 345.
16 Margaret Prang, 'Some Opinions of Political Radicalism in Canada Between the Two

World Wars,' (MA thesis, University of Toronto 1953) 54. See also United Church of Canada, Board of Evangelism and Social Service, *Christianizing the Social Order* (1934); R.C. Stewart Crysdale, *The Industrial Struggle and Protestant Ethics in Canada* (1961) 76–136; Roger Hutchinson, 'The Canadian Social Gospel in the Context of Christian Social Ethics,' in *The Social Gospel in Canada*, ed. Richard Allen (Ottawa 1975) 296–8. The only recent work of importance on the FCSO has been done by Roger Hutchinson, 'The Fellowship for a Christian Social Order: A Social Ethical Analysis of a Christian Socialist Movement,' (THD thesis, University of Toronto 1975).

17 'At last a Contribution from Our Intellectual Radicals,' *Mail and Empire*, 24 Mar. 1934. Grube Papers, 'Report of the Toronto Branch, 1934.' H.M. Cassidy, 'Report of the Research Committee of the LSR National Executive to the National Convention, Feb. 10, 1934.'

18 Caplan, *Dilemma of Canadian Socialism*, 66. Underhill Papers, Spry to Underhill, 7 July 1934. Scott Papers, Spry to Scott, 8 and 12 Mar. 1934. Graham Spry to the author, 24 Mar. 1968.

19 'G. Pierce' [Stewart Smith], *Socialism and the CCF* (Montreal 1934) 15, 150–1. See also Penner, *The Canadian Left*, 149–56.

20 Underhill Papers, E.A.Beder to Underhill, 24 Oct. 1934.

21 Underhill Papers, Scott to Underhill, 24 Nov. 1934; Underhill to E.A. Beder, 6 Dec. 1934, copy.

22 LSR Papers, Minutes, Toronto branch executive meeting, 20 Dec. 1934. See also Young, *Anatomy of a Party*, 261–5; Ivan Avakumovic, *The Communist Party in Canada: A History* (1975) 99–106.

23 Cassidy Papers, Scott to Cassidy, 23 Feb. 1935; Scott Papers, Cassidy to Scott, 7 Mar. 1935. Scott to E.O. Hall, 4 Mar. 1935, copy.

24 Cassidy Papers, Leonard Marsh to Cassidy, 27 July 1935.

25 Underhill Papers, [P.C. Armstrong], *A Criticism of the Book Written by Eugene Forsey, J. King Gordon, Leonard Marsh, J.F. Parkinson, F.R. Scott, Graham Spry and Frank H. Underhill and Published by the League for Social Reconstruction Under the Title 'Social Planning for Canada'* (n.p., n.d. [Montreal? 1935]); Underhill Papers, P.C. Armstrong to Leonard Marsh, 12 Nov. 1935; Scott to Underhill, 17 Nov. 1935; Marsh to Underhill, 14 Jan. 1935 [sic]. Scott Papers, S.B. Watson to Scott, 18 Dec. 1935, 24 Sept. 1936. Grube Papers, royalty statements from Thomas Nelson & Sons.

Although they offer no evidence, the surviving signatories of *Social Planning* still believe that the booklet added significantly to sales. Quite possibly the attack led newspapers to take the book more seriously than they might otherwise have done, and thus gave it publicity. Businessmen may also have bought copies for curiosity's sake. See F.R. Scott and others, 'An Introduction,' *Social Planning for Canada* (reprint ed., *The Social History of Canada*, no. 26, 1975) xviii.

26 *CCF Research Review* 3 (Dec. 1935) 18, 20. Salem Bland, 'A Great Event for Canadian Christianity,' *The New Outlook*, 13 Nov. 1935, 1104.

27 Leonard Marsh Papers (privately held), reviews scrapbook, Wallis Lefeaux, review in *B.C. Clarion*, n.d.; Robert Connell, 'The Clarion and the CCF,' *B.C. Commonwealth*, 21 Feb. 1936. Tim Buck, 'Socialist Planning – Under Capitalism?' *The Worker*, 15 Feb. 1936.

28 H.A. Innis, 'For the People,' *University of Toronto Quarterly* 5 (Jan. 1936). G.V.F., 'The CCF Bible,' *Winnipeg Free Press*, 29 Nov. 1935. B.K. Sandwell, 'Social Planning,' *Saturday Night* (19 Oct. 1935), 'The Domesday Book of Canada,' *Mail and Empire*, 28 Sept. 1935. R.A. MacKay, in *Dalhousie Review* 16 (Jan. 1937) 528.

29 Young, *Anatomy of a Party*, 71–2.

30 Escott Reid Papers (privately held), 'A Foreign Policy for the CCF'; Underhill to Reid, 3 and 8 July 1934; Scott to Reid, 5 July 1934; Scott Papers, Underhill to Scott, 3 July 1934; Scott to Woodsworth, 11 July 1934, copy. Underhill to Scott, 23 July 1934.

31 CCF Records, Minutes, National Council meeting, Ottawa, 8–9 February 1935. Underhill Papers, Scott to Underhill, 26 Feb., 28 Feb., 5 Mar. 1935; 'Proposed Amendment to Be Added to the B.N.A. Act, sec. 148.'

32 [F.H. Underhill], 'Notes and Comments,' *CF* 15 (Aug. 1935) 330; see also, in the same issue, Graham Spry, 'Politics.'

33 F.H. Underhill, 'English Labour and the CCF,' *CF* 13 (Apr. 1933); 'Notes and Comments,' *CF* 15 (Aug. 1935). See, in *The New Republic*, 'If the Elephant Dies' (21 Nov. 1934) and 'Toward a New Party' (22 May 1935). *SPC*, 487.

34 PAC, J.W. Dafoe Papers, Spry to Dafoe, 19 July 1935. See also Caplan, *Dilemma of Canadian Socialism*, 72–5.

35 Scott Papers, Scott to Warren K. Cook, 23 Oct. 1935, copy; Cook to Scott, 26 and 31 Oct. 1935.

36 Woodsworth Papers, Underhill to Woodsworth, 26 Nov. 1935.

CHAPTER 5

1 J.S. Woodsworth, 'President's Address,' *Saskatchewan CCF Bureau [Review]* 1 (Aug. 1933) 3.

2 Penner, *The Canadian Left*, 213. Interview with F.H. Underhill, Jan. 1967.

3 League for Social Reconstruction, *Canada and Socialism* (n.d. [1935]) 4.

4 *SPC*, 39.

5 Ibid., 37.

6 Ibid., 101. The description is derived from *The Modern Corporation and Private Property* (1932), by the American social scientists A.A. Berle and Gardiner C. Means. The LSR's disapproval of the great power exercised by the magnates had something

in common with the attitude of agrarian radicals in the West. J.M. King's *CCF Research Review* in Saskatchewan, in which LSR members occasionally published, drew attention in 1934 to the 'Fifty Big Shots' who allegedly owned and ran Canada. *Who Owns Canada* appeared as a pamphlet after being serialized in the *CCF Research Review*. Its author was Louis Rosenberg, a statistician with the Canadian Jewish Congress; he used the *nom de plume* Watt Hugh McCollum. An earlier publication with the same title had been published in 1913 by the *Grain Grower's Guide*. An updated version of Rosenberg's pamphlet was prepared by Donald MacDonald, then research director of the national CCF, in 1946.

7 *SPC*, 157. R.H. Tawney, *Religion and the Rise of Capitalism* (New York 1947 [1926]) 221.

8 *SPC*, 191–2, 195, 196. This line of argument is clearly influenced by the British Marxist, John Strachey. See his *The Coming Struggle for Power* (London 1933) 53–157. See also Hans Jaeger, 'Business in the Great Depression,' in *The Great Depression Revisited*, ed. Herman van der Wee (The Hague 1972).

9 *SPC*, 198, 199. See Richard H. Pells, *Radical Visions and American Dreams: Culture and Social Thought in the Depression* (New York 1973) 82–95.

10 *SPC*, 211, 212. See also Irene M. Biss, *The Industrial Revolution in Canada* (1933), and Eugene Forsey, *Unemployment in the Machine Age: Its Causes* (1935).

11 Rein Peterson, *Small Business: Building a Balanced Economy* (Erin, Ont. 1977) 136.

12 Tom Kent, 'The Climate of Socioeconomic Change,' Paper presented to the Canadian Public Relations Society, Halifax, June 1977, quoted by Arnold Edinborough, *The Financial Post*, 3 Sept. 1977. Kent is president of the Sydney Steel Corporation. For a recent discussion of the problems discussed in *Social Planning for Canada*, see Charles E. Lindblom, *Politics and Markets: The World's Political-Economic Systems* (New York 1977).

13 Martin Kitchen, *Fascism* (London 1976) 68. Thomas Childers, 'The Social Bases of the National Socialist Vote,' *Journal of Contemporary History* 11 (Oct. 1976), 29. The entire October 1976 issue of this journal is devoted to 'Theories of Fascism.'

The only published study of Canadian fascism is Lita-Rose Betcherman's interesting but badly flawed *The Swastika and the Maple Leaf* (1975).

14 L.P. Carpenter, *G.D.H. Cole: An Intellectual Biography* (Cambridge 1973) 154. A.F.W. Plumptre, review in *Economic Journal* 46 (Mar. 1936).

15 F.H. Underhill, 'The Webbs on Russia,' *CF* 16 (May 1936) 26. George Orwell, quoted in David Caute, *The Fellow-Travellers* (London 1973) 4. League for Social Reconstruction, Research Committee, *DNS* (1938) vi.

16 *SPC*, 218.

17 Underhill, 'Bentham and Benthamism,' *Queen's Quarterly* 39 (Nov. 1932) 668. See also Underhill, 'Fabians and Fabianism,' *CF* 25 (March–April 1946); and, for a useful discussion, Carl Berger, 'F.H. Underhill and the Tenacity of Liberalism,' *CF* 51 (Nov. 1971).

18 *SPC*, 237, 266–7, 388. On Guild socialism, see Carpenter, *G.D.H. Cole*, 46–111, 169–70
19 *SPC*, 243.
20 *DNS*, 51.
21 *SPC*, 331.
22 Lorne T. Morgan, 'The Origins and Development of Fascism,' in *Essays in Political Economy in Honour of E.J. Urwick*, ed. H.A. Innis (1938) 188. See also the debate between E.A. Havelock and two critics of the LSR's non-revolutionary approach, O.B. Van der Sprenkel and Felix Walter, in the pages of *The Canadian Forum* 12 (May and June 1932).
23 *SPC*, 282.
24 Ibid., 285. 2 Thess. 3: 10.
25 LSR Papers, S.B. Watson to J.O. Elton, 28 Dec. 1936, copy. *SPC*, 37, 38. See also J. King Gordon, 'Socialism and Christianity,' *Saskatchewan CCF Research Review* 1 (May 1934).
26 Ross Terrill, *R.H. Tawney and his Times* (Cambridge, Mass. 1973) 265.
27 *SPC*, 299, 300. John Maynard Keynes, *Essays in Persuasion* (New York 1963 [1931]) 104. 'Inflation is unjust and Deflation is inexpedient. Of the two perhaps Deflation is, if we rule out exaggerated inflations such as that of Germany, the worse; because it is worse, in an impoverished world, to provoke unemployment than to disappoint the rentier. But it is not necessary that we should weigh one evil against the other. It is easier to agree that both are evils to be shunned.' (Ibid., 103).
28 *SPC*, 315. See Robert Heilbroner, *The Making of Economic Society* (Englewood Cliffs, N.J. 1962) 229.
29 *SPC*, 327. John Strachey, in *The Coming Struggle for Power*, gives a Marxist's contemporary interpretation of the events of 1929–31. See also Robert Skidelsky, *Politicians and the Slump: The Labour Government of 1929–31* (London 1967).
30 *SPC*, 344, 367.
31 Ibid., 371–2, 373. At the time *Social Planning for Canada* was written it was estimated that some 56.2 per cent of wage earners and other income receivers (excluding farm labourers) received less than $1,000 per annum. Only 3.2 per cent received between $3,000 and $10,000, and only 0.4 per cent got more than $10,000. (Ibid., 16).
32 *SPC*, 392, 401. See also Leonard Marsh, A.G. Fleming, and C.F. Blackler, *Health and Unemployment* (1938). This was one of the studies done under the aegis of the McGill Bureau of Social Research.
33 *SPC*, 404.
34 Ibid., 458. Angus L. Macdonald to R.B. Bennett, 11 May 1934; H.A. Bruce to R.B. Bennett, 10 Aug. 1934, and attachment, both in Horn, *The Dirty Thirties*, 191–8. See also Heilbroner, *The Making of Economic Society*, 229–30.
35 David Mitrany, *Marx Against the Peasant* (New York 1961 [1951]) 163.

36 [Stafford Cripps], 'Canada's Problems,' the *New Statesman and Nation* (8 Feb. 1936) 177–8.

Professors Ivan Avakumovic (*The Communist Party in Canada*) and Norman Penner (*The Canadian Left*) both indicate that the policy of the CPC on the agrarian question was incomplete. On the use-lease system, see Peter R. Sinclair, 'The Saskatchewan CCF: Ascent to Power and the Decline of Socialism,' *Canadian Historical Review* 54 (Dec. 1973) 424–5.

37 *SPC*, 417, 418. There is a footnote reference in the latter passage to the chapter on foreign trade. I propose to deal with that subject in my discussion of the LSR's policy on foreign relations, below.

See also Michael Tracy, 'Agriculture in the Great Depression: World Market Developments and European Protectionism,' in *The Great Depression Revisited*, ed. Van der Wee.

38 *SPC*, 422–3, 424. See also Abraham Rotstein, 'Innis: The Alchemy of Fur and Wheat,' *Journal of Canadian Studies* 12 (Winter 1977), esp. 17–26.

39 *SPC*, 439. For a fascinating recent discussion, whose message is that small business can more than hold its own provided governments do not load the dice against it and in favour of large corporations, see Peterson, *Small Business*.

40 *SPC*, 284.

41 Ibid., 464, 465, 474, 477. The difference of views between Underhill and Good was fully aired in *The Canadian Forum* of August 1933. See also W.C. Good, *Farmer Citizen* (1958) chaps. 11–12.

42 *SPC*, 485, 486, 494–5.

43 Ibid., 67, 69.

44 *DNS*, 140, 143.

45 Robert Michels, *Political Parties*, trans. E. and C. Paul (Glencoe, Ill. 1949 [1915]) 402–3. Interview with Mr. Stuart Legge, July 1977.

46 An excellent discussion of co-operation and related issues can be found in the recent book by Richard E. Leakey and Roger Lewin, *Origins* (New York 1977), particularly in the last two chapters on 'Aggression, Sex, and Human Nature,' and 'Mankind in Perspective.' On the village, see 'George Bourne' (George Sturt), *Change in the Village* (London 1955 [1912]), esp. 96–7.

47 H.A. Innis, 'For the People,' *University of Toronto Quarterly* 5 (Jan. 1936) 283.

48 Pells, *Radical Visions and American Dreams*, 69–76, 89. Carl Berger, *The Writing of Canadian History: Aspects of English-Canadian Historical Writing, 1900–1970* (1976) 61–7. Arthur Mann, 'British Social Thought and American Reformers of the Progressive Era,' *Mississippi Valley Historical Review* 42 (Mar. 1956), Kenneth McNaught, 'American Progressives and the Great Society,' *Journal of American History* 53 (Dec. 1966).

49 Ned Rorem, 'The Music of the Beatles,' *New York Review of Books* (18 Jan. 1968) 26.

50 Interviews with Professor F.H. Underhill, Jan. 1967, and Professor Earle Birney, April 1967. Eugene Forsey, 'A New Economic Order,' in *Towards the Christian Revolution*, eds. R.B.Y. Scott and Gregory Vlastos (London 1937 [1936]) esp. 158, 162. See also, in the same volume, 'Propheticus' (Martyn Estall), 'The Marxist Challenge.' David Lewis, 'Marx to the Communist International,' *CF* 14 (Mar. 1936) 27. A.F.W. Plumptre, in *Economic Journal* 46 (Mar. 1936) 157.

51 Donald G. Creighton, 'Presidential Address,' *Canadian Historical Association Report* (1957) 6–7, 12. Penner, *The Canadian Left*, 201. Stanley Pierson, *Marxism and the Origins of British Socialism* (Ithaca, N.Y. and London 1973) 112–39.

52 See A.M. McBriar, *Fabian Socialism and English Politics, 1884–1914* (Cambridge 1962) 65 ff; Pierson, *Marxism and British Socialism*, 133 ff.

Tim Buck, *Yours in the Struggle: Reminiscences*, ed. William Beeching and Phyllis Clarke (1977) 344, 402–4.

53 R.T. Naylor, 'The Ideological Foundations of Social Democracy and Social Credit,' and Gary Teeple, '"Liberals in a Hurry": Socialism and the CCF-NDP,' in *Capitalism and the National Question in Canada*, ed. Gary Teeple (1972). Peter R. Sinclair, 'Class Structure and Populist Protest: The Case of Western Canada,' *Canadian Journal of Sociology* 1 (Spring 1975). Penner, *The Canadian Left*, 2, quoting O.D. Skelton, *Socialism: A Critical Analysis* (Boston 1911). Robert L. Heilbroner, 'Reflections on the Future of Socialism,' *Between Capitalism and Socialism* (New York 1970) 81–2.

54 Kenneth R. Minogue, *The Liberal Mind* (New York 1968 [1963]) vii, 65–8.

CHAPTER 6

1 *SPC*, 229.

2 McNaught, *A Prophet in Politics*, 176–80. F.R. Scott, 'The Development of Canadian Federalism,' Canadian Political Science Association (CPSA), *Papers and Proceedings* 3 (1931) 247.

3 F.R. Scott, *Social Reconstruction and the B.N.A. Act* (1934) 7–8; see also 19.

4 Norman McL. Rogers, 'LSR, CCF, and BNA,' *CF* 14 (June 1934). F.H. Underhill, in 'Round Table: Constitutional Amendment in Canada,' CPSA, *Papers and Proceedings* 6 (1934) 249–50.

5 *SPC*, 502, 505–6.

6 Ibid., 507, 508. Sections 51 and 51A deal with representation in the Dominion Parliament, 92(1) deals with provincial control over provincial constituion, 92 (12) with the solemnization of marriages in the provinces, 93 with education, and 133 with the use of the French language. *SPC* mistakenly used the number 135.

On minority rights and the 'compact theory,' see F.R. Scott, 'The Privy Council and Minority Rights,' *Queen's Quarterly* 37 (Autumn 1930); Norman McL. Rogers, 'The Compact Theory of Confederation,' CPSA, *Papers and Proceedings* 3 (1931). For the best recent discussion, see Ramsay Cook, *Provincial Autonomy, Minority Rights and the Compact Theory of Confederation, 1867–1921* (Ottawa 1969).

7 *SPC*, 509.

8 Ibid., 511. Eugene Forsey, the only leading member of the LSR to make it into the Senate so far, had by 1969 reached the conclusion that any federation must have two houses, one to represent 'the constituent communities (states or provinces) as such.' See his letter to *The Globe and Mail*, 7 Sept. 1977.

9 F.R. Scott, 'Goodbye Dominion Status,' *CF* 16 (Mar. 1937) 6. See also, by Scott, 'The Privy Council and Mr. Bennett's "New Deal" Legislation,' *Canadian Journal of Economics and Political Science* 3 (May 1937); 'The Consequences of the Privy Council Decisions,' *Canadian Bar Review* 15 (June 1937).

10 League for Social Reconstruction, *Canada – One or Nine? The Purpose of Confederation* (n.p., n.d. [Toronto 1938]) 2–3, 8, 10. The only copy of the printed booklet I have been able to find is in the E.A. Beder Papers, York University Archives. Mimeographed copies are in several collections of papers. The brief is most accessible in the pages of *The Canadian Forum* (March–May 1938).

11 *Canada – One or Nine?* 11, 13.

12 See W.L. Morton, 'Confederation 1870–1896: The End of the Macdonaldian Constitution and the Return to Duality,' *Journal of Canadian Studies* 1 (May 1966); Bruce W. Hodgins, 'Disagreement at the Commencement: Divergent Ontario Views of Federalism, 1867–71,' in *Oliver Mowat's Ontario*, ed. Donald Swainson (1972).

13 *Canada – One or Nine?* 13, 14–15, 16.

14 Ibid., 17. The brief is surely right in suggesting that the Canada of the latter nineteenth century was economically more 'open' than the Canada of the 1930s, though great disparities of wealth, as Michael B. Katz, J.T. Copp, and others have shown, existed in the earlier period as well. However, Canada only gradually became a political democracy during its first half-century, culminating in the extension of the federal franchise to adult women in 1919. In implying otherwise, here and in *Social Planning* (502), that Canada was a political democracy in 1867, the LSR was wrong. See W.L. Morton, 'The Extension of the Franchise in Canada,' Canadian Historical Association *Report* (1943).

15 *Canada – One or Nine?* 18, 21–2.

16 Ibid., 28, 32. Frank Scott to the author, 20 Apr. 1978.

17 *SPC*, 475. Frank H. Underhill, 'Some Observations upon Nationalism and Provincialism in Canada,' in *Problems in Canadian Unity*, ed. Violet Anderson (1938) 70.

18 *Canada – One or Nine?* 29. Underhill, 'Some Observations …,' 75.

19 Maxwell Cohen, 'Couchiching,' *CF* 20 (Oct. 1940) 202. In *The Canadian Forum*, see also 'Canada – One or Nine?' (June 1940); F.H. Underhill, 'The Sirois Commission as Historians' (Nov. 1940); G.M.A. Grube, 'Some Weaknesses of the Sirois Report' (Feb. 1941).

20 See, for example, F.R. Scott, 'The Constitution and the Post-War World,' in *Canada After the War*, ed. Alexander Brady and F.R. Scott (1943); David Lewis and Frank

Scott, *Make This YOUR Canada* (1943) esp. 151; F.H. Underhill, 'Dominion-Provincial Relations,' in *Planning for Freedom*, ed. Ontario CCF (1944).

21 F.H.U., 'O Canada,' *CF* 11 (June 1931) 333. But see Ralph Heintzman, 'Politics, Patronage, and the State of Quebec,' *Journal of Canadian Studies* 9 (May 1974), for a more informed assessment.

22 The earliest example of the use of the term *bicultural* that the research staff of the Royal Commission on Bilingualism and Biculturalism was able to track down was by Graham Spry, then national secretary of the Association of Canadian Clubs, in 1929. *Report* book one (Ottawa 1967), xxxi.

Frank Scott, quoted in the *Winnipeg Free Press*, 21 July 1933.

23 'Quebec Politics,' *CF* 11 (Mar. 1936) 5. *SPC*, 500, 501.

24 Eugene Forsey, 'Canada and Alberta: The Revival of Dominion Control Over the Provinces,' *Politica* 4 (June 1939) 123.

The Padlock Act was apparently prompted by the repeal in 1936 of Section 98 of the Criminal Code, dealing with sedition. The act was ultimately found to be *ultra vires* in 1957. See also D.A. Schmeiser, *Civil Liberties in Canada* (London 1964) 20, 202–3, 218–19.

25 *DNS*, 45.

26 Michael Oliver, 'The Social and Political Ideas of French Canadian Nationalists, 1920–1945' (PHD Dissertation, McGill University 1956) 225.

27 Scott Papers, Scott to J.S. Woodsworth, 30 Nov. 1938, copy.

28 Some Roman Catholics joined the CCF and were active in it, chief among them E.J. Garland, national organizer of the party for several years after his election defeat in 1935. See also Young, *Anatomy of a Party*, 211–13; Gregory Baum, 'Joe Burton: Catholic and Saskatchewan Socialist,' *The Ecumenist* 14 (July–Aug. 1976). I am grateful to Professor Baum for drawing this article to my attention.

29 See Joseph Levitt, 'The CCF and French Canadian "Radical" Nationalism' (MA Thesis, University of Toronto 1963) 147–55. Andrée Olssen, 'The Left in Quebec in the 1930's' (PHD Dissertation, Duke University 1972) 101–28.

30 Underhill, 'Some Observations ...,' 77. Underhill, 'The Conception of a National Interest,' *Canadian Journal of Economics and Political Science* 1 (Aug. 1935) 408.

31 Alan Cairns, 'The Judicial Committee and Its Critics,' *Canadian Journal of Political Science* 4 (Sept. 1971). Brooke Claxton, 'Social Reform and the Constitution,' *Canadian Journal of Economics and Political Science* 1 (Aug. 1935) 429–30, 434.

32 Donald Creighton, 'Eugene Alfred Forsey: An Introduction,' in Eugene Forsey, *Freedom and Order: Collected Essays* (1974) 3.

33 Margaret Prang, 'The Origins of Public Broadcasting in Canada,' *Canadian Historical Review* 46 (Mar. 1965), 2. Graham Spry, 'The Origins of Public Broadcasting in Canada: A Comment,' *Canadian Historical Review* 46 (June 1965) 136.

34 Margaret Prang, 'Nationalism in Canada's First Century,' Canadian Historical Associa-

tion *Report* (1968) 114. Douglas Cole, 'The Problem of "Nationalism" and "Imperialism" in British Settlement Colonies,' *Journal of British Studies* 10 (May 1971) 181. Forsey, 'Canada: Two Nations or One?' [1962], in *Freedom and Order*, 252.

35 Anthony D. Smith, *Theories of Nationalism* (New York 1972) 216–17.

36 J.W. Noseworthy, 'Education – A National Responsibility,' *CF* 18 (Feb. 1939).

37 H.A. Innis, 'The Rowell-Sirois Report,' *Canadian Journal of Economics and Political Science* 6 (Nov. 1940) 568–9.

CHAPTER 7

1 Scott Papers, 'Report of the National Convention of the League for Social Reconstruction, 22–23 February 1936.' This is evidently a condensed version of Scott's presidential address.

2 See Ronald Liversedge, *Recollections of the On-to-Ottawa Trek*, ed. Victor Hoar (1973). A briefer documentary account is to be found in Horn, *The Dirty Thirties*, part 5.

3 Leo Heaps, *The Rebel in the House: The Life and Times of A.A. Heaps, MP* (London 1970) 117.

4 H. Blair Neatby, *William Lyon Mackenzie King*, vol. 3, *1932–1939: The Prism of Unity* (1976) 158. CCF Records, 'Confidential Report of Discussions Between the CCF Parliamentary Group and the LSR Executive, March 28–29, 1936,' attached to Helen Marsh to M.J. Coldwell, 3 Apr. 1936.

5 CCF Records, 'CCF-LSR Conference, May 24–25, 1936.' Major C.H. Douglas was the British engineer who founded the Social Credit system.

6 CCF Records, F.R. Scott to Harold Winch, 5 June 1936, copy. Attached to it is the 'Election Manifesto, 1936.'

7 Scott Papers, Harold Winch to Scott, 27 Oct. 1936; Scott to Winch, 3 Nov. 1936, copy.

8 The Winch-Connell split is best read about in a book by an eyewitness and participant, Dorothy G. Steeves, *The Compassionate Rebel: Ernest E. Winch and His Times* (Vancouver 1960) 107–12; and in an article by Walter Young, 'Ideology, Personality and the Origin of the CCF in British Columbia,' *B.C. Studies* (Winter 1976–77) 156–62.

9 Scott Papers, Harold Winch to Scott, 30 July 1937. LSR Papers, Minutes, executive committee meeting, 4 Feb. 1938. Dorothy Steeves writes that 'the objectionable financial plank was quietly dropped after a year of cooler reflection' (*The Compassionate Rebel*, 111).

10 CCF Records, Eugene Forsey to David Lewis, 4 Mar. 1937; Graham Spry to Lewis, 9 Dec. 1936, n.d. [Spring 1937]; Lewis to Spry, 19 Dec. 1936, copy. See also Frank Underhill, 'The CCF Takes Stock,' *CF* 16 (Aug. 1936); Young, *Anatomy of a Party*, 78–9.

11 Alan Plaunt gave substantial sums to the CCF from the mid-1930s until his death in 1941.

According to a letter written by the national treasurer of the CCF in 1942, Plaunt donated $5,000 annually from 1938 on in order to maintain the national office. PAC, H.R.C. Avison Papers, A.M. Nicholson to H.R.C. Avison, 24 July 1942. This was confirmed by Mr David Lewis in a conversation in February 1977. On Plaunt's gifts, see also Underhill Papers, Underhill to M.J. Coldwell, 20 Aug. 1936, copy.

David Lewis, quoted in *The New Commonwealth*, 20 Aug. 1938. F.R. Scott, 'The CCF in Convention,' *CF* 18 (Sept. 1938). See also Young, *Anatomy of a Party*, 147–8.

12 King Gordon, 'A Christian Socialist in the 1930's,' in *The Social Gospel in Canada*, ed. Richard Allen (Ottawa 1975) 149–50.

13 LSR Papers, Mary C. Needler to J.C. Risk, 16 Oct. 1936.

14 Underhill Papers, Hugh R. Dent to Underhill, 14 Oct. 1932; Underhill to Dent, 5 Nov. 1932, copy. See also A.G. Mills, '*The Canadian Forum*: 1920–1934' (PHD Dissertation, University of Western Ontario 1976).

15 Dafoe Papers, Spry to Dafoe, 19 July 1935.

16 Interviews with Mr Graham Spry, June and September 1968. Interview with Mr Morden Lazarus, March 1977.

17 Underhill Papers, Minutes, national executive meeting, 1 May 1936; E.A. Havelock and F.H. Underhill to Graham Spry, 11 May 1936, copy; Spry to Underhill, 12 May 1936. LSR Papers, Helen Marsh to A.F. Stevenson, 1 May 1936, copy.

18 Underhill Papers, Carlton McNaught to Underhill, 7 May 1936. Scott Papers, 'Report of the National Conference ..., 1936.' See also LSR Papers, G.M.A. Grube to Helen Marsh [3 May 1936].

19 Humphrey Carver, *Compassionate Landscape* (1975) 44.

20 LSR Papers, Mark Farrell to Helen Marsh, 12 Dec. 1936.

21 Underhill Papers, Leonard Marsh to Underhill, 28 Oct. 1937; LSR Papers, Underhill to Marsh, 30 Oct. 1937.

22 On the Sustaining Fund, see LSR Papers, E.A. Havelock to L. Marsh, 23 Mar. 1938; Underhill Papers, 'Memorandum on the Canadian Forum, 27 Nov. 1943,' and attachment, 'List of Contributors to the Sustaining Fund, 1938–1943.' See also LSR Papers, Carlton McNaught to Jacob Markowitz, 12 Sept. 1940, copy. UBC Archives, Alan B. Plaunt Papers, G.M.A. Grube to Plaunt, 7 July 1939, with note: 'Written Sunday 10th. Sending 500 to Havelock this week.'

23 Scott Papers, S.B. Watson to Scott, 25 Sept. 1935. 'Report of the National Conference ..., 1936,' LSR Papers, League for Social Reconstruction, *Proceedings of the Sixth Annual Convention, Toronto, March 20–21, 1937* (n.p., n.d.) 3.

24 Geo. S. Mooney, *Co-operatives Today and Tomorrow: A Canadian Survey* (Montreal 1938) 189.

25 LSR Papers, Eugene Forsey to Edgar Ritchie, 1 Aug. 1937, copy.

26 'The Spanish Cauldron,' *CF* 16 (Oct. 1936) 5. On the efforts of Graham Spry and his collaborators, see Dafoe Papers, Spry to Dafoe, 1 Sept. 1936; *The New Commonwealth*,

17 and 31 Oct. 1936, 9 Jan. 1937. Victor Hoar, *The Mackenzie-Papineau Battalion* (1969) 9–10.

27 CCF Records, F.M. Aykroyd to all Montreal branch members, Oct. 1936, copy; Eugene Forsey to David Lewis, 10 Nov. 1936. Woodsworth Papers, Frank Scott to Woodsworth, 3 Feb. 1937. See also Walter Young, 'The National CCF: Political Party and Political Movement' (PH D Dissertation, University of Toronto 1965) 307–8.

28 'Quebec's Iron Heel,' *CF* 16 (Nov. 1936); 'Quebec Fascists Show Their Hand,' *CF* 16 (Dec. 1936). CCF Records, Eugene Forsey to Graham Spry, 17 Mar. 1937, copy.

29 Duart Snow, 'The Holmes Foundry Strike of March 1937,' *Ontario History* 69 (March 1977). I.M. Abella, 'The C.I.O., the Communist Party, and the Formation of the Canadian Congress of Labour, 1936–1941,' Canadian Historical Association *Report* (1969).

On LSR fears, see 'Civil Liberties in Quebec' and 'Oshawa,' *CF* 17 (May 1937); Eugene Forsey, 'Clerical Fascism in Quebec,' and [F.H. Underhill], 'Our Class-Conscious Newspapers,' *CF* 17 (June 1937).

30 LSR Papers, Leonard Marsh and C.M. Lapointe to Rt Hon. W.L.M. King, 2 Feb. 1938, copy. CCF Records, Eugene Forsey to David Lewis, 29 Nov. and 6 Dec. 1937. E.A. Forsey to the author [June 1968].

On disallowance, see Hon. Ernest Lapointe to His Excellency the Governor General, 5 July 1938, in Horn, *The Dirty Thirties*, 689–93. Eugene Forsey, 'Mr. Lapointe and the Padlock,' *CF* 18 (Aug. 1938).

31 Scott Papers, Scott to David Lewis, 11 July 1937, copy. 'S' [F.R. Scott], 'Embryo Fascism in Quebec,' *Foreign Affairs* 16 (April 1938).

32 See Kingsley Martin, *Editor* (London 1968) 149–60; John Lewis, *The Left Book Club* (London 1970) 24–6 and passim.

33 *DNS*, 25, 34, 37.

34 Ibid., 40, 41, 42.

35 Ibid., 45, 143.

36 LSR Papers, J.F. Parkinson to C.M. Lapointe, 2 June 1937. *DNS*, 153. LSR Papers, Lapointe to David Lewis, 24 Feb. 1938. According to royalty statements in the Grube Papers, 2,400 copies of the book were sold over five years.

37 Scott Papers, Scott to Lewis, 11 July 1937, copy. King Gordon to Scott, 1 Aug. 1937 and 2 Oct. 1937. Caplan, *Dilemma of Canadian Socialism*, 83.

38 LSR Papers, J.C. Risk to Helen Marsh, 16 Oct. 1936. *Proceedings of the Sixth Annual Convention*, 2–3.

39 Leonard Marsh to the author, 5 Dec. 1967. For a copy of the 'Draft of a Revised Manifesto,' see the LSR Papers.

40 LSR Papers, Minutes, National Convention, Montreal, May 20–21, 1939.

The minutes of the national executive provide little enlightenment. On 13 September 1938, 'the president [Leonard Marsh] undertook to submit a final draft ... at the next meeting.' Two meetings passed without mention of the document; then, five weeks later, 'it was thought that the new draught [sic] of the LSR Manifesto should be given further consideration and in the meantime it was decided to have reprinted a supply of the old form.' No further information is available. York University Archives, Gordon H. Jack Papers, LSR Executive, Minutes of the meeting of 13 September 1938; LSR National Executive, Meeting of 18 October 1938.

41 Underhill Papers, form letter for funds sent out by G.M.A. Grube, E.A. Havelock, J.F. Parkinson, F.H. Underhill, and S.B. Watson [Feb. 1936], copy. Spry Papers, Spry to Lewis, 30 Apr. 1937, copy; see also Spry to Lewis, 17 May 1937, copy.

42 Spry Papers, Spry to his parents, 3 June 1937, copy. See also Underhill Papers, Spry to Underhill, 12 Aug. 1937. Interview with Mr Graham Spry, Sept. 1968.

43 LSR Papers, *Proceedings of the Sixth Annual Convention*, 5. R.E.K. Pemberton to C.M. Lapointe, 10 Nov. 1937; Lapointe to Pemberton, 20 Nov. 1937, copy; Pemberton to Lapointe, 13 March 1938; LSR London Branch, 'Report on Activities During the Season 1937–38.' Interviews with Prof. R.E.K. Pemberton, Mr and Mrs Selwyn Dewdney, and Mr Charles Buck, April 1967.

CHAPTER 8

1 Neatby, *The Prism of Unity*, 170–1 and passim.

2 F.H. Underhill, 'Goldwin Smith,' *University of Toronto Quarterly* 2 (April 1933). Underhill Papers, Underhill to John S. Ewart, 22 July 1932, copy. See also Underhill, 'The Political Ideas of John S. Ewart,' Canadian Historical Association *Report* (1933); J.W. Dafoe, 'The Ideas and Influence of John S. Ewart,' *Canadian Historical Review* 16 (June 1933).

3 J.W. Dafoe Papers, Graham Spry to Dafoe, 8 Feb. 1932. F.H. Underhill, 'Canadian Writers of Today: J.W. Dafoe,' *CF* 13 (Oct. 1932). See also Ramsay Cook, *The Political Ideas of John W. Dafoe and the Free Press* (1963) 126–86.

4 Douglas Cole, 'John S. Ewart and Canadian Nationalism,' Canadian Historical Association *Report* (1969).

5 McNaught, *A Prophet in Politics*, 197–203. G.M.A. Grube, 'Pacifism: The Only Solution,' *CF* 16 (June 1936). Frank H. Underhill, *In Search of Canadian Liberalism* (1960) x.

6 Escott Reid Papers, 'External Affairs,' 1933. Eugene Forsey to Reid, 1 July 1933; Frank Scott to Reid, 6 July 1933. [H.M. Cassidy?], Comment on Draft Article on 'External Affairs.'

7 *SPC*, 359–60, 348.

8 Ibid., 514, 515, 517.

9 Ibid., 517–8.

10 Ibid., 518, 519, 520, 521.

11 Ibid., 522. On the Nye Committee, see Manfred Jonas, *Isolationism in America 1935–1941* (Ithaca, N.Y. 1966) 144–8.

12 *SPC*, 523.

13 Ibid., 524.

14 Escott Reid, 'Did Canada Cause the Next War?' and 'League Must Give Justice as Well as Peace,' *Saturday Night* (28 Sept. and 5 Oct. 1935). See also Richard Veatch, *Canada and the League of Nations* (1975) 63.

15 [F.H. Underhill], 'Leadership in Foreign Policy,' *CF* 15 (Dec. 1935) 380. E.A. Havelock, 'The League of Nations,' *CF* 15 (Feb. 1936) 11. Interview with Prof. E.A. Havelock, April 1967.

16 Jonas, *Isolationism in America*, 116.

17 Richard Hofstadter, *The Progressive Historians* (New York 1968) 325. See also Berger, *The Writing of Canadian History*, 78–9.

18 Stafford Cripps, 'British Foreign Policy,' *CF* 16 (Dec. 1936); H.N. Brailsford, 'A Socialist View of the League,' *CF* 17 (May 1937). Interview with Prof. F.H. Underhill, June 1968. See also McNaught, *A Prophet in Politics*, 199.

19 Marvin Gelber, 'That Liberal Façade,' *CF* 16 (May 1936) 18; reply by Underhill on p. 4.

20 Escott Reid, 'Mr. Mackenzie King's Foreign Policy, 1935–1936,' *Canadian Journal of Economics and Political Science* 3 (Feb. 1937); Dafoe Papers, Dafoe to Reid, 10 Nov. 1936, copy.

21 Woodsworth Papers, Scott to Woodsworth, 3 Feb. 1937. The reference to South Africa concerns the Royal Seals and Signet Act, passed by the Parliament of the Union of South Africa in 1934. 'Its effect was to remove all limitations upon the delegation of the King's executive power. Under its provisions, it would be entirely in order that while the King's ministers in Great Britain were advising him to declare war, his ministers in South Africa should be advising his representative there to declare South Africa's neutrality.' Sir Keith Hancock, *Survey of British Commonwealth Affairs 1918–1939*, vol. 1, *Problems of Nationality 1918–1936* (Oxford 1964 [1937]) 280.

Angus MacInnis Papers, Scott to MacInnis, 22 Feb. 1937. But see, in the same location, Eugene Forsey to MacInnis, 22 Feb. 1937. Forsey disagreed with Scott's advice and suggested that if the objectionable Section 19 could not be amended, the CCF should oppose the act. For the text of the Foreign Enlistment Act, see Victor Hoar, *The Mackenzie-Papineau Battalion* (1969) 249–55.

22 *DNS*, 141–2. F.H. Underhill, 'Keep Canada Out of War' [1937], *In Search of Canadian Liberalism*, 185.

23 Underhill Papers, *Canadian Unity in War and Peace: An Issue of Responsible Government* (1939) 1.

24 F.R. Scott, *Canada Today* (1938) 126, 135.

25 Neatby, *The Prism of Unity*, 212 ff., 290.

26 G.M.A. Grube, 'The Chamberlain Way to War,' *CF* 18 (Apr. 1938); 'After Munich,' *CF* 18 (Nov. 1938) 230. Dislike of Prime Minister Chamberlain lasted into the war: [Underhill], 'The New British Government,' *CF* 20 (June 1940) esp. 68.

27 'The Scapegoat,' *CF* 18 (Jan. 1939) 292. 'The Refugee Problem,' *CF* 18 (Mar. 1939) 361. See also Gerald E. Dirks, *Canada's Refugee Policy: Indifference or Opportunism?* (Montreal and London 1977) 44–71.

28 Scott, *Canada Today*, 103. F.H.U., 'O Canada,' *CF* 10 (Dec. 1929) 79; 'O Canada,' *CF* 11 (Feb. 1931) 169.

29 Underhill, 'Canada Moves Left,' *The World Tomorrow* (25 Jan. 1933). Underhill and Scott, discussion of a paper by R.A. MacKay, 'The Nature of American Politics,' in *Conference on Canadian-American Affairs, 1935, Proceedings*, ed. W.W. McLaren, A.B. Corey, and R.G. Trotter (Boston 1936) 205, 209.

30 Scott, 'The Permanent Bases of Canadian Foreign Policy,' *Foreign Affairs* 10 (July 1932) 619. Escott Reid, 'Canada and the Next War,' *CF* 14 (Mar. 1934).

31 *SPC*, 512.

32 Ibid., 55. This manner of stating the case obscures the fact that there are differences between domestic and foreign businessmen. As a recent study puts it, 'the perspective of the foreign businessman differs due to the external ties which he has both to his parent company abroad and to any other affiliates in other countries.' I.A. Litvak and C.J. Maule, 'Foreign Subsidiaries as Instruments of Host Government Policy,' quoted in Peterson, *Small Business*, 167.

33 *SPC*, 56.

34 Underhill, 'The Outline of a National Foreign Policy,' in *World Currents and Canada's Course*, ed. Violet Anderson (1937) 137.

35 Graham Spry, 'Radio Broadcasting and Aspects of Canadian-American Relations,' in *Conference on Canadian-American Affairs, 1935, Proceedings*, 109.

36 F.H.U., 'O Canada,' *CF* 9 (July 1929) 341.

37 Scott, *Canada Today*, 84. Scott, *Canada and the United States* (Boston 1941) 74.

38 Neatby, *The Prism of Unity*, 287–8. James Eayrs, *The Art of the Possible* (1961) 40n. Interviews with Principal Escott Reid, Apr. 1967, Nov. 1968.

39 J.L. Granatstein, *Canada's War: The Politics of the Mackenzie King Government 1939–1945* (1975) 19.

40 The LSR exaggerated the causal relationship between capitalism and imperialism. On this subject, see George Lichtheim, *Imperialism* (New York 1971) esp. 134–50; Irving M. Zeitlin, *Capitalism and Imperialism* (Chicago 1972); D.K. Fieldhouse, *Economics and Empire 1830–1914* (London 1973) 138–62. Benjamin J. Cohen, *The Question of Imperialism* (New York 1973) 229–58.

CHAPTER 9

1 LSR Papers, E.A. Havelock to Louise Parkin, 2 Sept. 1939.

2 LSR Papers, Helen Howes to T.C. Douglas, 21 Nov. 1938, copy; to M.J. Coldwell, 8 Jan. 1939, copy; to R. Liddle, 8 Jan. 1939, copy; to A. Griffith, 8 Jan. 1939, copy; to H.I.S. Borgford, 30 June 1939, copy. Robert Liddle to Helen Howes, 11 Jan. 1939.

3 LSR Papers, Gordon Jack to Helen Howes, 5 June 1940; Kay Montagu to Howes, 15 May 1939. Interview with Mrs Kay Montagu Morris, Feb. 1967.

4 LSR Papers, E.E. Roper to Howes, 8 Jan. 1940. CCF Records, 'Calgary Club Expulsion'; Minutes, CCF National Executive, 15 May 1939. Grube Papers, Minutes, LSR National Convention, 8–9 June 1940.

5 LSR Papers, Minutes, LSR National Convention, Montreal, 20–21 May 1939. W. Jarvis McCurdy to Howes, 2 Dec. 1939; Howes to McCurdy, 10 Dec. 1939, copy.

6 McNaught, *A Prophet in Politics*, 257. Interviews with Prof. E.A. Havelock, April 1967; Mr J.F. Parkinson, June 1968; Prof. R.E.K. Pemberton, March 1967.

7 LSR Papers, W.J. McCurdy to Louise Parkin, 28 Aug. 1939. J.C. Risk to Leonard Marsh, 24 March 1937; C.M. Lapointe to Risk, 1 April 1937, copy.

8 Scott Papers, Louise Parkin to W.L.M. King, 6 Sept. 1939, copy; LSR Papers, King to Parkin, 25 Sept. 1939.

9 CCF Records, George Williams to David Lewis, 5 Apr. 1937. See also Young, *Anatomy of a Party*, 91 ff.

10 Scott Papers, 'National Council Meetings, 6 Sept. 1939.' These are F.R. Scott's own minutes of the first day's discussions.

11 CCF Records, Minutes, CCF National Council meeting, Ottawa, 6–8 Sept. 1939; Eugene Forsey, 'Memorandum on CCF Policy.' George Williams to Angus MacInnis, 7 Feb. 1940, quoted in Young, *Anatomy of a Party*, 94.

12 LSR Papers, Havelock to Parkin, 24 Sept. 1939. Interview with Mr J.F. Parkinson, Dec. 1966.

13 Grube Papers, Minutes, LSR National Convention, Montreal, 8–9 June 1940.

14 F.H. Underhill, 'O.D. Skelton,' *CF* 20 (Mar. 1941). F.R. Scott, 'Canada's Role in World Affairs,' *Food for Thought* 2 (Jan. 1942). Scott, 'Canadian Nationalism and the War,' *CF* 21 (Mar. 1942).

15 LSR Papers, G.M.A. Grube to Parkin, n.d. [Sept. 1939]; 8 Oct. 1939. On the fears of proscription, see Young, *Anatomy of a Party*, 96. The attack on Underhill and Grube will be discussed in the next chapter.

16 LSR Papers, Eleanor Godfrey to Helen Howes, 19 Mar. 1940; Carlton McNaught to Jarvis McCurdy, 21 Oct. 1940. Alan Plaunt Papers, McNaught to Plaunt, 24 July 1941.

17 Carlton McNaught, *Volume Thirty: A Retrospect*, reprint from *CF* 30 (April–June 1950) 7–8.

18 LSR Papers, Howes to Violet McNaughton, 8 Nov. 1939, copy. Underhill Papers, Parkin to Underhill, 31 Mar. 1940. Grube Papers, Agenda, LSR National Convention, 1940.

19 All quotations from Grube Papers, Minutes, LSR National Convention, Montreal, 8–9 June 1940.

20 LSR Papers, McNaught to Dr J. Markowitz, 12 Sept. 1940, copy.

21 Grube Papers, McCurdy to branch secretaries, 16 Sept. 1940, copy. David Lewis to Eileen Troop, 9 June 1941.

22 LSR Papers, Roma Goodwin to Eileen Troop, 9 Apr. 1941. National Secretary's Report, 8 June 1940.

23 R.A. Farquharson, 'War Effort is Criticized by Tories,' *The Globe and Mail*, 14 June 1941.

24 Grube Papers, Report of the National Secretary, 14 June 1941.

25 Underhill Papers, Forsey to Underhill, 4 May 1941; Underhill, 'L.S.R.,' 21 May 1941. Conversation with Prof. W.J. McCurdy, October 1977.

26 Grube Papers, Minutes, joint meeting of the national executive and the Toronto branch executive, 9 Nov. 1941. CCF Records, Frank Scott to David Lewis, 13 Mar. 1942. See also J.L. Granatstein, 'The York South By-Election of February 9, 1942,' *Canadian Historical Review* 48 (June 1967).

27 [Underhill], 'Meighen Redivivus,' *CF* 21 (Jan. 1942). CCF Records, Forsey to the editor, *The Canadian Forum*, 8 Jan. 1942, copy. David Lewis to Eleanor Godfrey, 10 Jan. 1942, copy; Godfrey to Lewis, 16 Jan. 1942.

The *Forum* carried Forsey's protest, but only after the election. It was deemed inexpedient to have it appear in the February issue.

28 Scott, 'Ten Years of the League for Social Reconstruction,' *Saturday Night* (24 Jan. 1942).

29 See Ramsay Cook, 'Canadian Freedom in Wartime, 1939–1945,' in *His Own Man: Essays in Honour of Arthur Reginald Marsden Lower*, ed. W.H. Heick and Roger Graham (Montreal 1974) esp. 47–8.

30 Young, *Anatomy of a Party*, 97.

31 'Tumult and Shouting,' *CF* 21 (Mar. 1942) 358.

32 CCF Records, David Lewis to H.D. Hughes, 20 Dec. 1945, copy. Lewis to Scott, 12 Jan. 1948, copy; Scott to Lewis, 21 Jan. 1948.

33 CCF Records, Donald C. MacDonald, 'Report of Executive Committee on Education,' submitted to the National Council of the CCF, 1 Oct. 1949. Paul Fox to Lorne Ingle, 18 Nov. 1950. Conversations with Professors Paul Fox and K.W. McNaught, 1967.

34 Michael Oliver, Preface to *Social Purpose for Canada* (1961) vi–vii.

35 Abraham Rotstein, Preface to *The Prospect of Change* (1965) vii.

36 *Nationalism in Canada*, ed. Peter Russell (1966); *Agenda 1970: Proposals for a Creative Politics*, ed. Trevor Lloyd and Jack McLeod (1968).

37 *Close the 49th Parallel etc.: The Americanization of Canada*, ed. Ian Lumsden (1970); *Thinking about Change*, ed. David Shugarman (1974).

38 *Capitalism and the National Question in Canada*, ed. Gary Teeple (1972); Leo Panitch, 'Editor's Preface,' *The Canadian State: Political Economy and Political Power* (1977) viii.

CHAPTER 10

1 W.H. Alexander, 'Will Radical Leadership Emerge from Canadian Universities?' *Saskatchewan CCF Research* 1 (July 1934) 15; Alexander, ' "Noli Episcopari": Letter to a Young Man Contemplating an Academic Career,' *CF* 19 (Oct. 1939) 223.
2 John Porter, *The Vertical Mosaic* (1965) 503; F.C. Engelmann and M.A. Schwartz, *Political Ideas and the Canadian Social Structure* (1967) 153; Ian Lumsden, 'Imperialism and Canadian Intellectuals,' in *Close the 49th Parallel*, 329.
3 Murray G. Ross, *The University: The Anatomy of Academe* (New York 1976) 196.
4 Robin Harris, *A History of Higher Education in Canada 1663–1960* (1976) 213; Canada, Department of Trade and Commerce, Dominion Bureau of Statistics, Education Statistics Branch, *Higher Education in Canada, 1938–1940* (Ottawa 1941).
5 W.P. Thompson, *The University of Saskatchewan: A Personal History* (1970) 123; H.T. Logan, *Tuum Est: A History of the University of British Columbia* (Vancouver 1958) 109–20.
6 See Underhill Papers, University Salaries file.
7 *Higher Education in Canada, 1938–1940*, tables 12 and 15.
8 Harris, *A History of Higher Education in Canada*, 357.
9 See Richard Hofstadter, *Anti-Intellectualism in American Life* (New York 1966 [1963]) 34–9.
10 Howard Ferguson to H.J. Cody, 6 April 1929, quoted in Peter Oliver, *Howard Ferguson: Ontario Tory* (1977) 327; also 242–3.
11 *The Varsity*, 1 Nov. 1929.
12 Howard Adelman, *The Holiversity* (1973); Northrop Frye, Conclusion to *Literary History of Canada*, ed. Carl F. Klinck (1965) 830.
13 The preceding two paragraphs are based on S.E.D. Shortt, *The Search for an Ideal: Six Canadian Intellectuals and their Convictions in an Age of Transition 1890–1930* (1976).
14 A.G. Bedford, *The University of Winnipeg: A History of the Founding Colleges* (1976) 126–39.
15 Sir Robert Falconer, *Academic Freedom* (1922) 13.
16 A.H. Halsey and M.A. Trow, *The British Academics* (Cambridge, Mass. 1971) 117.
17 Richard Hofstadter and Walter P. Metzger, *The Development of Academic Freedom in America* (New York 1955) 383–497. Laurence R. Veysey, *The Emergence of the American University* (Chicago 1965) 317 ff.
18 Donald C. Savage and Christopher Holmes, 'The CAUT, the Crowe Case and the Development of the Idea of Academic Freedom in Canada,' *CAUT Bulletin*, 24 (Dec. 1975).
19 'The Higher Politics,' the *Globe*, 16 Feb. 1922.
20 Queen's University Archives, Sir Joseph Flavelle Papers, Flavelle to G.M. Wrong, 20 Jan. 1931, copy.

21 Public Archives of Ontario (PAO), Records of the Prime Minister's Office, G.S. Henry Papers, Henry to H.J. Cody, 13 Feb. 1931, copy.

22 Underhill Papers, Sir Robert Falconer to Underhill, 26 June 1931. Underhill's article, 'Canada in the Great Depression,' appeared in the *New Statesman and Nation* on 13 June 1931. It was the concluding paragraph, on page 571, which offended the *Mail and Empire*: 'An Amiable Thrust from Academic Cloister,' 26 June 1931.

23 Underhill Papers, Underhill to Falconer, 24 Sept. 1931, copy.

24 Underhill Papers, Falconer to Underhill, 28 Sept. 1931.

25 Flavelle Papers, George M. Wrong to Flavelle, 21 Jan. 1931.

26 PAO, H.J. Cody Papers, G.S. Henry to Cody, 20 July 1932; Cody Papers, Cody to Dr Tutt, 20 Dec. 1932, copy. I am grateful to Prof. Douglas Francis for drawing these two letters to my attention.

Interviews with Prof. F.H. Underhill, Dec. 1966, and Prof. E.A. Havelock, Apr. 1967.

27 Underhill Papers, Norman Thomas to Underhill, 12 Jan. 1933; S. Delbert Clark to Underhill, 13 Jan. 1933. Kingsley Martin, *Harold Laski* (New York 1953) 87–91.

28 UTA, H.M. Cassidy Papers, Cassidy to L. Eckhardt [president, St Paul's CCF Club], 18 Oct. 1933, copy; Cassidy to D.M. LeBourdais, 18 Oct. 1933, copy; Cassidy to H.J. Cody, 22 June 1934, copy.

Cassidy did return to the University of Toronto at the end of the Second World War.

29 CCF Records, M.J. Coldwell to J.F. Parkinson, 9 Dec. 1935, copy; Parkinson to Coldwell, 20 Dec. 1935.

30 The *Gazette* (31 Mar. 1933). J. King Gordon, 'A Christian Socialist in the 1930's,' in: *The Social Gospel in Canada*, ed. Richard Allen (Ottawa 1975) 141–3.

31 *The New Outlook*, 11 Apr. 1934, 10 Oct. 1934, 26 Dec. 1934, 13 Feb. 1935, 8 May 1935.

32 Graham Spry, 'The Case of King Gordon,' *The New Commonwealth*, 27 Oct. 1934.

33 Underhill Papers, Eugene Forsey to Underhill, 30 Mar. 1933; see also Forsey to Underhill, 2 May 1941. Interview with Senator E.A. Forsey, Oct. 1972.

34 F.R. Scott to the author, 11 Sept. 1968; interviews with Prof. Scott, Dec. 1966, May 1978.

35 McGill University Archives, Principal's Office Files, Wilfrid Bovey to J.H. MacBrien, 17 Dec. 1932, copy; MacBrien to Sir Arthur Currie, 13 Feb. 1933. Ramsay MacDonald was British prime minister in 1924 and from 1929 to 1935. I am obliged to Professor Frank Scott for drawing these letters to my attention.

36 Interviews with Prof. Leonard Marsh, June 1967, Feb. 1979.

37 H. Martyn Estall to the author, 1 Dec. 1977. Interviews with Prof. Gregory Vlastos, Apr. 1967, Oct. 1978.

38 R.A. MacKay to the author, 4 Oct. 1972. See also Underhill Papers, H.L. Keenleyside to Underhill, 9 Nov. 1933.

Arthur R.M. Lower, *My First Seventy-Five Years* (1967) 193–4.

39 On the Alexander case, see Frank Underhill, 'On Professors and Politics,' *CF* 15 (Mar. 1936). On the King case, Underhill Papers, Carlyle King to Underhill, 6 Oct. 1938; [Helen Orpwood], 'Free Speech in Saskatchewan,' *CF* 18 (Dec. 1938).

40 LSR Papers, Grace MacInnis to Helen Howes, 8 July 1939.

41 Underhill Papers, H.L. Keenleyside to Underhill, 8 Sept. 1933. For a detailed account of Underhill's difficulties in the 1930s and early 1940s, see Douglas Francis, 'Frank H. Underhill, Canadian Intellectual' (PHD Dissertation, York University 1976).

42 Underhill Papers, G.M. Wrong to Underhill, 7 and 11 Dec. 1933.

43 Brian J. Young, 'C. George McCullagh and the Leadership League,' *Canadian Historical Review* 47 (Sept. 1966) 202.

44 Underhill Papers, Writings 1937, 'Freedom of the Press.'

45 'Professor Underhill "Educates,"' *The Globe and Mail*, 1 June 1937.

46 Underhill Papers, Underhill to Steven Cartwright, 4 June 1937, copy; Cartwright to Underhill, 18 June 1937.

47 [B.K. Sandwell], 'The Front Page,' *Saturday Night* (9 Nov. 1935).

48 Leopold Macaulay, quoted in the *Globe*, 31 Mar. 1936.

49 Sir Edward Beatty, 'Freedom and the Universities,' *Queen's Quarterly* 44 (Winter 1937–38) 470.

50 Underhill Papers, Eugene Forsey to Underhill, 16 Oct. 1937.

51 Jean-François Pouliot to W.L.M. King, cited in Neatby, *The Prism of Unity*, 236n. 'Free Speech and its Abuses,' the *Gazette*, quoted in Eugene Forsey, 'Paper Attacks McGill Professor,' *The New Commonwealth*, 27 Aug. 1938.

52 *The Globe and Mail*, 13 Apr. 1939. Grube subsequently agreed to be more circumspect in his comments on public affairs. Underhill Papers, G.M.A. Grube to the Provost, Trinity College, 27 Apr. 1939, copy.

53 Ibid., 14 Apr. 1939. The passage first appeared in 'Canada and the Organization for Peace,' a mimeographed document prepared by the Canadian Institute of International Affairs for the International Studies Conference, 1935. It was quoted in R.A. MacKay and E.B. Rogers, *Canada Looks Abroad* (1938); this is where Colonel Drew found it.

54 Underhill Papers, Underhill to H.J. Cody, 18 Apr. 1939, copy.

55 Plaunt Papers, Plaunt to Scott, 20 Apr. 1939, copy. Underhill Papers, B.S. Keirstead to Underhill, 15 Apr. 1939.

56 'Free Speech in Toronto,' *CF* 19 (June 1939) 72. W.H. Alexander, '"Noli Episcopari" ...,' *CF* 19 (Oct. 1939) 223.

57 Plaunt Papers, George A. Drew to Plaunt, 18 Apr. 1939.

58 Granatstein, *Canada's War*, 128.

59 Underhill Papers, Writings 1940, 'A United American Front.' The quotation is from the typescript that Underhill subsequently prepared for President Cody. At Lake Couchiching he spoke from two sheets of paper on which he had jotted main points only.

60 Arthur Meighen to Ernest Lapointe, 28 Aug. 1940, quoted in Roger Graham, *Arthur Meighen*, vol. 3, *No Surrender* (Vancouver and Toronto 1965) 123.

61 On Underhill's troubles in 1940–41, see Douglas Francis, 'The Threatened Dismissal of Frank H. Underhill from the University of Toronto, 1939–41.' *CAUT Bulletin* 24 (Dec. 1975); Berger, *The Writing of Canadian History*, 79–84; D.G. Creighton, 'The Ogdensburg Agreement and F.H. Underhill,' in *The West and the Nation: Essays in Honour of W.L. Morton*, ed. Carl Berger and Ramsay Cook (1976).

62 Underhill Papers, Universities file, 'Statement by Professor F.H. Underhill as to an interview between him and a committee of the Board of Governors on January 2, 1941.' See also Plaunt Papers, Underhill to Plaunt, 10 Jan. 1941.

63 Creighton, 'The Ogdensburg Agreement and Underhill,' 312.

64 [P.C. Armstrong], *A Criticism of the Book ... 'Social Planning for Canada'*, 6.

65 Porter, *The Vertical Mosaic*, 503. Adelman, *The Holiversity*, 40.

66 Interviews with Mr Graham Spry, Sept. 1968, and with Prof. F.R. Scott, May 1978.
H.A. Innis, 'Government Ownership and the Canadian Scene,' in R.B. Bennett *et al.*, *Canadian Problems as Seen by Twenty Outstanding Men of Canada* (n.d. [1933]) 69.

67 F.H. Underhill, 'The Conception of a National Interest,' *Canadian Journal of Economics and Political Science* 1 (Aug. 1935) 404, 406, 407.

68 H.A. Innis, '"For the People,"' *University of Toronto Quarterly* 5 (Jan. 1936) 285 ff. Donald G. Creighton, *Harold Adams Innis: Portrait of a Scholar* (1957) 92–3.

69 Underhill, 'On Professors and Politics,' 7.

70 H.A. Innis to H.J. Cody, 8 Jan. 1941, quoted in Francis, 'The Threatened Dismissal of Underhill,' 19.

71 Underhill Papers, Leopold Macaulay to Underhill, 6 Jan. 1941.

72 Innis, '"For the People,"' 286.

73 David Braybrooke, 'Tenure – Illusion and Reality,' quoted in Janet Scarfe and Edward Sheffield, 'Notes on the Canadian Professoriate,' *Higher Education* 6 (1977) 345.

74 Frank Underhill made an early attempt; its results were not flattering to Canada. 'Academic Freedom in Canada,' *AAUP Bulletin* 46 (Sept. 1960).

75 S.M. Lipset, *The First New Nation* (London 1964 [1963]) 249 ff. Gerald L. Caplan, 'The Failure of Canadian Socialism: The Ontario Experience, 1932–1945,' *Canadian Historical Review* 44 (June 1963) 106 ff.; Young, *Anatomy of a Party*, 200–3.

76 David V.J. Bell, 'The Loyalist Tradition in Canada,' *Journal of Canadian Studies* 5 (May 1970) 27–9. Granatstein, *Canada's War*, 409–10, 413.

77 Several of the comparisons were suggested to me as a consequence of reading Hofstadter, *Anti-Intellectualism in American Life*, esp. 41–2.

78 I.M. Abella, *Nationalism, Communism and Canadian Labour* (1973).

79 Charles Taylor, 'Herbert Norman,' *Six Journeys: A Canadian Pattern* (1977) 136–49.
The assessment that there were no card-carrying members of the CPC among professors in the inter-war years was made by my colleague Norman Penner, who was active in the party from the 1930s into the 1950s. Lest it be thought that he is himself an exception: he did not begin to prepare himself for a career in university teaching until the 1960s.

There was at least one Trotskyite in the LSR circle, Prof. Earle Birney. The fact was not widely known, however, and Prof. Birney always assumed a pseudonym when writing on politics. Interview with Prof. Birney, Apr. 1967.

CHAPTER 11

1 McNaught, *A Prophet in Politics*, 258. Richard Hofstadter, *The Age of Reform* (New York 1955) 141 and *passim*. See also Carl Berger, *The Sense of Power* (1970) 12–77.
2 Karl Mannheim, *Ideology and Utopia*, trans. Louis Wirth (New York 1966 [1963]) esp. 219–29 and 239–47.
3 Mustafer and Carolyn Sherif, *An Outline of Social Psychology*, quoted in J.A.C. Brown, *Techniques of Persuasion* (Harmondsworth 1967) 66; see also 66–7, 147–8.
4 Charles E. Lindblom, *Politics and Markets* (New York 1977) 204–5, 208, 211.
5 Gordon Allport, *The Nature of Prejudice* (Garden City, N.Y. 1958) 456 ff., esp. 458.
6 See Michiel Horn, 'The Great Depression: Past and Present,' *Journal of Canadian Studies* 11 (Feb. 1976) 48–9.
7 Howard Palmer, 'Nativism in Alberta, 1925–1930,' Canadian Historical Association *Report* (1974); Michiel Horn, 'Keeping Canada "Canadian": Anti-Communism and Canadianism in Toronto 1928–29,' *Canada* 3 (Autumn 1975).
8 'G. Pierce' [Stewart Smith], *Socialism and the CCF*, 150–1.
9 B.A. Trestrail, *Stand Up and Be Counted* (1944) 29. Text and illustrations must have appealed to whatever anti-intellectual and anti-Semitic prejudices existed among the book's readers. The LSR plotters either were thin and bespectacled and wore an academic cap and gown, or possessed a stereotyped Jewish nose. See also Caplan, *Dilemma of Canadian Socialism*, 120–9, 158–63.
10 Young, *Anatomy of a Party*, 30; McBriar, *Fabian Socialism and English Politics*, 339; Margaret Cole, *The Story of Fabian Socialism* (London 1963) 218.
11 Young, *Anatomy of a Party*, 289; B.K. Sandwell, quoted in Caplan, *Dilemma of Canadian Socialism*, 198. J.L. Ilsley, quoted in the *Globe*, 13 Feb. 1933.
12 See Alan C. Cairns, 'The Electoral System and The Party System in Canada, 1921–1965,' *Canadian Journal of Political Science* 1 (Mar. 1968). The LSR had no settled policy on proportional representation. Frank Underhill favoured it: 'Our Fantastic Electoral System,' *CF* 15 (Nov. 1935); Eugene Forsey opposed it: CCF Records, Forsey to David Lewis, 22 July 1937.
13 Young, *Anatomy of a Party*, 135.
14 Caplan, *Dilemma of Canadian Socialism*, 106.
15 Maurice Bruce, *The Coming of the Welfare State*, 4th ed. (London 1972 [1968]) 291.
16 Graham Spry Papers, J.W. Dafoe to Spry, 16 Apr. 1936.
17 F.R. Scott and others, Introduction to *Social Planning for Canada*, reprint (1975) xix.
18 Ibid., xix–xx.

19 Bruce, *The Coming of the Welfare State*, 327.

20 Alvin Finkel, 'Origins of the Welfare State in Canada,' in Panitch, *The Canadian State*, esp. 350 ff. E.A. Havelock, 'The Politics of Mr. Micawber,' *CF* 12 (May 1932) 286.

21 Alan Wolfe, *The Limits of Legitimacy* (New York 1977) 6. This book proved useful to me as I was reformulating my thoughts on the modern welfare state.

22 Granatstein, *Canada's War*, 249–93. Since Leonard Marsh had been one of the most active members of the LSR, his report is of more than passing interest to us. See Michiel Horn, 'Leonard Marsh and the Coming of a Welfare State in Canada,' *Histoire sociale/Social History* 9 (May 1976). This is a review article of the re-issue in 1975, in the *Social History of Canada* series, of the *Report on Social Security for Canada*.

23 David A. Dodge, 'Impact of Tax, Transfer, and Expenditure Policies of Government on the Distribution of Personal Income in Canada,' *Review of Income and Wealth* 21 (March 1975). W. Irwin Gillespie, 'On the Redistribution of Income in Canada,' *Canadian Tax Journal* 24 (July–August 1976), esp. 436. Early evidence suggests that during the 1970s the situation changed towards slightly greater inequality. See a reference to a very recent Carleton University Study in the *Globe and Mail*, 20 June 1980.

24 Lindblom, *Politics and Markets*, 199.

Bibliographical Note

The sources used are indicated in the notes. It may be useful to the reader, however, to have a list of the people with whom I have been in contact. I have also added a list of the documentary collections I consulted and a bibliography of LSR publications.

Interviews, conversations, correspondence

Miss Myrtle Adams, Mrs Joan S. Aykroyd, Prof. Eric Beecroft, Prof. Earle Birney, Mr Andrew Brewin, Mr Charles S. Buck, Mr Humphrey Carver, Mrs Beatrice Cassidy, Hon. M.J. Coldwell, Mr R.E.G. Davis, Mrs Irene Dewdney, Mr Selwyn Dewdney, Hon. T.C. Douglas, Prof. H. Martyn Estall, Senator Eugene Forsey, Prof. Paul Fox, Prof. J. King Gordon, Mr Ronald Grantham, Prof. G.M.A. Grube, Prof. E.A. Havelock, Prof. John Holmes, Dr H.L. Keenleyside, Mr Morden Lazarus, Mr Stuart Legge, Mr David Lewis, Prof. John Line, Prof. W.J. McCurdy, Mr E.D. MacInnes, Mrs Grace MacInnis, Prof. Edgar McInnis, Prof. R.A. MacKay, Mr F.J. McKenzie, Prof. Kenneth McNaught, Prof. Leonard Marsh, Mrs Kay Montagu Morris, Mr Lou Morris, Mrs Louise Parkin, Mr J.F. Parkinson, Prof. R.E.K. Pemberton, Principal Escott Reid, Prof. Frank R. Scott, Prof. R.B.Y. Scott, Mr Graham Spry, Prof. Irene M. Spry, Prof. K.W. Taylor, Prof. Frank H. Underhill, Prof. Gregory Vlastos, Mr Harry Wolfson.

Documentary collections consulted

Public Archives of Canada
H.R.C. Avison Papers, Brooke Claxton Papers, M.J. Coldwell Papers, CCF Records, J.W. Dafoe Papers, E.A. Forsey Papers, Grace MacInnis Papers, F.H. Underhill Papers, J.S. Woodsworth Papers

Public Archives of Ontario
H.J. Cody Papers, G.S. Henry Papers
University of British Columbia
Angus MacInnis Papers, Alan M. Plaunt Papers
Queen's University
Sir Joseph Flavelle Papers, G.M.A. Grube Papers
University of Toronto
Harry M. Cassidy Papers, Sir Robert Falconer Papers, J.S. Woodsworth Memorial Collection, including the LSR Papers deposited by Prof. W.J. McCurdy
Victoria University
E.A. Forsey Papers (Fellowship for a Christian Social Order)
York University
E.A. Beder Papers, Gordon Jack Papers, Edgar McInnis Papers
Privately held
J. King Gordon Papers, Leonard Marsh Scrapbooks, Lou Morris Papers (*The Canadian Forum*), Escott Reid Papers, Frank R. Scott Papers, Graham Spry Papers

Publications by the National Office of the LSR or its branches in chronological order within categories

Books
League for Social Reconstruction, Research Committee. *Social Planning for Canada*. Toronto: Thomas Nelson 1935
– *Democracy Needs Socialism*. Toronto: Nelson 1938

Pamphlets
League for Social Reconstruction, Vancouver Branch No 1. *The League for Social Reconstruction: A Programme for the New Social Order in Canada*. [Vancouver 1932]
League for Social Reconstruction. *Handbook*. [Toronto] 1933
Forsey, Eugene A. *Dividends and the Depression*. Toronto: Thomas Nelson 1934 (LSR Pamphlet No 1)
League for Social Reconstruction, Research Committee. *Combines and the Consumer*. Toronto: Nelson 1934 (LSR Pamphlet No 2)
Thomas, Ernest. *The Church and the Economic Order*. Toronto: Nelson 1934 (LSR Pamphlet No 3)
Scott, Francis R. *Social Reconstruction and the B.N.A. Act*. Toronto: Nelson 1934 (LSR Pamphlet No 4)

League for Social Reconstruction. *Proceedings of the Sixth Annual Convention, Toronto, March 20–21, 1937*. [Montreal 1937]
Forsey, Eugene A. *Does Canada Need Immigrants?* [Toronto 1937]
– *Recovery – for Whom?* [Toronto 1937]
Marsh, Helen, *Guide to L.S.R. Activities*. [Montreal 1937]
League for Social Reconstruction. *Canada – One or Nine? The Purpose of Confederation*. [Toronto 1938]
League for Social Reconstruction, Winnipeg Branch. *Pioneers in Poverty*. Winnipeg: Garry Press 1938
League for Social Reconstruction. *Poor Man Rich Man*. [Montreal]: Woodward Press [1941]

Leaflets
League for Social Reconstruction. *Manifesto*. Various printings. [Toronto, Montreal 1932ff]
– *What To Read: A Guide to Books and Articles on Current Social and Economic Questions*. [Toronto 1932]
League for Social Reconstruction, Research Committee. *Socialism or Social Credit?* Toronto: Stafford Printers [1935]
League for Social Reconstruction. *Canada and Socialism*. Toronto: Stafford Printers [1935–36]
– 'So You're Going to Study Co-operation.' Mimeographed. [1936]
Grube, G.M.A. and Olive Ziegler. *League for Social Reconstruction: Book Reviews*. Toronto: Stafford Printers [1936?]
League for Social Reconstruction. *We Want Member Groups!* [Montreal 1939?] (Leaflet No 1)
– *Why Social Reconstruction?* [Montreal 1939?] (Leaflet No 2)
– *What the Sirois Report Proposes* [Toronto 1941?]

Periodical
The Canadian Forum, May 1936–1942

Index